V&R unipress

Religion and Transformation in Contemporary European Society

Band 15

Herausgegeben von Kurt Appel, Christian Danz, Jakob Helmut Deibl, Rüdiger Lohlker, Richard Potz und Sieglinde Rosenberger

Die Bände dieser Reihe sind peer-reviewed.

Katharina Limacher / Astrid Mattes /
Christoph Novak (eds.)

Prayer, Pop and Politics

Researching Religious Youth in Migration Society

With 2 figures

V&R unipress

Vienna University Press

Bibliografische Information der Deutschen Nationalbibliothek
Die Deutsche Nationalbibliothek verzeichnet diese Publikation in der Deutschen Nationalbibliografie; detaillierte bibliografische Daten sind im Internet über http://dnb.d-nb.de abrufbar.

Veröffentlichungen der Vienna University Press erscheinen im Verlag V&R unipress GmbH.

Gedruckt mit freundlicher Unterstützung des Rektorats der Universität Wien.

Umschlagabbildung: „Between broken light" © Ines Mahmoud, Linz 2016
Druck und Bindung: CPI books GmbH, Birkstraße 10, D-25917 Leck
Printed in the EU.

Vandenhoeck & Ruprecht Verlage | www.vandenhoeck-ruprecht-verlage.com

ISSN 2198-5235
ISBN 978-3-8471-0979-2

Contents

Part III – Negotiating Religious Belonging in Migration Society

Katharina Limacher / Astrid Mattes / Christoph Novak

Introduction: Prayer, Pop and Politics*

As we write this introduction, 300 Catholic bishops meet in the Vatican to discuss how the Catholic Church can address the needs of younger generations, the Austrian government attempts to ban religious head-coverings in early childhood educational facilities and we witness religious youth activism that ranges from saving the lives of refugees in the Mediterranean sea to calls for an exclusively Christian Europe. That there are plenty of examples of conflicting interests between generations, political ideologies, and religious orientations, clearly calls for a scholarly investigation into what we subsume here under prayer, pop and politics. These terms put together do not just encompass those rare occasions when they manifest simultaneously, but they represent three dimensions, which, when studied in conjunction, allow us to grasp highly interwoven aspects of the lives of religious young people in a migration society.

Among scholars of various disciplines, there is an increasing interest in research on the religious engagement of young people in a migration society. While some are concerned with identity politics and processes of boundary drawing as well as minority representation and participation, others focus on issues of a changing religious landscape, the effects of pluralization and the diaspora situation of religious communities. Most scholarly perspectives share an interest in understanding the renewed role of religion in societies that have undergone secularization in their recent history and the ways in which young people shape and engage with religion today. Scientific interest might have remained limited to specialists in religious studies, if there was no wider politicization of religion and migration processes.

Religion, migration and politics are not only discursively interwoven but far too often lumped together by political actors and researchers alike. Recent years

* The editors want to thank the Research Centre "Religion and Transformation in Contemporary Society" for the opportunity to develop this book project. We thank Marlene Deibl and the RaT-Team for their wonderful support in the publication process. Also, we want to thank all contributors for their collegiality and responsiveness throughout this process.

saw a vast amount of research on religion and migration. Although often conducted with best intentions, such studies have frequently reproduced problematic notions and perspectives. When focussing on the religion of 'others', or on religion as a marker of otherness, researchers often ignore certain realities of contemporary societies, such as their longstanding history of (religious) diversity. Critical literature observes a racialization of religion in both politics and research, but often ignores that religion at the same time continues to be a relevant means in people's lives (Larsson / Spielhaus 2013; Brubaker 2013; Amir-Moazami 2018). Therefore we argue that empirical research on religious youth should take into account the delicate interrelationships between religion, race and age.

This edited volume brings together researchers who share an interest in reflecting on contemporary debates on migration, religion and youth, as well as in reassessing their own academic work with a focus on these shortcomings. Despite coming from different disciplines, we all know situations in our empirical work when we felt uneasy because we did not understand what young people meant when making what we might call a pop-cultural reference. We experienced moments of unexpected self-reflection when encountering spiritual practices and we met young people who found political causes to fight for through their religious engagement. In this light, prayer, pop and politics is exactly what we, as scholars of religious studies, political science, sociology, Islamic studies and educational sciences, encounter in our work. On a more abstract level, there is more to prayer, pop and politics than a fancy alliteration: With this book, we seek to address pressing political and societal issues at the intersection of religion, age and race while taking the agency of the people whose lives we are studying seriously and including our own research experiences in the outcome of our work.

Research on Religious Diversity in a Migration Society

When researching young religious people in contemporary society we come across a broad range of different religious traditions and religious practices in spatial proximity. This diversity has been associated with migration and therefore has been the stimulus for a vast amount of research on migration since the 1980s. A long-standing concept within migration studies is that of diaspora. It is inherently related to religion and interested in inter-group contact. Originating in the Jewish context, the concept of diaspora has had a stellar career in many fields of social sciences and humanities. First used to describe the dispersed Jewish community, diaspora soon designated any group of people, religious or not, on the grounds of a common history or the common experience of living away from a former homeland (Vertovec 1997, Baumann 2000, Mayer 2005, Somalingam 2017). The concept of diaspora therefore became an important analytical category to analyse a society shaped by migration.

Another way to analyse diversity in contemporary society is the concept of super-diversity. Steven Vertovec (2007) coined the term super-diversity to refer to a society that is diverse not only in terms of ethnicity but also as a result of the interplay of different variables, such as immigration statuses, labour market experiences, age, gender and spatial distribution (ibid., p. 1025).

As much as these and similar concepts try to grasp migration from an inclusive perspective, they have also been the subject of considerable controversy. Brubaker, for instance, is critical of the inflationary use of the term diaspora and fears that it makes the term conceptually irrelevant (Brubaker 2005). And the analytical category of super-diversity is criticized because it claims to represent a new approach to politics of identity when in fact it reproduces certain colonial hierarchies as it fails to consider global power relations and their influence on these categories of diversity (Ndhlovu 2015, p. 33). Nevertheless, super-diversity has resonated widely among critical migration scholars as it promotes an intersectional point of view and is considered a valuable descriptive model.

A concept that takes the intersectional perspective one step further and avoids the reproduction of symbolic boundaries is that of migration society, *Migrationsgesellschaft*, a term coined by Paul Mecheril, et al. (2013). We suggest conducting research on the complex linkages between migration and religion in the light of this concept. Mecheril et al. (2013) position themselves in the fields of education and critical migration studies and understand their work as an endeavour to analyse structures of domination. According to this perspective, migration is not an exception but the historical norm; migration is perceived as constituent of contemporary society:

> "There are good reasons for investigating and discussing contemporary society from the perspective of *migration society*, since the phenomenon of transgressing culturally, legally, linguistically and (geo-) politically significant borders is very important from a global perspective (albeit in different ways)." (Mecheril / et al. 2013, p. 8, our translation, emphasis added)[1]

With their approach, Mecheril et al. foster a specific view on migration. Migration should no longer be thought of or treated as an exception but instead as an inherent structural feature of society, past and present. The shift from migration

1 "Die Gegenwart kann also mit guten Gründen unter der Perspektive Migrationsgesellschaft untersucht und diskutiert werden, da Phänomenen der Überschreitung kulturell, juristisch, lingual und (geo-)politisch signifikanter Grenzen unter Bedingungen der Gegenwart weltweit (gewiss jedoch in unterschiedlicher Weise) sehr große Bedeutung zukommt" (Mecheril / et al. 2013, p. 8).

as something extraordinary has important consequences for questions of belonging (*Zugehörigkeit)* and identity. Through a notion of migration as the exception, questions of belonging arise and boundaries between a seemingly homogenous 'we' and differing 'others' are drawn (Broden / Mecheril 2007, 7), naturalized and racialized. We thus risk politicizing questions of belonging when we address migration as an exception rather than a normality. Consequently, if we see migration as an essential feature of society, we can move towards an analysis that refrains from politicizing questions of belonging and instead focuses on processes of politicization as such.

Approaching the topic from this perspective, Mecheril et al. (2013) list different goals of critical migration studies, two of which are especially important for research on religious youth: Researchers in critical migration studies are encouraged to take a self-reflective position and look at knowledge production in this domain not as a neutral process but as a social practice of normalization in a highly contested domain (Broden / Mecheril 2007, 7). Critical migration studies should moreover be aware of the potential changes in power structures that influence different forms of belonging (Mecheril / et al. 2013, p. 49).

Religion – Age – Race

This book presents research at the intersection of religion, age and race and gathers several different approaches to the broader question what it is like to be young and religious in a contemporary migration society. We can view age, race and religion as categories of difference that, together with an array of others, such as gender, class and ability, intersect and contribute to a person's societal situatedness (Haraway 1988). But there is more to the story than three (or more) overlapping categories that, depending on their manifestation as a marker of majority or minority, may or may not result in (multiple) discrimination. Each of these categories of difference emerges from processes of boundary drawing and is therefore subject to constant reproduction, discursive changes and shifting power structures. It is worthwhile exploring how the concepts of religion, age and race interlock, how this interdependence has come to colour our understanding of each one of them, as well as the ambiguities which have emerged for each of these concepts. While issues of gender, class and disability are no less important, we have deliberately chosen religious phenomena, age and race as our primary focus points, as we consider their intersections as particularly relevant for understanding contemporary social formations and political struggles.

Age, as Jenkins et al. argue, is one of the most overlooked categories of difference, as we perceive the limited inclusion of children or young adults as agents as quasi natural (2015, p. 40). Research on age and intersectionality emphasizes the relatively weak and vulnerable position of both very young and very old people (Calastani / King 2015). Being young is then a particular expression of age as an individual and group characteristic. However, age must not be considered a purely descriptive and therefore de-politicized term. Notions of childhood, adulthood, old age and so on have changed profoundly in recent decades and centuries (Ariès 1962; Cunningham 2014). From an intersectional perspective that evaluates situatedness with regard to power structures, being young means for the most part to be in a position of little influence on processes of boundary drawing, at least for boundaries dominant in mainstream, 'grown up' discourses. At the same time, young people are frequently drivers of change, bearers of political and social movements, and creative minds in terms of technical, artistic and societal innovation (Shadmehr / Haschke 2016; Ho / et al. 2015). Depending on context, youth may also be subject to romanticization and glorification (Mitchell 2017), and being young might open up windows of opportunity and allow taking unconventional ways. There is an inherent ambivalence to age, depending on context, individual dispositions and, importantly, on relation to other intersectional categories.

In a migration society, and thus within societal surroundings characterized by heterogeneity, as discussed in the beginning of this introductory chapter, belonging becomes politicized. Racialization and racisms structure the way and extent to which a person's membership is subject to politicization. Race is, however, a tricky category, as speaking of race is always at risk of solidifying a categorization that has no bearing in biological facts, while not making it explicit ignores the marginalization that actually occurs (Lentin 2008; Gilroy 1998). In particular, in a European context, the historic taboo of race frequently results in seemingly non- or even anti-racist public debates that reproduce patterns of exclusion and merely rename or shift boundaries. Although most people agree that biological racism lacks any basis in science whatsoever (Gilroy 2001, pp. 11 ff.), many scholars argue that racism did not simply disappear but transformed itself. This contemporary articulation of racism, cultural racism, considers attributed, essentialized cultural characteristics as the legitimate basis for social stratifications and hierarchies (Balibar 2005).Without going into details of research on race, we want to emphasize the critical perspectives this book promotes with regard to race, processes of racialization and racism. Although race is not the primary subject of our research, we take into account processes that build on racialization and transfer racial structures to culture (Lentin 2005), ethnicity and nationalism (Gilroy 2001; 2005; Brubaker 2009), or, as discussed in the next paragraph, religion.

As argued by many scholars, religion is an increasingly racialized category (El-Tayeb 2011; Grillo 2010; Modood 2009). In particular, women wearing headscarves become the visible other in a seemingly colour-blind Europe. At the same time, nationalist, populist and far-right actors claim Christianity as central to their own/national/European identity (Marzouki / et al. 2016; Hafez / Heinisch 2018). Meanwhile, some scholars speak of a post-Christian Europe, thereby emphasizing the inconsistency and contradictions in the ways that large parts of European societies deal with religion. "This is the paradox of Europe: its societies are marked as much by the Christian faith as by its abandonment and rejection", writes Evert van de Poll (2013, p. 251). In spite of all this, many political debates today ignore this ambivalent relation and put religion at the centre of identity politics. This makes a complex field, the governance of and conviviality in religious diversity, even more contentious.

This contention is by no means new and has led to complex forms of legal and institutional accommodation. Religion as a category of difference is frequently treated in special ways. Liberal theories of democracy, which have developed along the question of how to govern diversity in a just way, acknowledge religions as a form of "deep diversity" (Galston 2002) in need of legal establishment. In fact, religion is subject to special forms of legal protection, not only as a marker of difference (as such protected through anti-discrimination laws) and fundamental rights (freedom of religion and others), but also through particular institutional provisions (broadly referred to as state-religion relations). However, religion is not only a distinct category at the legal level.

Most importantly, at least in a liberal democratic context, religion as an individual attribute marks a personal decision. Although never fully free of constraints, people do choose their religion. Much more than race or age, religion is subject to individual choice. This is a crucial point, often overlooked in social-scientific work that treats religion at the intersection with race. While religion can also be an ascribed, constructed and racialized category, it often is an affiliation and agenda people choose willingly. It is therefore important to bear in mind the complexity of religion, as the result of both self-and other-identification, sometimes subject to racialization, as a fundamental right and an individual choice.

Moreover, as with all intersectionality, it is crucial to avoid a blind spot on the hegemonic expression of a category. When discussing the intersection of race, age and religion, we tend to think of younger persons of colour who follow minority religions. However, a white person has a race, a 40-year old has an age and a Christian has a religion as well. What differs are the experiences of normalization and otherness respectively. Depending on what kind of age, race and religion a person has or is associated with, processes of othering and boundary drawing may make a person painfully aware of his/her markers of difference or allow him/her to widely ignore them. Depending on the specifics of intersectional situatedness, age can be more of a benefit or more of a constraint, race will be experienced as affecting adolescence or be hardly perceptible and religion might reinforce or weaken these impacts. Here again, it needs to be emphasized that, much more than age and race, religion is (also) subject to voluntarism and choice.

Therefore the question of religion is somewhat trickier, as it has an additional dimension. Do non-religious people have a (non-)religious identity marker that is situated within the category of religion? When asking that question from a religious studies perspective, we might want to start a discussion on what non-religious means: non-affiliated, atheist, agnostic or just not interested, and what about implicit religion? But as we write a book about religion, youth and politics, it is sufficient for our scope to ask which kind of religion is relevant to political discourses, influencing societal situatedness and most importantly, relevant to the young people we engage with in our research.

Reflecting Methods

In the light of what has been said above, what does it mean to ask questions about prayer, pop and politics in migration societies? What does it mean to let such questions guide one's empirical research? Even taking up a 'critical' perspective is not without its inherent pitfalls, as it still requires navigating conceptual dilemmas and taking responsibility for one's own situatedness in the field. How do we, as academics doing research, contribute to the problematization and thereby the politicization of our research subjects? We have argued that the pivotal concepts framing the topic, religion, age and race, are themselves ambiguous and problematic constructions, entangled with discursive powers and deployed in the service of very different, often diametric political interests. As we see the need for researchers to take responsibility for their particular standpoint, account for their interests and intentions, as well as for the social positions they have come to occupy through discursive processes of attributing powers, entitlements and privileges, how can we with a clear conscience do this kind of research?

Actually, we cannot and must not free us of those doubts. Instead, they should constitute the basis for a constant, critical assessment of our research practice and work as knowledge producers. As we find ourselves trapped in a situation where we are constantly in danger of contributing to the very reproduction of the problematic concepts which we are investigating 'critically', we ought to cultivate those worries to become better researchers. Many academics have addressed these problems of empirical research practice by pointing out different problematic spheres: the chimera of methodological nationalism (Glick Schiller / Çağlar 2009; Wimmer / Glick Schiller 2003), the uncritical reproduction of racial classifications (Ladner 1998; Zuberi / Bonilla-Silva 2008), and the equally problematic construction of ethnic groups (Brubaker 2002; Glick Schiller / et al. 2006). Gillespie, Howarth and Cornish summed up the problem of using social categories in research by pointing out that social categories are: "(1) perspectival, (2) historical, (3) disrupted by the movement of people, and (4) re-constitutive of the phenomena they seek to describe." (Gillespie et al. 2012, p. 392) Researchers, we argue, must not discard this criticism lightly, nor should they stop doing research. Instead we ought to make use of the privileges we enjoy to work against the grain, which means using our creative capacities and scientific knowledge to work towards the dissolution of problematic social phenomena and categories we investigate and use in our research.

This leads to the second issue: How are researchers positioned and how can they position themselves vis-à-vis their research subject? A neutral or objective stance is unattainable to any researcher given the discursive baggage one carries around all of the time. This baggage is performed (e.g. through internalized gendered or classed behavioral patterns) and embodied (e.g. through being associated with dominant gender constructions). It materializes in legal documents, such as passports or birth certificates, in how one is seen (and categorized) by others, but also in how one perceives one's social surroundings. Researchers ought to account for their particular situation as part of their research practice, whether they share a location with their research participants or are positioned very differently. This "situated knowledge" (Haraway 1988) needs to inform our research practice. This requires discarding the notion of the researcher as an invisible, neutral observer and taking one's particular standpoint, emerging from meta-discourses (on race, age, religion, etc.), seriously into account. Reflecting on one's social location in such a way involves acknowledging that the characteristics one is associated with, do not have a fixed meaning but are contextual and socially constructed. This is not the same as assuming that those characteristics are not real. Rather, their specific meaning has not emerged from the characteristics as such, but involved human activities that attributed meaning to them (Sprague 2005, p. 51). It is this attached, flexible, socially constructed and context specific meaning through which those characteristics receive their discursive power and eventually have real impact on one's life and research practice. At this point, we have gone full circle, as it becomes clear that religion, race and age are not meaningful categories by themselves, but are imbued with power only through political processes that have turned those terms into meaningful categories with real-life implications.

This effectively means that we, as researchers, need to reflect critically on our own research interests and practices. We should ask ourselves, how did our interest in the research subject emerge and whose problem perspectives did we intentionally or unintentionally apply in formulating our research questions? Whose concerns are we addressing with our research? What are our own (implicit) assumptions about the lives of others, through which we come to our hypotheses or perceptions of what seems to be the problem with regard to a specific phenomenon?

We also should question ourselves on what being positioned in some way (e. g. in terms of religion) means in different social contexts relating to our research. What kind of discursive baggage do we bring with us into our research, which entitlements and privileges have become so 'normal' to us that we have stopped being aware of the particular socio-historic trajectory upon which they rest? Experiences some of us consider normal and 'natural' might be far from normal for research participants. How do these privileges influence the research process and how can we still do valid research in spite of this?

Finally, yet importantly, we need to be critical of our own engagement with research participants and ask in which ways we can make our research valuable for them, so that it acknowledges and maybe addresses their problem perspectives as well. We should also ask what role the participants play in shaping the research trajectory and/or the interpretation of data. Even more radically, we may ask how we can find ways to let our research be guided by the actual problem perspectives of research participants. How can we realize such critical perspectives, not only as researchers, but also as knowledge producers, when writing up our research? Are there ways to represent participants, or to let them represent themselves, in the written-up results of research?

None of these questions relate exclusively to religion, age and race. They are equally relevant in spheres like gender, ability/disability, class and respectability, to name just a few. However, as the focal points of this volume, religion, age and race play a particularly important role – in one way or another – in all the contributions presented here. None of the questions we just raised are to be answered with certainty, but they ought to make us aware of some of the most problematic issues in empirical research practice and, at the same time, stimulate our creative capacities to come up with new ways to do research in spite of the entanglements and fallacies of our situatedness.

This book covers a wide spectrum of subjects, each connected to its own body of literature and to specific challenges. The articles are grouped in three main sections. The first section deals with methodological reflections already hinted at above. The first paper, authored by Christoph Novak, examines forms of privileges, which emerge from different social positionings of researchers and research participants. Based on his own research experiences with young, self-identified Muslims in Zurich and Vienna, he sketches an approach that seeks to account for the researcher's privileges in qualitative interview encounters. The second contribution takes a complementary stance and addresses the position as in-group researcher. Farid Hafez and Linda Hyökki discuss challenges of boundary-drawing as peer researchers in Muslim communities in Austria and Finland. While they see peer research as a means to avoid othering and culturalization, they emphasise that in the light of an acknowledged fluidity of identity as well as different lines of differences, a critical reflection of the researcher's subjectivity is important. The third chapter in this section provides a perspective on quantitative social research on identity and youth. Anastas Odermatt critically assesses the operationalization of concepts of identity and youth by means of a comparison of two large-scale research projects. He shows that the use of concepts such as identity and youth tend to be over-simplifying or imprecise and asks for a clearer theoretical positioning to enhance the explanatory power of research on identity in adolescents and young adults in quantitative research.

The second section of this volume addresses questions of online identifications and the role of social media when researching religious youth. The first paper by Astrid Mattes develops a conceptual framework for the analysis of identifications of religious youth in digital spaces. Bringing together research on religious belonging and politics of belonging, the author suggests a multi-dimensional research framework to analyse identifications of young people growing up as digital natives. Giulia Evolvi shares this interest for digital media and explores the concept of *hypermediated religious spaces* in her paper. Using the hashtag #NousSommesUnis, which was created in response to the 2015 Paris terrorist attacks, she dissects the various aspects of identification processes of religious youth. The third contribution, by Rüdiger Lohlker, describes the embedding of an activist's project in academic research: the production of alternative narrations to Jihadi narratives by means of the YouTube video clips of *Jamal al-Khatib.* It is an example of participatory action research that creates the possibility for young Muslims to express a critical position in collaboration with researchers, social workers and a professional film crew.

The third section gathers case studies that look more broadly at negotiations of religious belonging in migration society. Katharina Limacher's contribution analyses different forms of religious knowledge of Hindu youth in Zurich and Vienna. Using Bourdieu's distinction of different forms of capital, she characterizes young people's assessment of their own religious knowledge in the light of a society shaped by privileges for certain religious communities. The second contribution, by Andreas Tunger-Zanetti, Silvia Martens and Jürgen Endres, dissects the religious orientation of young Muslims in Switzerland. Analysing data from a qualitative research project, the authors register a shift away from the religious community as a place of collective authority to individual actors. The third article in this section investigates the place of religion in identification processes of Vietnamese Buddhist youth in Switzerland and Germany. Through the analysis of two biographies, Rebekka Khaliefi demonstrates the different forms that religious identification processes take in predominantly Christian societies. Jana Wetzel's chapter presents a critical reading of European research on self-identified Muslim youth from the perspective of de- and post-colonial theories. In reference to her own research in mosques, the author advocates taking different concepts of religiosity and religion as well as the spatial dimensions more seriously. The section concludes with a paper by Dilek Aysel Tepeli and Martina Loth on Alevi youth in Germany. The authors shine a light on different aspects that influence Alevi identity constructions among young Alevis in Germany and in the light of the political developments in Turkey.

Given this diversity of subjects and approaches, we will not be able to answer all the questions described above. However, we are confident to introduce a book that manages to treat religious young people as actors with agency. For the field of racial studies, which is equally concerned with marginalization and racialization, Robbie Shilliam argues:

> [M]y main point is that this research agenda is dominated by one story – what the master does unto the sufferers – and addressed to one politics – can the master redeem the detritus of his humanity? What of the sufferers and their stories and politics? Are they merely fragments of raw data? Or do they have an epistemic part to play in the research agenda on race and racism? (2013, p. 156)

We equally find such a "master's narrative", as Shilliam calls it, in the scholarly literature on youth identifications and religious belonging. It is this particular criticism that we want to overcome by treating the subjects of our research as agents who determine their own (identity) politics through their actions and choices. We as researchers are not in the position of granting this agency but merely able to observe it carefully while taking into consideration our own role as situated individuals.

References

Amir-Moazami, Schirin (ed.) (2018): *Der inspizierte Muslim: zur Politisierung der Islamforschung in Europa.* Bielefeld: Transcript.

Ariès, Philippe (1962): *Centuries of childhood. A social history of family life.* New York, NY: Vintage Books.

Balibar, Etienne (2005): Difference, Otherness, Exclusion. In *Parallax* 11 (1), pp. 19–34. https://doi.org/10.1080/1353464052000321074.

Baumann, Martin (2000): "Diaspora: Genealogies of Semantics and Transcultural Comparison." In: *Numen*, 47 (3), pp. 313–337. https://doi.org/10.1163/156852700511577.

Broden, Anne / Mecheril, Paul (eds.) (2007): *Re-Präsentationen. Dynamiken der Migrationsgesellschaft.* Informations- und Dokumentationszentrum für Antirassismusarbeit in Nordrhein-Westfalen. Düsseldorf: IDA-NRW.

Brubaker, Rogers (2002): "Ethnicity without groups." *European Journal of Sociology* (43), pp. 163–189. https://doi.org/10.1017/S0003975602001066.

– (2005): "The 'diaspora' diaspora." *Ethnic and Racial Studies* 28 (1), pp. 1–19. https://doi.org/10.1080/0141987042000289997.

– (2009): "Ethnicity, Race, and Nationalism". *Annual Review of Sociology*, 35 (1), pp. 21–42. https://doi.org/10.1146/annurev-soc-070308-115916.

– (2013): "Categories of analysis and categories of practice: a note on the study of Muslims in European countries of immigration". *Ethnic and Racial Studies*, 36 (1), pp. 1–8. https://doi.org/10.1080/01419870.2012.729674.

Calastani, Toni / King, Neil (2015): "Age and Intersectionality". In: Twigg, Julia / Wendy, Martin (eds.): *Routledge Handbook of Cultural Gerontology*. New York: Routledge, pp. 193–201.

Cunningham, Hugh (2014): *Children and Childhood in Western Society since 1500*. Hoboken: Taylor and Francis.

El-Tayeb, Fatima (2011): *European others: queering ethnicity in postnational Europe*. Minneapolis: University of Minnesota Press.

Galston, William A. (2002): *Liberal pluralism: the implications of value pluralism for political theory and practice*. Cambridge, UK; New York: Cambridge University Press.

Gillespie, Alex / Howarth, Caroline S. / Cornish, Flora (2012): "Four problems for researchers using social categories." *Culture & Psychology*, 18 (3), pp. 391–402. https://doi.org/10.1177/1354067X12446236.

Gilroy, Paul (1998): "Race Ends Here". *Ethnic and Racial Studies*, 21 (5), pp. 838–47. https://doi.org/10.1080/014198798329676.

– (2001): *Against race. Imagining political culture beyond the color line*. Cambridge, Massachusetts: The Belknap Press of Harvard University Press.

– (2005): *Postcolonial melancholia*. New York: Columbia University Press (The Wellek lectures).

Glick Schiller, Nina / Çağlar, Ayșe / Guldbrandsen, Thaddeus C. (2006): "Beyond the ethnic lens. Locality, globality, and born-again incorporation." *American Ethnologist* 33 (4), pp. 612–633. https://doi.org/10.1525/ae.2006.33.4.612.

Glick Schiller, Nina / Çağlar, Ayse (2009): "Towards a Comparative Theory of Locality in Migration Studies. Migrant Incorporation and City Scale." *Journal of Ethnic and Migration Studies*, 35 (2), pp. 177–202. https://doi.org/10.1080/13691830802586179.

Grillo, Ralph (2010): "British and Others. From 'Race' to 'Faith'". In: Vertovec, Steven / Wessendorf, Susanne (eds.): *The Multiculturalism Backlash: European Discourses, Policies and Practices*. New York: Routledge, pp. 50–71.

Hafez, Farid / Helnisch, Reinhard (2018): "Breaking with Austrian Consociationalism: How the Rise of Rightwing Populism and Party Competition Have Changed Austria's Islam Politics". *Politics and Religion*, 11 (03), pp. 649–78. https://doi.org/10.1017/S1755048318000172.

Haraway, Donna (1988): "Situated Knowledges. The Science Question in Feminism and the Privilege of Partial Perspective." *Feminist Studies*, 14 (3), pp. 575–599. https://doi.org/10.2307/3178066.

Ho, Elaine / Clarke, Amelia / Dougherty, Ilona (2015): "Youth-led social change: Topics, engagement types, organizational types, strategies, and impacts." *Futures*, 67 (march), pp. 52–62. https://doi.org/10.1016/j.futures.2015.01.006.

Jenkins, Henry / Itō, Mizuko / boyd, danah (2015): *Participatory culture in a networked era: a conversation on youth, learning, commerce, and politics*. Cambridge, UK; Malden, MA: Polity Press.

Ladner, Joyce A. (Ed.) (1998): *The Death of white sociology. Essays on race and culture.* [Black Classic Press ed.]. Baltimore: Black Classic Press.

Larsson, Göran / Spielhaus, Riem (2013): "Narratives of Inclusion and Exclusion: Islam and Muslims as a Subject of European Studies". *Journal of Muslims in Europe*, 2 (2), pp. 105–13. https://doi.org/10.1163/22117954-12341272.

Lentin, Alana (2005): "Replacing 'race', historicizing 'culture' in multiculturalism". *Patterns of Prejudice*, 39 (4), pp. 379–96. https://doi.org/10.1080/00313220500347832.

– (2008): "Europe and the Silence about Race". *European Journal of Social Theory*, 11 (4), pp. 487–503. https://doi.org/10.1177/1368431008097008.

Marzouki, Nadia / McDonnell, Duncan / Roy, Olivier (Eds.) (2016): *Saving the People: How Populists Hijack Religion.* London: Hurst & Company.

Mattes, Astrid (2017): "Who We Are Is What We Believe? Religion and Collective Identity in Austrian and German Immigrant Integration Policies." *Social Inclusion*, 5 (1), pp. 93–104. https://doi.org/10.17645/si.v5i1.766.

Mayer, Ruth (2005): *Diaspora. Eine kritische Begriffsbestimmung.* Bielefeld: Transcript.

Mecheril, Paul / Thomas-Olalde, Oscar / Melter, Claus / Arens, Susanne / Romaner, Elisabeth (Eds.) (2013): *Migrationsforschung als Kritik? Konturen einer Forschungsperspektive.* Wiesbaden: Springer VS.

Mitchell, Claire (2017): *Religion, Identity and Politics in Northern Ireland: Boundaries of Belonging and Belief.* Milton: Taylor & Francis.

Modood, Tariq (2009): "Muslims and the Politics of Difference". In: Hopkins, Peter / Gale, Richard (eds.): *Muslims in Britain: Race, Place and Identities.* Edinburgh University Press, pp. 191–209.

Ndhlovu, Finex (2015): "A decolonial critique of diaspora identity theories and the notion of superdiversity." *Diaspora Studies*, 9 (1), pp. 28–40. https://doi.org/10.1080/09739572.2015.1088612.

Poll, Evert Van de (2013): *Europe and the Gospel: Past Influences, Current Developments, Mission Challenges.* Berlin: De Gruyter.

Shadmehr, Mehdi / Haschke, Peter (2016): "Youth, Revolution, and Repression." *Economic Inquiry*, 54 (2), pp. 778–93. https://doi.org/10.1111/ecin.12293.

Shilliam, Robbie (2013): "Race and research agendas". *Cambridge Review of International Affairs*, 26 (1), pp. 152–58. https://doi.org/10.1080/09557571.2013.770298.

Somalingam, Thusinta (2017): *Doing Diaspora. Ethnonationale Homogenisierung im transnationalen Bildungsraum der Tamil Diaspora.* Wiesbaden: Springer VS.

Sprague, Joey (2005): *Feminist Methodologies for Critical Researchers. Bridging Differences.* Lanham: AltaMira Press.

Vertovec, Steven (1997): "Three Meanings of 'Diaspora'. Exemplified among South Asian Religions." *Diaspora* 6 (3), pp. 277–299. https://doi.org/10.1353/dsp.1997.0010.

– (2007): "Super-diversity and its implications." *Ethnic and Racial Studies*, 30 (6), pp. 1024–1054. https://doi.org/10.1080/01419870701599465.

Wimmer, Andreas / Glick Schiller, Nina (2003): "Methodological nationalism and beyond. Nation-state building, migration and the social sciences." *International Migration Review*, 37 (3), pp. 576–610. https://doi.org/10.1111/1471-0374.00043.

Zuberi, Tukufu / Bonilla-Silva, Eduardo (Eds.) (2008): *White Logic, White Methods. Racism and Methodology.* Lanham: Rowman & Littlefield Publishers.

Part I –
Methodological Reflections at the Intersection of Age, Race and Religion

Christoph Novak

Facing Privilege in Qualitative Interview Settings. The A-B-C-D-Approach

"The central argument is that what distinguishes critical from uncritical research is not the method used, but how the method is used, both technically and politically."
Joey Sprague 2005, p. 27

Abstract
Most people are bestowed with social privileges, whether they want them or not. Carrying specific racialised and gendered characteristics, being associated with some religious groups, being raised in certain socio-economic conditions, being categorised in specific age groups and performing a certain professional role come with different, context specific advantages. Manifestations of such privileges not only show in social interactions (e.g. being attended well by a waiter), but also influence lived-realities quite fundamentally (e.g. never having experienced sexual harassment). Often privileges are working to one's advantage so seemingly naturally, that one does not only take them for granted for oneself, but one is inclined to assume that one's privileged experiences constitute the norm, rather than an exception.
While investigations of privilege and privileged groups have become labeled as Privilege Studies under the influence of Peggy McIntosh, knowledge of privilege is only slowly making its entry into critical research practice. This chapter addresses this gap by identifying some areas in which privilege can have a problematic impact on data generated in one-on-one research encounters, particularly qualitative interviews. The issues raised relate primarily to situations in which privilege differentials between researchers and researched exist. Based on these reflections, in the second part of the chapter I develop the A-B-C-D-approach, which ought to help researchers integrate a critical self-assessment of privilege in research design, practice and analysis. The four steps proposed are (1) the assessment of privilege, (2) the balancing of the influence of privilege through research design, (3) the act of communicating the knowledge about privileging structures as a way to control for its influence and signal one's critical position to research participants, and (4) the deconstruction of the influence of privilege throughout analysis.

This chapter develops a structured process of self-reflection, which invites researchers to see themselves as social beings embedded in social power relations and as having context-specific privileges. By privileges, I refer to advantages, which originate in social interactions and have their basis in material living conditions and/or hegemonic discursive formations. Those advantages can be linked, for example, to how someone is perceived by others (e.g. based on stereotypes) and the particular experiences one has due to those perceptions.

Knowledge of one's context-specific privileges is important for methodological reasons (as this knowledge can be used to reduce bias throughout data collection and interpretation) as well as from a normative perspective (since having privileges needs to be accounted for as something influencing research on many levels).

I realised the need to confront my embodied and performed privileges while doing research with young self-identified Muslims in Zurich and Vienna. Already during a pilot interview, I became aware of several aspects influencing the interview situation, which I had not yet taken adequately and structurally into account. When reviewing the conversation, it became clear to me, that the interview would have progressed very differently, if I had not been identified as a young, white, male, non-Muslim researcher from Austria, but as being seen as bearing other characteristics. There was clearly no point in trying *not* to be identified this way, since it is impossible to make others perceive oneself detached from social power relations. (Spillers 1987) While there is no feasible way to prevent the formation of implicit assumptions about a person with whom one engages, the central question is this: If it cannot be avoided, how can aspects which might lead to serious biases within data be controlled for in a scientific process?

The solution I came up with comprises four steps: (1) *assessing* the discursive meaning that I inadvertently brought to the interview situation; (2) *balancing* my influence on the research process and provided more autonomy to research participants; (3) *clarifying* my motivation for the research and the reflexive process which it involved when meeting research participants; (4) *deconstructing* my influence in the process of data analysis. The *A-B-C-D-approach* is the focus of the second part of the chapter. I start, however, with discussing privilege conceptually, highlighting different spheres of privilege (particularly those relevant for the general topic in this volume) and how they influence qualitative interviewing contexts. (Gubrium / Holstein 2003; Rosenthal / Fischer-Rosenthal 2010)

As this chapter addresses the effects of privilege differentials emerging from different social positionings occupied by researcher and researched, it complements Hafez and Hyökki's contribution (this volume) who discuss the situation of researchers sharing certain characteristics with their research participants (see also: Kubica 2016). However, while they emphasize the relevance of the social construction of in- and out-groups, my chapter follows Joey Sprague's (2005) standpoint theory, developed from critical realist epistemologies (Bhaskar 2008; Archer / et al. 2013). Sprague, like other researchers, emphasises that detailed knowledge of the scientific tools and methods is essential for knowing which questions can be asked and what data eventually emerges from the research encounter. Social scientists working within a field responsive to their presence (e.g. in interview situations) need to realise that their major research tool is their own physique (body) and performance (actions) (Archer 2013, pp. 200f.), which also influences which questions can be asked and what can emerge as knowledge, eventually.[1] Nevertheless, I argue that the applicability of the A-B-C-D-approach is not limited to critical realist perspectives, but stretches to other approaches as well.

Defining Privilege

While being privileged provides the basis for very particular experiences, it has largely remained out of focus of mainstream social research. This is so because a central property of privilege is its ability to obscure its genesis in power relations, hide its un-naturalness and non-transcendence. (Pease 2013)[2] Consequently, it was not until Peggy McIntosh's (1988) seminal self-reflection, that privilege as a scientific concept received broader attention. McIntosh defines white privilege as "an invisible package of unearned assets that I can count on cashing in each day, but about which I was 'meant' to remain oblivious." (1988, n.p.) In a later work, McIntosh complements this by comparing white privilege to a "bank account which I was given at birth, and did not ask for […]. And because it is white privilege it will automatically refill even after I spend it down." (McIntosh 2012, p. 196).

While McIntosh's metaphors help in making privilege comprehensible, they are not sketching it in great conceptual depth. Looking at privilege more systematically, Winddance Twine and Gardner (2013b) identify several interconnected characteristics of privilege.

Privilege manifests as a form of power. Rather than seeing oneself as part of a privileged racialised, gendered, etc. group, characteristics, which allocate to its bearer a position of power, tend to be naturalised and rendered unremarkable. Media scholar Richard Dyer summed this up by stating that: "There is no more

1 With respect to the relationship between social constructionism and critical realism, it is good to keep in mind that critical realists do not deny the role of one's socially constructed positions and privileges as part of reality. Instead, they emphasise that "the fact that [a discourse, a social practice, or physical reality] is socially defined and produced does not make a societal phenomenon any less real." (Alvesson / Sköldberg 2012, p. 41)

2 Nevertheless, in some scientific traditions, interest for studying privilege is not particularly new. Already around 1900, W.E.B. DuBois interrogated white privilege in the United States. DuBois' works are among the earliest examples of the change of perspective, which has become paradigmatic for privilege studies, namely the debasement of white, adult, male, heterosexual, Christianity as the supposedly "neutral" standpoint of most social research (Winddance Twine / Gardener 2013b, 9; Du Bois 1990; Du Bois / Sundquist 1996; Ferber 2012; McIntosh 2012).

powerful position than that of being 'just' human. The claim to power is the claim to speak for the commonality of humanity. Raced people can't do that – they can only speak for their race. But non-raced people can, for they do not represent the interests of a race." (Dyer 1997, p. 2). Dyer makes clear that being able to consider oneself as *normal*, comes itself with very concrete social privileges and discursive powers, including the privileged access to negotiating what falls within and outside of the norm. That means that people who have certain privileges also have better access to participate in the social construction of privilege. (Ferber 2012) Pratto and Stewart (2012) argue that *hyper-privileged* individuals (who benefit from a culmination of several privileges) tend to perceive themselves as the core of a given society, and worthier of political consideration than others (in spite of the fact that demographically they usually do not constitute a majority). What is even more important for privileged researchers, is that privileged individuals lack a considerable amount of the experiences other people have (e.g. with discriminatory practices and systems) and often perceive such phenomena rather as the exception than the norm (Pratto / Stewart 2012, p. 31; Winddance Twine / Gardner 2013b, pp. 8f.).

Privilege renders itself invisible, at least for those who benefit from it. Liu / et al.'s (2007) psychological study shows that privilege emerges from social constructions, particularly whenever "one's social identities (i.e., religious, race, social class) are considered normative and therefore not questioned by peers, family, or society." This results in an "insulated worldview" which is perceived as "normative, universal and ubiquitous," while those "not subscribing to the privilege[d] person's worldview are considered deviant." (Liu / et al. 2007, p. 196; Winddance Twine / Gardner 2013b, p. 9)

Privilege appears in several different social environments and relationships (class, race, gender, ability, sexual orientation, etc.), is highly contextual and constantly transforming. Privilege can manifest in various social constructions. In the West at least, such privileging constructions are, for example, whiteness, cis-genderedness, maturity, being associated with a dominant Christian faith group, being seen as part of middle, upper-middle, or upper-classes, and so on. Paired with the invisibility of privilege, this explains the phenomenon, that the privileged position is still widely perceived as the norm and often treated as the null-hypothesis against which those lacking certain privileges can be measured in their supposed – sometimes even naturalised – inferiority and deficiency. (Winddance Twine / Gardner 2013b, p. 10)

Privilege stands in a dialectic relationship with oppression. Like Winddance Twine and Gardner, Pease Pease (2013) and Pratto and Stewart (2012) also maintain, that where there is privilege, there also exists an oppressed or disadvantaged group (Pratto /Stewart 2012). Studying privilege or privileging systems consequently means highlighting the constructedness of those advantages, showing the dialectic relationship between privilege and oppression, how privilege has been maintained, how it has been challenged and asking for the effects privilege has on social and political practices, institutions and participation. (Winddance Twine / Gardner 2013b, p. 10; Pease 2013, pp. 13 ff.)

The privileged and the disadvantaged are both positioned through relationships of meta-discursive power. Dismantling privilege is not an individual act. One might have privileges by adhering to certain norms or lose it by disturbing said norms, but challenging the super-structure of privilege and oppression can happen exclusively on a meta-discursive level. (Winddance Twine / Gardener 2013b, pp. 8 ff.) Implicit social norms cultivated through hegemonic perspectives on society and history, constitute the discursive fabric from which privilege gains its power. In this sense, privilege is connected to the legacies of the colonialism, the hierarchies of gender and race, notions of capability, respectability and normalcy.

So far, I discussed privilege in the abstract, as a phenomenon emerging from the unequal distribution of discursive power and material resources, and as being based on the construction of implicit norms. I will now look at different areas in which privilege has manifested and which hold particular relevance for the qualitative, empirical studies collected in this volume, but also qualitative research in general.

Spheres of Privilege

Facing privilege means to de-centralise and de-normalise its occurrence and to perceive particular experiences as social phenomena rendered by privileging positionings and their entanglements with social power. Taking the effects of privilege in social research seriously means that the life-worlds of privileged individuals must no longer serve as the null-hypothesis for assessing social relations and conditions; it requires discarding privileged perspectives as the supreme scientific positions for "objective" research. Researchers need to reflect critically upon experiences which were rendered possible by privilege, and which have come to characterise their life-worlds. It is key to perceive those experiences and privileges as social phenomena in need of scientific inquiry and explanation. (Sprague 2005, pp. 22 ff.; Haraway 1988; Pease 2013)

Here, I will briefly sketch the rationale and possible influence of some privileging characteristics. Furthermore, I highlight the need for the researcher's reflexivity, to control for the influences privilege has on interview data and to generate reliable results. To this end, I provide sets of questions, which ought to help assessing one's privileges in different areas. None of the categories occurs naturally, but instead, they receive their meaning and normative capacity as socially constructed categories of difference (Berger / Luckmann 1991; Burr 2015). While it is true that those categories are constantly (re)negotiated, they emerge from specific socio-historic trajectories and cannot be easily subverted. Awareness of those genealogies allows researchers to follow Donna Haraway's emphasis on cultivating one's situated knowledge:

> "I am arguing for politics and epistemologies of location, positioning, and situating, where partiality and not universality is the condition of being heard to make rational knowledge claims. [...] I am arguing for the view from a body, always a complex, contradictory, structuring, and structured body, versus the view from above, from nowhere, from simplicity." (Haraway 1988, p. 589)

Consequently, getting to terms with one's privileges means acknowledging one's position within the social fabric of power relations on a societal level, and taking responsibility for its effects within micro publics (such as interview settings). The following discussion highlights spheres of privilege relevant to the volume's foci. Each of those embodied and performed privileges might affect research processes unintendedly, if not taken into account. I rely on a critical perspective on "the West" (Hall 2011), whereby I acknowledge that privileges articulate very differently in different discursive contexts. While I discuss the spheres as ideal types, it should be noted that privilege does not surface in isolation, but needs to be thought of as intersectional phenomenon, where the co-occurrence and interferences of different privileges and disadvantages exhibit strong effects.

Age privilege as "grown-ups"

> "Childhood was not 'discovered' in the nineteenth century; rather, it was produced through new rationalities and techniques of government that acted on children's psyches, their bodies and their minds, and in doing so produced them as particular kinds of psychic, corporeal and intellectual subjects." (Wells 2011, p. 18)

Age is a particularly naturalised, but at the same time very powerful category of privilege. In contemporary social sciences the predominant focus lies on researching ageism against old people (Lyons / et al. 2017; Nelson 2004; Ayalon / Tesch-Römer 2018). However, adults are usually perceived as having reached a status of being physically and psychologically developed and capable of rational behaviour and thinking. In contrast, children and young people are perceived as still having to go through a maturing process (Zhao / et al. 2011). The dominant view of children stands in dialectic relationship with the construction of adults as intellectually superior human beings, able to make informed decisions (James / James 2011, pp. 74ff, p. 200). While some aspects connected to being a young person might be considered an empirical fact, e.g. rapid bodily changes during puberty (James / James 2011, pp. 18ff.), it is highly doubtful, whether adulthood should be automatically equated with having reached static grown-up-ness (Wells 2011). In any case, the notion of being fully developed is a privileged position, as it exclusively assumes the ability to correctly assess risks for oneself and others and make informed, rational decisions. This assumption manifests, for example, in age restrictions and their inherent underpinnings.[3] While specific regulations differ between countries, the dominant view in the West seems to be, that a young person is in need of caring and schooling. Both requirements are perceived to be best met in specific institutional settings (nuclear, bourgeoisie families and schools) in order for young people to become valuable members of society (James / James 2011, pp. 144ff.). Here it is worth mentioning, that both institutions – the family and schools – in their contemporary form, were themselves outcomes of the socio-economic rearrangements beginning with industrialisation in the 19th century (Brockliss / Montgomery 2010, p. 11). In contrast, young people who execute their agency by engaging in other social spheres or do not follow the hegemonic, institutionalised path towards adulthood, are often problematized and criminalized.

Juvenile ageism, first sketched by Jack Westman (1991), describes such institutional forms of discrimination (e.g. social systems ignoring the interests of young people), as well as individual forms of discrimination (e.g. carer's neglect). However, Westman makes some assumptions, which seem difficult to maintain today, such as assuming children to be essentially "helpless" (Westman 1991, p. 238) which seems a normative rather than an empirical position. In addition, Westman reproduces the view, which Zhao / et al. (2011, p. 249) later identified as tendency to construct children as "primitive" social beings.

This volume's focus on the study of young people, makes age gaps a source of privilege for the *adult* researcher, as childhood and youth is mostly constructed as phase of dependency on older people, who are those young people should obey in order to learn how to be a grown-up. Adolescence is perceived as a transitional phase towards adulthood, in which bodily changes have already happened, but in which young people still lack behind intellectually and are not yet completely able to make informed decisions autonomously. (Wells 2011)

The notion of children as passive social beings with little intellectual resources, who lack genuine political agency seems unwarranted and paternalistic, as it reproduces a notion of young people as pre-political beings, (Zhao / et al. 2011) while adults are constructed as capable of canny political action (Raby 2007). Since such assumptions are still pervasive, it seems clear that research

3 While age restrictions on drinking and smoking might be based on the higher harm certain substances can have on a young person's body, it also assumes that young people are not capable of making informed decisions and take care of themselves.

with children and young adults is inflicted with power imbalances, and therefore needs thorough reflections on questions of age, and what it means in specific social contexts.[4]

Questions to assess one's age-privileges:
- How has my age / maturity influenced how people perceive me throughout my life?
- How have I benefitted from being considered of a particular age at different points in my life?
- How do I treat people who I consider "not my age"? What do I expect from them? What are the underlying assumptions for these expectations?
- Am I more sceptical / critical towards statements of young people than of people I consider "grown-up"? If so, what are my underlying assumptions? Are those assumptions based on empirical observations, or do they have a good theoretical underpinning? If so, which alternative approaches to research with young people could I use to generate data that are more accurate?

Racial privilege as whites

> "Eddy is white, and we know he is because nobody says so." (Morrison 1993, p. 72)

Being identified as white comes with several social benefits, many of which Peggy McIntosh (1989) included in a still incomplete list of more than 30 everyday situations in which McIntosh felt being identified as white was advantageous. More systematic studies also showed racial privilege in the West, as they found that people identified as white were less likely to experience discrimination based on their racial affiliation, e.g. to be found guilty by criminal courts (Uhrig 2016) or being the target of racial profiling (Liu 2017).

Particularly important for the interview context, white people are rarely expected to speak for "their" racial group, while non-white people are often made into representatives of the racial group they are affiliated with (by the interviewer), which can be considered a form of reverse-racism (Mizock / et al. 2011). While in doing so, one might acknowledge the existence of racism, one also denies individuality to those targeted by racist discourses. Instead, racism is made into a pathology, which "overdetermines" (Fanon 2008, p. 95) the individual and constructs it primarily as a victim and product of racism. In other words, everything a person targeted by racism does and feels could be in-

4 For a particularly good reflection on this issue in empirical research practice, see Thorstensson Dávila's (2014) study on refugee youth.

terpreted as a response to having experienced racist discrimination. Racism is reified as the singular force, which engenders the individual, its experiences, troubles, hardships, and even its agency. This perpetuates the racist dogma, that only whites are truly agentive, creative and autonomous, while the agency, creativity and autonomy of non-white people is conditioned by them being targets of racist discrimination. This assumption over the devastating effect of racism on the psyche and agency of non-white individuals becomes even more problematic if one assumes, that the person having white privilege probably might has had little to no first-hand experience with racist discrimination.[5]

Questions to assess one's racial-privilege:
- How have notions of racial identity or racism influenced my perception of people I identify with other "races"?
- How has my racial affiliation influenced how people perceive me in different contexts?
- How have I benefitted from being considered of a particular race throughout my life?
- How do I treat people who I identify as being of a particular racial / ethnic group? What assumptions do I make about their lives and what is the role I attribute to experiences of racism? How are those assumptions based on empirical observations or have theoretical underpinnings?

Religious privilege as Christians

> "[Christianity qua concept] is a relationship of power. It is a structure of possible actions, the enactment of essential divisions and their distribution across a hierarchical differential of power." (Anidjar 2009, p. 392)

Christian privilege is likely to manifest in at least two distinctive forms. First, Christian privilege can refer to structural and individual advantages which come from being associated with a Christian heritage. This actual privilege, referred to in the literature as *christonormativity*, functions particularly through "the normalization and privileging of Christianity as the dominant religious and spiritual culture" (Ferber 2012, p. 70). Much of the current research on christonormativity has been undertaken in the United States, where the cultural entanglement of

5 Frantz Fanon (2008) famously raised those objections against Jean-Paul Sartre's point that the emerging anti-colonial artistic expressions – the *Negritude* literary movement in particular – were essentially only manifestations of class struggle, which would then make the artistic expression merely into a response to the general progression of history and society towards the classless-society. Fanon fiercely criticised this point as being essentialist and denying true agency to anti-colonial/post-colonial political activists and artists. (Fanon 2008, pp. 89ff.)

Christian-Protestant traditions with political culture has become increasingly visible within the past decades (Deckman / et al. 2017; Williamson / et al. 2011). Lewis Schlosser (2003), analogous to Peggy McIntosh, listed privileges emerging from being Christian in the United States. For a Western European context, such a list might also include having one's religious holidays as general public holidays, but also being able to change one's religious affiliation without the act being pathologised as a kind of seeking refuge from one's "pre-modern" religion.

While in Europe it seems that in a few countries (such as France) atheism is an even more advantageous position to be associated with (Salton 2012), European national histories tend to link Christianity to European heritage (e. g. seeing Europe's history connected to the fate of the empire of the Catholic kings, rather than the Muslim Empire, which reigned over considerable parts of the Iberian Peninsula for over 700 years). While in many Western European countries, the connection between religiosity and politics is far less pronounced than in the United States today, debates over the scope of Europe's "Judeo-Christian" heritage and foundations indicate the normalisation of a particular religious heritage and its framing as the basis of European identity. This connects quite well with orientalist tropes and discourses, which have a long tradition in Western culture (Said 2003), and still inform anti-Muslim sentiments today. Several authors emphasize that in the eyes of many non-Muslim Westerners, Islam has ceased to be seen as a personal religious conviction, but that it has been ethniciszed (Thielmann 2013), or racialized (Considine 2017; Galonnier 2015; Selod / Embrick 2013). In such discourses, Islam itself is constructed as an antipode to *Europe*, while disregarding the heterogeneity of Islamic believe systems worldwide, and the influence of Muslims on "European" science and culture. Therefore, it is unsurprising that Muslims are often accused of not being truly loyal to the Western nation states they live in or are citizens of, but instead are looked upon with suspicion (Brown 2010; Modood / et al. 2006; Schiffauer 2006; Hassan 2015). Here christonormativity intersects with anti-Muslim racism, which falls in line with Ferber's (2012, p. 70) observation, that Christianity has informed and legitimised a multiplicity of privileging and oppressive forces, such as gender and racial hierarchies, anti-Semitism, ageism, classism, and so on.

Christian privilege can also be understood in an ontological sense, as having greatly informed a dominant Western and by this also hegemonic scientific understanding of religion. For Gil Anidjar the normalization of Christianity resulted in the estrangement and exotisation of other religions, particularly so-called ethnic or indigenous religions, which became the focus of anthropological research, whereas anthropological interest for European Christianity has remained scarce (Anidjar 2009, 2015). Consequently, as researchers, we need to be critical of the relationship of Christianity with dominant political culture in Europe. In addition, we must be aware that religion itself is a culturally framed, vague and therefore problematic concept. Being critical of christonormativity means being aware of, first, the normalisation of Christianity and its constitutive role in constructions of "Western" culture and values, second, the privileges that emerge from being associated in one way or another with Christianity, and third, the role of Christianity in influencing our basic understandings of what religion is.

Questions to assess one's religious-privileges:
- How has a Christian notion of religion influenced my thinking about religion in general?
- How has my religious affiliation (whether I intend to be identified with it or not) influenced how people treated me?
- How do I treat people, which I consider as members of a particular religious group? What do I think about their lives? What are the underlying assumptions for these suppositions?
- How have I benefitted from people assuming that I belong to a certain religious group?

Gender privileges as cis-gendered, heterosexual male

> "Genders [...] can be neither true nor false, neither real nor apparent. And yet, one is compelled to live in a world in which genders constitute univocal signifiers, in which gender is stabilized, polarized, rendered discrete and intractable." (Butler 1988, 528)

Feminist standpoint theory has argued that under the cover of seemingly objective and unbiased research, it was actually undisclosed male, patriarchal, colonial, situated knowledge, which informed science over centuries (Haraway 1988; hooks 1992). Since this criticism started to be acknowledged in the late 1980s, the call for critical self-assessment has strongly resonated particularly, but by far not exclusively in gender-related research (Lang 2011; Leino / Peltomaa 2017; Selod / Embrick 2013; Stoetzler / Yuval-Davis 2002). Still, this critical stance has not yet resulted in a more critical approach to research in general. (Woodward 2008, p. 548)

There are two manifestations of gender privilege, which I want to address very briefly. On the one hand, patriarchal structures provide the basis for the production and reproduction of dominance of men over people identifying or being identified as non-male (Liu 2017; Orelus 2010; Pittman 2010; Eberhardt 2017). Such privileges can manifest in interactions between people who have learned to identify and are socially identified as male and non-male individuals. On the other hand, looking at the performative aspect of gender, gender is not only a system of dominance, but also an instrument of social control, as Judith Butler (1988) emphasises. Behaving within socially assigned and sanctioned gendered norms comes with specific privileges, whereas non-heteronormative behaviour is considered deviant and pathological.

As interviewers and listeners, we have to realise, that we might enforce these regulatory, controlling mechanisms unconsciously through our gendered demeanour. Avoiding such patterns during interviews, but also controlling for them during analysis, is absolutely key for a self-critical assessment of one's own performance and the influence one has on the conversation. However, interviewees might also have internalised gendered expectations towards, for example, a male interviewer (e. g. waiting until he* introduces the next topic or asks a question, instead of leading the conversation). Such patterns should also be taken into account before, during and after the interview. (Cameron 2011; Talbot 2011; Brody 2000)

Apart from paying attention to gendered ways of speaking and acting, gender also has effects on the respective life-worlds of speakers and listeners, creating particular experiences, expectations and problem perspectives. (Orelus 2010) For example identifying as non-binary can be highly problematic, when one is expected to identify as either male or female only. Therefore, gender must not be automatically perceived as self-evident or essentially binary. Equal consideration is also warranted for people who have non-heterosexual sexual orientations, as such practices are often stigmatised (Herek 1997), frequently constitute grounds for legal discrimination and makes one more likely to be physically assaulted. (Waaldijk / Bonini-Baraldi 2006; Earley 2016)

Questions to assess one's gender- and sexual orientation-privileges:
- How has the notion of the existence of gender dichotomy influenced me?
- How has the notion of heteronormativity (the notion that heterosexuality is the only "normal" sexual orientation) influenced me?
- How have patriarchal structures in family and society influenced my thinking about gender relations and "natural" gendered entitlements?
- How has my gender affiliation or sexual orientation, whether I intended to be identified with it or not, influenced how people treat me and how have I benefitted from this?
- How do I treat people which I consider having a particular gender or sexual orientation, or those which I cannot put in one of the dominant categories? What do I assume about their lives, and what are the underlying assumptions for these suppositions?

Socio-economic privilege as member of the upper / upper-middle class

> "[C]lass is a phenomenon (and lived experience) that is organized through hard-core structural, resource-based political processes, but equally, through the cultural, representational practices of everyday social life." (Thurlow / Jaworski, 2017 539)

Quite obviously, material living conditions, economic status and educational background – the elements which are widely perceived to be constitutive of "class" as a socio-economic phenomenon – come with their specific sets of social entitlements and restrictions (Liu / et al. 2007; Sanders / Mahalingam 2012; Skeggs 2004; Thurlow / Jaworski 2017). Researchers have to be aware of those aspects when doing interviews with people who are denied class-specific privileges, which the researcher has.

Socio-economic privileges can take various forms. Often educational achievement is influenced by the socio economic situation of one's parents. Some studies find that even within the same school, educational achievements differ along class divisions (Thiel 2012). Consequently, it is fair to say that in many contexts educational achievement is conditioned by class privilege. Equally, being socialized in a privileged socio-economic environment allows for privileged aspirations. For Liu / et al., an "upward mobility bias" is characteristic for white middle-class privilege and assumes that "individuals are constantly interested in upward social mobility, achievement, and success." (2007, p. 197) This petit bourgeoisie notion of socio-financial aspiration needs critical assessment in two ways. First, there is no reason to assume, that the desire of upward mobility is a universal human virtue, even though contemporary capitalism seems to nurture this assumption through its implicit imperative of self-optimisation (Sennett 2006). Second, structurally disadvantaged individuals might have learned that this upward mobility narrative is mediated by class: "[E]xperiences have taught people who are poor or less privileged that they are less likely to receive bank loans, that they are more likely to encounter discrimination in stores, and that they have little influence in their work situations." (Liu / et al. 2007, p. 198). Taking these points seriously, researchers must take classed aspirations and experiences critically into account, and recognise them as particular, rather than universal.

Another point researchers should keep in mind is that socio-economic stigma determines the accessibility of space (e.g. for homeless people), as MacDonald and Winddance Twine (2013, pp. 221 ff.) discuss in their article on (semi-)public spaces in Boston. This can be a serious issue for researchers looking for a place to meet with research participants. Researchers have to keep in mind that it might be *their* privilege, which gives their research participants access to spaces which otherwise they would not usually enter (e.g. university buildings), or might even be prevented from entering (e.g. certain commercial spaces for people not appearing as potential customers). In any case, researchers should reflect upon the class privileges, which regulate access to different resources. Further socio-economic privileges, identified by Liu / et al. (2007, pp. 205f.) relate to particular classed experiences, e.g. housing and financial resources, sociostructural support (e.g. assuming that government has one's interest in mind), social power and familiarity with classed behavioural norms (e.g. knowing social etiquette) to name just a few.

Questions to assess one's class-privileges:
- How has the class I was born into influenced my life's trajectory?
- How have different socio-economic conditions, which I have experienced in my life so far, influenced my perception of the world?
- How has the social class I belong to, or people associate me with, worked to my advantage in different social settings and influenced how people treated me?
- How do I treat people, which I consider as having a particular socio-economic / class background? What do I think about their lives? What are the underlying assumptions for these suppositions?

Occupational privilege of the researcher as a writer

> "There is an intricate web of morality, rigor, and responsibility that art, that writing itself, imposes on a writer. It's singular, it's individual, but nevertheless it's there. At its best, it's an exquisite bond between the artist and the medium. At its acceptable end, it's a sort of sensible co-operation. At its worst, it's a relationship of disrespect and exploitation." (Roy 2001, p. 6)

So far, I have looked at categories of difference relating to age, race, religion, gender and social class. For each of those spheres, I discussed the construction of a privileged position in a Western context, and briefly pointed out how such notions have come to influence what many of us have come to perceive as the norm. (Muhammad / et al. 2015; Pratto / Stewart 2012) As researchers, we are responsible to consider these aspects, reflect on them self-critically and make informed decisions concerning the social power relations, which exist in society as a whole, as well as in the micro publics of research environments. Meeting informed decisions must come from a process of serious, self-critical assessment and reflection, and needs to result in a deliberate decision on the use of methods. (Sprague 2005, p. 27)

However, alongside those privileges, we also have to take responsibility for being located at a relatively powerful position within the economy of knowledge production. As we are professional knowledge producers, our work has some kind of credibility, which – warranted or not – comes with a considerable amount of discursive power and social prestige.[6] Importantly, our work might have influence on the lives of individuals unaffected by the research process itself, as policy makers tend to use scientific findings to legitimise policy. In sum, the ability to present something as knowledge is, in essence, the greatest privilege of the researcher.

Consequently, we are not only responsible for raising our awareness of racialised, gendered, etc. privileges, but also reflect on those, which come through our profession. They, as well, can have serious implications on researching and writing. Research participants might project a lot of importance into a research collaboration, particular in the case of projects, which addresses a problem they encounter in their daily lives. Sometimes they expect results in the form of changes in policy, a different media coverage, and there like. While such an immediate effect is hardly ever the case, researchers should be aware, that participants might want to make use of this perceived privilege of the researcher to trigger social change. This momentum – that people provide answers from which they expect social change to emerge in the way they hope for – also needs to be taken into account by researchers.

As is true for other spheres of privilege, Arjun Appadurai (2006, but also other postcolonial theorists such as: Ladner 1998; Mohanty 1984; Spivak 2010) points out that researchers' privilege is highly intersectional, meaning that it is far less powerful, if it is not paired with other privileges. Researchers, which are identified as non-white, for example, might have their credibility challenged when writing about racist violence, simply by the fact that they are assumed of not presenting a scientific assessment, but as speaking exclusively as a representative of a disadvantaged group, expressing political opinions rather than making scientific statements. Similarly a religious scholar writing on Christianity might have the credibility of her_his work drawn into question, if being identified as Muslim.[7]

Questions to assess one's privileges as a researcher:

- How has being identified as a researcher influenced how other people (non-academics in particular) interact with me?
- How do I treat people, which I consider non-academics, particularly when it comes to research contexts, but also when it comes to sharing scientific in-

6 According to US data, scientists have a rather good reputation also among the public. (Funk 2017; National Academies Press (US) 2015)

7 This happened to religious scholar and author of a book on Jesus of Nazareth, Reza Aslan when being interviewed on TV in 2013. Rather than discussing the argument of the book, the host questioned Aslan's credibility as scientist and ability to write about Jesus, bringing up his Muslimness as a reason.

formation? What do I think their concerns are? What are the underlying assumptions for these suppositions?
- How has my capacity as researcher, worked to my advantage in different social settings?
- Which position do I claim when interacting with research participants and how do I represent them in my writing?

The A-B-C-D-Approach

While the first part of the chapter aimed at familiarising the reader with a few areas in which unacknowledged privilege might pose problems for interpersonal exchanges in general and qualitative interviewing encounters in particular, this section develops a structured operationalisation of those reflections in empirical research projects. Therefore, I propose four steps, each accompanying different stages of the research process: (1) *assessing* the privileges I have vis-à-vis the research participants in the specific context in which the interview takes place, (2) *balancing* the effects of privileges through the use of specific research methods and a particular research design, (3) *clarifying* one's awareness of privilege differentials in conversation with research participants. This can help to reduce misunderstandings and control for one's influence on the research context, and (4) *deconstructing* the effects of privilege in the analytical process. These four steps I call the *A-B-C-D-approach.* This approach is intended to serve as an initial guideline for researchers trying to incorporate a critical acknowledgment of their own privileges in their research design and practice. It systematically incorporates reflexivity in research and aims at improving the quality of data and analysis (Wolcott 2001, p. 163; Guber 2001; da Silva / Webster 2018)[8]. On the following pages, I present each of those four steps in more detail, based on their application in my own qualitative research with young, self-identified Muslims in Zurich and Vienna.

Assessing privilege – knowing oneself

Data do not emerge from a social vacuum, but are embedded and engendered by power relations, experiences, discursive orders and social positionings which materialise in the research setting and the interaction between researcher and participant (Esin / et al. 2014; Gubrium / Holstein, 2003; Foucault 1981). Among

8 Without a notion of privilege at its conceptual core, ethnographic accounts discussed questions of researcher positionality, standpoint and reflexivity extensively.

those factors, privileges of researchers are often overlooked, which can, however, lead to unwarranted suppositions, problem perspectives and conceptual frameworks, which do not align with the life-worlds of research participants and effectively result in distorted data and analysis. Internalised notions emerging from being brought up in a privileging environment might shape ideas about the interviewee's life and thinking. (Mizock / et al. 2011; Sanders / Mahalingam 2012) Identifying and controlling for those influencing factors is crucial in order to collect and analyse data in the best, most truthful way. For sure, it is highly unlikely that a researcher exclusively occupies privileged positions vis-á-vis a research participant. Mostly spheres of privilege and disadvantage intersect. Nevertheless, while a lack of privilege is something individuals recognise quite easily and readily account for in their research practice, privileges tend to hide themselves from the person having those privileges (Sprague 2005, pp. 127ff., pp. 165ff.; Wildman / Davis 1995, pp. 885ff.; Dyer 1997; Pease 2013).

Consequently, the first step for researchers is to develop an understanding of their own privileges. Inspired by the work by Peggy McIntosh, activists came up with lists of items relating to different privileges.[9] Choosing a different approach, I familiarised readers with ways to assess their privileges through asking specific questions. Thereby, researchers should get an idea how privileges might have influenced their lives. Researchers should begin to assess how experiences affected by privilege were responsible for how they think about their research subject(s) today. (Muhammad / et al. 2015) Are assumptions over a certain issue reasonably warranted, or are they based on privileged suppositions and second-guessing regarding *the experiences of the Others?*

- Be aware that a privileged socialisation also means having learned to misinterpret the privileges one has as the result of one's own making, rather than the product of social forces.
- Be aware that from a global perspective, there are more people lacking core privileges than there are people who can rely on being privileged in most contexts of life. Particularly, privileged people can more easily avoid situations in which they are not equipped with privilege.

9 Such lists can be found on various online platforms and usually consist of diverse items, ranging from being right-handed to having one's "ancestor's history" taught in school history classes, from never having been dependent on social benefits, to not having a second thought about calling the police when in trouble.

Balancing privilege – developing a research design and choosing research methods

How does one's approach to research might help in balancing the influence privilege has on the research encounter? Alternative research methods, which provide greater expressive possibilities and give more autonomy to research participants, can loosen the discursive grip of the privileged researcher (Brotherton 2011)[10], by putting less emphasis on the interrogating character of conventional one-on-one interviews (Mizock / et al. 2011). They can also reduce the pressure on interviewees, who are expected to understand the intention of the researcher's question, reply accordingly, and perform as knowledgeable subjects or experts (Gubrium / Holstein 2003, pp. 30f.). Some established modes of interviewing, such as narrative interviewing (Andrews / et al. 2013; Riessman 2008; Rosenthal / Fischer-Rosenthal 2010; Scheibelhofer 2008), tend to be "more open and adaptable" to research participants, and generally more reflexive of the "meaning-making work and communicative conditions of interviewing" (Gubrium / Holstein 2003, p. 32). However, they still fall short in preventing from the interrogating gaze and performance of the interviewer. The research participant is likely to respond consciously or unconsciously to the internalised behavioural patterns of the privileged researcher. In this sense, most, if not all, attempts to get rid of the researcher's influence will fail.

To avoid this dead end, I want to put forward a radical reinterpretation of research participant and researcher. Research participants must not only be perceived as monadic experts or informants on a single issue, but as authors and creative users of discourse, who deliberately construct an account tailored to the particular audience and the setting, their individual time resources and the topic. Without falling into either the role of an interrogator nor of a passive receptor, the researcher ought to constitute the primary audience while also consciously co-constructing the account through verbal and non-verbal cues (Sprague 2005, pp. 165ff.).[11]

In my own research, I decided to work with a photo interview technique, adopted from Bettina Kolb (2008; see also: Harper 2002; Hurworth / et al. 2005), which stands in the tradition of Participatory Action Research (Ozanne / Saatcioglu 2008) and more specifically photo voice approaches (Seed, 2016; Wang / et

10 Here, I refer in particular to gendered ways of behaving (talking, gesturing), but also the effect, simply being identified as male, already has on a research context. You might think of the unease a male research participant might have in discussing aspects of his life with a female researcher or vice versa.

11 In this regard, we can only speak of a researcher if the researcher is also, in fact, the addressee of those creations of world. In other words, the voyeuristic perspective of the unengaged, non-located, invisible observer is not a location from which knowledge can be acquired.

al. 1996; Wang / Burris 1997; Wang / Redwood-Jones 2001). After having conducted a narrative, biographical interview, I invited participants to take part in a photo project. I asked them to take 10–15 pictures of important objects, places or spaces in their everyday life over the course of approximately one month. Thereby, participants had time to reflect on the task given to them and re-interpret it so that it would make sense to them. As a result, I received a very heterogeneous set of pictures. Some used the photo project to depict stages of their lives (the schools they attended, the houses they lived in, etc.), while others focused more on the present and what was important to them in the here and now (food, street art, the night sky, etc.). Of course, even without the gaze of the researcher over their shoulder, participants had been informed, and were aware, that they were taking pictures for a subsequent photo-interview. Resembling the depicted heterogeneity, accounts to the pictures varied greatly; some used their pictures to talk quite explicitly to the topic of the project, while others represented themselves in a more personal, general way.

The novelty and particular strength of this approach concerning levelling the researcher's privilege lies in its openness, which provides research participants authorship in the considerate or spontaneous construction of their visual accounts. Consequently, in the photo-interview, interviewees, through their selection of visual content, have more power over the agenda setting of the interview, while the research interest of the researcher is less prominent.[12]

Also in other aspects privilege can be balanced through choices relating to research design. In my own research, when it came to setting up a meeting for an interview, I asked participants where *they* wanted to meet. I followed their lead and trusted them with choosing the place and setting, in which they thought, they could express themselves in the way they wanted. Thereby I acknowledged that particular places are not generally accessible to everyone (e.g. while for most men* meeting in coffee houses and pubs is rather easy, this might not be the case for women* as some of those spaces are rather gender-exclusive). Certain places also require adhering to behavioural codes, the knowledge of which can be a matter of privileged socialisation. (Goffman 1990) The choice of setting might include the presence of other people. As I assume that spoken utterances are co-

12 Nevertheless, this method is not without its critics (Allan 2012). Many people working with similar visual methods in the context of research with young people emphasize the potential of such approaches as enabling participants to make their voices heard and assume a process of empowering to take place (Harper 2002; Kolb 2008; McIntyre 2010; McLees 2013; Nykiforuk / et al. 2011; Wang / Redwood-Jones 2001). Other researchers, however, questioned those empowering effects, as empirical data on those effects does not exist (Block / Bukkingham 2007; Luttrell 2010; Piper / Frankham 2007). Whether or not such positive effects are empirically detectable, it can still be maintained, that such an approach allows research participants to have a greater say in the research project themselves and can diminish the researcher's influence on meaning-making processes.

produced (Riessman 2008), even a passive third party can affect the conversation. While in most methodologies, such a situation might be interpreted as problematic, the interviewee's wish to speak not with the interviewer alone, but with another person present, can also be thought of as a specific performative choice, as taking up a specific role for which this third party is considered important by the interviewee.

- Try to reflect on how the speaker constructs you as the audience. To whom are the utterances addressed (to you as a sympathetic, empathetic individual, to policy makers, to the public in general, to a specific group…)?
- When collecting demographic meta-information, avoid forcing people to identify with hegemonic gendered, racialised, etc. categories (e.g. male or female). Instead, allow for open-ended expressions of such affiliations. (Do not assume to be able to identify a person's ethnicity, gender, or religious identity, without having asked them.)
- In some cases, it can be a good idea to give research participants considerable time to think and reflect on a research question and / or execute a certain task (like taking pictures).
- Develop a research design which includes tasks, which deliberately invites participants to make the research meaningful to themselves. By doing so, research participants have a chance to challenge your problem perspective, which you would enforce much more strongly in a conventional interview setting.

Clarifying privilege – countering the invisibility discourse

Apart from the research design, privilege also materialises intersubjectively in the interpersonal contact between the research participant and the researcher (Stoudt / et al., 2012, p. 179; Pease 2013, pp. 33ff.). In their study on the discursive resources available to speak about social class privilege, Sanders and Maligham (2012) show that while disadvantaged individuals might be very well aware of the existence of other people's privileges, they often feel hesitant to address their experiences of being disadvantaged vis-á-vis (hyper-)privileged individuals, as such accounts are rather unusual in dominant discourses. In being consciously or unconsciously aware of the privileges of the researcher, research participants might also have prejudices against them. Participants might suppose that the researcher has a biased problem perspective oneself due to unacknowledged privileges (Muhammad / et al. 2015). Such unaddressed suppositions can lead to serious misunderstandings and biased data. Even without this degree of reflexivity on behalf of research participants, they might be irritated by a research project, which does not answer to what they consider problematic or urgent. Consequently, tesearch participants might not feel taken seriously in their personal situation.[13] This impression of ignorance towards the lived experiences and realities might result in incoherent or superficial data, due to research participants' lack of commitment to the project. (Mizock / et al. 2011)

In order to control better how research participants construct the researcher (in one's role as primary audience) it is advisable to position oneself explicitly before an interview. This might also include stating one's intentions behind the research, one's academic interests so far, one's intellectual path (when one started to consider something as problematic and why) and so on. The declaration of privilege should be part of the initial clarification by the researcher. Importantly, however, it should not be a blunt declaration of oneself as anti-racist/sexist/etc., but should include clarifying one's critical awareness of the unequal distribution of privileges and its real life manifestations. Such a clarification may take the form of a straight forward acknowledgment that life-worlds are different (and unfairly so) due to the ways people are born and raised under specific, human-made, political circumstances upon which both, researcher and research participants have had limited influence.[14] Through this discursive positioning one can better prevent misunderstandings, as it introduces a discourse the interviewee can make use of to address issues of privilege and disadvantage. Ideally, this should provide for an open interview atmosphere. (Sanders / Mahalingam 2012). Indicating the researcher's awareness of structures of privilege, signals to participants that accounts of structural or individual oppression won't be met with categorical disbelieve by the researcher.

The importance of such an act can be seen in Mizock / et al.'s (2011) study on narrative interviews on traumatic experiences. They point out that racialised research participants might find it easier to speak about racism to people who they feel might have made similar experiences. However, one must take care not to "overdetermine" (Fanon 2008) research participants as inherently disadvantaged. Instead, one may signal that it is peculiar that media portrays representatives of minority populations in a stereotypical way, or that women of colour are rarely listened to, but often talked about. As it is important to indicate one's general awareness of the existence of such privileges in society it does not

13 The difficulties that come with this are also pointed out by Alexandra Allan, who did a photo and film-project with young people from two private colleges in England. Whereas Allan was aware of the class privilege of the participants, as well as the privilege enjoyed as a researcher, the video project turned out to be rather unsatisfying. Allan had the impression, students made use of the resources provided by the project without seriously engaging in discussions on their material. (Allan 2012, p. 5.12f.) It appears as if the problem perspective or interests of the researcher and the research participants did not align and resulted in less commitment to the project.

14 When doing so, make sure to use the same concepts, better the same wording in all the interviews.

necessarily have to relate to an assumed privilege the researcher has in contrast to the research participant. Nevertheless, such a statement should refer to a phenomenon the participant is likely to be familiar with in some way.

- Be aware, that people might not want to be put in the category you want to locate them in, even if they are categories you consider meaningful for anti-racist, anti-sexist, etc. struggle.[15] Anticipate your world-view being challenged.
- Be critical of your own way of speaking and avoid dominating speech patterns.
- Do not pathologise people who you think must frequently experience forms of discrimination. Be aware that people will have developed strategies to avoid or fight against such forms of being disadvantaged.[16]
- Instead, closely follow the research participant's own assessment of the effects discriminations have had in the past and present.
- Try to create an appreciative and respectful environment by avoiding devaluing and violent speech and metaphors (Summy 1998).

Deconstructing privilege – controlling for the effects of privilege

As a last step, controlling for the effects of privilege remains key. This process, which helps to increase the validity and reliability of research findings, requires to deconstruct the effects of privilege on research data (Ramazanoglu / Holland, 2002, pp. 116ff.). To do so, it can be helpful to interpret data collaboratively with research participants. This also helps to level the researcher's privilege by giving participants a chance to contribute to the analytical process. Of course, such an endeavour needs a certain degree of commitment on behalf of the research participants, and maybe also some methodological instructions (e.g. stating what to focus on and how to analyse). (Ozanne / Saatcioglu 2008)

In my own research project, I followed this approach by doing photo-interviews. While I could have analysed the pictures as independent data, I relied on the interpretation of the photographers and invited them to tell me what the

15 How then research the effects of oppression, if a research participant resists acknowledging racist, sexist, etc. categorisations? It should be clear that oppression can have devastating, pathological and lasting effects on one's psyche, just as a number of other traumatic experiences. However, for most individuals, oppression will be only one aspect among many, which characterise their lives. Individual desires, plans, actions and creativity tend to characterise an individual's life more, than the fact that people struggle against oppressive power structures. Approach people who have experienced discrimination as the experts they are when it comes to describing what oppression does to their life (and what it does not).

16 Such strategies are most likely embedded in everyday practices, such as avoiding certain places, confronting racists head on, not disclosing a position lacking privileges, if it can be avoided, etc.

pictures showed and what about the motif was important to them. Subsequently, when analysing the photo-interviews, I strongly focused on collaborative meaning-making processes and the interactions between interviewee and interviewer (Harper 2002). To do so systematically, I applied a Narrative Constructionist Analytic framework (a variation of Narrative Analysis) developed by Cigdem Esin, Matoureh Fathi and Corinne Squire (2014). For this approach, the emphasis lies on the context specificity of narratives, as the interviews are the social phenomenon to be analysed. Non-verbal cues (gestures, laughter, etc.), the use of local vernacular, gendered language, the use of different concepts, modes of voice, etc., are considered relevant aspects which might influences the way narratives are constructed. Apart from the level of performance and positioning (Davies / Harré 1990), Esin, Fathi and Squire also emphasise taking socio-political and historical aspects into account, which allows asking and interrogating, for example, the influence of gender, whiteness and other aspects on the co-construction of narratives.

This, of course, is but one methodological path to follow in order to assess one's performance and gendered presence as relevant aspects in collaborative meaning-making processes. Other approaches might rely on Critical Discourse Analysis (Fairclough 2013; Wodak 2009), feminist standpoint theory (Haraway 1988; Ramazanoglu / Holland 2002), or critical realist approaches (Sprague 2005, pp. 165ff.), to name just a few.

- Follow research participants in their assessment of their lived experiences, and avoid challenging participants' interpretation of an act. (Ramazanoglu / Holland 2002)
- Control for enacted power in interaction: Who introduces new topics? Does somebody narrate extensively or does somebody only reply briefly on questions asked? Who interrupts who, when, and what seem to be the effects of such interruptions? (Riessman 2008)
- Control for gendered speech patterns. (Talbot 2011)

Conclusion

This article engaged in a discussion of the effects of privilege on qualitative research, particularly on interview encounters between privileged researchers and research participants lacking certain privileges. First, I invited readers to reflect on spheres in which they might be privileged (relating to age, race, religion, gender, class and their profession as researchers). Second, I highlighted a path to incorporate a critical awareness of privilege in research practice. The A-B-C-D-approach, which I developed, can help researchers in generating data that are more reliable. Furthermore, it presents a structured approach to work with and control for privilege throughout the analytical process.

What this chapter calls for, is a perpetual process of critical self-assessment as inherent part of research practice. As social (power) relations constantly change and different contexts engender different privileges, we, as researchers, have to continue questioning ourselves and how our privileges might play out with various people, at different points in time and space. Learning to see one's own privileges and the effects they have on scientific knowledge production, as well as finding new approaches to do research, while being critically aware of one's own influence on the research environment, are skills, which need development and constant practice. This also acknowledges that there is no path to get rid of privileges once and for all, but instead, that we need to control for their effects and take responsibility for them. With this knowledge, we should look for creative ways to generate data with new, experimental methods attuned to the relation of researcher and research participants in a specific project.

Nevertheless, the proposed way of doing research, must not be mistaken for an attempt to secure the place of white, male, Christian, cis-gendered, mature, etc. researchers in the field. On the contrary, it invites everybody to assess one's privileges, make the assessment a part of the research project and improve one's research. Furthermore, these guidelines may also provide a measuring tape against which research can be assessed regarding its incorporation of a critical assessment of the author's own social position.

Despite the gravity of the problem, there has been little awareness of the effects of privilege on research encounters yet. This might have to do with a fear researchers have, namely that acknowledging their carefully cultivated and internalised privileges would sabotage their own scientific standing and credibility. (Pease 2013) However, the opposite concern should be far more unsettling, which is that unacknowledged privilege emits a biasing effect on research data which one can hardly control for in hindsight, if one has not controlled for it from the start.

References

Allan, Alexandra (2012): "Power, participation and privilege. Methodological lessons from using visual methods in research with young people." *Sociological Research Online*, 17 (3). https://doi.org/10.5153/sro.2662.

Allievi, Stefano (2006): "How the Immigrant has Become Muslim." *Revue Européenne des Migrations Internationales*, 21 (2), pp. 135–163. https://doi.org/10.4000/remi.2497.

Alvesson, Mats / Sköldberg, Kaj (2012): *Reflexive methodology. New vistas for qualitative research.* Los Angeles: SAGE.

Andrews, Molly / Squire, Corinne / Tamboukou, Maria (eds.) (2013): *Doing narrative research*, London / et al., SAGE.
Anidjar, Gil (2009): "The idea of an anthropology of Christianity." *Interventions*, vol. 11, no. 3, pp. 367–393. https://doi.org/10.1080/13698010903255718.
– (2015): "Christianity, Christianities, Christian." *Journal of Religious and Political Practice*, 1 (1), pp. 39–46. https://doi.org/10.1080/20566093.2015.1047687.
Anthias, Floya (2009): "Intersectionality, belonging and translocational positionality. Thinking about transnational identities." In: Rosenthal, Gabriele / Bogner, Artur (Eds.): *Ethnicity, belonging and biography. Ethnographical and biographical perspectives.* Berlin: Lit, pp. 229–249.
Appadurai, Arjun (2006): "The right to research." *Globalisation, Societies and Education*, 4 (2), pp. 167–177. https://doi.org/10.1080/14767720600750696.
Archer, Margaret (2013): "Introduction. Realism in the Social Sciences." In: Archer, Margaret / Bhaskar, Roy / Collier, Andrew / Lawson, Tony / Norrie, Alan (Eds.): *Critical Realism. Essential Readings.* Hoboken: Taylor and Francis, pp. 189–205.
Archer, Margaret / Bhaskar, Roy / Collier, Andrew / Lawson, Tony / Norrie, Alan (Eds.) (2013): *Critical realism. Essential Readings.* Hoboken: Taylor and Francis.
Ayalon, Liat / Tesch-Römer, Clemens (Eds.) (2018): *Contemporary perspectives on ageism.* Cham: Springer International Publishing.
Berger, Peter L. / Luckmann, Thomas (1991): *The social construction of reality: A treatise in the sociology of knowledge.* Harmondsworth: Penguin books.
Bhaskar, Roy (2008): *A realist theory of science.* London: Verso.
de Block, Liesbeth / Buckingham, David (2007): *Global children, global media: Migration, media and childhood.* Basingstoke: Palgrave Macmillan.
Bonds, Anne / Inwood, Joshua (2016) "Beyond white privilege." *Progress in Human Geography*, 40 (6), pp. 715–733. https://doi.org/10.1177/0309132515613166.
Brockliss, Laurence W. B. / Montgomery, Heather (eds.) (2010): *Childhood and violence in the Western tradition.* Oxford: Oxbow Books.
Brody, Celeste M. (2000): *Gender consciousness and privilege.* London, New York: Falmer Press.
Brotherton, Dawn B. (2011): "Rehumanizing Race-Related Research in Qualitative Study of Faith-Based Organizations: Case Studies, Focus Groups, and Long Interviews." In Stanfield, John H. (Ed.): *Rethinking Race and Ethnicity in Research Methods.* Walnut Creek: Left Coast Press, pp. 235–251.
Brown, Katherine E. (2010): "Contesting the securitization of British Muslims." In *Interventions* 12 (2), pp. 171–182. https://doi.org/10.1080/1369801X.2010.489690.
Burr, Vivian (2015): *Social constructionism.* London: Routledge.
Butler, Judith (1988): "Performative acts and gender constitution. An essay in phenomenology and feminist theory." *Theatre Journal* 40 (4), pp. 519–531. http://www.jstor.org/stable/3207893.
Cameron, Deborah (2011): "Performing gender identity: Young men's talk and the construction of heterosexual masculinity." in Mooney, A. (ed.): *The language, society and power reader.* London, New York: Routledge, pp. 179–191.
Considine, Craig (2017): "The racialization of Islam in the United States. Islamophobia, hate crimes, and 'flying while brown'." *Religions*, 8 (9), 165. https://doi.org/10.3390/rel8090165.

Davies, Bronwyn / Harré, Rom (1990): "Positioning. The discursive construction of selves." *Journal for the Theory of Social Behaviour* 20, pp. 43–63.
Davis, Ashley / Mirick, Rebecca / McQueen, Barbara (2015): "Teaching from privilege." *Affilia*, 30 (3), pp. 302–313. https://doi.org/10.1177/0886109914560742.
Deckman, Melissa / Cox, Dan / Jones, Robert / Cooper, Betsy (2017): "Faith and the free market. Evangelicals, the Tea Party, and economic attitudes." *Politics and Religion*, 10 (1), pp. 82–110. https://doi.org/10.1017/S1755048316000420.
Du Bois, W. E. B (1990): *The souls of black folk.* New York: Bantam Classics.
Du Bois, W. E. B. ; Sundquist, Eric J. (1996): *The Oxford W.E.B. Du Bois reader.* New York, et al.: Oxford Univ. Press.
Dyer, Richard (1997): *White.* London et al.: Routledge.
Earley, Frances (2016): *Sexual orientation.* Hauppauge: Nova Science Publishers Inc.
Eberhardt, Maeve (2017): "Gendered representations through speech. The case of the Harry Potter series." *Language and Literature* 26 (3), pp. 227–246. https://doi.org/10.1177/0963947017701851.
Esin, Cigdem / Fathi, Mastoureh / Squire, Corinne (2014): "Narrative analysis: The constructionist approach." In: Flick, Uwe (ed.): *The SAGE handbook of qualitative data analysis.* London: SAGE, pp. 203–216.
Fairclough, Norman (2013) *Critical discourse analysis: The critical study of language.* London: Routledge.
Fanon, Frantz (2008): *Black skin, white masks.* New York: Grove Press.
Ferber, Abby L. (2012): "The culture of privilege. Color-blindness, postfeminism, and Christonormativity." *Journal of Social Issues*, 68 (1), pp. 63–77. https://doi.org/10.1111/j.1540-4560.2011.01736.x.
Foucault, Michel (1981): The Order of Discourse. In Robert Young (Ed.): *Untying the text. A post-structuralist reader.* Boston: Routledge & Kegan Paul, pp. 48–78.
Funk, Cary (2017): "Real Numbers: Mixed Messages about Public Trust in Science." *ISSUES in Science and Technology,* 34 (1). available: http://www.issues.org/34-1/real-numbers-mixed-messages-about-public-trust-in-science/ [07.08.2018].
Galonnier, Juliette (2015): "The racialization of Muslims in France and the United States. Some insights from white converts to Islam." *Social Compass*, 62 (4), pp. 570–583. https://doi.org/10.1177/0037768615601966.
Goffman, Erving (1990): *The presentation of self in everyday life.* New York et al.: Doubleday.
Guber, Rosana (2001): *La etnografía. Método, campo y reflexividad.* Bogotá.
Gubrium, Jaber F. / Holstein, James A. (2003): *Postmodern interviewing*, Thousand Oaks, London: SAGE.
Hall, Stuart (2011): "The West and the Rest. Discourse and power." In Hall, Stuart (ed.): *Formations of modernity.* Cambridge: Polity Press pp. 275–332.
Haraway, Donna (1988): "Situated knowledges. The science question in feminism and the privilege of partial perspective." *Feminist Studies*, 14 (3), pp. 575–599. https://doi.org/10.2307/3178066.
Harper, Douglas (2002): "Talking about pictures: A case for photo elicitation." *Visual Studies*, 17 (1), pp. 13–26. https://doi.org/10.1080/14725860220137345.

Hassan, Said (2015): "Law-abiding citizen. Recent fatwas on Muslim minorities' loyalty to Western nations." *Muslim World,* 105 (4), pp. 516–539. https://doi.org/10.1111/muwo.12109.

Herek, Gregory M. M. (1997): *Stigma and sexual orientation. Understanding prejudice against lesbians, gay men and bisexuals.* Thousand Oaks: SAGE.

Hill Collins, Patricia (1998): "It's all in the family. Intersections of gender, race and nation." *Hypatia* 13 (3), pp. 62–82. https://www.jstor.org/stable/3810699.

hooks, bell (1992): *Black looks: Race and representation.* London: Turnaround.

Hurworth, Rosaling / Clark, Eileen / Martin, Jenepher / Thomsen, Steve (2005): "The use of photo-interviewing. Three examples from health evaluation and research." *Evaluation Journal of Australasia,* 4 (1&2), pp. 52–62. https://doi.org/10.1177/1035719X05004001-208.

James, Allison / James, Adrian (2011): *Constructing childhood: Theory, policy and social practice.* Houndmills: Palgrave Macmillan.

Kleinman, Sherryl (2007): *Feminist fieldwork analysis.* Thousand Oaks: SAGE.

Kolb, Bettina (2008): "Involving, Sharing, Analysing – Potential of the Participatory Photo Interview." *Forum Qualitative Sozialforschung,* 9 (3), Art. 12. available: http://www.qualitative-research.net/index.php/fqs/article/view/1155/2574 [15.08.2018].

Kubica, Grazyna (2016): How 'native' is my 'native anthropology'? Positionality and the reception of the anthropologist's work in her own community – A reflexive account. In *Cargo* 14 (1–2), pp. 81–99.

Ladner, Joyce A., (ed.) (1998): *The death of white sociology: Essays on race and culture.* Baltimore: Black Classic Press.

Lang, James C. (2011): "Epistemologies of situated knowledges. 'Troubling' knowledge in philosophy of education." *Educational Theory,* 61 (1), pp. 75–96. https://doi.org/10.1111/j.1741-5446.2011.00392.x.

Leino, Helena / Peltomaa, Juha (2017): "Situated knowledge–situated legitimacy. Consequences of citizen participation in local environmental governance." *Policy and Society,* 31 (2), pp. 159–168. https://doi.org/10.1016/j.polsoc.2012.04.005.

Liu, William M. (2017): "White male power and privilege: The relationship between White supremacy and social class." *Journal of Counselling Psychology,* 64 (4), pp. 349–358. https://doi.org/10.1037/cou0000227.

Liu, William M. / Pickett, Theodore / Ivey, Allen E. (2007): "White middle-class privilege: Social class bias and implications for training and practice." *Journal of Multicultural Counselling and Development,* 35 (4), pp. 194–206. https://doi.org/10.1002/j.2161-1912.2007.tb00060.x.

Luttrell, Wendy (2010): "'A camera is a big responsibility': A lens for analysing children's visual voices." *Visual Studies,* 25 (3), pp. 224–237. https://doi.org/10.1080/1472586X.2010.523274.

Lyons, Anthony / Alba, Beatrice / Heywood, Wendy / Fileborn, Bianca / Minichiello, Victor / Barrett, Catherine / et al. (2017): "Experiences of ageism and the mental health of older adults." In *Aging & mental health,* pp. 1–9. https://doi.org/10.1080/13607863.2017.1364347.

MacDonald, Melissa / Winddance Twine, France (2013): "Residential mobility and the market value of whiteness in Boston." In Winddance Twine, France / Gardener, Bradley (eds.): *Geographies of Privilege.* Hoboken: Taylor and Francis.

McIntosh, Peggy (1988): "White privilege and male privilege. A personal account of coming to see correspondences through work in Women's Studies." *Wellesley, Wellesley College: Center for Research on Women* (Working Paper 189). Available: http://www.iub.edu/~tchsotl/part2/McIntosh%20White%20Privilege.pdf [20.08.2018].

– (1989): "White privilege. Unpacking the invisible knapsack." Women's International League for Peace and Freedom, *Peace and Freedom*, July / August, pp. 10–12.

– (2012): "Reflections and Future Directions for Privilege Studies." *Journal of Social Issues*, 68 (1), pp. 194–206. https://doi.org/10.1111/j.1540-4560.2011.01744.x.

McIntyre, Alice (2010): "Through the eyes of women. Photovoice and participatory research as tools for reimagining place." *Gender, Place & Culture*, 10 (1), pp. 47–66. https://doi.org/10.1080/0966369032000052658.

McLees, Leslie (2013) "A postcolonial approach to Urban Studies. Interviews, mental maps, and photo voices on the urban farms of Dar es Salaam, Tanzania." *The Professional Geographer*, 65 (2), pp. 283–295. https://doi.org/10.1080/00330124.2012.679449.

Mizock, Lauren / Harkins, Debra / Ray, Sukanya / Morant, Renee (2011): "Researcher race in narrative interviews on traumatic racism." *Journal of Aggression, Maltreatment & Trauma*, 20 (1), pp. 40–57. https://doi.org/10.1080/10926771.2011.537597.

Mohanty, Chandra T. (1984): "Under western eyes. Feminist scholarship and colonial discourses." *boundary 2*, 12 (3), pp. 333–358. https://doi.org/10.2307/302821.

Modood, Tariq / Triantaphyllidu, Anna / Zapata-Barrero, Ricard (eds.) (2006): *Multiculturalism, Muslims and citizenship. A European approach.* London: Routledge.

Morrison, Toni (1993): *Playing in the dark: Whiteness and the literary imagination.* New York, Vintage Books.

Muhammad, Michael / Wallerstein, Nina / Sussman, Andrew / Avila, Magdalena / Belone, Lorenda / Duran, Bonnie (2015): "Reflections on researcher identity and power. The impact of positionality on Community Based Participatory Research (CBPR), processes and outcomes." *Critical Sociology*, 41, (7–8), pp. 1045–1063. https://doi.org/10.1177/0896920513516025.

National Academies of Sciences, Engineering, and Medicine (2015): "Trust and Confidence at the Interfaces of the Life Sciences and Society. Does the Public Trust Science? A Workshop Summary." Washington: National Academies Press.

Nelson, Todd D. (ed.) (2004): *Ageism. Stereotyping and prejudice against older persons.* Cambridge: MIT Press.

Nykiforuk, Candace / Valliantos, Helen / Nieuwendyk, Laura (2011): "Photovoice as a method for revealing community perceptions of the built and social environment." *International Journal of Qualitative Methods*, 10 (2), pp. 103–124. https://doi.org/10.1177/160940691101000201.

Orelus, Pierre (2010): "Chapter 1: Unmasking male, heterosexual, and racial privileges. From naive complicity to critical awareness and praxis." *Counterpoints*, 351, pp. 17–62. https://www.jstor.org/stable/i40115892.

Ozanne, Julie / Saatcioglu, Bige (2008): "Participatory action research." *Journal of Consumer Research*, 35 (October), pp. 423–439. https://doi.org/10.1086/586911.

Pease, Bob (2013): *Undoing privilege. Unearned advantage in a divided world.* London: Zed Books.

Piper, Heather / Frankham, Jo (2007): "Seeing voices and hearing pictures. Image as discourse and the framing of image-based research." *Discourse: Studies in the Cultural Politics of Education*, 28 (3), pp. 373–387. https://doi.org/10.1080/01596300701458954.

Pittman, Chavella T. (2010): "Race and gender oppression in the classroom. The experiences of women faculty of color with white male students." *Teaching Sociology*, 38 (3), pp. 183–196. https://doi.org/10.1177/0092055X10370120.

Pratto, Felicia / Stewart, Andrew L. (2012): "Group dominance and the half-blindness of privilege." *Journal of Social Issues*, 68 (1), pp. 28–45. https://doi.org/10.1111/j.1540-4560.2011.01734.x.

Raby, Rebecca (2007): Across a Great Gulf? Conducting Research with Adolescents. In Best, Amy L. (Ed.): *Representing youth. Methodological issues in critical youth studies.* New York: New York University Press, pp. 39–59

Ramazanoglu, Caroline / Holland, Janet (2002): *Feminist methodology: Challenges and choices.* London, Thousand Oaks: SAGE.

Riessman, Catherine K. (2008): *Narrative methods for the human sciences*, Thousand Oaks et al.: SAGE.

Rosenthal, Gabriele / Fischer-Rosenthal, Wolfram (2010): "The analysis of narrative-biographical interviews." in Flick, Uwe / Kardorff, Ernst von / Steinke, Ines (eds.): *A companion to qualitative research.* London: SAGE. pp. 259–265.

Roy, Arundhati (2001): *Power Politics.* Cambridge: South End Press.

Said, Edward W. (2003): *Orientalism*, London: Penguin.

Salton, Herman T. (2012): "Unholy union. History, politics and the relationship between church and state in modern France." *Review of European Studies*, 4 (5), pp. 135–147. https://doi.org/10.5539/res.v4n5p135.

Sanders, Melissa R. / Mahalingam, Ramaswami (2012): "Under the radar. The role of invisible discourse in understanding class-based privilege." *Journal of Social Issues*, 68 (1), pp. 112–127. https://doi.org/10.1111/j.1540-4560.2011.01739.x.

Scheibelhofer, Elisabeth (2008): "Combining narration-cased interviews with topical interviews. Methodological reflections on research practices." *International Journal of Social Research Methodology*, 11 (5), pp. 403–416. https://doi.org/10.1080/1364557070 1401370.

Schiffauer, Werner (2006): "Enemies within the gates. The debates about the citizenship of Muslims in Germany." In Modood, Tariq / Triantaphyllidu, Anna / Zapata-Barrero, Ricard (eds.): *Multiculturalism, Muslims and citizenship. A European approach.* London: Routledge. pp. 94–116.

Schlosser, Lewis Z. (2003): "Christian privilege. Breaking a sacred taboo." *Journal of Multicultural Counselling and Development*, 31 (1), pp. 44–51. https://doi.org/10.1002/j.2161-1912.2003.tb00530.x.

Seed, Natalie (2016): "Photovoice. A patricipatory approach to disability service evaluation." *Evaluation Journal of Australasia*, 16 (2), pp. 29–35. https://doi.org/10.1177/1035719X1601600205.

Selod, Saher / Embrick, David G. (2013): "Racialization and Muslims. Situating the Muslim experience in race scholarship." *Sociology Compass*, 7 (8), pp. 644–655. https://doi.org/10.1111/soc4.12057.

Sennett, Richard (2006): *The culture of the new capitalism.* New Haven: Yale University Press.

da Silva, Sofia Marques / Webster, Joan Parker (2018): "Positionality and Standpoint. Situated Ethnographers Acting in On- and Offline Contexts." In Beach, Dennis / Bagley, Carl / da Silva, Sofia Marques (Eds.): *Wiley Handbook of Ethnography of Education.* Newark: John Wiley & Sons Incorporated, pp. 501–512.

Skeggs, Beverley (2004): *Class, self, culture.* London: Routledge.

Smith, Andrea (2013): "Unsettling the privilege of self-reflexivity." In Winddance Twine, France / Gardener, Bradley (eds.) *Geographies of privilege.* Hoboken: Taylor and Francis, pp. 263–279.

Spillers, Hortense J. (1987): "Mama's baby, papa's maybe: an American grammar book." *Diacritics* 17 (2), pp. 64–81. DOI: 10.2307/464747.

Spivak, Gayatri C. (2010): "Can the subaltern speak?" (revised edition, from the "History" chapter of Critique of Postcolonial Reason). In Morris, Rosalind C. (ed.): *Can the subaltern speak? Reflections on the history of an idea.* New York: Columbia Univ. Press, pp. 21–80.

Sprague, Joey (2005): *Feminist methodologies for critical researchers. Bridging differences.* Lanham: AltaMira Press.

Stanfield, John H. (ed.) (2011): *Rethinking race and ethnicity in research methods.* Walnut Creek: Left Coast Press.

Stoetzler, Marcel / Yuval-Davis, Nira (2002): "Standpoint theory, situated knowledge and the situated imagination." *Feminist Theory,* 3 (3), pp. 315–333. https://doi.org/10.1177/146470002762492024.

Stoudt, Brett G. / Fox, Madeline / Fine, Michelle (2012): "Contesting privilege with critical participatory action research." *Journal of Social Issues,* 68 (1), pp. 178–193. https://doi.org/10.1111/j.1540-4560.2011.01743.x.

Summy, Ralph (1998): "Nonviolent speech." *Peace Review,* 10 (4), pp. 573–578. https://doi.org/10.1080/10402659808426206.

Talbot, Mary (2011): "'I wish you'd stop interrupting me!' Interruptions and asymmetries in speaker-rights in equal encounters." in Mooney, Aannabelle (ed.) *The language, society and power reader.* London, New York: Routledge, pp. 164–178.

Thiel, Oliver (2012): "Socio-economic diversity and mathematical competences." *European Early Childhood Education Research Journal* 20 (1), pp. 61–81. DOI: 10.1080/1350293X.2012.650012. DOI: 10.1080/1350293X.2012.650012.

Thielmann, Jörg (2013): "Islamic fields and Muslim techniques of the self in a German context." In Behloul, Samuel-Martin / Leuenberger, Susanne / Tunger-Zanetti, Andreas (eds.): *Debating Islam: Negotiating religion, Europe, and the self.* Bielefeld: transcript.

Thorstensson Dávila, Liv (2014): "Representing Refugee Youth in Qualitative Research. Questions of Ethics, Language and Authenticity." *Diaspora, Indigenous, and Minority Education* 8 (1), pp. 21–31. DOI: 10.1080/15595692.2013.803466.

Thurlow, Crispin / Jaworski, Adam (2017): "The discursive production and maintenance of class privilege: Permeable geographies, slippery rhetorics." *Discourse & Society,* 28 (5), pp. 535–558. https://doi.org/10.1177/0957926517713778.

Uhrig, Noah (2016): *Black, Asian and minority ethnic disproportionality in the criminal justice system in England and Wales.* UK: Ministry of Justice.

Vanner, Cathrine (2015) "Positionality at the center." *International Journal of Qualitative Methods,* 14 (4), pp. 1–12. https://doi.org/10.1177/1609406915618094.

Waaldijk, Kees / Bonini-Baraldi, Matteo (2006): *Sexual orientation discrimination in the European Union. National laws and the employment equality directive.* The Hague: Asser Press.

Wang, Caroline C. / Burris, Mary A. (1997): "Photovoice. Concept, methodology, and use for Participatory needs assessment." *Health Education & Behavior*, 24 (3), pp. 369–387. https://doi.org/10.1177/109019819702400309.

Wang, Caroline C. / Burris, Mary A. / Xiang, Yue, (1996): "Chinese village women as visual anthropologists. A participatory apporach to reaching policymakers." *Social Science and Medicine*, 42 (10), pp. 1391–1400. available: http://isites.harvard.edu/fs/docs/icb.topic463254.files/November_18/Wang_Photonovella.pdf.

Wang, Caroline / Redwood-Jones, Yanique A. (2001): "Photovoice ethics. Perspectives from Flint photovoice." *Health Education & Behavior*, 28 (5), pp. 560–572. https://doi.org/10.1177/109019810102800504.

Wells, Karen (2011): "The politics of life. Governing childhood." *Global Studies of Childhood*, 1 (1), pp. 15–25. https://doi.org/10.2304/gsch.2011.1.1.15.

Westman, Jack (1991): "Juvenile ageism. Unrecognized prejudice and discrimination against the young." *Child Psychiatry and Human Development*, 21 (4), pp. 237–256. https://doi.org/10.1007/BF00705929.

Wildman, Stephanie M./ Davis, Adrienne D. (1995): "Language and Silence. Making Systems of Privilege Invisible." *Santa Clara Law Review* 35 (3), 881–906.

Williamson, Vanessa / Skocpol, Theda / Coggin, John (2011): "The Tea Party and the remaking of republican conservatism." *Perspectives on Politics*, 9 (1), pp. 25–43. https://doi.org/10.1017/S153759271000407X.

Winddance Twine, France / Gardener, Bradley (eds.) (2013a): *Geographies of privilege.* Hoboken: Taylor and Francis.

– (2013b): "Introduction." in Winddance Twine, F. / Gardener, B. (eds.) *Geographies of privilege.* Hoboken: Taylor and Francis, pp. 1–17.

Windsong, Elena Ariel (2017): "Incorporating intersectionality into research design. An example using qualitative interviews." *International Journal of Social Research Methodology* 21 (2), pp. 135–147. https://doi.org/10.1080/13645579.2016.1268361.

Wodak, Ruth, (ed.) (2009): *Methods of critical discourse analysis.* Los Angeles: SAGE.

Wolcott, Harry F. (2001): *The art of fieldwork*. Walnut Creek: AltaMira Press.

Woodward, Kath (2008): "Hanging out and hanging about: Insider / outsider research in the sport of boxing." *Ethnography*, 9 (4), pp. 536–560. https://doi.org/10.1177/1466138108096991.

Yancy, George, (ed.) (2004): *What white looks like: African-American philosophers on the whiteness question.* New York, Routledge.

– (2008): *Black bodies, white gazes: The continuing significance of race*, Lanham, Md., Rowman & Littlefield.

Zhao, Gouping (2011): "The modern construction of childhood. What does it do to the paradox of modernity?" *Studies in Philosophy and Education*, 30 (3), pp. 241–256. https://doi.org/10.1007/s11217-010-9213-8.

Zuberi, Tukufu / Bonilla-Silva, Eduardo (eds.) (2008): *White logic, white methods. Racism and methodology.* Lanham: Rowman & Littlefield Publishers.

Farid Hafez / Linda Hyökki

Researching Sisters and Brothers: Implications of In-Group Research to Fieldwork Among Muslims

Abstract
Methodological reflections are an integral part of every qualitative study. Hereby the notion of a researcher's positionality vis-à-vis the researched has become crucial, especially since the reflexive turn in social sciences. While traditional ethnography used to problematize the notion of "going native", now qualitative studies are done by "peer researchers" who share with the research participants a world of experiences that goes beyond mere gender or national identities. Hence, such "in-group interviews" aim to research those exact experiences emerging from the membership for instance of a sexual, ethnic or religious community. Even more, in small communities the researcher might well have personal relationships with his/her interviewees or is at least somewhat known which brings new questions of interpersonal hierarchies in research. Applicable to such research settings, the critical paradigm calls for discussions that alongside positionality also reflect accountability and partiality of the researcher. These three aspects emphasize questions of emancipation and the imperative of disclosing social injustices, as the critical paradigm is generally applied to investigate the lifeworld and practices of marginalized and oppressed communities. This article is a methodological discussion on in-group interviews conducted in Muslim communities in Austria and Finland by two researchers who identify themselves with the respective communities. The discussion explores the three aforementioned elements as well as issues of access and rapport. The article seeks to answer the question whether the researcher can ever really take the position of an "insider". This question is examined by looking into how in the micropolitics of the research endeavour in in-group interviews. The article discusses the limits of a "peer researcher" sharing the world of experiences with the researched and shows how positionality is always dependent on the particularities of each research setting, reflecting the intersectional, fluid, and socially constructed identities of both the researcher as well as the researched.

Introduction

The significant role in knowledge construction played by the field has been long acknowledged in ethnographic study approaches. The natural setting in which the studied community or participants live and gain their experiences is an integral part of the Heideggerian understanding of humans' perception which is shaped by every individual's "historicality", i.e. their personal background and the socio-cultural context in which they live and consequently interpret encounters and phenomena. However, methodological discussions of a conscious researcher doing a qualitative study with methods such as interviewing, and observation go hand in hand with the researcher's reflection on his or her positionality within the research setting. While early ethnographers understood the researcher to inquire through an objective lens, freed from bias and pre-commitment, the purpose of their research endeavours became entangled in the wider agenda of creating discourses of the Other for the colonial enterprise (Davies 1999, p. 45). Even after the notion of reflexivity was introduced into the political dimension of ethics in qualitative research, techniques were used to eliminate the impact of the researcher on the research setting (e.g. in participant observation) or the interview situation (Davies 1999, p. 7) in the quest for neutrality in the inquiry, data and results. Moreover, such research also meant that the analyses would stay on the descriptive and interpretive level and therefore the engagement of the researcher with the field would end with data collection and the researcher would not take any stance on the status quo of his/her participants.

The contemporary ethnographic approach to inquiry entails, however, a constructivist understanding of epistemology that shifts our understanding of the role of the researcher away from the traditional imperative of a "detached" observer. Knowledge production within the interview situation is hence understood to be co-constructed by the researcher/interviewer and the participant/interviewee (Borer / Fontana 2012, p. 48). The civil rights movements of the 1960's and 1970's set up a new political consciousness among academics (Bhavnani et al. 2014, p. 165) and in the last few decades, the critical approach in qualitative research has been applied explicitly to ethnographic research methods as well (Creswell 2007; Madison 2005). The critical paradigm is inspired by the tradition of the Frankfurt School that emerged from the legacy of Marxist theory and thus embodied the imperative for research to contribute to social change. Therefore, the critical paradigm, or the Critical Theory paradigm, contrasts itself with two other major paradigms to qualitative research — the post-positivist and interpretivist — in its political and value-oriented objective to "make domination and subjugation obvious and to help oppressed groups to emancipation" (Willis 2007, p. 48). As Foley (2002, p. 470) illustrates his own "becoming" a critical ethnographer in the 1960's and 1970's, he explains how American anthropologists came to realize how their works had been part of the international 'development' projects that promoted global capitalism of a discipline that was "founded upon liberal, humanist doctrines of ameliorism, orientalism, colonialism, and racism." Critical ethnography thus settled as a distinctive branch with its own methodology (cf. Thomas 1993; Madison 2005; Carspecken 1996), and with its value-oriented and political objective it has been well applicable for studies on sexual, linguistic, and religious minorities (cf. King 2010; Heller 2011; Bakali 2016; Miled 2017) that have been historically – or still are – oppressed and marginalized in their respective local and global contexts.

With the 'critical' in the paradigm also came the acknowledgement of the researcher's complex identity, i. e. the intersectionality of race, gender, social class, sexual orientation etc., and the ways in which these would affect the choices made during data collection procedures and analysis. Consequently, the reflection on positionality was extended beyond criticizing the notion of objectivity to critiquing the subjectivity of the researcher (Madison 2005, p. 8). This article draws upon the experiences of two researchers: a convert Muslim researcher conducting interviews within her own religious community in Finland and a co-founding member of a Muslim youth organisation who conducted research on this youth organisation years after he left. On one hand, this article offers reflections of Linda Hyökki on how the "nativeness" of the marginalized group of converts and religious minority played a role in the decisions she had to make throughout the fieldwork. Her research asked how the interviewees have perceived Islamophobia, how they made sense of these experiences, and how they finally coped with them in their everyday lives. It was her understanding from the beginning that she would seek to uncover a portion of injustices experienced by convert Muslims in Finland and amplify the voices of her participants whose stories are otherwise unheard. Her research is framed within the critical paradigm in which she seeks to challenge dominant discourses about Islam and Muslims and address the issues of power and control that are embedded in Islamophobia as a form of racism. On the other hand, Farid Hafez has published numerous articles on the Austrian Muslim Youth (AMY) as well as an edited volume. As a male researcher with a background in a Muslim youth organisation and as a scholar who repeatedly intervenes as a critical voice, he reflects on his own positionality along different questions when he researches the history and recent activism of this youth organization. Are there different questions to be raised from an insider perspective? What is the role of trust given to a scholar activist?

Peer-researchers: inside or out?

One main shared method of inquiry was the interview. Linda Hyökki specifically chose the semi-structured interview which Kvale and Brinkmann (2008, p. 3) define as having a "purpose of obtaining descriptions of the lifeworld of the interviewee in order to interpret the meaning of the described phenomena."

While Hyökki was interested in her participants' experiences through the way in which they perceived, made sense of and coped with Islamophobia in society, Hafez was interested in the current leadership's self-awareness and framing of politics as well as their understanding of identities within the organisation. Hyökki drew on her research questions and literature review on Islamophobia and previous studies on convert Muslims in European countries and pre-determined a set of themes she wanted to cover during the interview. Thus, the semi-structured interview took a more specific form of what Hirsjärvi and Hurme (2008) have called "theme interviews." Hafez chose different types of interviews for different research questions. On identity issues, Hafez drew on participant observation (Hafez 2017a). For history, he drew on narrative interviews (Hafez 2017b), and for politics of the AMY (Hafez 2017c), he drew on expert interviews next to content analysis.

The positionality of the researcher plays a role all the way through the research process from research design to the decisions made for publishing results and has a critical role in shaping the micropolitics of the research especially if the research is done on a marginalised and oppressed group, such as an ethnic, religious or sexual minority. Thus, while "semi-structured" describes the interview design, "in-group interview"[1] (Juvonen 2017) is what we can call settings in which the interviewer him/herself is part of the community that is being researched and shares the "world of experiences" with the interviewees, or as Ryan et al. (2011) define such researchers as "peer researchers." The critical paradigm is often applicable to peer researchers or in-group interviews in indigenous studies and queer research. This means that the interviewer and the interviewee(s) share a certain feature of their identity that goes beyond mere gender or national identities, such as membership in an ethnic, sexual or religious minority, but it could also be a membership in a smaller and more exclusive community such as a sports association, etc. The researcher's position as an "insider" of the social group under study, the researcher's expertise on the topic, previous first-hand experiences from the field, and experiential knowledge are an integral part of the research design. Importantly, in in-group interviews the aim is to explore questions pertaining to the exact experience emerging from the membership of the respective community or to study how the members give and share meaning to particular events or concepts (Juvonen 2017, p. 406). This

1 For the lack of a better translation in English, Hyökki has proposed adopting the term "in-group interview" as suggested by Dr. Tuula Juvonen in an email correspondence (12.20.2017). Juvonen, a scholar of Gender Studies, used the Finnish term "sisäpiirihaastattelu" in her article (Juvonen 2017) on interview settings in which the interviewer shares with the interviewees a lifeworld that is based on a certain characteristic such as religious affiliation or sexual orientation. The Finnish term thus connotes an interview that is done within an exclusive social circle, an "in-group".

converges with Hyökki's research questions about convert Muslim experiences on Islamophobia in Finland, and with Hafez's questions on negotiating identity and doing politics in Austria.

Whereas traditional ethnography saw notions such as "going native" in the field as a hindrance to the ever-sought objectivity (Davies 1999, p. 71), critical ethnography/approach has embraced *native* researchers, individuals who themselves might come from a history of colonisation and disenfranchisement. From this perspective, both Hyökki's and Hafez's positions were characterised by a certain degree of "insiderness", which helped to avoid othering the research participants/community due to biased readings of history and literature review (cf. Hyvärinen 2017, p. 22) and hence this highlights the instrumentality of a critical approach in such studies.

The critical paradigm acknowledges the plurality of "truths" — that identities are complex, fluid, and socially constructed — and the consequent impact of intersectionality in race, gender, social class, and sexual orientation on the researcher's subjectivity in the field. The critical paradigm calls for reflecting beyond the "insider/outsider" status, which has traditionally been regarded as the degree to which the researcher shares commonalities with the participants and how the established degree of "closeness" affects access to the field and rapport. In the critical paradigm, the context of the research endeavour itself and its micropolitics play a significant role and thus the ethnographer is asked to question aspects such as what will be done with the research and who will benefit from it (Madison 2005, p. 7). Considering that critical ethnography is never apolitical, these questions find their underpinnings oftentimes vis-á-vis discussions of historical, societal oppression, inequalities, and questions of power. As Spencer et al. (2014, p. 91) note, research methods of the critical paradigm consider context as essential to the subjectivity of the researcher. Muslims in both geographical contexts of Austria and Finland have endured historical oppression and marginalisation and continue to be othered. The critical paradigm brings "insider researchers" and the imperative to not reproduce narratives that are generally dominant in media and politics and in no way contribute to the emancipation of these communities. Instead, the objective was to challenge such narratives and the status quo.

Doing interviews as a critical Muslim researcher

Bhavnani et al. (2014, p. 172) have outlined three elements of critical qualitative research and the process of questioning dominating representations, one of which is partiality. In this regard, Hyökki decided to especially take into consideration the different representations of "ethnic Muslims" and "white Muslims" and how those have led to racialisation and inevitably to marginalisation of the latter in the society. Hence, her research aimed to offer counter-narratives of belonging and normalisation of religious diversity in Finnish society. This was especially important in her research which was seeking to find new narratives about Finnish converts going beyond the question of *hijab* through which especially Muslim women are oftentimes passivized and instead concentrating on the aspect *agency*. Hafez opted for a historical lens going beyond 9/11 to discuss the process of negotiating identity (Hafez 2017a). Also, he escaped the trap of 'religionization' when researching the founding years of the AMY. Hafez asked not seemingly obvious questions on religion to understand the founding moments of a religious youth organisation, but instead focused on lifestyle, politics and youth culture far beyond religion to find hip hop culture as a central dimension while not neglecting religion (Hafez 2017b).

Secondly, regarding the notion of accountability (Bhavnani et al. 2014), from the beginning Hyökki did not want to engage in "hit and run" research, meaning that she would merely *use* her participants for her own benefit, i. e. authoring the PhD thesis. Instead, she wanted to ensure that whatever knowledge about the social realities of Finnish convert Muslims was created during the research process she would take beyond her writing desk and bring it into the activism that she has embraced in the last few years against Islamophobia. Moreover, her accountability towards her research participants also meant that she would offer each interviewee the possibility of having some sort of input in the way she depicted them in her research report. For instance, that meant giving them the opportunity to choose their own aliases with the acknowledgement of how for some converts deciding for or against an Islamic name is part of the identity construction process. Hafez' paper, 'Muslim Protest against Austria's Islam law: An Analysis of Austrian Muslim's Protest against the 2015 Islam Law' reflects the will to give a voice to the Muslim actors. Next to well-documented press releases, it also presents other mechanisms of protest and, most importantly, gives a voice to understand the motives and configuration of different modes of protest by having group interviews. Group interviews for collective actors also ensured to reflect the heterogeneity of the groups involved in these protests.

Lastly, in concordance with other authors of critical qualitative research, Bhavnani et al. (ibid.) also mention positionality and the meaning of socio-historical/political context. For Hyökki's research this meant not only considering a critical literature review on studies about Muslims and Islam in Finland but also the global context of the Orientalist tradition that has had a significant impact on the formation of the contemporary Islamophobic discourse. Furthermore, pertaining to the question of "the field" and the problem of defining any heterogenous community within limits, Hyökki considered the question of demographic diversity within the Muslim minority in Finland, including the "first Muslims of Finland", the Tatars, and the diverse ethnicities within the Muslim immigrant community as well as the diversity within the convert community itself. The objective of disclosing counter-narratives about "who Finnish Muslims are" opposes the way in which Muslims in Finland have been represented as a homogenous entity, especially in discussions on policies concerning governance of Islam. Having been involved in the protest against the Islam Act, Hafez was an organic part of this movement and could thus discern the nuances of certain modes of protest. At the same time, this creates the pitfall of evaluating those actors, who would not join in solidarity with this struggle. These actors might not talk to Hafez, at least that openly, or would talk to him not as a scholar, but as a political subject to either convince him of their position or the like. In any intensive political struggle, this clearly creates boundaries and the scholar must know them to also be able to set his academic boundaries. In such a situation, a team of scholars can be of great help, although the political nature of a potential interviewee does not fade away only with the framing of the respective interviewer.

Finding new horizons: asking new questions

The starting point of Hyökki's fieldwork was the identification of eligible participants. Since she was only interested in narratives of convert Muslims, her sampling was purposive (Morgan 2008, p. 797) and she had identified as eligible interviewees Muslim converts residing in Finland with "white" Finns as both parents. These were thus Finnish Muslims, who had later in their life converted to Islam, i. e. they were not "born to a Muslim family", whether they had previously been Evangelic Lutheran or atheists. She chose to include both female and male converts out of two main reasons. First, experiences of Muslim women on discrimination and victimization as a racialized and marginalized group gains much attention (cf. Van Nieuwkerk 2009; Suleiman, 2013; Anway 2000) especially at a time during which several European countries have applied legislative bans on Muslim women's attire in public spaces (cf. Brems 2016; Vakulenko 2007)[2]. Second, even in previous qualitative studies on Western converts, the quota of male interviewees tended to remain much lower than that of female interviewees (Roald 2004; Moosavi 2015; Özyürek, 2015) apart from Galonnier's

2 Studies on the impact of such legislations on the grassroots level also have been published in 2016 by the European Network against racism (ENAR), "Forgotten Women : the impact of Islamophobia on Muslim women" (http://www.enar-eu.org/Forgotten-Women-the-impact-of-Islamophobia-on-Muslim-women) and in 2018 by Open Society Foundations "Restrictions on Muslim Women's Dress in the 28 EU Member States" (https://www.opensocietyfoundations.org/reports/restrictions-muslim-women-s-dress-28-eu-member-states).

comparative study (2015). Male converts can be classified in many local contexts a "hidden" population and more demanding in terms of recruitment strategies (cf. Ellard-Gray / et al. 2015; Hennink / et al. 2011).

One major difference between Muslim men and women in research, which in Hyökki's view has received less attention so far, is the mere fact that due to less visible attire, convert men are rarely recognisable as Muslims and thus, in comparison to female converts, the victimisation of Muslim convert men is a rare phenomenon. The male converts are thus less easily "racialised" and their personal experiences with Islamophobia especially on street level is expected to differ from that of their female fellows (cf. Chakraborti / Zempi 2012; Allen 2015). As Hyökki knew from her personal experiences living as a hijab-wearing woman in Finland and having friends who embraced the most distinct Islamic attire, even the levels of harassment could vary from woman to woman based on the degree of their "visibility" as Muslims. Moreover, as Islamophobia manifests not only as verbal or physical attacks in the public, but many Muslims are exposed to it due to online hate speech and structural discrimination, Hyökki wanted to include the voices of male converts to find out to what extent convert male and female Muslims experience Islamophobia in different manners and how their reactions to it and strategies to deal with it vary.

For Hafez, his insider knowledge allowed him to ask questions that other outside observers would possibly not have raised. Hafez does not belong to the first generation of the founding fathers of the AMY who developed the foundation of the AMY, but to the second generation who founded the AMY in its current legal status. Hence, he knew the first founding fathers personally, was well connected to them and knew about their lives. This allowed him to shed light on issues which had been previously completely out of sight. One is the central role of hip-hop music and African-American political culture, to which he dedicated a full article (Hafez 2017b). While African-American figures such as Malcolm X and the Black Panthers are recognized today, they definitely do not hold the influence they did in the founding years. The same can be said about hip hop culture, which was the basic social milieu from which the founding fathers of the AMY emerged. Highlighting this fundamental but less visible aspect of the AMY relies on insider knowledge beyond general knowledge of the organisation. This knowledge is very much related to personal life stories, the biographies of the founding fathers as well as the pillars of youth activism in the founding years.

Also, Hafez's collaborative effort in editing a volume with other members of the AMY next to observers from the outside allowed him to shed light on many neglected aspects. This ranges from internal theological discourses that are nearly unavailable in written form (Bauer 2017; Hofer 2017; El-Abd 2017) to participant observers of very specific fields of action like inter-religious dialogue (Wansch 2017), refugee aid work (Abuzahra 2017) and musical life (Ulu 2017).

Reflecting upon the 'insider' position

The benefits of an in-group interview in fieldwork according to Juvonen (2017) are easier access to the field and rapport with the interviewees. However, it is important that the researcher does not fall victim of relaxed ideas about "privileged" positionality. As for Hyökki's own status in the field, she realised that as a member of the Muslim convert community, she did share the religious affiliation with her participants, but not the notion of the "world of experiences" as mentioned in the definition of in-group interviews since many other factors such as her gender, her socio-economic background, the fact that she is currently an expat living abroad and not in Finland, as well as her religious interpretations would create divisions between her and the participants. As for Hafez, he had left the Austrian Muslim Youth organisation nearly 10 years ago and the organisation had significantly changed. This becomes evident through the new leadership who represent a whole new generation, the sociological composition of its members, and its political involvement in daily Austrian politics. Also, Hafez has become an international scholar with stays abroad from Indonesia to the United States, leaving the borders of the Austrian nation state behind. Discussing and reflecting on issues (which might also be relevant to members of the AMY) informed by the literature and experiences outside of Austria also set the scholar apart from local actors and enriched the perspective. Therefore, regarding such multi-layered identities and the way in which each of them shape the experience of both the researcher and the researched, Bhavnani et.al. (2014, pp. 170–172) express their dissatisfaction and note that critical researchers should be aware of "fabricated positionalities" that imply unchangeable identities of both sides and what they call a "homogenised field." Taking that into consideration, questions of "access" and "rapport" become more relative and contested, even to the "insider" researcher.

Hyökki has been a member of the Finnish convert Muslim community since 2007 and along with a relatively wide network of friends, acquaintances and Facebook contacts she also has access to private platforms for Muslim women on social media which are otherwise closed to outsiders, i. e. non-Muslims. She therefore recruited her participants by using social networking strategies, specifically research-based recruitment, informal networks and snowballing. She also recruited female participants from two focus groups in which she had previously conducted interviews regarding everyday-lives of convert Muslims in Finland. Hyökki asked the focus group participants whether they would be interested in participating in individual in-depth interviews that would be part of her PhD thesis and she had taken the names and contacts of those who agreed. Hyökki sent them private messages either through Facebook or WhatsApp when she started recruitment for the interviews in September 2017 and followed up on their willingness to participate. She believes that the recruitment channels were the biggest advantage that she as an "insider" researcher had. An "outsider" researcher, however, who may not possibly have any personal contacts to use as gatekeepers to such groups[3], would have to reach out to open platforms such as mosques or community centres and through the management personnel – who then function as gate keepers – to gain contact information of interested participants. Hyökki however, was able to merely post her recruitment letter in the women's Facebook groups and invite interested participants to contact her privately.

It should be noted that the informal social networks Hyökki used were comprised of Muslim women from all ethnic backgrounds. Therefore, in her communication she used for recruitment purposes, she explained that she was looking for "ethnic Finns" who had converted to Islam and not, for example, Muslims of immigrant origin from Somalia, Arab countries and so on[4]. Purposive sampling follows from the essential objective of qualitative research to explore a specific phenomenon. The researcher aims at understanding the dynamics of this phenomenon in the society and any subjective meanings individuals give to it. Hence, the imperative is to obtain data that emerges from lives of people who share specific characteristics linked to the phenomenon (Hennink / et al. 2011, p. 84; see also Palys 2008).

Soon after Hyökki had initiated her recruitment in social media, she realized that her membership in the community did not guarantee an avalanche of responses from interested participants. At this point, Hyökki had to set aside her assumption that being "a privileged insider" interviewer and researcher which she had thought would automatically mean that her recruitment would run more smoothly than the one by "an outsider" researcher who does not share the religious affiliation with the researched community of converts. So, she wanted to explore how different identities and loyalties affected the process of recruitment, starting with female participants, and the ways gender affected recruitment of male participants.

3 Often in these groups some members have been privately contacted by a researcher and asked to distribute a recruitment letter for a researcher who is interested in interviewing (convert) Muslim women.

4 Hyökki encountered a rather embarrassing situation in the beginning of her fieldwork when a friend, whom she had asked for contacts of Muslim male converts, asked whether she would also be interested in his story. He is a convert to Islam, whose parents migrated to Finland from Africa. However, he considers himself a Finn as he was born in Finland and has a strong cultural identification with Finland and Finns. Hyökki was embarrassed to tell him that he would not "qualify". It was not only the embarrassment of having to use his "race" against him but also the situation in which she had to turn down his voice and story from her research. However, she explained her friend the research question and its focus on whiteness as a category, which he understood, and they laughed away the awkward situation.

Being at the time of her research a PhD candidate at a Turkish university, Hyökki had left her home country 12 years prior to her PhD research. The time she had spent abroad as an expat revealed itself as a disconnecting element in her degree of closeness to the participants. She learned to understand after all that she was not that connected to the networks and local communities like she thought, except for her Facebook friendships with several dozen convert Muslim women as well as her private friendships she had cultivated. Hyökki was an expat who visited the country once or twice a year, never participated in weekly events or Friday prayers of the mosques nor had she a fixed group of "sisters", or a clique, around her. Thus, she was not really a member of any particular community but had some contacts across the country and in different communities. Her friendships with other convert women were mostly based on long-time friendships prior the time she left Finland, so she had less connection with women who had converted recently. This made her rethink her status as an "insider" to the community and she realized that she could be more of an "outsider" than she initially thought she was.

An existing insider status of the researcher also has an impact on the level of trust the researcher can have with the interviewees (Sherry 2008, 433). Therefore, after realising the alienation that Hyökki had gone through after so many years from the "turf" of the community to which she felt attached, she had to rethink the question "Who do *I think I am* and *why* should anyone trust me as a researcher?" How could she feel guaranteed that her mere religious affiliation would win immediate trust and willingness of her "sisters" to share their stories with her? To many, she was after all, as much of a stranger to them as a non-Muslim researcher. The interpersonal element of the fieldwork with in-group interviews drew her to the heterogenous community in which she was working. Hyökki reflected on the fact that if she was going to rely on social networks such as the Facebook groups for her recruitment, she would have to accept that her social media persona, the things she had posted in the groups, the image she gave of herself in her profile pictures, etc. might not necessarily be of help in the process. The Muslim community just like the convert community in Finland is as diverse as it could get and thus differences in interpretation of religious issues are inevitable. How could she be sure that even though she personally did not know every convert member in the group that they would not have already formed an opinion about her as a person, as a *Muslim* and this would affect the potentiality of her gaining any "trust" among these sisters?

Finally, Hyökki's background in academia could easily pigeonhole her — how could she claim to share the world of experience with these women who lived the life of a Muslim in the Finnish context each day, when her perspective on the country's internal affairs was mostly based on observations from abroad? Thus, after having started the interviews and listening to a few first stories from the women, Hyökki came to the point in which she had to rethink the role of her literature review. She had, for instance, read much about the concept of racialisation (Meer / Modood 2010) and how it is connected to Islamophobia, and how convert Muslims come to lose their "whiteness" (cf. Moosavi 2015; Galonnier 2015). This also reflects in the various micro-aggressions that Muslims encounter. However, her participants did not largely account similar experiences to those that literature on other European contexts such as United Kingdom or Germany (Özyüerek 2015; Moosavi 2015) reported. Thus, although theme interviews are theory-oriented, it was real world experience and the objective of qualitative interviews that provided a first-order understanding of phenomena for her (Brinkmann 2014, p. 287). Upon this realization, Hyökki stepped out of her literature bubble and gave space to the accounts of her study participants. After all, they were the experts of Islamophobia in Finland, not her.

The impact of gender on her position as a researcher changed her recruitment strategy when it came to finding male participants. She could not make use of informal social networks, since she had neither developed tight personal relationships with Finnish male converts nor was she a member of any social media groups in which this subgroup of the community would be heavily represented. This was mostly due to the mere fact that adherence to distanced gender relations had kept her mainly connected with female converts. Moreover, male converts in Finland can be described as a "hidden" population group (cf. Hennink et al. 2011, p. 100), in the sense that due to their scarce number, lack of even informal networks, and "invisibility" among the public, they are more difficult to identify. This also impacted her chances at finding eligible participants. Hyökki thus reached two participants using a common friend to ask for a permission to establish contact and complemented that strategy with snowball sampling. For the latter, trusted and familiar individuals – both female and male – connected to the community of male converts helped to spread the word about her research and forwarded the contact details of potential male participants who otherwise would have been out of reach.

The social etiquette in the Muslim community relating to gender relations highlights the relativity of ease in contacting potential participants even for a Muslim-researcher. In qualitative fieldwork the researcher needs to be sensitive towards cultural factors already in the recruitment phase (Jensen 2008, p. 2; Hennink et al. 2011, p. 69). Varying interpretations of appropriate gender relations exist, however, and as a researcher Hyökki had to be prepared and respect the fact that not all male participants would be willing to have private conversations with her. Hyökki decided to proceed rather carefully as she did not want to cause her interviewees at any stage to feel uncomfortable in participating in her study. For instance, she wanted to approach a convert man of whom she knew from social media. In order not to appear intrusive and bold, she asked a mutual friend of theirs to first check whether it would be appropriate that she do so. Indeed, one male interviewee did not respond after many attempts at contact (even though he had been referred to her by his friend) and she found out from other male participants that he had reservations of meeting with her for the interview in a one-on-one setting. Even though some qualitative research manuals (cf. Hirsjärvi and Hurme 2008) encourage persuading less responsive participants – who have expressed initial interest in the study – for an interview, the aforementioned case made Hyökki consider where she should draw the line between setting an interview while not pressuring the participants.

Hafez has another position. While he has left the AMY, he is still connected to the discourse as a scholar activist (Suzuki / Mayorga, 2014), regularly publishing op-eds and speaking on radio and TV on issues around Muslims in Austria and Europe and Islamophobia. Hence, although he might not be in touch with many people from the AMY, many know him from public lectures and as a public figure. Especially when it came to his interviewees, it was not very difficult to find trust, which was critical (Sherry 2008, p. 433). One particularly crucial incident in the lives of many politically aware Muslims, the implementation of the Islam Act 2015, created many opportunities for Farid Hafez. As a leading voice against the new act, which was criticised as institutionalising Islamophobia, Hafez received wide recognition from the larger Muslim community. This helped him in conducting research which was based on group interviews with members of two front groups that acted against the act, the AMY and the Network of Muslim Civil Society (Hafez 2017c). Although the leadership of the AMY was new and had no relationship to Hafez, this scholar activism was very helpful in getting not only direct access to the leading actors on behalf of the AMY, but also in receiving trust. This was especially the case due to long time members of the AMY, who knew Hafez personally from his past activism, who helped in connecting him to the new leadership. As for the members of the Network of Muslim Civil Society, a heterogenous group of people that formed around the protest against the Islam Act of 2015, there were no personal connections and more importantly, no back-dating relationship.

Here, the scholar activism and the members knowing that Hafez was on the 'right side of the struggle' was a reason to gain trust. The 'insider'-position was thus much wider in its scope and based on a shared period of activism and fighting the same struggle, which connected Hafez to the two organisations. Unlike Hyökki, Hafez played a more organic role in the protest, which he was also interested in researching. He was not an alien to the community, although he was neither a formal member of any of these associations nor a participant, but rather a scholar who introduced his own perspective, tried to frame the discourse along his own analysis, intervened in op-eds and was an invited expert by an opposition party in the parliament. So, he was part of the struggle of those he researched in the sense of supporting their specific objectives, but also through his own writings.

Conclusion

This article has discussed the way in which a researcher who belongs to the same minority group which he/she is studying faces questions of positionality, accountability and partiality in research design and fieldwork. The two research contexts explored in this article both concern Muslim communities in European contexts. On the one hand, this article shows the necessity of peer-research to avoid othering and culturalization, to provide a deeper view of the topic as well to make possible a representation not for a group, but out of the group. On the other hand, the article reveals the difficulty to represent subaltern positions with a classical understanding of an "insider" researcher. In the case of Hafez, it was his political activity more than his status as a researcher that produced the "sameness" of researcher and interviewee, hence clearly putting other markers behind.

The authors agree that in contemporary times, which are marked by prevailing societal and institutionalised anti-Muslim racism, it is imperative that any qualitative studies regarding these marginalised communities should be framed within the critical paradigm. Questions of emancipation, the objective of disclosing social injustices, and a personal commitment of connecting academic research with social activism motivate the authors to question the ways in which Muslim communities are represented in academic studies. This article has also reflected upon the notions of access and rapport and how these are intertwined with the understanding of an "insider"-position. The article established that sharing the religious identity or being a member of the very minority under study does not automatically give the researcher a privileged position. The fluidity of identity both of the researcher and of the study participants needs to be considered and any shared commonalities – or differences – should not be taken granted. A shared history of common struggles and a scholar activist position helps but sets boundaries at the same time. It helps in terms of trust and gives the scholar insights into nuances. Thus, it provides a deep insight into these struggles, with which the researcher can represent agency of marginalised groups. At the same time, it may not allow access to every actor and thus forces the researcher to either set boundaries for the research or operate in a team of researchers, such as in the case of Linda Hyökki's study. This shows that individual researchers hold differences dependent on context. Even though in our cases, the religion, ethnic background (and gender) seems to be the same, in the context of research, researcher and interviewee are always in an unequal position of power. Hence "peer-research" is also context-dependent. The critical paradigm necessitates a critical reflection on the researcher's subjectivity throughout the study. Who speaks for whom and in whose voice is one of the most important questions that qualitative researchers need to pose to challenge any othering and exoticisation of oppressed minorities.

References

Abuzahra, Nora (2016): "Es kommen Menschen. Flüchtlingsarbeit der Muslimischen Jugend Österreich." In: Hafez, Farid / Heinisch, Reinhard / Kneucker, Raoul / Polak, Regina (eds.): *Jung, muslimisch, österreichisch. Einblicke in 20 Jahre Muslimische Jugend Österreich.* Vienna: New Academic Press, pp. 344–357.

Allen, Chris (2015): "'People hate you because of the way you dress': Understanding the invisible experiences of veiled British Muslim women victims of Islamophobia." *International Review of Victimology,* 21(3), pp. 287–301. https://doi.org/10.1177/0269758015591677.

Anway, Carol A. (2000): "American Women Choosing Islam". In: Yazbeck Haddad, Yvonne / Esposito, John L. (eds.): *Muslims on the Americanization Path?* Oxford: Oxford University Press, pp. 146–160.

Bakali, Naved (2016): *Islamophobia: Understanding Anti-Muslim Racism Through the Lived Experiences of Muslim Youth.* Rotterdam: Sense Publishers.

Bauer, Wolfgang (2016): "Kerninhalte der Muslimischen Jugend Österreich. Eine theologische Legitimation?" In: Hafez, Farid / Heinisch, Reinhard / Kneucker, Raoul / Polak, Regina (eds.): *Jung, muslimisch, österreichisch. Einblicke in 20 Jahre Muslimische Jugend Österreich.* Vienna: New Academic Press, pp. 98–112.

Bhavnani, Kum-Kum / Chua, Peter / Collins, Dana (2014): "Critical Approaches to Qualitative Research" In: Patricia, Leavy (ed.): *The Oxford Handbook of Qualitative Research.* Oxford: Oxford University Press, pp. 165–178.

Birgit Hofer (2016): "Die Fiqh-Praxis der Muslimischen Jugend Österreich." In: Hafez, Farid / Heinisch, Reinhard / Kneucker, Raoul / Polak, Regina (eds.): *Jung, muslimisch, österreichisch. Einblicke in 20 Jahre Muslimische Jugend Österreich.* Vienna: New Academic Press, pp. 113–133.

Brems, Eva (ed.) (2014): *The Experiences of Face Veil Wearers in Europe and the Law.* Cambridge: Cambridge University Press.

Brinkmann, Svend (2014): "Unstructured and Semi-Structured Interviewing." In: Patricia, Leavy (ed.): *The Oxford Handbook of Qualitative Research.* Oxford: Oxford University Press, pp. 277–299.

Carspecken, Francis (1996): *Critical Ethnography in Educational Research: A Theoretical and Practical Guide.* Abingdon: Routledge.

Chakraborti, Neil / Zempi, Irene (2012): "The veil under attack: Gendered dimensions of Islamophobic victimization." *International Review of Victimology,* 18(3), pp. 269–284. https://doi.org/10.1177/0269758012446983.

Creswell, John W. (2007): *Qualitative Inquiry & Research Design. Choosing Among Five Approaches.* Thousand Oaks: SAGE Publications.

Davies, Charlotte A. (1999): *Reflexive Ethnography. A Guide to researching selves and others.* London/New York: Routledge.

El-Abd, Gudrun (2016). "Glaube und soziales Handeln. Eine islamisch-theologische Betrachtung." In: Hafez, Farid / Heinisch, Reinhard / Kneucker, Raoul / Polak, Regina (eds.): *Jung, muslimisch, österreichisch. Einblicke in 20 Jahre Muslimische Jugend Österreich.* Vienna: New Academic Press, pp. 134–150.

Ellard-Gray, Amy / Jeffrey, Nicole K. / Choubak, Melisa / Crann, Sara E. (2015): "Finding the Hidden Participant: Solutions for Recruiting Hidden, Hard-to-Reach, and Vulnerable Populations." *International Journal of Qualitative Methods,* 2015, pp. 1–10. https://doi.org/10.1177/1609406915621420.

Foley, Douglas E. (2002): "Critical ethnography: The reflexive turn." *International Journal of Qualitative Studies in Education,* 15(4), pp. 469–490. https://doi.org/10.1080/09518390210145534.

Galonnier, Juliette (2015): "The racialization of Muslims in France and the United States: Some insights from white converts to Islam." *Social Compass,* 62(4), pp. 570–583. https://doi.org/10.1177/0037768615601966.

Hafez, Farid (2017a): "Whose Austria? Muslim Youth Challenge Nativist and Closed Notions of Austrian Identity." *Anthropology of the Middle East,* 12(1) Summer 2017, pp. 38–51.

– (2017b): "From Harlem to the Hoamatlond. Hip Hop, Malcolm X, and Muslim Activism in Austria." *Journal of Austrian-American History,* 1(2), pp. 159–180. https://doi.org/10.5325/jaustamerhist.1.2.0159.

– (2017c): "Muslim Protest against Austria's Islam law. An Analysis of Austrian Muslim's Protest against the 2015 Islam Law." *Journal of Muslim Minority Affairs,* 37(3), pp. 267–283.

Heller, Monika (2011): *Paths to Post-Nationalism. A Critical Ethnography of Language and Identity.* Oxford: Oxford University Press.

Hennink, Monique M. / Hutter, Inge / Bailey, Ajay (2011): *Qualitative Research Methods.* Thousand Oaks: SAGE.

Hirsjärvi, Sirkka / Hurme, Helena (2014): *Tutkimushaastattelu: teemahaastattelun teoria ja käytäntö.* Helsinki: Gaudeamus Helsinki University Press.

Hyvärinen, Matti (2017): "Haastattelun maailma." In: Hyvärinen, Matti / Nikander, Pirjo / Ruusuvuori, Johanna (eds.): *Tutkimushaastattelun käsikirja.* Tampere: Vastapaino, pp. 11–45.

Jensen, Devon. (2008): "Access". In: Given, Lisa M. (ed.): *The SAGE Encyclopedia of Qualitative Research Methods, Volumes 1 & 2.* Thousand Oaks: SAGE, pp. 2–3.

Juvonen, Tuula (2017): "Sisäpiirihaastattelu." In: Hyvärinen, Matti / Nikander, Pirjo / Ruusuvuori, Johanna (eds.): *Tutkimushaastattelun käsikirja.* Tampere: Vastapaino, pp. 398–410.

King, James R. (1999): "Am not! Are too! Using queer standpoint in postmodern critical ethnography." *International Journal of Qualitative Studies in Education,* 12(5), pp. 473–490. https://doi.org/10.1080/095183999235908.

Kvale, Steinar / Brinkman, Svend (2008): *InterViews: Learning the Craft of Qualitative Research Interviewing.* Thousand Oaks: SAGE.

Madison, D. Soyini (2005): *Critical Ethnography: Method, Ethic, and Performance.* SAGE Publications.

Meer, Nasar / Modood, Tariq (2010): "The Racialisation of Muslims." In: Sayyid, Salman / Vakil, Abdoolkarim (eds.): *Thinking through Islamophobia: Global Perspectives.* London: Hurst Publishers, pp. 69–83.

Miled, Neila (2017): "Muslim researcher researching Muslim youth: reflexive notes on critical ethnography, positionality and representation." *Ethnography and Education*, https://doi.org/10.1080/17457823.2017.1387063.

Moosavi, Leon (2015): "The Racialization of Muslim Converts in Britain and Their Experience of Islamophobia." *Critical Sociology*, 41(1), pp. 41–56. https://doi.org/10.1177/0896920513504601.

Morgan, David L. (2008): "Sample". In: Given, Lisa M. (ed.): *The SAGE Encyclopedia of Qualitative Research Methods, Volumes 1 & 2.* Thousand Oaks: SAGE, pp. 797–798.

Özyürek, Esra (2015): *Being German, Becoming Muslim. Race, Religion and Conversion in the New Europe.* Princeton: Princeton University Press.

Palys, Ted (2008): "Purposive sampling". In: Given, Lisa M. (ed.) *The SAGE Encyclopedia of Qualitative Research Methods, Volumes 1 & 2.* Thousand Oaks: SAGE, pp. 697–698.

Ryan, Louise / Kofman, Eleonore / Aaron, Pauline (2011): "Insiders and outsiders: working with peer researchers in researching Muslim communities." *International Journal of Social Research Methodology* 14(1), pp. 49–60. https://doi.org/10.1080/13645579.2010.481835.

Sherry, Mark (2008): "Insider/Outsider Status". In: Given, Lisa M. (ed.): *The SAGE Encyclopedia of Qualitative Research Methods, Volumes 1 & 2.* Thousand Oaks: SAGE.

Spencer, Renée / Pryce, Julia M. / Walsh, Jill (2014): "Philosophical Approaches to Qualitative Research." In: Leavy, Patricia (ed.): *The Oxford Handbook of Qualitative Research.* Oxford: Oxford University Press, pp. 81–98.

Suleiman, Yasir (2013): *Narratives of Conversion to Islam in Britain. Female Perspectives.* University of Cambridge.

Suzuki, Daiyu / Mayorga, Edwin (2014): "Scholar-Activism: A Twice Told Tale." *Multicultural Perspectives*, 16(1), pp. 16–20. https://doi.org/10.1080/15210960.2013.867405.

Thomas, Jim (1993): *Doing Critical Ethnography.* Thousand Oaks: SAGE.

Ulu, Yasin (2016): "Kick the truth, to the young 'Muslim' youth! Hip Hop & MJÖ." In: Hafez, Farid / Heinisch, Reinhard / Kneucker, Raoul / Polak, Regina (eds.): *Jung, muslimisch, österreichisch. Einblicke in 20 Jahre Muslimische Jugend Österreich.* Vienna: New Academic Press, pp. 358–374.

Vakulenko, Anastasia (2007): "Islamic Dress in Human Rights Jurisprudence: A Critique of Current Trends." *Human Rights Law Review.* Oxford University Press. https://doi.org/10.1093/hrlr/ngm024.

Van Nieuwkerk, Karin. (ed.). (2009): *Women embracing Islam: Gender and conversion in the West.* Austin: University of Texas Press.

Wansch, Peter (2016): "Vom Reden zum Handeln. Das Dialogverständnis der MJÖ." In: Hafez, Farid / Heinisch, Reinhard / Kneucker, Raoul / Polak, Regina (eds.): *Jung, muslimisch, österreichisch. Einblicke in 20 Jahre Muslimische Jugend Österreich.* Vienna: New Academic Press, pp. 328–343.

Willis, Jerry (2007): *Foundations of qualitative research: Interpretive and critical approaches.* Thousand Oaks: SAGE.

Anastas Odermatt

Identität bei Jugendlichen und jungen Erwachsenen im Spiegel quantitativer Migrations- und Religionspädagogikforschung

Abstract
Identity Among Youth and Young Adults in the Light of Quantitative Migration and Religious Education Research
Religion, identity, their relationship to each other and consequently ideas of *one's self* and the *others* are central questions in academic research and debate. With a view to future developments, *identity*, *migration* and *youth* have increasingly attracted research interest. Especially in quantitative research, it is of utmost importance *which* theoretical concepts are quantified and operationalized *how*. Theoretically formulated premises become obsolete through individual operationalizations too quickly. This makes the ability to connect to the used theory fragile too. And individual strands of research are unknown or unrecognized in their own field and corresponding opportunities and chances are simply overlooked and forgiven.
In the first part of the chapter, the contribution oriented to identity theory describes *identity* and *youth* from a theoretical point of view. In the second part two empirical studies are presented: the TIES project (The Integration of the European Second Generation) and the RaLP project (Religion and Life Perspectives). In the third part, a comparison between the theoretical premises and the conceptions of *identity* and *youth* used in the field of research will be presented. Coming from the central questions of this book, the premises and implications used are reflected and discussed in the conclusion.

Einleitung

Religion, Identität und ihr Verhältnis zueinander, folglich auch Vorstellungen von Eigenem und Fremdem, sind zentral erforschte und diskutierte Themen. Im Blick auf zukünftige Entwicklungen sind dabei „Identität“, „Migration“ und „Jugend“ vermehrt ins Forschungsinteresse gerückt. Gerade in der quantitativen Forschung ist es von höchstem Belang, *welche* theoretischen Konzepte *wie* quantifiziert und operationalisiert werden. Nur allzu schnell werden durch einzelne Operationalisierungen theoretisch formulierte Prämissen (wissentlich oder unwissentlich) hinfällig; damit wird aber die Anschlussfähigkeit an die jeweils in Anschlag gebrachten Theorien brüchig. Am Phänomen Religion interessierte Wissenschaften (Religionswissenschaften, Religionssoziologie, Religionspädagogik, Theologie etc.) sind an „Identität" interessiert, da einerseits Religiosität und damit unter anderem Lebens-, Welt- und Wertvorstellungen aufs engste mit Identitätsfragen gekoppelt sind. Anderseits sind sie an „Identität" interessiert, da diese nicht nur auf der individuellen Mikroebene von Interesse ist, sondern auch auf Meso- und Makroebene in den sozialen Identifizierungs- und Abgrenzungsprozessen eine gewichtige Rolle spielt (siehe hierzu exemplarisch Liedhegener 2016). Dieses Interesse am Integrations- aber auch am Abgrenzungs- und Exklusionspotential von Identität teilen die am Phänomen Religion interessierten Wissenschaften u. a. mit der Migrationsforschung. Identität ist hier einerseits ebenfalls auf der gesellschaftlichen Ebene von Interesse. Anderseits stehen auf individueller Ebene die Frage nach Veränderung von Identität durch Migration und die entsprechenden Herausforderungen im Fokus der Forschung.

Der identitätstheoretisch ausgerichtete Beitrag leitet im *ersten* Teil „Identität" und „Jugend" sozialwissenschaftlich bzw. entwicklungspsychologisch her. Im *zweiten* Teil werden zwei empirische Studien aus den Forschungsfeldern Migration und Religionspädagogik vorgestellt: das TIES Projekt (The Integration of the European Second Generation) für Ersteres und das RaLP Projekt (Religion and Life Perspectives) für Zweiteres. Im *dritten* Teil wird ein Vergleich zwischen den theoretischen Ausgangsprämissen und den in den beiden Forschungsfeldern konkret verwendeten Identitätstheorien und -konzepten vorgenommen. Mit Blick auf die zentralen Fragestellungen des Buches werden die in Anspruch genommenen Prämissen und Implikationen hinsichtlich „Identität" und „Jugend" reflektiert und diskutiert.

„Identität" und „Jugend": Theoretische Einbettung

Identität: Vielfalt und analytische Engführung

Der Begriff *Identität* wird gegenwärtig äußerst inflationär gebraucht und die Abgrenzungen zu Konzepten des Individuums und der Person erfolgen häufig, wenn überhaupt, nur schwammig. Hinzu kommt, dass dieser Begriff je nach Wissenschaftsbereich und Diskurs tatsächlich auch Unterschiedliches bedeutet (Müller 2011, S. 19; Teichert 2000; Zurawska 2007, S. 22f.).

So ist Identität in der *Philosophie* zunächst ein Begriff der Logik (Teichert 1999, S. 3). Er ist ein „Terminus zur Bezeichnung einer vollständigen oder absoluten Gleichheit" (Prechtl / Burkhard 2008, S. 257). Er wird eingesetzt, um bei einem Vergleich zweier Entitäten sowohl räumlich als auch zeitlich eine entsprechende Aussage über ihre Gleichheit zu machen. Der Begriff ist in der

Philosophie mit jenem der Person verhängt: *Personale Identität* ist eine komplexe, historisch gewachsene Zusammensetzung aus dem formaltheoretischen Begriff *Identität* und dem praktischen Begriff *Person* (Teichert 1999). Die *Psychologie* und die mit ihr verbundene *Psychiatrie* stellen ihrerseits die Frage nach der Entstehung, Aufrechterhaltung und Wiederherstellung der spezifischen Identität einzelner Menschen. Und in den *Kultur- und Sozialwissenschaften* steht sodann die Frage im Vordergrund, ob und wie Identität kontextuell verortet und konstruiert wird und welche Folgen und Wirkungen sich daraus auf Darstellungs- oder Kommunikationsebene ergeben.

Mit Blick auf die eingangs gestellte Frage, *welche* theoretischen Konzepte in der „Migrationsforschung" und „Religionspädagogik" *wie* quantifiziert und operationalisiert werden, ist eine sozialwissenschaftliche Konzeption von Identität zentral.

Sozial- und kulturwissenschaftliche Verortung

Historisch gesehen gehen die meisten heute verwendeten sozialwissenschaftlichen Begriffe auf drei Theorietraditionen zurück: auf die Psychoanalyse, auf den symbolischen Interaktionismus und auf die kognitivistische Entwicklungspsychologie (Zurawska 2007, S. 27).

Die *psychoanalytische* Tradition im Anschluss an Erik Erikson (1973) versteht Identität als Bewusstsein des Individuums von sich selbst und als Kompetenz zur Meisterung des Lebens (Abels 2010, S. 276). Mit Erikson (1973, S. 106ff.) kann gezeigt werden, wie sich Identität im Lebenszyklus entwickelt und welche spezifischen Entwicklungsstufen sich in den unterschiedlichen Lebensphasen ergeben.

Der *symbolische Interaktionismus* beruht auf den Arbeiten von William James (1909) und George Herbert Mead (1968) und der Unterscheidung zwischen *I* und *Me* und später *self*. Demnach entsteht *Identität* durch symbolische Interaktion zwischen Menschen. Das *I* ist eine Reaktion auf Haltungen der anderen, wobei sich diese Haltungen, Einstellungen und Erwartungen der anderen im *Me* widerspiegeln und sammeln. Um *Identität* zu erreichen, müssen sich das *I* und das *Me* in einem *Self* kumulieren, wobei das *Self* zuständig ist für die Vermittlung zwischen *I* und *Me* (Zurawska 2007, S. 39; Müller 2011, S. 37, 90). Identität ist demnach analytisch betrachtet dreiteilig: es gibt ein *I* (*personale Identität*), ein *Me* (*soziale Identität*) und ein *Self* (*Ich-Identität*) (ebd., S. 37).

Die *kognitivistische Entwicklungspsychologie* baut auf der psychoanalytischen Tradition und auf den begrifflichen Neuerungen des symbolischen Interaktionismus auf. Sie geht dabei von einem psychoanalytischen Modell im Sinne Eriksons aus, in welchem die Entwicklung schon angelegt ist, und von der Unterscheidung der Identität in *I*, *Me* und *Self* aus dem symbolischen Interaktionismus. Aus dieser Kombination ergibt sich die Frage, wie *I*, *me* und *Self* entwicklungspsychologisch entstehen und wie sich eine *stabile* Identität bildet. Die hierzu eingeführten zentralen Begriffe *Assimilation*, *Akkommodation* und *Äquilibration* und die darauf aufbauenden Thesen gehen auf den Entwicklungspsychologen Jean Piaget (1967) zurück. „Als immer anzustrebendes Ziel der Identitätsentwicklung gilt ein Gleichgewicht zwischen der Identitätsassimilation (Identitätsstabilisierung durch Anpassung neuer Erfahrungen an die bestehende Identität) und der Identitätsakkommodation (Identitätsänderung durch Anpassung der bestehenden Identität an neue Erfahrungen)" (Zurawska, S. 33 f.). Die Schaffung dieses Gleichgewichts beschreibt Piaget als Äquilibration. *Stabile Identität* ist in diesem Sinne die stetige Herstellung und Aufrechterhaltung dieses Gleichgewichts.

Neben diesen häufig verwendeten Zugängen zu Identität gibt es noch diverse weitere Zugänge, die im jeweiligen Forschungskontext von Belang und je nach Forschungsfrage zielführender sein können. Auch im Vorliegenden Band finden sich weitere, unterschiedliche Identitätskonzeptionen, die in ihrer jeweiligen Anwendung spannende Aspekte eines großen und nur schwer zu fassenden Themenkomplexes aufzeigen können. Und es gibt auch Forschende, welche die hier vorgestellte analytische Identitätskonzeption eher ablehnen und stattdessen *fluidere* Konzepte vorschlagen (z. B. Gilroy 1997). Dass Identität *fluid* oder auch *multipel* sein kann, wiederspricht dem hier vorgestellten Identitätskonzept meines Erachtens nicht. Vielmehr geht es um andere, aus meiner Sicht komplementäre Forschungszugänge. Es muss jeweils genau hingeschaut werden, inwieweit die jeweiligen Konzeptionen wofür tragfähig sind, und wofür nicht (Liedhegener 2016, S. 72).

Die hier vorgestellte Engführung ist ausgerichtet auf die empirische Sozialforschung. Hierfür ist insbesondere das Identitätskonzept des symbolischen Interaktionismus relevant.

Konzeption von Identität im symbolischen Interaktionismus

Der symbolische Interaktionismus geht davon aus, dass die Identität eines Individuums durch symbolische Interaktion zwischen Menschen entsteht und sich im Laufe der Zeit durch Wechselbeziehungen entwickelt (Müller 2011, S. 36). Er unterscheidet analytisch zwischen der personalen Identität ‚*I*', der sozialen Identität ‚*me*' und der Ich-Identität ‚*self*' (vgl. Abb. 1).

Personale Identität (‚I') meint jene persönlichen Merkmale, die ein Individuum als einzigartig erscheinen lassen (ebd., S. 90). Darunter fallen insbesondere seine individuelle Biographie sowie alle biopsychosozialen Merkmale wie Körper, Geschlecht, Fähigkeiten, Interessen und psychische Persönlichkeitsmerkmale. Personale Identität ergibt sich aus der Wechselwirkung des Individuums mit seiner natürlichen Umwelt.

Soziale Identität (‚me') entsteht in der Wechselwirkung des Individuums mit seiner sozialen Umwelt. Sie umfasst Positionen, die im sozialen Beziehungsgefüge eingenommen werden, und bildet Zugehörigkeiten zu kollektiven Identitäten sowie Rollen-Identitäten ab (ebd., S. 76f, 90). Auch die Fremdbildwahrnehmung, das heißt das Bewusstsein darüber, wie man von anderen gesehen wird und welche Erwartungen damit verbunden sind, sowie die eigene symbolisch-materielle Darstellung, das heißt die symbolisch-materielle Identität, gehören zur sozialen Identität (ebd.). „In ihrer Gesamtheit drückt sie die Verortung des Individuums im sozialen Beziehungsgefüge sowie in umfassenderen gesellschaftlichen Einheiten aus" (ebd., S. 83).

Die *Ich-Identität (‚self')* entsteht in der Wechselwirkung zwischen der personalen und der sozialen Identität. Sie stellt ein Referenz- und Ordnungsschema dar, das bei intrapsychischen Divergenzen und Konflikten zwischen personaler und sozialer Identität vermittelt und Orientierung bezüglich Einstellungen und Handlungen stiftet (ebd., S. 85ff.).

Die verschiedenen Komponenten der Identität entstehen und bestehen in der Spannung zur jeweiligen Umwelt, beziehungsweise in der Spannung untereinander. So entsteht soziale Identität in der Wechselwirkung mit der sozialen Umwelt und aufgrund des individuellen sozialen Horizonts. Personale Identität entsteht und besteht in der Wechselwirkung mit der natürlichen Umwelt beziehungsweise aufgrund des biopsychosozialen Horizonts. Und die Ich-Identität entsteht einerseits in der Dialektik zwischen sozialer und personaler Identität und anderseits in Wechselwirkung mit der normativ-kulturellen Umwelt, beziehungsweise aufgrund des moralischen Horizonts des Individuums. Der biopsychosoziale, soziale und moralische Horizont ergibt sich aus den individuellen, äußeren biopsychosozialen, sozialen und moralischen Bedingungen und den damit gemachten Erfahrungen (Müller 2011, S. 82).

Das dialektische Verhältnis und die äußeren Bedingungen, aus denen Identität entspringt, lassen sich anhand der biographisch temporalen Komponente der Identität vertieft erläutern. Die biographische Komponente leitet sich demnach ab aus dem Zusammenspiel zwischen personaler und sozialer Identität: Konfigurationen der personalen Identität ermöglichen oder hemmen die Ausbildung der sozialen Identität. Umgekehrt beschränken oder fördern Konfigurationen der sozialen Identität Entwicklungen der personalen Identität. Die biographische Komponente der Identität unterstreicht die hohe Bedeutung der äußeren, gesellschaftlichen Bedingungen sowie die Tatsache, dass Identität der zeitlichen Veränderung unterliegt.

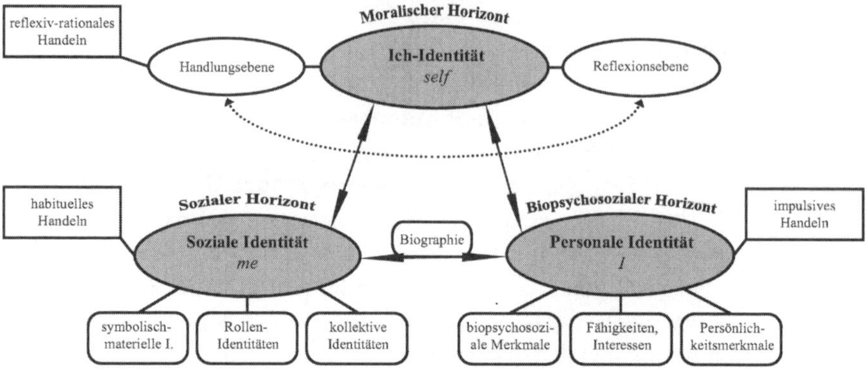

Abbildung 1: Identitätskonzeption. *Quelle: eigene Darstellung nach Müller (2011, S. 73)*

Soziale Identität als Kristallisationspunkt der Sozialforschung

In der Sozialforschung ist insbesondere die Soziale Identität von Interesse. Diese drückt in ihrer Gesamtheit die Verortung des Individuums im sozialen Beziehungsgefüge sowie in umfassenderen gesellschaftlichen Einheiten aus (Müller 2011, S. 83). Gemäß der *Social Identity Theory (SIT)* u.a. nach Tajfel (1982, S. 102) entsteht sie aus dem Wissen des Individuums um seine Mitgliedschaft in sozialen Gruppen und aus dem Wert der abgeleiteten emotionalen Bedeutung, mit der diese sozialen Identitäten besetzt sind. Ich unterscheide innerhalb der sozialen Identität nach Müller (2011, S. 77f.) zwischen symbolisch-materiellen, an Rollen angelehnten und kollektiven Identitäten.

Kollektive Identitäten sind ausgehandelte Konfigurationen eines gemeinsamen Wir-Gefühls, das Gleichförmigkeit ausdrückt und sich mittels Lebensstil und symbolisch-materiellen Elementen zur Schau stellt (ebd.). Der Aushandlungsprozess wird nicht nur durch jene Mitglieder gestaltet, die sich mit der jeweiligen kollektiven Identität identifizieren (Mikro-Ebene). Er wird auch durch all jene beeinflusst, die sich zwar nicht mit ihr identifizieren, sie aber sehr wohl kategorisieren und erfassen, beurteilen und artikulieren (auf Meso- und Makro-Ebene). Auch kollektive Identitäten unterliegen demnach einer Selbst- und einer Fremdwahrnehmung. Beispiele für kollektive Identitäten sind Nationalitäten, Fangruppen, Religionen, aber auch Vereine oder Verbände.

Rollen-Identitäten beziehen sich per se nicht auf ein Kollektiv, sondern auf eine spezifische Position, an die bestimmte Verhaltenserwartungen gerichtet sind (ebd., S. 78). Rollen-Identitäten können aber an kollektive Identitäten angebunden sein, wenn diese entsprechende Positionierungen umfassen. Beispiele für Rollen-Identitäten sind die Rollen der Angestellten, der Nachbarin oder der Mutter.

Mit *symbolisch-materiellen Identitäten* werden Zugehörigkeiten, das heißt Identifizierungen mit kollektiven Identitäten und Rollen-Identitäten, ausgedrückt. Das Tragen einer Tracht definiert auf symbolisch-materieller Ebene die Zugehörigkeit zu einer kollektiven Identität. Das Eintreten in einen Laden mit suchendem Habitus drückt die Rollen-Identität eines Kunden aus und ist verknüpft mit der Erwartung, dass beim Finden des Gesuchten eine Kaufhandlung erfolgt. In der Überlagerung zwischen übernommenen kollektiven Identitäten, erlernten Rollen-Identitäten und entsprechenden symbolisch-materiellen Identitäten zwecks Selbstdarstellung ergibt sich die Gesamtlage einer sozialen Identität.

Individuen streben in ihrer Selbstdarstellung nach einem möglichst positiven Selbstbild (Müller 2011, S. 77, 82). Um dieses Ziel zu erreichen, identifizieren sie sich mit möglichst positiv assoziierten kollektiven Identitäten und machen diese zu eigenen sozialen Teil-Identitäten (Hutnik 1985, S. 298). Durch den moralischen Horizont, den Individuen besitzen, können sie kollektive Identität normativ bewerten (ebd.); sie kategorisieren und ordnen auf Grundlage dieses Horizonts die verschiedenen kollektiven Identitäten (Müller 2011, S. 79).

Ohne eine ausgebildete Ich-Identität ist sowohl das Streben nach einem positiven Selbstbild als auch der Vorgang der Kategorisierung und Identifizierung sozialer Teil-Identitäten auf Grundlage eines moralischen Horizonts nur schwer möglich. Aus diesem Grund sind die Phase der Jugend und die damit verbundene Ausprägung der Ich-Identität so wichtig. In der Jugend gemachte und in die Entwicklung der Ich-Identität aufgenommene Identitäts- und Rollenerfahrungen bilden die Grundlage für Orientierung und Einordnung zukünftiger Erfahrungen und Handlungen.

Jugend

Die „Jugend" als gesellschaftlich anerkannte Lebensphase ist historisch erst in der Neuzeit entstanden und hat die Tendenz, sich zeitlich weiter auszudehnen (Hurrelmann / Quenzel 2013, S. 17). Entwicklungspsychologisch bezeichnet Jugend die Zeit zwischen der Pubertät und dem Ende des zweiten Lebensjahrzehnts (ebd., S. 236). Das zentrale Merkmal dieser Phase ist die Herausbildung der Ich-Identität. Auf die Jugendphase folgt das junge und mittlere Erwachsenenalter, wobei sich die Abgrenzung zwischen Jugendphase und der Phase des jungen Erwachsenenalters nicht klar ziehen lässt (ebd., 260). Zentrale Merkmale für das junge Erwachsenenalter sind Volljährigkeit, Autonomie, Eintritt ins Berufsleben und Familiengründung (ebd.).

In der gegenwärtigen Jugendforschung fließen die Jugendphase und das frühe Erwachsenenalter auf der Ebene der Altersdefinition häufig zusammen. Das ist methodologisch insofern relevant, als damit ein zentrales Kriterium der jeweils zu definierenden Grundgesamtheit in den Blickwinkel gerät. In der Forschungsrealität gibt es eine Vielzahl von Möglichkeiten, wie „Jugend" definiert wird. So bezieht sich beispielsweise die Shell-Jugendstudie (2010, S. 361) auf Jugendliche im Alter zwischen 12 und 25 Jahren. Die VROID-MHAP-Studie von Käppeler und Morgenthaler (2013) untersucht im qualitativen Teil Jugendliche im Alter zwischen 14 und 16 Jahren, im quantitativen Teil Jugendliche im Alter zwischen 13 und 17 Jahren. Und Sellmann (2012, S. 26) definiert die Jugend in seinen Überlegungen als Lebensphase zwischen 14 und etwa 26 Jahren.

Identitätsentwicklung in der Jugend

Identität entwickelt sich und besteht im Spannungsfeld zwischen dem Individuum und seiner sozialen, kulturellen und natürlichen Umwelt. Jugend ist eine von mehreren chronologisch gedachten Phasen im Lebensverlauf eines Menschen (Hurrelmann / Quenzel 2013, S. 11ff.; Erikson 1973, S. 106ff.; Schneider 2012, S. 159ff., 235ff.). Soll Identität bei Jugendlichen genauer erfasst werden, wird auf die Entwicklung der Identität während dieser Lebensphase fokussiert. Eriksons (1973) Theorie fußt auf dem prozesshaften Charakter der Identitätsbildung. Dabei ist der Prozess der Identitätsbildung eine Aneinanderreihung von Krisen und Entwicklungsaufgaben, die zu bewältigen sind (ebd., S. 275ff; Schneider 2012, S. 52). Er unterscheidet dabei acht Stadien mit je spezifischen Konflikten, Krisen und Themen (vgl. Tabelle 1).

Tabelle 1: Entwicklungsstadien nach Erikson

Stufe	**Anspruch der Identität**	**Konflikt**
Säuglingsalter	Ich bin, was man mir gibt.	Vertrauen vs. Misstrauen
Kleinkindalter	Ich bin, was ich will.	Autonomie vs. Scham / Zweifel
Spielalter	Ich bin, was ich mir vorstellen kann.	Initiative vs. Schuldgefühle
Schulalter	Ich bin, was ich lerne.	Wertsinn vs. Minderwertigkeit
Jugendphase	Wer bin ich, wer bin ich nicht?	Identität vs. Rollendiffusion
Frühes Erwachsenenalter	Ich bin, was ich einem anderen gebe und was ich in ihm finde.	Intimität vs. Isolation
Erwachsenenalter	Ich bin, was ich mit einem Anderen zusammen aufbaue und erhalte.	Generativität vs. Stagnation
Reifes Erwachsenenalter	Ich akzeptiere, was ich geworden bin.	Ich-Integrität vs. Verzweiflung

Quelle: eigene Tabelle in Anlehnung an Erikson (1973, S. 106ff.), Abels (2010, S. 275ff.) und Schneider (2012, S. 52).

Die Phase der Jugend startet mit den starken körperlichen und neurologischen Veränderungen der Pubertät (Erikson 1973, S. 106; Schneider 2012, S. 238ff.). Diese Veränderungen zwingen den Jugendlichen, seine sozialen Rollen neu zu definieren, und treiben ihn in eine Identitätskrise (Erikson 1973, S. 106). Diese Krise löst den Bildungsprozess der Ich-Identität aus: „Die Integration, die nun in der Form der Ich-Identität stattfindet, ist mehr als die Summe der Kindheitsidentifikationen. Sie ist das innere Kapital, das zuvor in den Erfahrungen einander folgender Entwicklungsstufen angesammelt wurde, wenn eine erfolgreiche Identifikation zu einer erfolgreichen Ausrichtung der Grundtriebe des Individuums auf seine Begabung und seine Chancen geführt hat" (ebd., S. 107). Die soziale und personale Identität haben sich bis zur Phase der Jugend schon zu einem gewissen Grad entwickelt. Die Ich-Identität entfaltet sich dann, ganz im Sinne des symbolischen Interaktionismus, im Wechselspiel zwischen sozialer und personaler Identität. Mit der Entwicklung der Ich-Identität tritt das reflexive Selbst einer Identität in den Vordergrund: Selbst-, Fremd- und Idealbilder werden reflektiert und auf Grundlage des moralischen Horizonts kategorisiert; Identifizierungen mit kollektiven Identitäten und Rollen-Identitäten werden hinterfragt, bewusst eingegangen und erprobt.

Wichtig in dieser Phase werden die *Peers*, das heißt gleichaltrige Freunde (Schneider 2012, S. 247). Eine bedeutsame Rolle spielt die tastende Suche nach einer eigenen Identität: Gewohntes wird abgelehnt, wobei dem Abgelehnten noch nicht unbedingt eine eigene Sinngebung entgegengesetzt werden kann. Das damit entstandene Vakuum kann mit einer Identifizierung mit den kollektiven Identitäten der Peers überbrückt werden (ebd.). Die soziale Identität spielt daher bei Jugendlichen eine bestimmende Rolle.

Quantitative Studien

In den empirischen Sozialwissenschaften beschäftigen sich unterschiedliche Forschungszweige mit dem Schnittbereich Identität, Jugend und Religion: so die Jugend- und Werteforschung (u.a. Gensicke 2011; Kriesi / et al. 2007; Shell 2011), die Migrationsforschung (u.a. Aicher-Jakob 2010; Allenbach 2011; Crul 2012), die Religionspädagogik (u.a. Helbling 2010; Ilg / et al. 2018; Schweitzer 1993; 2009; Schweitzer / et al. 2018; Ziebertz 2005; 2006 2009; 2011) sowie die Religionssoziologie (Collins-Mayo 2010; Gareau / et al. 2018; Käppler / et al. 2013; Müller 2011; Wippermann 1998; Young / et al. 2018; Zurawska 2007). Die verschiedenen Forschungsstränge verlaufen mehrheitlich voneinander losgelöst und beziehen sich nur marginal aufeinander. Es sollen hier nicht alle vorgestellt werden. Vielmehr werden zwei Studien aus unterschiedlichen Forschungssträngen ausgewählt und mit Blick auf ihre verwendeten Identitäts- und Jugendkonzeptionen beschrieben und analysiert: mit Blick auf die *Migrationsforschung* das TIES Projekt (The Integration of the European Second Generation) und mit Blick auf die *Religionspädagogik* das RaLP Projekt (Religion and Life Perspectives). Diese Studien sind insofern interessant, als sie jeweils eigene größere länderübergreifende Erhebungen umfassten und für das jeweilige Forschungsfeld im deutschsprachigen Raum von hohem Interesse waren. Der Fokus bei den Vorstellungen liegt weniger auf den Ergebnissen an sich als auf den verwendeten Identitäts- und Jugenddefinitionen.

TIES (The Integration of the European Second Generation)

Das TIES-Projekt (The Integration of the European Second Generation) startete 2005 als Forschungsprojekt zur *zweiten Generation* in mehreren europäischen Staaten unter der Leitung des Institute for Migration and Ethnic Studies (IMES) der Universität Amsterdam und des Netherlands Interdisciplinary Demographic Institute (NIDI).[1] Fokussiert wurde auf Nachkommen von Einwanderern aus der Türkei, dem ehemaligen Jugoslawien sowie aus Marokko. Das TIES-Projekt war wohl die erste große internationale Studie, die den Migrationshintergrund und nicht die Staatsangehörigkeit zum Selektionskriterium erhob. Leitende Forschungsfrage waren die strukturelle Integration von Kindern von Immigrantinnen und Immigranten in unterschiedlichen Ländern und die Frage, welche Kontextfaktoren die besten Aufstiegschancen („upwards mobility") für die zweite Generation ermöglichen (Crul / Schneider 2012, S. 375).

Methodik des TIES-Projekts

Die Datenerhebung erfolgte mittels CAPI- und PAPI-Surveys[2]. Da es sich bei Migration aus Sicht der Studienautoren um ein größtenteils urbanes Phänomen handelt, wurden die Surveys in 15 Städten in acht europäischen Ländern durchgeführt (Crul / et al. 2012, S. 13). Dies sind Stockholm in Schweden, Berlin

1 Die Projektdarstellung beruht einerseits auf der Publikation der Gesamtergebnisse von Crul / et al. (2012), anderseits auf den noch verbliebenen Projektseiten: www.nwo.nl/en/research-and-results/research-projects/i/04/2204.html (geprüft am: 10.10.2018); https://www.imis.uni-osnabrueck.de/forschung/abgeschlossene_projekte/the_integration_of_the_european_second_generation_ties.html (geprüft am: 10.10.2018). Die Hauptprojekt-Website www.tiesproject.eu wurde in die Website des Nachfolgeprojekts überführt: https://www.elitesproject.eu/ (geprüft am: 10.10.2018).

2 CAPI steht für *Computer Assisted Personal Interview:* Befragungsart, bei der die Interviewerinnen und Interviewer die Antworten der Zielpersonen über ein entsprechendes Computerprogramm erfassen; PAPI steht für *Paper and Pencil Interviews:* Schriftliche Fragebögen werden verteilt oder postalisch verschickt.

und Frankfurt am Main in Deutschland, Amsterdam und Rotterdam in den Niederlanden, Brüssel und Antwerpen in Belgien, Paris und Straßburg in Frankreich, Madrid und Barcelona in Spanien, Wien und Linz in Österreich sowie Zürich und Basel in der Schweiz.

In den meisten Städten wurden jeweils drei verschiedene Gruppen unterschiedlicher ethnisch-nationaler Herkunft befragt, namentlich zwei Gruppen der zweiten Generation und eine Kontrollgruppe autochthoner Herkunft. Die jeweiligen Gruppen der zweiten Generation waren türkischer und marokkanischer Herkunft in den Niederlanden und Belgien sowie türkischer und jugoslawischer Herkunft in Deutschland, Österreich und der Schweiz. In Frankreich und Schweden wurden nur die zweite Generation türkischer Herkunft und die Kontrollgruppe untersucht, in Spanien nur Jugendliche marokkanischer Herkunft der zweiten Generation und die Kontrollgruppe.

Zielpersonen für die einzelnen Surveys waren Personen zwischen 18 und 35 Jahren. Für die Untersuchung der Nachkommen von Einwandererinnen und Einwanderern aus den drei besagten Ländern bzw. Regionen wurde das Kriterium „zweite Generation" definiert als Kinder von Einwandererinnen und Einwanderern, die im Einwanderungsland der Eltern geboren wurden und leben (Crul / et al., S. 12).

Das Sampling erfolgte, wenn immer möglich, auf Grundlage von Bevölkerungsregistern mit entsprechend erfassten Daten (Groenwold / Lessard-Phillips, S. 50). Falls dies, wie in den meisten Fällen, nicht möglich war, wurde auf „Simple Random Sampling without Replacement" (SRSWOR) in Kombination mit Straßen- bzw. Quartieranalyse, auf onomastische Verfahren oder im Fall von Barcelona gegen Ende der Erhebungsphase zwecks Ausschöpfung auf Schneeballakquisition via Immigrantenorganisationen gesetzt.[3]

Ergebnisse aus dem TIES-Projekt

Die Ergebnispräsentation der Studie erfolgte einerseits mittels länderspezifischer Auswertungsbände, z.Bsp. jenem von Fibbi et. al. (2015) für die Schweiz oder die Auswertung von Sürig und Wilmes (2011) für Deutschland. Anderseits gab es einen länderübergreifenden Auswertungsband von Crul / et al. (2012). Des Weiteren wurde im Nachfolgeprojekt „ELITES" aufbauend auf den quantitativen Ergebnissen qualitative Forschung betrieben.

Die leitende Forschungsfrage der TIES-Studie mit Blick auf die Resultate war, in wie weit die Kontextfaktoren die Aufstiegschancen („upwards mobility") für die zweite Generation beeinflussen bzw. ermöglichen. Um diese Frage gesamt-

3 Onomastische Sampling-Verfahren leiten für eine entsprechende Stichprobe die regionale bzw. nationale Herkunft einer Zielperson von ihrem Namen ab.

haft zu beantworten, wurde im Rahmen der Ergebnispräsentation erstens nur auf die türkischen Befragten abgestellt, da diese in den meisten Städten befragt wurden. Und zweitens wurden unter den Befragten jene herausgefiltert, deren Eltern ein tiefes Bildungsniveau mitbrachten. So konnte ländervergleichend die Forschungsfrage beantwortet werden. Die Resultate gruppieren sich entlang der Bereiche *Bildung*, *Arbeitsmarkt*, *soziales Umfeld*, *Nation – Stadt – Quartier* und *Religion und Kultur.*

Hinsichtlich der *Bildung* wurde festgestellt, dass in Deutschland, Österreich und Belgien rund ein Drittel der Türkischstämmigen zweiter Generation mit Eltern mit tiefem Bildungsniveau den Bildungsweg frühzeitig[4] verlassen. Dies im Gegensatz zu Frankreich, Schweden und den Niederlanden: hier sind die Aufstiegschancen im Bildungsbereich klar größer; daher ist auch der prozentuale Anteil jener, die eine Berufsbildung, einen höheren sekundären Bildungsabschluss bzw. einen tertiären Bildungsabschluss erlangen, höher.[5] Zusammenfassend stellen Crul und Schneider (2012, 381) fest: „National and local educational opportunity structures are thus crucial for children of immigrants and their real-life chances, not least because they also determine in how far family background characteristics foresee ultimate educational outcomes".

Für die Integration in den jeweiligen *Arbeitsmärkten* stellten Crul und Schneider (ebd., S. 383) zweierlei fest: Einerseits sind rund ein Viertel bis ein Drittel der Türkischstämmigen zweiter Generation nach der Schule entweder arbeitslos oder auf dem Arbeitsmarkt nicht aktiv (v.a. Frauen), was auf eine schlechte Arbeitsmarktintegration hindeutet. Anderseits konnten die Hälfte bis zwei Drittel sehr wohl Fuß fassen und einen besseren Job als ihre Eltern erlangen (ebd., S. 387). Haupttreiber, ob jemand den Aufstieg schafft oder nicht, ist die Bildung.

Das *soziale Umfeld* wurde u.a. mittels einer Analyse der engsten Freundschaften beleuchtet. Die meisten gemischten *Freundschaften* wurden in Zürich, Basel und in Paris gefunden, dies aufgrund der verhältnismäßig kleinen Stadtgrößen bzw. des spezifischen Typus der lokalen Community (ebd., 398). So leben die Türkischstämmigen zweiter Generation in Zürich und Basel sehr verstreut und in Paris ist die Community sehr klein im Vergleich zu anderen ethnischen Minderheiten. Im Gegensatz dazu steht Berlin mit der größten türkischen Community in Europa: Hier ist es demographisch schlicht unwahrscheinlicher,

4 Mit „early school leavers" sind jene gemeint, „who have a lower secondary school degree at most" (Crul / Schneider 2012, S. 378).

5 Problematisch anzumerken ist, dass Schulabschlüsse nur bedingt länderübergreifend verglichen werden können. So kommen Crul und Schneider (2012, S. 382) zum Schluss, dass die sekundären Bildungsabschlüsse in Frankreich und in Schweden aufgrund der anschließenden Berufschancen im Vergleich mit jenen in Deutschland, Österreich und den Niederlanden wohl eher zu den tieferen Bildungsabschlüssen zu zählen sind.

mit anderen Ethnien in Kontakt zu kommen, und tendenziell finden die Kontakte innerhalb der Community statt.

Die Autoren fanden drei Typen ethnisch-übergreifender Freundschaften (ebd. S. 390):

1. Freundeskreis innerhalb der türkischen Community (Rotterdam, Wien, Linz, Berlin und Frankfurt)
2. Freundeskreis, ethnisch gemixt aber „non-white“: Amsterdam, Paris, Strasbourg und Stockholm)
3. Freundeskreis ethnisch gemixt inkl. gebürtigen Einheimischen: Zürich und Basel

Hinsichtlich ethnisch übergreifender Heiraten zeigen Crul und Schneider (ebd., S. 390) auf, dass der Großteil der Türkinnen und Türken in zweiter Generation einen Partner bzw. eine Partnerin aus der gleichen ethnisch-nationalen Gruppe heiratet (zwischen 86 % in Frankreich und 97 % in Schweden).

Hinsichtlich eines *nationalen* Zugehörigkeitsgefühls („Österreicher sein“, „Deutscher sein“ etc.) ist dies überall nicht allzu stark, bzw. die Werte für jene, die ein schwaches oder sehr schwaches Zugehörigkeitsgefühlt aufweisen, scheinen überall relativ hoch:

Tabelle 2: Nationales Zugehörigkeitsgefühl

	AUT	CHE	DEU	FRA	NLD	SWE
Schwach oder sehr schwach	25.7 %	15.4 %	19.8 %	23.9 %	24.8 %	23.6 %

Anmerkung: Schwache oder sehr schwache Gefühle der nationalen Zugehörigkeit unter Türkischstämmigen zweiter Generation mit Eltern mit tiefem Bildungsniveau. *Quelle: Crul / Schneider 2012, 391, TIES Survey 2007–2008*

Aufgrund der Tatsache, dass das Zugehörigkeitsgefühl in den verschiedenen Ländern auf der einen Seite überall relativ gleich schwach ist, dass aber auf der anderen Seite unterschiedliche Einbürgerungsregimes herrschen, die Beziehungsnetzwerke unterschiedlich formiert und auch die sozio-ökonomischen Ausgangsbedingungen unterschiedlich sind, kommen die Autoren (ebd., S. 391) zum Schluss, dass diese keinen direkten Einfluss auf die Stärke des Zugehörigkeitsgefühls hätten. Der relevante Treiber seien hier vielmehr die Akzeptanz und die soziale und strukturelle Offenheit der Aufnahmegesellschaft und dabei spielen entsprechende öffnende bzw. schließende Identitätsmechanismen eine Rolle. Im Gegensatz zu den nationalen kollektiven Identitäten, die in diesem Sinne mehrheitlich geschlossen scheinen, stehen die Zugehörigkeitsgefühle zur spezifischen Stadt oder zum Quartier: In allen elf Städten zeigte die Zielgruppe ein höheres Zugehörigkeitsgefühl zur Stadt bzw. zum Quartier als die Kontrollgruppe (daher die „einheimische“ Bevölkerung):

„In six out of the eleven cities we surveyed, second-generation Turks showed a stronger identification with the city than did their respective comparison groups. In the five other cities, we found the same result when going down to the neighbourhood level. This shows that weak national identity does not mean that this group would not feel ‚at home' where they grew up and live." (dies. 392)

Die Stadt- bzw. Quartier-Identitäten sind also offenere und inklusivere Identitätskategorien als nationale Identitäten (ebd., S. 393).

Mit Blick auf die *Religiosität* unterscheiden sich gemäß Crul und Schneider (ebd., S. 393) die untersuchten Gruppen am meisten, wobei Türkischstämmige der zweiten Generation religiöser seien als die Vergleichsgruppe.[6] Die meisten Türkischstämmigen der zweiten Generation sehen sich als „muslimisch", wobei diese Identifikation per se nichts mit entsprechendem Verhalten oder Glauben zu tun haben muss. So sagen in Frankreich, in Schweden, in der Schweiz und in Belgien rund ein Drittel der Türken zweiter Generation, die sich selbst als „muslimisch" bezeichnen, dass sie nie beten würden, ein Fünftel davon geht auch nie in eine Moschee (ebd., S. 394). In der Schweiz praktizieren zwei Drittel all jener, die sich als „muslimisch" bezeichnen, nicht. Im Gegensatz dazu scheinen in Österreich, in den Niederlanden und in Deutschland die religiös aktivsten Musliminnen und Muslime zu leben (ebd., S. 395): Drei Viertel der Zielpersonen in Wien halten den Ramadan ein, essen halal oder vollziehen ihre täglichen Gebete. In Amsterdam ist diese Gruppe mit zwei Dritteln ebenfalls groß.

Crul / Schneider (ebd.) unterscheiden zwischen einem „politischen" und einem „modernen" Islam. Der ersteren Kategorie ordnen sie jene Zielpersonen zu, die der Aussage zustimmen, dass die Religion die höchste politische Autorität sei, der zweiten jene, die dieser Aussage widersprechen *und* gleichzeitig der Aussage zustimmen, dass Religion eine private Angelegenheit sei (ebd.).[7]

6 Kritisch ist hier anzumerken, dass nicht ganz klar ist, was die Autoren unter „religiös" verstehen: So ist an einer Stelle die Rede von „Zugehörigkeit" (S. 393 oben), an anderer Stelle von „Praxis" (Tabelle 10.13 in Schneider und Crul 2012, S. 393) und in deren Interpretation von „Religiosität" die Rede. Dasselbe Problem bildet sich auch auf Fragebogenebene ab: So wird die Zugehörigkeitsfrage des „Basic Questionnaires" im Deutschen Fragebogen mit der Frage übersetz, ob die Zielperson aktuell religiös sei (Pott 2014). Im Gesamtdatensatz ist folglich die Validität nicht mehr gegeben. Die gemachte Aussage hinsichtlich der Differenz ist aber insofern akzeptabel, als dass entsprechende Binnen-Differenzen untersucht wurden. Länderübergreifende Vergleiche und vertiefte Analysen können aber nicht gemacht werden.

7 Die konkreten Aussagen lauteten: „Religion sollte die einzige und letztgültige politische Autorität sein." bzw. „Religion sollte eine private Angelegenheit zwischen dem/der Gläubigen und Gott sein." Ungeklärt bleibt in dieser Typologie, was mit jenen ist, die Religion zwar nicht als höchste politische Instanz, aber sehr wohl als öffentliche Angelegenheit betrachten.

Tabelle 3: „Politischer" vs. „Moderner" Islam

	AUT	BEL	CHE	DEU	FRA	NLD	SWE
„Moderner" Islam	64.6 %	64.7 %	85.5 %	57.9 %	77.1 %	63.9 %	89.9 %
„Politischer" Islam	11.8 %	17.2 %	7.7 %	27.9 %	14.3 %	10.4 %	5.6 %

Anmerkung: Verteilung eines politischen bzw. modernen Islams unter religiösen Türkischstämmige zweiter Generation (in Prozent). *Quelle: Crul / Schneider 2012, S. 395, TIES Survey 2007–2008*

Crul und Schneider (ebd., S. 395f.) erklären die insbesondere hohe Rate jener, die einen „politischen Islam" in Deutschland vertreten, einerseits mit dem Bildungsniveau: Ein „politischer Islam" ist für Musliminnen und Muslime mit tieferer Bildung attraktiver als für jene mit höherer Bildung. Anderseits erklären sie sich die hohe Rate mit länderspezifischen institutionellen Rahmenbedingungen des jeweiligen Islam: So konnten sie für Deutschland einen positiven Zusammenhang zwischen Koranschulen-Besuch und väterlichem Moscheebesuch und der Einstellung zum „politischen" Islam konstatieren. Dies im Gegensatz zu den Niederlanden: dort gab es einen negativen Zusammenhang. Die religiösen Institutionen scheinen in den beiden besagten Ländern als unterschiedliche Treiber zu fungieren, wobei die Autoren offenlassen, ob dies mit den unterschiedlichen Religionspolitiken zu tun hat oder mit anderem und hier entsprechenden Forschungsbedarf anmelden.

Zusammenfassend kommen Crul und Schneider (ebd.) zum Schluss, dass die Integration der Türkischstämmigen der zweiten Generation mit Eltern mit tiefen Bildungsniveau in Europa zwar auf zweierlei Weise interpretiert werden könne, in den Medien und in der Politik aber vor allem jene Interpretation, dass sie nicht oder nur schlecht integriert seien, kolportiert würde. Die Autoren (ebd., S. 399) wiedersprechen dieser Interpretation mit der Feststellung, dass eine beachtenswerte Gruppe von Türkinnen und Türken zweiter Generation insbesondere in der Bildung und in der Arbeitswelt aufgestiegen ist und dass spezifische institutionelle Rahmenbedingungen dafür die entsprechenden Treiber sind. Der länderspezifische Kontext scheint ganz allgemein einen weniger starken Einfluss auf Indikatoren auf Mikro-Ebene (z.Bsp. Partnerwahl) und Gruppenzugehörigkeitsgefühlen auf Meso-Ebene („ethno-nationale" Zugehörigkeiten) zu haben denn auf entsprechende Zuschreibungen auf Makro-Ebene (nationale Zugehörigkeiten).

Identitätsbegriff im TIES-Projekt

Schneider et. al (2012, S. 286ff.) liefern für das TIES-Projekt eine umfangreiche Theoretisierung von Identität(en). Im Anschluss an Devereux (1978) und Brubaker (2004) definieren sie Identität zunächst als „‚labels' for belonging to certain categories, though these labels can be quite disconnected from actual cultural and social practices." Dieses Labelling außerhalb spezifischer Kontexte vollzieht sich in dreierlei Hinsicht: *Erstens* via Selbst-Beschreibung des Individuums, *zweitens* auf Ebene der Kategorie bzw. der Gruppe selbst und drittens in der ‚Außenwelt', das heißt in der Fremdwahrnehmung außerhalb der Kategorien bzw. Gruppen. Gleichzeitig seien die unterschiedlichen Labels sehr wohl verwoben mit spezifischem kulturellen und sozialen Handeln, wobei dieses in drei Dimensionen stattfinden kann: in einer symbolische Dimension (dazu zählen Symbole wie Fahnen etc. wie auch symbolische Performanz wie Nationalfeiertage, Zeremonien etc.), in einer interagierenden Dimension (‚self' – ‚others') und in einer diskursiven Dimension, die auf die definitorischen Mechanismen und Narrative unterschiedlicher „Labels" verweist. Diese Definition wird dann in der Forschungsrealität eingeholt vom tatsächlich Möglichen:

> „Addressing identity issues in a survey such as TIES proves difficult because the aforementioned dimensions – symbolical, interactional and discursive – cannot really be concreticised. Surveys do not address individual strategies for self-positioning nor, even less so, do they account for the individuals' personal politics of identity. The statistical distribution of ‚feelings of belonging' in different domains and their degree of correlation with background variables and interrelation with other relevant domains (e.g. social relations, language, religion, social participation) are indicators of the structural dimension within the identificational incorporation of children of immigrants into urban societies in Europe." (Schneider / et al., S. 289).

Schließlich bezieht sich Identität in der TIES-Studie auf unterschiedliche soziale Zugehörigkeiten und auf die entsprechenden Selbstzuschreibungen der Zielpersonen zu Kategorien wie Ethnie, Land, Stadt und Religion. Diese Zugehörigkeiten werden in der Analyse kombiniert sowohl mit sozio-demographischen Variablen wie Alter, Geschlecht, Bildung oder dem sozio-ökonomischen Status der Eltern als auch mit Handlungsmustern (religiöse Praxis, Sprache, Partizipation und Zugehörigkeit). Die Selbstzuschreibungen werden mit Fragen zum Zugehörigkeitsgefühl zu verschiedenen Kategorien erkundet. Identität wird im TIES-Projekt als vielschichtiger Indikator von Gefühlen zu und als Konstruktion unterschiedlicher kollektiver Identitäten betrachtet. Zu betonen ist, dass sich trotz dieser praktischen Einschränkungen die Studienautoren vertieft mit Identität auseinandergesetzt haben und sie sich entsprechend dieser Einschränkungen bewusst sind und die Schwächen auch reflektiert haben.

Jugenddefinition des TIES-Projekts

Jugend wird von Crul / et al. (2012, S. 12) zunächst definiert im Rahmen einer Altersdefinition von 18–35 Jahren. Für die Analyse werden regelmäßig zwei Alterskohorten gebildet, konkret jene zwischen 18–25 und jene zwischen 26–35.

Diese Altersbegrenzung erfolgte primär aus praktischen Gründen: einerseits aus den zu Verfügung stehenden Akquise-Möglichkeiten im Rahmen der durchgeführten Surveys (ebd., 18), anderseits aus der Definition der Zielgruppe, folglich aus der Wahrscheinlichkeit, von einem „Gastarbeiter" abzustammen und die gesamte Schullaufbahn im Migrationsland absolviert zu haben. Die Tatsache, dass „nur" über 18-jährige Zielpersonen befragt wurden, ist den Studienautoren bewusst; so greifen sie mittels zeitlichen Rückgriffs-Fragen auf die Biographie und entsprechende Erfahrungen unter 18 Jahren zurück (ebd., S. 164).[8]

Des Weiteren kommt „Jugend" im Rahmen der Erfassung der Freundschaftskreise zur Sprache[9]. So stellen die Studienautoren fest, dass Peers in der Adoleszenz eine wichtige Rolle spielen (ebd., S. 160). Der Einfluss der Peers ist sogar wichtiger als jeder andere Einfluss einer Gruppe einschließlich der Kernfamilie. Darüber hinaus findet in dieser Phase die Identitätsfindung statt; identitätsstiftende ethnische und kulturelle Selbstzuordnungen werden in Freundschaften und freundschaftlichen Verbindungen geformt, aber auch in der Auswahl möglicher Beziehungen widergespiegelt (ebd.).

RaLP (Religion and Life Perspectives)

Das RaLP Projekt ist schon etwas älter und hat seinen Anfang im Jahr 2000 genommen. Es nahm aus theologischer, pädagogischer und soziologischer Perspektive die Lebenseinstellungen und die Religiosität von Jugendlichen („young people") in den Fokus. Forschungsleitend war die Frage, welchen Einfluss sozio-demographische Gegebenheiten (unabhängige Variable UV 1), Persönlichkeit (UV 2) und Sozialisation (UV 3) auf Religiosität (abhängige Variable AV 1) und Lebenseinstellungen (AV 2) haben (Ziebertz / Kay 2009, S. 10).

Methode des RaLP-Projekts

In zehn Ländern (Deutschland, Großbritannien, Türkei, Polen, Niederlande, Schweden, Finnland, Irland, Kroatien und Israel) wurden gesamthaft n=9'854 Zielpersonen zu ihrer Religiosität und zu ihren Lebenseinstellungen befragt (ebd., S. 27). Als Zielpersonen wurden Schülerinnen und Schüler auf sekundärer Bildungsstufe mit einem Durchschnittsalter von 17–18 Jahren gewählt, die voraussichtlich die Hochschulreife erlangen (ebd.). Zwar sei die untersuchte

8 So wird mit einer Frage, wie es „damals" während der Sekundarschulzeit war, entsprechend zurückgegriffen.

9 Der Freundeskreis wird hier mittels Abfrage des besten, zweitbesten und drittbesten Freundes und der jeweiligen Herkunft (eigene ethnische Gruppe; Deutsch/Schweiz; andere ethnische Gruppe) operationalisiert (Crul / et al., S. 161).

Gruppe damit nicht repräsentativ für Jugendliche allgemein, dafür seien sie die „future opinion formers“ und würden Europa zukünftig mitprägen.

Das Sampling erfolgte je nach Land über eine Zufallsstichprobe aus Schulen mit einzelnen Schneeballelementen (Schulen empfehlen sich gegenseitig) oder aufgrund geographischer Schichtung ausgewählter Schulen. Die PAPI-Fragebögen wurden über entsprechenden Schulen und Lehrpersonen verteilt.

Zentrale Ergebnisse aus dem RaLP-Projekt

Die vielfältigen Ergebnisse wurden in mehreren Bänden dargestellt (Ziebertz / Kay 2005; 2006; Ziebertz / Kay / Riegel 2009). Was gesamthaft betrachtet leider fehlt, sind konsolidierte Ergebnis-Aussagen mit Blick auf das zu Beginn der Untersuchung eingeführte Modell. In diesem Sinne erfolgt hier eine nur äußerst kleine und selektive Auswahl, beschränkt auf die beiden Bereiche religiöse Zugehörigkeit und religiöse Sozialisierung.

Mit Blick auf die *religiösen Zugehörigkeiten* kommen Ziebertz und Kay (2006, 247, S. 264) zum Schluss, dass das Feld der untersuchten 17–18-jährigen Jugendlichen in Europa sowohl innerhalb der einzelnen Religion als auch zwischen den Ländern äußerst vielfältig ist (vgl. Tab 4.).[10]

Tabelle 4: Zugehörigkeit zu einer Religionsgemeinschaft

	Zugehörigkeit		
Land	**Nein**	**Ja**	**Summe**
Niederlande	37.7 %	62.3 %	100.0 %
Vereinigtes Königreich	23.5 %	76.5 %	100.0 %
Deutschland	21.7 %	78.3 %	100.0 %
Schweden	18.8 %	81.2 %	100.0 %
Israel	16.8 %	83.2 %	100.0 %
Kroatien	8.5 %	91.5 %	100.0 %
Finland	5.8 %	94.2 %	100.0 %
Irland	2.3 %	97.7 %	100.0 %
Polen	-	100 %	100.0 %
Türkei	-	100 %	100.0 %

Anmerkung: „Do you belong to a church or religious community?“. *Quelle: Ziebertz / Kay 2006, Tabelle 13.1, S. 341*

10 Die Trennlinie Religionszughörigkeit Ja/Nein ist für die religiöse Landschaft Europas insbesondere für West-Europa sicherlich zentral. Religiöse Vielfalt wird aber allgemein auf Ebene der unterschiedlichen Religionszugehörigkeiten gemessen, wobei sich hier gerade mit Blick auf West- und Osteuropa unterschiedliche Entwicklungen abzeichnen. Siehe hierzu ausführlich die Ergebnisse der Swiss Metadatabase of Religious Affiliation (SMRE) von Liedhegener / Odermatt (2018).

Die länderspezifischen Unterschiede werden einerseits mit entsprechend verschiedenen historischen Hintergründen erklärt, anderseits mit der Vermutung, dass die Modernisierung unterschiedlich weit fortgeschritten sei.

Hinsichtlich *religiöser Sozialisation* stellen sich Ziebertz und Kay (ebd., S. 249) die Frage, wie säkularisiert die Familienstrukturen in den einzelnen Ländern sind. Hierzu werden vier Fälle unterschieden: (1) Familien, in denen die Jugendlichen ihre Eltern als auch sich selbst als religiös beschrieben („religious in the 2nd generation"); (2) Familien, in denen die Jugendlichen ihre Eltern als religiös, sich selbst aber als nicht-religiös beschreiben („secularised in the 1st generation"); (3) Familien, in denen die Jugendlichen sowohl ihre Eltern als auch sich selbst als nicht religiös bezeichnen („secularised in the 2nd generation"); und (4) Familien, in denen die Jugendlichen ihre Eltern als nicht-religiös, sich selbst aber als religiös bezeichnen („religious in the 1st generation").

Tabelle 5: Grad der Säkularisierung anhand religiöser Sozialisierung

	Grad der Säkularisierung			
Land	**Rel. in 2nd Gen. (1)**	**Rel. In 1st Gen. (4)**	**Sec. In 1st Gen. (2)**	**Sec. In 2nd Gen. (3)**
Schweden	13.7 %	2.2 %	24.9 %	59.2 %
Niederlande	14.2 %	2.2 %	37.9 %	45.7 %
Deutschland	22.6 %	2.7 %	38.9 %	35.8 %
Finnland	35.7 %	6.6 %	31.8 %	25.9 %
Vereinigtes Königreich	37.4 %	2.8 %	31.5 %	28.3 %
Israel	48.1 %	1.2 %	35.9 %	14.9 %
Irland	59.5 %	1.1 %	34.2 %	5.2 %
Kroatien	62.3 %	2.6 %	24.8 %	10.3 %
Polen	80.5 %	0.9 %	16.8 %	1.8 %
Türkei	81.6 %		18.4 %	

Quelle: Ziebertz / Kay 2006, Tabelle 13.3, S. 342

Kontinuierliche religiöse Familientraditionen finden sich in der Türkei (81.6 %) und in Polen (80.5 %) und noch immer mehrheitlich in Kroatien (62.3 %) und Irland (59.5 %) (vgl. Tab. 5). Im Gegensatz dazu sind die religiösen Sozialisierungsprozesse innerhalb der Familie in Schweden (13.7 %) und den Niederlanden (14.2 %) sehr gering. In allen untersuchten westeuropäischen Ländern (Niederlande, Deutschland, Vereinigtes Königreich und Irland) bezeichnet sich rund ein Drittel der Jugendlichen als nicht religiös, wobei diese gleichzeitig ihre Eltern als religiös beschreiben. Eindeutig kleiner ist diese Gruppe in Polen (16.8 %) und in der Türkei (18.4 %). Die Anteile jener Jugendlichen, die sich selbst als nicht-religiös bezeichnen und die auch ihre Eltern als nicht-religiös beschreiben, sind in Schweden (59.2 %) und in den Niederlanden (45.7 %) am größten. Eine religiöse Sozialisierung innerhalb der Familie findet in diesen beiden Ländern mehrheitlich nicht mehr statt. Erwähnenswert sind die 6.6 % jener Jugendlichen in Finnland, die sich selbst als religiös bezeichnen, ihre Eltern aber als nicht-religiös.

Die untersuchten Länder sind also, was die religiöse Zugehörigkeit anbelangt, sehr unterschiedlich und auch die familiären Sozialisierungsmechanismen hinsichtlich Religion funktionieren ganz unterschiedlich (oder eben nicht).

Identitätsbegriff im RaLP-Projekt

Es gibt keine explizite theoretische Verortung hinsichtlich Identität. Jedoch lassen die verwendeten Analysekategorien und Operationalisierungen Rückschlüsse auf die mitgetragene Identitätstheorie zu:

- Mit der analytischen Unterscheidung zwischen einer Mikro-, Meso- und Makroebene wird das Individuum auf der Mikroebene lokalisiert und gleichzeitig in einer Meso- und Makroebene eingebettet.
- Im Bereich Religion werden sowohl Zugehörigkeit als auch Selbstbezeichnungen abgefragt. Es gibt also Zugehörigkeiten zu Gruppen.
- Hinsichtlich Persönlichkeit werden die Persönlichkeitsausprägungen Neurotizismus, Extraversion und Psychotizismus erhoben (P-E-N Modell). Persönlichkeit wird unterschieden von anderen Analysekategorien wie z.Bsp. Soziodemographie etc. Diese Persönlichkeitsausprägungen werden in den Auswertungen nicht vertieft verwertet.
- Hinsichtlich Sozialisierung wird insbesondere die religiöse Sozialisierung erfragt. Identität wird damit prozedural als mit der Biographie verhängt betrachtet.

Mit diesen Hinweisen kann Identität im RaLP-Projekt wie folgt herauskristallisiert werden: prozedural und biographisch; Persönlichkeit und Zugehörigkeiten werden unterschieden; das Individuum ist eingebettet in ein größeres Ganzes (Meso- und Makro-Ebene).

Jugenddefinition im RaLP-Projekt

Als „Youth People“ werden, wie oben beschrieben, Schülerinnen und Schüler auf sekundärer Bildungsstufe mit einem Durchschnittsalter von 17–18 Jahren gewählt, die voraussichtlich die Hochschulreife erlangen. Es wird explizit eingestanden, dass dies nicht für die ganze „Jugend“ repräsentativ sei. Der Fokus liege vielmehr auf den zukünftigen Entscheidungsträgerinnen und Entscheidungsträgern.

Was von der Theorie übrigbleibt: Abgleich zwischen Theorie und Forschungspraxis

Nachdem im ersten Teil „Identität“ und „Jugend“ sozialwissenschaftlich verortet und im zweiten Teil zwei große Forschungsprojekte aus den Bereichen „Migrationsforschung“ und „Religionspädagogik“ analytisch vorgestellt wurden, erfolgt in diesem dritten Teil ein Vergleich zwischen den theoretischen Ausgangsprämissen und den im Forschungsfeld konkret verwendeten Identitäts- und Jugendkonzepten.

Vergleich Theorie – Forschungsfelder

Die sozialwissenschaftliche Verortung von *Identität*, wie sie in diesem Beitrag konzipiert wurde, setzte an der Unterscheidung von *I*, *me* und *self* an, wobei sich Identität allgemein im Spannungsfeld zwischen Individuum und Umwelt entwickelt und das *self* spezifisch in der Jugendphase (vgl. dazu und folgend Tabelle 6).

Tabelle 6: Identität Vergleich

	Identität	**Jugend**	**Weiteres**
Soz.-wiss. Verortung	- I – me – self - *Me:* Rollen / Symbolische I. / Kollektive I. - Entwicklung im Spannungsfeld Ind. – Umwelt	- Lebensphase unter mehreren mit spez. Herausforderungen - Pubertät am Ende des 2. Lebensjahrzehnts - Entwicklung *self*	
TIES	- Labels der Zugehörigkeit zu verschiedenen Kategorien - Operationalisierungen: Abfrage von Zugehörigkeits- und Identitätsgefühlen zu verschiedenen Kategorien	- 18–35 Jahre - Peer-Orientierung - Rückgriff auf „damals“	Reflektierter Umgang mit den Begrifflichkeiten und mit den zur Verfügung stehenden Erhebungsmethoden und -instrumenten; keine eigene Verortung von „Jugend“
RaLP	- Prozedural, biographisch; - Persönlichkeit und Zugehörigkeiten werden unterschieden; - Individuum eingebettet in ein größeres Ganzes (Meso- und Makro-Ebene)	- Schülerinnen und Schüler auf sekundärer Bildungsstufe - 17–18 Jahre - Hochschulreife	Keine eigene theoretische Verortung von „Identität“ und „Jugend“ – Rückgriff auf Operationalisierungen

Quelle: Eigene Tabelle.

Sowohl das TIES- als auch das RaLP-Projekt messen dem *me*, der sozialen Identität und damit auch den kollektiven Identitäten, hohe Bedeutung zu. Das RaLP-Projekt erhebt auf der Ebene der Operationalisierungen zwar das *I*, die personale Identität, verwertet es aber dann nicht tiefer. Beide Projekte beachten das *self* als gerade im Jugendalter entstehende Kategorie nicht weiter.

Beide sozialwissenschaftlichen Projekte konzentrieren sich offensichtlich auf die soziale Identität. Sie verstehen sie als Verweis auf kollektive Identität mit Blick auf unterschiedliche Labels und Zugehörigkeiten. Das RaLP-Projekt hebt, da es sich um eine religionspädagogische Studie handelt, erwartungsgemäß die entwicklungspsychologischen Momente (Identität als Prozess, Sozialisierung) stärker hervor. Im Gegensatz dazu stellt das TIES-Projekt die Zugehörigkeiten klarer in den Vordergrund.

Jugend wird als Lebensphase unter mehreren betrachtet, in der das *Self* – die Ich-Identität – entwickelt wird. Zeitlich wird *Jugend* in der Pubertät am Ende des zweiten Lebensjahrzehnts verortet. Jugend wird in den beiden Projekten unterschiedlich definiert. Die schon festgestellte Überlagerung von Jugendalter und der Phase der jungen Erwachsenen zeigt sich auch im TIES-Projekt (18–35 Jahre). Und auch die Peer-Orientierung ist im TIES-Projekt von Wichtigkeit (soziales Umfeld, Freunde). Das RaLP-Projekt fokussiert sich demgegenüber auf die 17–18-jährigen mit Hochschulreife.

Diskussion

Identität wird in der sozialwissenschaftlichen Forschung häufig auf die soziale Identität eingeengt. Das ist insofern bedauerlich, als damit Chancen vergeben werden. Drei Punkte sind für weiterführende Forschung zentral:

1. Die sozialwissenschaftliche Forschung beschäftigt sich unter der Prämisse, dass Handlungen von Identität ausgehen, sui generis mit Identität. Der Begriff wird gegenwärtig inflationär gebraucht. Umso wichtiger ist eine jeweils klare theoretische Verortung mit Anknüpfungspunkten an bestehende Identitätstheorien. Eine eindeutige theoretische Verortung hilft auch, entsprechende Operationalisierungen zu entwickeln und im Anschluss an Erhebungen zu interpretieren und zu verstehen.
2. Entwicklungspsychologische Phasen müssen in der empirischen Sozialforschung, in der Alter eine sozio-demographischen Grundvariable *par excellence* ist, mitbedacht werden. Gerade Alters- bzw. Generationeneffekte könnten vor diesem Hintergrund zielführender analysiert und interpretiert werden.

3. Mit der Hinzunahme von „I“ und „self“ können interdisziplinäre Felder und Chancen eröffnet werden. Gerade die Sozialpsychologie bietet hier vielfältige Anknüpfungsmöglichkeiten. Zwar besteht das Risiko, dass man sich schnell verliert, da die unterschiedlichen Forschungsstränge im ersten Augenblick von außen betrachtet sehr vielfältig und unübersichtlich erscheinen.[11] Gleichwohl sind, mit Blick auf mögliche Kontroll- und Erklärungsvariablen, entsprechende Konzepte und die jeweiligen Operationalisierungen als Chancen mitzudenken.
   So werden zum Beispiel in der politikwissenschaftlichen Forschung die Big Five als Messkonzept für personale Identität („I“) verwendet (z.Bsp. Freitag 2017, zu den Big Five: Gerlitz / Schupp 2005 oder Lang / Lüdtke 2005).[12] Und das von Rammstedt und John (2007) entwickelte BFI-10 kam schon in verschiedenen Untersuchungen des *International Social Survey Programme* zum Einsatz, unter anderem in den Modulen *National Identity* (2003) und *Religion* (2008).
   Und für das „self“ könnten entsprechende Skalen zur Selbstwahrnehmung oder ähnliches in Anschlag gebracht werden. Auf alle Fälle ist hier weiter (interdisziplinäre) Forschung nötig.
   Zwar mögen einzelne Zusammenhänge nicht wirklich überraschen („wenn jemand introvertiert ist, wird sein soziales Umfeld tendenziell wohl kleiner sein“). So geht es aber vielmehr um die Kombination mehrerer Konzepte und ihre Verwendung als Kontroll- und Erklärungsvariablen um die Erklärungskraft entsprechender Modelle zu erhöhen und zu verbessern.

Auch mit dem *Jugend*-Begriff wird tendenziell unreflektiert umgegangen. Stets sollte zunächst erörtert werden, was darunter verstanden wird. Ist es „nur“ eine Altersspanne? Oder geht es um spezifische Herausforderungen, welche die „Jugend“ kennzeichnen und in der Forschung auch berücksichtigt werden könnten? Oder handelt es sich um Phänomene der jüngeren Generation allgemein, das heißt von Jugendlichen und jungen Erwachsenen? Die „Jugend“ erforschen, das tönt stets gut; sie sei ja die „Zukunft“. Jedoch ist hierbei die Prämisse enthalten, dass sich bestimmte Eigenschaften über die Jahre mittragen und damit Generationeneffekte sind; aber auch Alterseffekte müssen mitbedacht werden. In diesem Sinne ist zu reflektieren, warum überhaupt Jugend erforscht wird. Genau dies hat sich dieses Buch in dankenswerter Weise zur Aufgabe gemacht.

11 Aber in welchem Forschungsfeld ist das von außen betrachtet nicht so?

12 Bei den Big Five handelt es sich um ein analytisches Modell aus der Persönlichkeitspsychologie. Dem Modell zufolge gibt es fünf Hauptdimensionen der Persönlichkeit und jeder Mensch lässt sich entsprechend einordnen. Die fünf Dimensionen sind Offenheit für Erfahrungen, Gewissenhaftigkeit, Extraversion, Verträglichkeit sowie Neurotizismus.

Zusammenfassung

Der vorliegende Beitrag hat „Identität“ und „Jugend“ aus der empirischen Sozialforschung hergeleitet. Die Verortung von *Identität* setzt an der Unterscheidung James (1909) und Meads (1968) von I, me und self an. Dabei entwickelt sich Identität im Sinne Piagets (1967) im Spannungsfeld zwischen Individuum und Umwelt und das self entfaltet sich nach Erikson (1973) spezifisch in der Jugendphase. *Jugend* gilt demnach als eine Lebensphase unter mehreren und wird biographisch in der Pubertät am Ende des zweiten Lebensjahrzehnts verortet.

Das Forschungsinteresse des Beitrags liegt darin, zu untersuchen, wie weit die theoretisch erörterten Begriffe auch im Feld quantitativer Sozialforschung Anwendung finden. Zu diesem Zweck wurde aus dem Bereich der Migrationsforschung das TIES-Projekt und aus dem Bereich der Religionspädagogik das RaLP-Projekt vorgestellt – und die beiden wurden miteinander verglichen. Die Auswahl dieser Bereiche ist einerseits der Forschungsperspektive und Forschungsarbeit des Autors geschuldet.[13] Anderseits entspricht sie der Tatsache, dass er über eigene Erfahrungen als Lehrperson für (überkonfessionelle, religionswissenschaftlich ausgerichtete) Religionskunde auf Gymnasialstufe verfügt und zugleich als Politiker in der kantonalen Legislative (Parlament) des Kantons Zug regelmäßig auch auf politischer Ebene mit Migrationsthemen in Berührung kommt. Er sieht nun seine Felderfahrungen durch die Ergebnisse des RaLP-Projekts bestätigt: Die Zugehörigkeit zu Religion ist an sich vielfältig und die Sozialisation ist insbesondere in westeuropäischen Ländern tendenziell brüchig. Die Resultate des TIES-Projekt sind in einer anderen Hinsicht spannend: Sie zeigen die Schweiz gerade im politischen Diskurs hinsichtlich Migration als Land mit hohem Anteil an Personen mit Migrationshintergrund; „Integrationsprobleme“ im Sinne von Herausforderungen sind sicherlich vorhanden, werden aber auch diskursiv konstruiert. Nach den Ergebnissen des TIES-Projekts kann die Schweiz im Vergleich zu anderen Ländern wohl als „Best Practice“ betrachtet werden. Das bestätigt die entsprechenden Erfahrungen. Das TIES-Projekt kam zum Schluß, dass Jugendliche und junge Erwachsene der zweiten Generation in Europa zu einem grossen Teil in der Bildung und im Arbeitsfeld einen Sprung nach vorne schaffen und so eine „Aufwärtsmobilität“ erfahren.

Der Vergleich zwischen beiden untersuchten Projekten und Feldern bringt zu Tage, dass „Identität“ in der empirischen Sozialforschung häufig als „soziale Identität“ betrachtet und damit verkürzt wird. Daraus ergeben sich Forderungen für die Forschungsarbeit: Die theoretischen Konzepte sind klar zu verorten und

13 Der Autor ist wissenschaftlicher Mitarbeiter im internationalen DFG-/SNF-Forschungsprojekt *Social Groups and Religious Identities in Civil Society (RESIC).*

es ist aufzuzeigen, welche Anschlüsse sich insbesondere im Blick auf die benachbarten Disziplinen der Entwicklungs- und Sozialpsychologie ergeben. Damit wird es möglich, erprobte Konstrukte und Operationalisierungen zu adaptieren und als neue Erklärungs- und Kontrollvariablen für entsprechende Modellbildung einzuführen.

Literatur

Abels, Heinz (2010): *Identität. Über die Entstehung des Gedankens, dass der Mensch ein Individuum ist, den nicht leicht zu verwirklichenden Anspruch auf Individualität und die Tatsache, dass Identität in Zeiten der Individualisierung von der Hand in den Mund lebt.* 2. Aufl. Wiesbaden: VS.

Aicher-Jakob, Marion (2010): *Identitätskonstruktionen türkischer Jugendlicher. Ein Leben mit oder zwischen zwei Kulturen.* Wiesbaden: VS.

Allenbach, Brigit (2011): *Jugend, Migration und Religion. Interdisziplinäre Perspektiven.* Baden-Baden: Nomos.

Brubaker, Rogers (2004): *Ethnicity without Groups.* Cambridge: Cambridge University Press.

Burkard, Franz P. / Prechtl, Peter (2008): *Metzler Lexikon Philosophie. Begriffe und Definitionen.* 3. Aufl. Stuttgart: J.B. Metzler.

Collins-Mayo, Sylvia (Hg.) (2010): *Religion and youth.* Farnham, Surrey, England: Ashgate Pub. Ltd (Theology and religion in interdisciplinary perspective series).

Crul, Maurice / Lelie, Frans / Schneider, Jens (Hg.) (2012): *The European Second Generation Compared. Does the Integration Context Matter?* Amsterdam: Amsterdam University Press.

Crul, Maurice / Schneider, Jens (2012): Conclusions and implications. The integration context matters. In: Maurice Crul, Frans Lelie und Jens Schneider (Hg.): *The European Second Generation Compared. Does the Integration Context Matter?* Amsterdam: Amsterdam University Press, S. 375–404.

Devereux, George (1978): *Ethnopsychoanalyse. Die komplementaristische Methode in den Wissenschaften vom Menschen.* Frankfurt am Main: Suhrkamp.

Erikson, Erik H. (2013 (1973)): *Identität und Lebenszyklus. Drei Aufsätze.* Unter Mitarbeit von Käte Hügel. 26. Aufl. Frankfurt am Main: Suhrkamp.

Fibbi, Rosita (Hg.) (2015): *The new second generation in Switzerland. Youth of Turkish and former Yugoslav descent in Zurich and Basel.* Amsterdam: Amsterdam University Press.

Freitag, Markus (2017): Die Psyche des Politischen. Was der Charakter über unser politisches Denken und Handeln verrät. Zürich: *Neue Zürcher Zeitung* NZZ Libro (Politik und Gesellschaft in der Schweiz, Band 6).

Gareau, Paul L. / Culham Bullivant, Spencer / Beyer, Peter (2018): *Youth, religion, and identity in a globalizing context. International perspectives.* Leiden: Brill (Youth in a Globalizing World, 8).

Gensicke, Thomas (2011): Werteorientierung, Befinden und Problembewältigung. In: Shell Deutschland Holding (Hg.): *Jugend 2010. Eine pragmatische Generation behauptet sich.* Frankfurt am Main: Fischer, S. 187–242.

Gerlitz, Jean-Yves / Schupp, Jürgen (2005): Zur Erhebung der Big-Five-basierten Persönlichkeitsmerkmale im SOEP. Dokumentation der Instrumententwicklung BFI-S auf Basis des SOEP-Pretests 2005. In: *DIW Research Notes* (4).

Gilroy, Paul (2014 (1997)): Diaspora and the detours of identity. In: Kathryn Woodward (Hg.): *Identity and difference.* London: Sage; The Open University (Culture, media and identities), S. 301–343.

Groenewold, George / Lessard-Phillips, Laurence (2012): Reserach methodology. In: Maurice Crul, Frans Lelie und Jens Schneider (Hg.): *The European Second Generation Compared. Does the Integration Context Matter?* Amsterdam: Amsterdam University Press, S. 39–56.

Helbling, Dominik (2010): *Religiöse Herausforderung und religiöse Kompetenz. Empirische Sondierungen zu einer subjektorientierten und kompetenzbasierten Religionsdidaktik.* Zürich: LIT-Verlag.

Hurrelmann, Klaus / Quenzel, Gudrun (2013): *Lebensphase Jugend. Eine Einführung in die sozialwissenschaftliche Jugendforschung.* 12. Aufl. Weinheim: Beltz Juventa.

Hutnik, Nimmi (1985): *Aspects of Identity in a multi-ethnic society.* In: Neo Community 12 (2), S. 298–309.

Ilg, Wolfgang / Pohlers, Michael / Schweitzer, Friedrich / Gräbs Santiago, Aitana (2018): *Jung – evangelisch – engagiert.* Gütersloher Verlagshaus.

James, William (1909): *Psychologie.* Leipzig: Quelle & Meyer.

Käppler, Christoph / Morgenthaler, Christoph / Brodbeck, Kathrin (Hg.) (2013): *Werteorientierung, Religiosität, Identität und die psychische Gesundheit Jugendlicher.* Stuttgart: Kohlhammer (Praktische Theologie heute, Bd. 126).

Kriesi, Irene / Malti, Tina / Buchmann, Marlis (2007): *Wertorientierungen Jugendlicher und junger Erwachsener in der Schweiz. Auswertungen des Schweizerischen Kinder- und Jugendsurvey COCON im Auftrag der Stiftung Zürcher Unternehmerforum.* Hg. v. Stiftung Zürcher Unternehmerforum. Zürich.

Kropač, Ulrich / Meier, Uto / König, Klaus (Hg.) (2012): *Jugend, Religion, Religiosität. Resultate, Probleme und Perspektiven der aktuellen Religiositätsforschung. Internationales und Interdisziplinäres Forschungssymposion „Jugend – Religion – Religiosität. Resultate, Probleme und Perspektiven der aktuellen Religiositätsforschung“.* Regensburg: Pustet.

Lang, Frieder R. / Lüdtke, Oliver (2005): Der Big Five-Ansatz der Persönlichkeitsforschung: Instrumente und Vorgehen. In: Siegfried Schumann (Hg.): *Persönlichkeit. Eine vergessene Größe der emprischen Sozialforschung.* Wiesbaden: VS, S. 29–39.

Liedhegener, Antonius (2016): Religiöse Identitäten als Problem wechselseitiger Identifizierungen und Kategorisierungen. Aktuelle theoretische Konzepte und Fragen ihrer Operationalisierung in der empirischen Religionsforschung. In: Ines-Jacqueline Werkner und Oliver Hidalgo (Hg.): *Religiöse Identitäten in politischen Konflikten.* Wiesbaden: Springer VS (Politik und Religion), S. 65–82.

Liedhegener, Antonius / Odermatt, Anastas (2018): *Religious Affiliation as a Baseline for Religious Diversity in Contemporary Europe. Making Sense of Numbers, Wordings, and Cultural Meanings.* Luzern. Online verfügbar unter https://www.smre-data.ch/en/content/publications, zuletzt geprüft am 16.10.2018.

Mead, George Herbert (1968): *Geist, Identität und Gesellschaft aus der Sicht des Sozialbehaviorismus.* Frankfurt am Main: Suhrkamp.

Müller, Bernadette (2011): *Empirische Identitätsforschung. Personale, soziale und kulturelle Dimensionen der Selbstverortung.* Wiesbaden: VS.

Piaget, Jean (1992): *Biologie und Erkenntnis. Über die Beziehungen zwischen organischen Regulationen und kognitiven Prozessen.* Frankfurt am Main: Fischer.

Rammstedt, Beatrice / John, Oliver P. (2007): Measuring Personality in One Minute or less: A 10-Item Short Version of the Big Five Inventory in English and German. In: *Journal of Research in Personality 41*, S. 203–212.

Schneider, Jens / Fokkema, Tineke / Matia, Rquel / Stojcic Snezana / Ugrina, Dusan, Vera-Larrucea, Constanza (2012): Identities. Urban belonging and intercultural relations. In: Maurice Crul, Frans Lelie und Jens Schneider (Hg.): *The European Second Generation Compared. Does the Integration Context Matter?* Amsterdam: Amsterdam University Press.

Schneider, Wolfgang (2012): *Entwicklungspsychologie.* 7. Aufl. Weinheim: Beltz.

Schumann, Siegfried (Hg.) (2005): *Persönlichkeit. Eine vergessene Größe der empirischen Sozialforschung.* Wiesbaden: VS.

Schweitzer, Friedrich (1993): Wer sind die Konfirmanden? Neuere Forschungsergebnisse zur Persönlichkeitsentwicklung und religiösen Entwicklung im Konfirmandenalter. In: *Pastoraltheologie.*

Schweitzer, Friedrich (Hg.) (2009): *Konfirmandenarbeit erforschen. Ziele – Erfahrungen – Perspektiven.* 1. Aufl. Gütersloh: Gütersloher Verl.-Haus (Konfirmandenarbeit erforschen und gestalten).

Schweitzer, Friedrich / Wissner, Golde / Bohner, Annette (2018): *Jugend – Glaube – Religion. Eine Repräsentativstudie zu Jugendlichen im Religions- und Ethikunterricht* (Glaube – Wertebildung – Interreligiosität).

Sellmann, Matthias (2012): Jugendliche Religiosität als Sicherungs- und Distinktionsstrategie im sozialen Raum. In: Ulrich Kropač, Uto Meier und Klaus König (Hg.): *Jugend, Religion, Religiosität. Resultate, Probleme und Perspektiven der aktuellen Religiositätsforschung.* Regensburg: Pustet, S. 25–55.

Shell Deutschland Holding (Hg.) (2011): *Jugend 2010. Eine pragmatische Generation behauptet sich.* Frankfurt am Main: Fischer.

Tajfel, Henri (1982): *Social identity and intergroup relations.* Cambridge / New York / Paris: CUP (European studies in social psychology).

Teichert, Dieter (2000): *Personen und Identitäten.* Berlin: De Gruyter.

Weber, Max (1972 (1921)): *Wirtschaft und Gesellschaft. Grundriss der verstehenden Soziologie.* Tübingen: Mohr Siebeck.

Werkner, Ines-Jacqueline / Hidalgo, Oliver (Hg.) (2016): *Religiöse Identitäten in politischen Konflikten.* Springer Fachmedien Wiesbaden. Wiesbaden: VS (Politik und Religion).

Wilmes, Maren / Sürig, Inken (2015): *The Integration of the Second Generation in Germany. Results of the TIES Survey on the Descendants of Turkish and Yugoslavian Immigrants.* Amsterdam: Amsterdam University Press.

Wippermann, Carsten (1998): *Religion, Identität und Lebensführung. Typische Konfigurationen in der fortgeschrittenen Moderne; mit einer empirischen Analyse zu Jugendlichen und jungen Erwachsenen.* Opladen: Leske + Budrich.

Woodward, Kathryn (Hg.) (2014 (1997)): *Identity and difference.* London: Sage; The Open University (Culture, media and identities).

Young, Pamela Dickey / Shipley, Heather (2018): *Religion, Gender and Sexuality among Youth in Canada: Summary and Selected Findings.* Online verfügbar unter http://religionanddiversity.ca/media/uploads/rgsy_final_project_report_final.pdf, zuletzt geprüft am 20.09.2018.

Ziebertz, Hans-Georg (Hg.) (2011): *Praktische Theologie – empirisch. Methoden, Ergebnisse und Nutzen.* Berlin: Lit-Verl. (Empirische Theologie, 24).

Ziebertz, Hans-Georg / Kay, William K. (Hg.) (2005): *Youth in Europe I. An international empirical study about life perspectives.* Münster: Lit (International practical theology, 2).

Ziebertz, Hans-Georg / Kay, William K. (2006): Religiosity of Youth in Europe. In: Hans-Georg Ziebertz und William K. Kay (Hg.): *Youth in Europe II. An international empirical Study about Religiosity.* Münster, Berlin: Lit (International practical theology, 4), S. 246–265.

Ziebertz, Hans-Georg / Kay, William K. (Hg.) (2006): *Youth in Europe II. An international empirical Study about Religiosity.* Münster, Berlin: Lit (International practical theology, 4).

Ziebertz, Hans-Georg / Kay, William K. / Riegel, Ulrich (Hg.) (2009): *Youth in Europe III. An International Empirical Study about the Impact of Religion on Life Orientation.* Münster, Berlin: Lit (International practical theology, 10).

Ziebertz, Hans-Georg / Riegel, Ulrich (2011): Weltbilder Jugendlicher. Quantitative Analysen von Daten der internationalen RaLP-Studie zu Religiosität und Lebenseinstellungen Jugendlicher. In: Hans-Georg Ziebertz (Hg.): *Praktische Theologie – empirisch. Methoden, Ergebnisse und Nutzen.* Berlin: Lit-Verl. (Empirische Theologie, 24), S. 149–175.

Zurawska, Wioleta (2007): *Religiosität und Identität. Eine vergleichende Analyse bei Jugendlichen und deren Eltern in Polen und Deutschland.* Dissertation. Universität zu Köln, Köln.

Part II –
Religious Youth and Digital Spaces

Astrid Mattes

Conceptualizing Digital Identifications of Religious Youth in Migration Society

Abstract
Young people, ever increasingly, negotiate and pursue multiple, flexible belongings and create manifestations of their lives through an ongoing curation of online content in delimited digital spaces. This chapter aims to conceptualize identifications of religious youth in digital spaces in migration society. Starting from the observation that religious diversity is becoming an ever more politicized issue, I am interested in how young religious people negotiate their religiousness through the lens of a politics of belonging. I focus on identifications in digital spaces, as they are increasingly relevant to younger generations and a particularly rich resource for analysis. Discussing belonging at the intersection of politics and religion requires taking into consideration both the extensive literature on religious belonging and on the politics of belonging. Relating these two rather separate scholarly debates and sketching the potential gains from merging them is the goal of my paper. In a second step, I review research on digital identifications of young people and identify methodological and theoretical concepts that help systematize research in digital spaces. Thirdly, I combine the theoretical insights from religious studies and political science with insights from digital communication studies to propose a conceptual framework for the analysis of digital identifications of religious youth in migration society.

Introduction: Why we need to look at digital identifications of religious young people

Migration society, and thus a societal surrounding in which diversity is the norm and not the exception, is the background against which this volume investigates religious young people and their political and pop-cultural expressions. The young people we are interested in are aware of the religious pluralism and different ethnic backgrounds of their peers and the multiple languages used among them. Much more than for their parents, their identification processes take place in a super-diverse (Vertovec 2007) and digitally delimited environment. As is the case with future generations, contemporary youth religiousness will not only be decisive for the further development of religious communities but also for governing diversity in societies that are shaped by plurality. Without fueling a utopian or dystopian debate about youth and new media, the investigation of contemporary identifications of religious youth opens up opportunities to better understand the extent and direction of profound societal changes we experience with regard to digitalization, religion as a public/private matter and politicization of diversity.

Although the numbers of religiously affiliated youth have been stagnating or shrinking across Europe, the meaning that religion is ascribed to in public discourses as well as in personal positionings has gained importance. In contrast to the very idea of secularization thesis, being religious in a secular world is becoming less of a private matter. As scholars of religion argue, the declaration of religiousness is no longer a self-evident private matter, but due to its exceptional character a somewhat public act of self-positioning. Grace Davie writes about the changing character of Christian confirmation ceremonies, which become "a very significant event for those individuals who choose this option, […] in fact an opportunity to make public what has often been an entirely private activity" (Davie 2007, 174). Christel Gärtner (2016), whose empirical work focuses on Catholics of different ages, voices similar views. Rogers Brubaker argues that being "'Muslim' is increasingly reflexively embraced rather than simply taken for granted", due to the politicized interplay of self-identification and other-identification as a follower of Islam (2013, 3). In the spirit of postmodernity, being explicitly religious (as opposed to invisible, implicit or other forms of religiosity as discussed by Luckmann 1967 and others) is widely de-privatized.

On the individual level, this deprivatization of religion has particular implications for identification processes and concepts of belonging. A somewhat coherent majority understanding of explicit belief is no longer available. Even among Catholics in Catholic majority settings, to name only one example, beliefs are becoming increasingly pluralized. As is the case for society as a whole, we can observe a polarization between liberal/cosmopolitan and traditionalist/nationalist views. What is more, identifying oneself as a religious person clearly has different implications depending on the kind of religion people grow up with and/or choose for themselves.

Among migrant minority religions, the developments are even more diverse, considering the inner-religious pluralism, the different world regions of origin, the equally observable liberal-vs.-traditionalist polarization, and, for Islam, an extraordinary politicization of religion. To some extent, the individual consumer of religion chooses from a market of different understandings of religion, often within one religious tradition. In Europe, unlike in the US, this market is not primarily formed by a multitude of denominations, but by a flexible consumption of services of established religious institutions and alternative forms of the religious (see Hödl 2003) as well as non-religious offers (therapy, retreats, etc.). This is particularly true for religion in digital spaces. As Paul McClure states, "the assumptions implicit in the Internet – that one is free to choose and tinker with affiliations [...] – may intensify or map onto broader cultural shifts." (2017, 485)

As is the case with most aspects of life, digital spaces gain importance for religious belonging and processes of identification in general. Chiara Pattaro writes that "[d]igital media have transformed the conditions and possibilities for the consumption and production of knowledge and culture, and the perception that people have of their place in the world and of their memberships and belonging." (2015, 298) This is equally true for the identifications of religious youth, who might experience their religion as some kind of stigma or, in more neutral terms, as an exceptional feature of their self in widely secular surroundings. As research on online behavior of young people shows, we can understand social media use as a careful and ongoing curation and performance of selfhood (Cover 2014), dependent on social positions, context and audiences (Pitcan, Marwick, and boyd 2018) and thereby inextricably linked to, but not necessarily identical with, offline identifications and manifestations of self.

While (religious) identifications and multiple belongings are becoming more complex, the political understanding of identity (and the role of religion within it) is increasingly rigid. Dominant political discourses discuss European/national identity, common values and "Christian heritage" as opposed to populations of migrants who are seen as not (yet) sharing said identity, values and heritage (see Mattes 2017). As addressed in multiple chapters of this edited volume, religion is a category that is becoming more and more discursively connected to race. Scholars of racial studies such as Fatima El Tayeb have argued that we can speak of a racialization of religion when Muslim women in particular become "the visible other" to a white European self (2011). For young religious people, these developments clearly affect their situatedness with regard to religion and race.

It is this politicization and its effects on young people's lives that make religious belonging and its digital expression a pressing issue. The codification of common values and mandatory value courses as well as the symbolic positioning of crucifixes and the simultaneous restriction of Islamic symbols in the public sphere are very real implementations of this rigid identity politics, a development that has been discussed by political scientists referring to "illiberal politics" (Berezin 2009; Dzihic 2016; Guild 2009; Orgad 2010). Such illiberal politics question the liberal paradigm (in essence, the maximization of individual freedom and equality) and, consequently, challenge universal human rights approaches. This puzzle – complex religious belongings expressed on- and offline opposed by rigid identity politics, which results in a limited ability to accommodate difference – challenges liberal democracy and the governing of (religious) diversity across Europe, and it will continue to do so.

This paper aims to provide a conceptual research framework for the empirical analysis of digital identification of religious youth in order to develop a better understanding of multiple belongings in diverse and networked surroundings. For this purpose, I discuss approaches to belonging in religious studies/sociology of religion and political science/migration studies in the following chapter.

Politics, religion and belonging: disciplinary perspectives

Belonging, religious belonging and the politics of belonging are widely used concepts. The concept of religious belonging is increasingly found in the study of religion (Davie 2007) but rarely related to the politics of belonging in a more widely used sense, which is embedded in postcolonial, feminist theory (Yuval-Davis 2011). This article aims to link these two bodies of literature by explicitly putting the theoretical lens on the issue of belonging of religious people (as discussed by Levitt 2004; Voss Roberts 2010; Krause 2011). In doing so, I hope to contribute to a theoretical development of belonging, which is necessary particularly because of its extensive use. As Floya Anthias argues, "[b]elonging and identity are words overused and under-theorized in the context of population movements and translocation." (2006, 19) This is equally true for the field of religion. I will therefore start by broadly defining belonging as a claiming of membership in (socially constructed) collectivities through processes of identification (see Guibernau 2013).

Religious belonging and its manifold understandings

Sociology of religion mostly considers religious belonging in relation to processes of secularization. Famously, Grace Davie described the difference between belonging and believing in relation to religious communities and the increasing trend of religion as a vicarious phenomenon (Davie 2007). Belonging without believing is equally a phenomenon that scholars of religion have observed (Mountford 2011). In both cases, believing stands for the identification with religious ideas and concepts of a religious community and tradition, while belonging stands for the membership as well as identification with institutionalized religion.

Another conceptualization of religious belonging deals with those who claim or are attested multiple religious belonging. In her review of existing theoretical approaches to multiple religious belonging, Michelle Voss Roberts discusses three strands of research: "(1) the dogmatic reflections of religious elites; (2) popular ritual participation; and (3) the hybrid identities of communities on the borders of traditions and cultures" (2010, 47). The first describes the experience of persons deeply rooted in one, for them, clearly defined religious tradition and their encounter with and acceptance of other religious concepts. The second discusses multiple lived religious practices, often without conceptual reflection. The third strand describes hybrid religiosity as the result of religious pluralism.

Both the ideas on multiple religious belonging and concepts of dissenting membership and identification address complex cases of religious belonging and thereby implicitly transport the notion of a one-dimensional form of religious belonging that is seen as the norm or some form of original condition. Despite the analytical value for the described developments, these concepts imply the idea of a form of religiosity where believing and belonging (in the singular) match. In order to avoid this implicit oversimplified understanding of religion, Abby Day provides a different perspective on belief and belonging. She attempts "relocating belief to the social", as she argues that belief is an expression of belonging and a performative act of doing religion (2011, 93). This relates to the growing relevance of sociological approaches to religion that look at practices and discourses that constitute the religious rather than express it.

While the scientific study of religion spent a great deal of its disciplinary development attempting to define religion, either substantially or functionally, a praxeological approach provides a conceptual alternative (Limacher 2018, 235). Religious belonging, in that sense, can be located through the analysis of bodily and communicative religious practices. In a way, it refers to the implicit knowledge that praxeological approaches attest: Religious practices are based on implicit knowledge that individuals employ in the course of performing the practice. Only through observing a practice is it possible to ask about the implicit knowledge it is based on, which, in turn, allows us to draw conclusions about individuals holding that knowledge (see Reckwitz 2003, 292). Despite its significance in a wider sociological sense, a problem that is not solved by a praxeological approach is the question of where to start. What is a religious practice and why?

The so called "lived religion" approach starts by focusing on ordinary individuals and asks about "everyday practices of sacralization that may or may not coincide with institutionalized or collective definitions of the sacred" (Ammerman 2016; see also Edgell 2012). Coming back to a profane-sacred divide might not only seem unsatisfactory to scholars of religion, it also reminds us of phenomenological approaches to religion that have long been rejected (Pylajew and Antonow 2015). While I definitely do not want to make a plea for a phenomenological approach to the study of religion, I would also not abandon a lived religion approach due to its orientation along the category of the sacred.

The definition of the sacred, here, lies with the individual. Consequently, researchers have to treat their objects of investigation as experts in the subject they intend to study. "Religion is what individuals choose on their own authority. [...] lived religion is about personalized, often hybridized practices that are chosen by the individual. This is religion where personal agency can be exercised." (Ammerman 2016, 8) Ammerman refers to implicit knowledge that individuals make explicit. Scholars of praxeology would not neglect individual agency but add that through the application of implicit knowledge in the course of practices in certain contexts individuals create and give meaning to their surroundings, although the explicit rules that result might differ substantially from the implicit knowledge the practices are based on. An individual is able to make sense of a practice (e. g. by calling it a religious practice) because there is a relation between its occurrence in everyday life and the acquisition of knowledge about it, or in other words, its contextuality (see Limacher 2018, 21).

Neither praxeological nor "lived religion" approaches will result in a conceptual answer to what religion is but they make it possible to understand how individuals, and consequently social collectivities, agree to call it. Such research rather sees more than one had originally asked for, than excluding what has so far not been conceptually related to religion. Religious belonging, then, is what individuals express in their practices and are able to explicate because of the contexts they learned about. The implicit knowledge embedded in those practices most likely exceeds what people explicate as religious belonging. Researching this practical knowledge and its emergence makes it possible to understand changing practices of religious belonging beyond the individual case.

A "lived religion" approach seems particularly useful when interested in digital identifications of religious youth, as it emphasizes the aspect of personal agency and fits the very idea of belonging as an individual's deliberate claim to membership to socially constructed collectivities (following Guibernau 2013). Theories of multiple religious belonging often view the individuals they discuss as exceptions to the rule of concise followers of a clearly demarcated religious tradition. Believing-without-belonging/belonging-without-believing approaches view secularization processes as wreckers of equally wholesome religious affiliations. A "lived religion" approach, by contrast, is centered around individuals who are actively involved in practices of identification that lead up to religious belonging.

Politics of belonging

Political scientists as well as scholars of race, gender and migration increasingly treat the politics of belonging as a distinct field of interest that subsumes questions of membership, boundary drawing and identity politics (Brubaker 2010; Wimmer 2013; Klandermans 2014). While questions of membership have always been essential to any political system and nation state societies in particular, phenomena of globalization, most importantly international migration (Castles and Miller 2009), and liberal democratic developments aiming at equality for marginalized groups, often initiated by political movements, international institutions and courts rather than governments, add fuel to identity conflicts.

Politics of belonging is not only about formal politics, but, as Hedethoff and Hjort put it, "belonging constitutes a political and cultural field of global contestation (anywhere between ascriptions of belonging and self-constructed definitions of new spaces of culture, freedom and identity), summoning a range of pertinent issues concerning relations between individuals, groups and communities." (2002, x) Individual processes of identification, individual and collective processes of boundary drawing as well as formal politics of membership play into the politics of belonging.

Intersectional theories that ask "how the differential situatedness of different social agents affects the ways they affect and are affected by different social, economic and political projects" (Yuval-Davis 2011, 4) form the basis for analyzing politics of belonging. This situatedness is important for understanding belonging, the identifications that lead to it and the implications it has for individuals. In the study of religion, intersectional perspectives can be found far too rarely. This results in an often isolated view on religion as a standalone sphere of life, rather than one that is interwoven in a complex net of intersecting identifications, affiliations and ascriptions.

However, researching the intersectional occurrence of categories of difference also brings with it new analytical and methodological challenges, in particular with regard to categories of analysis. As Leslie McCall writes in her critical review of intersectional research, one way to analyze intersectionality "begins with the observation that there are relationships of inequality among already constituted social groups", and she emphasizes the necessity to take these group categories as a starting point, "as imperfect and ever changing as they are". Making these relationships the center of analysis is promising but makes it necessary "to explicate those relationships, and doing so requires the provisional use of categories." (2005, 1785f.) This reminds us of the problems scholars of religion encounter when asking about religious belonging. In both cases, the provisional use of categories cannot be avoided but requires researchers to "respect the demand for complexity" (ibid.). Concerning the questions addressed in this edited volume, age, religion and race are relevant categories that name and constitute social groups and as such are related to but distinct from processes of religious identification. Especially religion and race in their multiple combinations are suitable for systematic comparison in order to develop a better understanding of how religious belonging affects and is affected by individual situatedness.

Intersectional theory is the basis of approaches to the politics of belonging. However, what is understood as a politics of belonging differs among studies and no widely used framework for its analysis is available. Scholars have emphasized a variety of important aspects of the politics of belonging and have brought attention to the issue of locality of belonging (Lovell 2003; Youkhana 2015; Levitt 2004; Askins 2015; Taylor 2012). Also, particularities of social collectivities and collectivization beyond rough group identities have been a focus of research (Pitcan, Marwick, and boyd 2018; Stahl and Habib 2017), and political activism as a particular aspect in the politics of belonging has been emphasized in recent years.

For analytical purposes, we can group these relevant aspects of the politics of belonging into different dimensions that are not sharply demarcated but interrelated and interdependent. Discussing the concept of belonging, Nira Yuval-Davis suggests differentiating between social locations (affiliations with intersectional categories of difference), "identifications and emotional affiliations" (narrations of belonging) and political views (2006). As I will argue, due to the specifics of religious belonging and the lacking incorporation of intersectional situatedness so far, it is helpful to contrast intersectional categories explicitly with the different dimensions discussed in the politics of belonging. Furthermore, I want to follow the shift in politics of belonging approaches proposed by Youkhana and others and include space as an analytical dimension. Together with narrations of belonging and political views, the inclusion of space results in the differentiation of three analytical dimensions in the politics of belonging[1].

As belonging always has a *spatial dimension*, sometimes also referred to as the territorial dimension of place (Neville/ et al. 2014) or locality of belonging (Lovell 2003), it is worth including it in the analytical framework. This spatial dimension refers to geographical locations but nowadays it is increasingly complemented by virtual places and digital spaces. "A space-sensitive theorization of social relations and belonging opens up new perspectives on the question of how social collectives are naturalized and by whom, and under which conditions they open up to new forms of belonging; it thus brings forth new findings about collectivization, social mobilization, and change." (Youkhana 2015, 10) It allows for the analytical inclusion of marginalized spaces, concepts of trans-locality, diaspora and global perspectives of belonging, which are equally relevant to the other two dimensions discussed below.

Collectivization also concerns what we could call the *narrative dimension of*

1 Others choose different groupings, see for (Dietz 2011).

belonging, which includes identifications with all kinds of collective identity narratives, stories about senses of community, acceptance and pride (see Neville/ et al. 2014). Nira Yuval-Davis writes that "not all of these stories are about belonging to particular groupings and collectivities; they can be, for instance, about individual attributes, body images, vocational aspirations or sexual prowess. However, even such stories often relate, directly or indirectly, to self and/or others' perceptions of what being a member in such a grouping or collectivity (ethnic, racial, national, cultural, religious) might mean. The identity narratives can be individual or they can be collective, the latter often a resource for the former." (2006, 202) While practices of identification with identity narratives are grouped into the narrative dimension of belonging, the concepts mentioned are also important for the political dimension of belonging.

The *political dimension of belonging* refers to challenging membership both in a formal, rights-based sense (Senders 1996), in an informal sense (as discussed by Brubaker 2010), with regards to universal human rights (Morondo Taramundi 2016) and beyond conventional understandings of citizenship (Isin 2008). Especially studies that link intersectional perspectives of belonging to activism look at agency in relation to power and, consequently, how the personal becomes political (Ålund 2014). Voicing claims about one's own or others' situatedness, being affected by intersectional categories and visions for change build on the identification with identity narratives and make them explicit. Often, studies on the politics of belonging only draw on the latter dimension, although in terms of a more general view on issues of belonging the political dimension is, metaphorically speaking, only the tip of the iceberg.

Politics of belonging then includes negotiations over position and power in all of the aspects I grouped into the three dimensions of belonging. Combined with the intersectional categories that the perspective of a politics of belonging builds on, we will find different outcomes with regard to the situatedness of individuals depending on their ascribed, performed, proclaimed and practiced identifications.

Combining the two: What can we gain?

The scientific study of religion is often somewhat trapped between social scientific research that mostly applies a pragmatic, if not oversimplifying concept of religion and theology, which lacks the distance to the research subject that religious studies claim for their discipline. In-between these larger research traditions, the impressively nuanced understanding of and sensitivity for religion that this discipline has developed is frequently lost. Research on religion conducted by social scientists benefits from a broader understanding of religion as one of many social phenomena, categories of difference and societal institutions but mostly lacks religious studies' sensitivity. Moreover, while it is definitely worth carefully scrutinizing whether religion is a special case, it often proves to be so. Be it the fundamental rights protection of religious freedom, the intergenerational robustness of religious difference or the fact that many people willingly choose to be religious, rather than just being born into a religion (see Mattes 2016), many aspects of religion function differently than other categories of difference.

A combination of a nuanced "lived religion" approach with the intersectional perspectives that the politics of belonging provide might be able to avoid both disciplinary shortcomings. Therefore, it is necessary to include religion as defined by the individuals involved in research *and* as a (provisional) category of difference that they engage in with their practices of identification.

Here, we can look at spatial aspects in relation to religious belonging when practices link to sacred places, communities of believers, and religious institutions as they may open up new and unusual spaces for religious youth, depending on the intersectional categories of religion as well as race. When asking about the social dimension of religious belonging, we can do so in relation to identifications with age groups, religious communities as well as less formal collectivities and associated identity narratives. Regarding the political dimension of religious belonging, practices of resistance and claims for rights that refer to or are derived from religious concepts and communities are of particular interest. A comparative perspective concerning age, religion and race and their intersections is a promising approach to disentangling the complexity of relationships among and between social groups that are subsumed under religious youth.

Youth and belonging in digital spaces

Although "digital" often serves as a buzzword that is used to conjure up associations with freshness, innovativeness and youth, it is worth discussing this connection and scrutinizing the fact that empirical studies on identity/belonging in digital space overwhelmingly investigate youth and young adults. Most obviously, the argument of "digital natives" (as opposed to "digital immigrants") as well as the attested "growing digital generation gap" (Buckingham 2000) make young adults a particularly interesting population for the study of digital aspects of belonging. Digital natives engage differently in digital spaces than older generations do. What is more, studies on identity and identification generally focus mostly on teenagers and young adults. This young age is seen as a formative phase. Scholars like Gabriele Rosenthal and Arthur Bogner (2009) argue that belonging matters particularly at biographical turning points, which occur more frequently at a younger age (e. g. choice of education and profession).

Age is also a category that I aim to investigate from an intersectional perspective in this edited volume. As Mimi Itō writes, "age is one of the most naturalized forms of oppression that we have. It's cross cultural and the least questioned among our structural forms of oppression like race, class and gender." (Jenkins, Itō, and boyd 2015, 40) From the perspective of politics of belonging, age is a relevant factor and an intersectional category. Young people's agency is often neglected or subject to stiff headwind. As Itō's co-author danah boyd argues, "although moral panics predate conversations about teenagers, youth became the focus of most mid- to late twentieth century moral panic" (2015, 33). Such moral panics have concerned youth and religion in the past (Barker 1993) as well as youth and digitalization (Buckingham 2000). Here, social psychology views "transitions in the social, economic or moral order of the Society", as well as "threats to existing hierarchies; status competition; the impact of social change upon established ways of life; and the breakdown of previously existing structures of control" as relevant factors (Garland 2008, 14).

The belonging of religious youth in digital spaces connects many of these issues, which makes it an interesting case for the study of societal transformation processes. Not only is "youth" frequently the subject of collective worries, if not panics, digitalization and new media are as well. When further combined with worries about transformation processes of religion, both more trivial issues, such as tinkering with religion and its consequences for affiliations as described by McClure, and very serious problems, such as young people falling for jihadist terrorist groups (as addressed by Lohlker in this volume), come to mind and illustrate the relevance of research in this field.

Concepts of digital belonging

The search for the self is a deeply human behavior. While unstable identification is typical for this kind of search, social and cultural demands ask us to overcome that instability and become a distinct, recognizable, coherent self. Here, Rob Cover argues "that social networking sites are popular because they are the most effective means to achieve this cultural demand and respond to contemporary anxieties around subject intelligibility and recognizability." (Cover 2014, 57) In line with this book's aim, Cover emphasizes the importance of "the refinement of theories of identity performativity into methodologies of investigation" (ibid.).

Research on belonging and digital spaces, or more accurately digital expressions of belonging, is a growing field. A multitude of empirical studies emerged over the last decade. In reviewing them, we can find some aspects worth scrutinizing. First, as stated by Cover (2014, 55), too many studies on digital identity/belonging focus on a single channel. While these studies are valuable within their particular research frame, they limit their concept of identity/belonging to a certain form of expression, overseen by the respective social media channel. A second aspect often overlooked in studies on digital belonging is the sense of audience and awareness of context that young people have. Marwick and boyd show how their study participants "have a sense of audience in every mediated conversation, whether on instant messenger or through blog comments" (2011, 115). While it has become common to view digital expression as an ongoing construction of subjectivity, it is also a performative act, characterized by self-censorship, curation and context-specific identifications (Pitcan, Marwick, and boyd 2018). Thirdly, and related to this, although most studies observe the participatory character of digital spaces, many lack differentiation concerning the purpose of online activities. Itō et al. have demonstrated the significant difference among what they call "genres of participation" (2010) for digital learning outcome, and other studies have adapted this concept to questions of belonging (Wargo 2017).

Therefore, when talking about online identification of religious youth, we have to take into account expressions made by individuals through multiple channels rather than through one particular channel. We should investigate the (imagined) audiences young people aim to address through their curation of profiles and posts as discussed in the next section and consider "genres of participation", which will be further explained in the section on research approaches.

Situatedness online

Since we are concerned with intersectionality and the politics of belonging, issues of situatedness are equally relevant in digital spaces. We find that the participatory culture that opens up online affects social situatedness in multiple ways. As discussed in the section on politics of belonging, online spaces provide opportunities for political activism, the voicing of minority claims and civic engagement. At the same time, online spaces are not separated from offline realities, and intersectional situatedness, power relations and marginalization are equally present. The empowering potential that lies within online activities must be assessed under the influence of intersectional situatedness.

In studies on imagined audiences, we can find one way in which research has taken into account this interrelatedness of online and offline situatedness. Building on Joshua Meyrowitz' work, the challenges people have in discussing media artefacts (vacation photos) with multiple audiences (1986), danah boyd developed the concept of conflict collapse. In digital spaces, it is no longer possible to curate behavior to a specific context; rather, people speak to imagined audiences, similarly to the way in which writers do so. This requires new curation skills. "In choosing how to present themselves before disconnected and invisible audiences people must attempt to resolve context collapses or actively define the context in which they are operating."(boyd 2014, 32)

Related to this, Pitcan et al. (2018) interviewed young people of low socio-economic status about their imagined audiences and the ways in which they curate their social media contents to cater to them. Discussed through the lens of respectability ("a continuum of behaviors and attitudes that reproduce dominant norms, and strategies for producing a counter-narrative to negative stereotypes placed upon subordinated groups", ibid.), the study shows how awareness about expectations as well as attempted upward social mobility influence the identifications that participants made online. Such findings are highly useful when considering situatedness in online identifications. Crucially, such studies rely on methods that do not limit the subject of analysis to media artefacts that were produced online but include the producers as experts.

Research approaches: online ethnography and participatory methods

Aside from quantitative big data and text-based analyses, many studies on online behavior make use of qualitative methods like discourse analysis, various interview techniques and, in particular, digital ethnography. The first method is often criticized for putting texts rather than subjects at the center of attention, thereby leaving out any chance to grasp agency as well as the interdependencies of offline and online identifications. Interviews are not only used as an isolated method but also conducted by both discourse analysts and ethnographers. The third method, digital ethnography, refers to approaches that enjoy great popularity in communication studies and reach out to many other fields of research. Most pioneering research on online behavior has relied on ethnography, and, increasingly, there have been efforts to systematize digital ethnographic approaches (Pink/ et al. 2016).

Digital ethnography is based on a definition of ethnography as a method that acknowledges the role of theory, strongly reflects the researcher's own role and considers humans as both subjects and objects of research and respects the irreducibility of the human experience (O'Reilly 2005, 3f.). Digital ethnography transfers the broad set of methods used by conventional ethnography (e.g. watching, listening, asking questions) to the analysis of digital expressions (see Pink/ et al. 2016, 3). However, certain considerations have to be made with regard to the mediatedness of digital spaces that limit opportunities for personal encounters.

Not least due to such limitations, digital ethnography is often combined with participatory methods. Participatory methods involve participants in the production and reflection of research (Torre, Cahill, and Fox 2015). As in the study on respectability quoted above, young individuals might first be interviewed by project staff and later become interviewers themselves (Pitcan, Marwick, and Boyd 2018). The benefit of such approaches is particularly obvious when access to the subjects and objects of research are limited due to the age, race, class or gender of the researcher. However, when taken one step further than mere field access, participatory methods allow for an invaluable reality check concerning the interpretation of the collected data. Often, participatory approaches also emphasize their potential to facilitate social change (Gubrium and Harper 2013; Kindon, Pain, and Kesby 2007; Mitlin and Thompson 1995).

An example of how digital ethnography helps to develop tools of analysis for its very own purpose is Mimi Itō's study on "genres of participation". Based on Henry Jenkins' idea of fandom as "participatory media cultures", Itō introduces her genres that allow for structuring media participation according to actors' engagement rather than according to media platforms or text styles. Her approach views media as "embodiments of social and cultural relationships that in turn shape and structure our possibilities for social action and cultural expression" (2010, 4). As a result, it is possible to differentiate between friendship-driven and interest-driven genres of participation. Itō claims that this differentiation corresponds to different genres of youth culture and social network structure and therefore remains somewhat fluid. While more friendship-driven modes ("hanging out" while gaming) can transition to more interest-driven genres (e.g. recreational gaming), more friendship-driven practices (social media profiles, photos with friends) can be a step towards what Itō calls "messing around" (early interest-driven modes of media production).

Similarly to "messing around", David McClure discusses "tinkering with technology and religion" and describes in his study on religious belonging that "as a pluralizing force, the Internet creates a new space through which individuals must navigate competing truth claims and ideas about what is ultimately important. Because of the overwhelming variety of worldviews, beliefs, and religious ideas that are part and parcel of one's online experience, the Internet encourages tinkering with an assortment of spiritual options" (2017, 494), also in terms of technical opportunities. Although both studies differ greatly in their methodology, also McClure's study points out the relevance of individual strategies of online navigation for processes of identification.

Working with genres of participation informed by studies on religious belonging in digital spaces is a promising approach as it puts individuals and their media engagement at the center of attention. Combined with a participatory approach, the mediatedness that challenges digital ethnographic methods can be somewhat limited. Moreover, similarly to a "lived religion" approach, agency lies with the research subject. A widely heard criticism of ethnographic approaches is the lack of systematization. The downside of ethnography's openness is its risk of becoming somewhat random. Especially for digital ethnography, it is crucial to limit the research field in order to avoid simply browsing through online spaces. Therefore, a close linkage to theory is crucial. In the following chapter, the presented theoretical concepts will be combined to introduce a conceptual research framework for the study of digital identifications of religious youth in migration society.

Towards a conceptual research framework

Nira Yuval-Davis argues that constructions of self can "in certain historical contexts, be forced on people. In such cases, identities and belonging/s become important dimensions of people's social locations and positioning, and the relationships between locations and identifications can become empirically more closely intertwined." (2006, 203) This is the case with religious youth. Their social location, as part of a religious group in times when religion is strongly politicized, forces them to identify accordingly. This chapter discusses concepts that form the basis of a conceptual framework for the analysis of digital identifications of religious youth in migration society.

Such a research framework aims at addressing the following research question: *How can we grasp practices of religious belonging and acknowledge the specificity of its manifestation in digital spaces and its relation to offline conceptualizations of self in the light of the situatedness with regard to race, religion and age?* In order to do answer this question, we need to investigate the relation of intersectional categories, which are both subject to self- and other-identification (Brubaker 2013), to communicative practices of religious belonging.

Starting from a "lived religion" concept, rather than using religion as a category of difference or making it subject to formal membership etc., we can avoid pitfalls of conventional approaches to religious belonging in the study of religion that too often transport an institution-centered and implicit notion of what religion is or should be. As discussed throughout this paper, it is crucial to establish a relation between communicative practices of religious belonging that we can observe in digital spaces and societal situatedness that determines the politics of belonging. Thus far, approaches to religious belonging widely fail to do so. Therefore, it is useful to include religious belonging as our research

		Communicative practices of religious belonging				
		Curating what kind of religious belonging?			For whom?	By which means?
Intersectional categories	Age	Spatial dimension	Narrative dimension	Political dimension	(imagined) Audiences	Genres of participation
	Religion					
	Race					

Table 1: Conceptual research framework for the analysis of online identifications of religious youth

interest separate from religion as an intersectional category like age and race and investigate their relationships.

Age, religion and race, the intersectional categories addressed in this book, are presumed to affect the communicative practices of religious belonging that can be observed in digital spaces. In order to grasp these communicative practices of religious belonging, the conceptual framework presented here draws on dimensions of belonging as discussed in the politics of belonging to describe the contents of religious identifications. Here again, spatial, narrative and political dimensions relate to intersectional situatedness and call for analysis and interpretation. The investigation of the spatial dimension of belonging may highlight religious youth areas on- and offline. Equally, diasporic aspects of religion, and racialized spatial experiences of religious youth can be brought to attention. Identity narratives of religious young people might include narrations about religious collectivities such as the *Ummah*, global Catholicism and its ideas. Especially with regard to age and race, concepts of respectability are of interest. In the political dimension, claims for religious rights and (un)equal treatment might be related to the intersectional category of religion. A vision for change with regard to inclusion/exclusion is likely the dominating issue when focusing on the category of race in the political dimension of belonging. Regarding age, political claims of religious youth might challenge religious authorities or simply define their own ones (see Tunger / et al. in this volume).

Following what recent research on the relevance of audiences has shown, it is furthermore useful to ask for whom young people curate their online identifications and relate these audiences to the intersectional categories relevant for them. Concerning age, it is interesting to see how religious youth curate content for peers and different groups of adults. The perspective of race raises questions of curating for a minority or majority as well as young people's relations to potentially marginalized positions. In a similar vein, religious young people may curate contents for religious peers, non-religious or other-religious audiences. Here, qualitative interviews are a necessary tool for accessing such information but participatory approaches are also a promising methodological tool.

Finally yet importantly, the question of which means young people use to curate their online identifications can be assessed by using the concept of "genres of participation". Religious youth might use more friendship- or interest-driven practices when addressing their situatedness with regard to religion, race and age as well as practices of tinkering or messing around. How the means of communicative practices of belonging relate to the contents and audiences of identification remains to be explored but constitutes a promising field of research.

The present conceptual research framework is a first attempt at structuring a complex and rather chaotic field in which a multitude of concepts, often similarly named but substantially different in content, are in use. Designed for a participatory approach of digital ethnography that avoids the problems of mediatedness and arbitrariness that are often held against ethnographic works, the conceptual framework makes it possible to explore religious belonging through the lens of a politics of belonging. This is promising for scholars of religion, who lack concepts of religion applicable to empirical research, and social scientists, who lack approaches to religion that are not oversimplifying.

Conclusion: potential pitfalls and promising perspectives

Identity and belonging are hybrid, fluid concepts that are becoming ever more politicized. When talking about religious belonging in migration society, we talk about research in a contentious field. As a consequence, there are not only political interests at play, but also complex situations of individuals and groups that experience this politicization of their faith. While there is wide scholarly interest in questions on how politicization of religion affects institutionalized religion and practices of inclusion and exclusion, there is much less interest in the ways in which it affects practices of religious belonging.

The presented conceptual framework aims at facilitating research that makes it possible to develop situated concepts of religious belonging. The intersectionality of age, religion and race is a suitable case for exploring options for situating religious belonging. Although it is rather complex, the presented framework aims to provide a structure for approaching an otherwise amorphous phenomenon.

This exploration concerns a highly sensitive field of research that needs to consider privacy issues, legal aspects of online research, and the vulnerable situation of young people, who are potentially racialized in their religious position. The complexity is not limited to scholarly concepts but includes research ethics and demands a sensitive implementation. If executed well, the results of such an exploration open up multiple interesting research perspectives for the scientific study of religion, most importantly with regard to comparative studies of practices of religious belonging beyond a minority focus, religious belonging in (post)secular times and last but not least theoretical reflections on the discipline's subject itself.

References

Ålund, Aleksandra (2014): "Politics of Belonging: A Narrative on Activism in Sweden." *NORA – Nordic Journal of Feminist and Gender Research,* 22 (4), pp. 330–37. https://doi.org/10.1080/08038740.2014.965199.

Ammerman, Nancy T (2016): "Lived Religion as an Emerging Field: An Assessment of Its Contours and Frontiers." *Nordic Journal of Religion and Society,* 1 (02), pp. 83–99. https://doi.org/10.18261/issn.1890-7008-2016-02-01.

Anthias, Floya (2006): "Belonging and Identity Are Words Overused and Under-Theorised in the Context of Population Movements and Translocation." In: Yuval-Davis, Nira/ Kannabiran, Kalpana / Vieten, Ulrike (eds.): *The Situated Politics of Belonging.* London: Thousand Oaks, pp. 365–388.

Askins, Kye (2015): "Being Together: Everyday Geographies and the Quiet Politics of Belonging". *ACME: An International E-Journal for Critical Geographies,* 14, pp. 461–69.

Barker, Eileen (1993): "Neue religiöse Bewegungen. Religiöser Pluralismus in der westlichen Welt." In: Bergmann, Jörg/ Hahn, Alois/ Luckmann, Thomas (eds.): *Religion und Kultur,* Opladen: Westdt. Verlag, pp. 231–48.

Berezin, Mabel (2009): *Illiberal Politics in Neoliberal Times: Culture, Security and Populism in the New Europe.* Cambridge, UK; New York: Cambridge University Press.

Brubaker, Rogers (2010): "Migration, Membership, and the Modern Nation-State: Internal and External Dimensions of the Politics of Belonging Migration and Membership." *Journal of Interdisciplinary History,* 41, pp. 61–78. https://doi.org/10.1162/jinh.2010.41.1.61.

Brubaker, Rogers (2013): "Categories of Analysis and Categories of Practice: A Note on the Study of Muslims in European Countries of Immigration." *Ethnic and Racial Studies,* 36 (1), pp. 1–8. https://doi.org/10.1080/01419870.2012.729674.

Buckingham, David (2000): *After the Death of Childhood: Growing up in the Age of Electronic Media.* Cambridge, UK; Malden, MA: Polity Press.

Castles, Stephen/ Miller, Mark J. (2009): *The Age of Migration: International Population Movements in the Modern World.* Basingstoke: Palgrave Macmillan.

Cover, Rob (2014): "Becoming and Belonging: Performativity, Subjectivity, and the Cultural Purposes of Social Networking". In Poletti Anna/ Rak Julie (eds.): *Identity and Technologies. Constructing the Self Online*, London: University of Wisconsin Press, pp. 25–41.

Davie, Grace (2007): "From Believing without Belonging to Vicarious Religion". In:-Pollack, Detlef/. Olson, V.A: (eds.): *The Role of Religion in Modern Societies*, London: Routledge, pp. 165–78.

Day, Abby (2011): *Believing in Belonging: Belief and Social Identity in the Modern World.* Oxford; New York: Oxford University Press.

Dietz, Angelika (2011): *Dimensions of Belonging and Migrants by Choice: Contemporary Movements between Italy and Northern Ireland.* Münster: Waxmann.

Dzihic, Vedran (2016): "IllIberal Democracy. A European Issue." In Najmowicz, Alexandrina (ed.): *Active citizenship – Values/Democracy/Citizenship.* Paris: European Civic Forum, pp. 30–40.

Edgell, Penny (2012): "A Cultural Sociology of Religion: New Directions". *Annual Review of Sociology,* 38 (1), pp. 247–65. https://doi.org/10.1146/annurev-soc-071811-145424.

El-Tayeb, Fatima (2011): *European Others: Queering Ethnicity in Postnational Europe.* Minneapolis: University of Minnesota Press.

Taylor, Yvette (2012): *Fitting into Place? Class and Gender Geographies and Temporalities.* Londin: Routledge.

Garland, David (2008): "On the Concept of Moral Panic". *Crime, Media, Culture: An International Journal* 4 (1), 9–30. https://doi.org/10.1177/1741659007087270.

Gubrium, Aline, and Krista Harper (2013): *Participatory Visual and Digital Methods.* Milton, Abingdon: Taylor and Francis.

Guibernau, Montserrat (2013): *Belonging: Solidarity and Division in Modern Societies.* Cambridge, UK: Polity.

Guild, Elspeth (ed.) (2009): *Illiberal Liberal States: Immigration, Citizenship and Integration in the EU.* Farnham: Ashgate.

Hedetoft, Ulf/ Hjort, Mette (2002): *The Postnational Self: Belonging and Identity.* Minnesota: University of Minnesota Press.

Hödl, Hans Gerald (2003): "Alternative Formen des Religiösen". InFigl, Johann (ed.): *Handbuch Religionswissenschaft: Religionen und ihre zentralen Themen.* Vandenhoeck & Ruprecht, pp. 485–525.

Isin, Engin F (2008): "Theorizing Acts of Citizenship". In: Isin, Engin F. /Nielsen, Greg Marc (eds.): *Acts of Citizenship.* London; New York: Zed Books Ltd, pp. 15–43.

Itō, Mizuko (ed.) (2010): *Hanging out, Messing around, and Geeking out: Kids Living and Learning with New Media.* Cambridge, Mass: MIT Press.

Jenkins, Henry/ Itō, Mizuko/boyd, danah (2015): *Participatory Culture in a Networked Era: A Conversation on Youth, Learning, Commerce, and Politics.* Cambridge, UK; Malden, MA: Polity Press.

Kindon, Sara/ Pain, Rachel / Kesby, Mike (eds.) (2007): *Participatory Action Research Approaches and Methods: Connecting People, Participation and Place.* London: Routledge.

Klandermans, P. G. (2014):"Identity Politics and Politicized Identities: Identity Processes and the Dynamics of Protest." *Political Psychology,* 35 (1), pp. 1–22. https://doi.org/10.1111/pops.12167.

Krause, Kristine (2011): "Cosmopolitan Charismatics? Transnational Ways of Belonging and Cosmopolitan Moments in the Religious Practice of New Mission Churches." *Ethnic and Racial Studies,* 34 (3), pp. 419–35. https://doi.org/10.1080/01419870.2011.537355.

Levitt, Peggy (2004): "Redefining the Boundaries of Belonging: The Institutional Character of Transnational Religious Life". *Sociology of Religion,* 65 (1), pp. 1. https://doi.org/10.2307/3712504.

Limacher, Katharina (2018): *Doing Mandir, Doing Kōvil Eine Empirische Rekonstruktion Hinduistischer Tempelpraktiken in Der Schweiz Und in Österreich.* Luzern: Universität Luzern.

Lovell, Nadia (2003): Locality and Belonging. London: Routledge.

Marwick, Alice E./ boyd, danah (2011): "I Tweet Honestly, I Tweet Passionately: Twitter Users, Context Collapse, and the Imagined Audience". *New Media & Society,* 13 (1), pp. 114–33. https://doi.org/10.1177/1461444810365313.

Mattes, Astrid (2016): *Integrating Religion: The Roles of Religion in Austrian, German and Swiss Immigrant Integration Policies.* Wien: Universität Wien.

Mattes, Astrid (2017): "Who We Are Is What We Believe? Religion and Collective Identity in Austrian and German Immigrant Integration Policies". *Social Inclusion,* 5 (1), pp. 93. https://doi.org/10.17645/si.v5i1.766.

McCall, Leslie (2005): "The Complexity of Intersectionality". *Signs,* 30 (3), pp. 1771–1800. http://www.jstor.org/stable/10.1086/426800.

McClure, Paul K (2017): "Tinkering with Technology and Religion in the Digital Age: The Effects of Internet Use on Religious Belief, Behavior, and Belonging." *Journal for the Scientific Study of Religion* 56 (3), pp. 481–97. https://doi.org/10.1111/jssr.12365.

Meyrowitz, Joshua (1986): *No Sense of Place: The Impact of Electronic Media on Social Behavior.* . New York, NY.: Oxford Univ. Press.

Mitlin, Diana/ Thompson, John (1995): "Participatory Approaches in Urban Areas: Strengthening Civil Society or Reinforcing the Status Quo?" *Environment and Urbanization,* 7 (1), pp. 231–50. https://doi.org/10.1177/095624789500700113.

Morondo Taramundi, Dolores (2016): "Identity, beolonging and human rights: cultural cues in integration processes. An introduction."*The Age of Human Rights Journal,* no. 7 (December), pp.1–5.

Mountford, Brian (2011): *Christian Atheist – Belonging without Believing.* Winchester: O-Books.

Neville, Helen A./Oyama, Kathleen E./ Odunewu, Latifat O./Huggins Jackie G. (2014): "Dimensions of Belonging as an Aspect of Racial-Ethnic-Cultural Identity: An Exploration of Indigenous Australians." *Journal of Counseling Psychology* 61 (3), pp. 414–26. https://doi.org/10.1037/a0037115.

O'Reilly, Karen (2005): *Ethnographic Methods.* London; New York: Psychology Press.

Orgad, Liav (2010):"Illiberal Liberalism Cultural Restrictions on Migration and Access to Citizenship in Europe." *The American Journal of Comparative Law,* 58 (1), pp. 53–105. http://www.jstor.org/stable/25652685.

Pattaro, Chara (2015): "New Media & Youth Identity. Issues and Research Pathways." *Italian Journal of Sociology of Education,* 7 (1), pp. 397–327.

Pink, Sarah/Horst, Heather A., Postill, John/ Hjorth, Larissa/ Lewis, Tania/Tacchi, Jo (eds.) (2016): *Digital Ethnography: Principles and Practice.* Los Angeles: SAGE.

Pitcan, Mikaela/ Marwick, Alice E. / boyd, danah (2018): "Performing a Vanilla Self: Respectability Politics, Social Class, and the Digital World." *Journal of Computer-Mediated Communication,* 23 (3), pp. 163–79. https://doi.org/10.1093/jcmc/zmy008.

Pylajew, Maxim/ Antonow, Konstantin (2015): "Die Kategorie Des Heiligen in Der Religionsphänomenologie, Theologie Und Philosophie Des 20. Jahrhunderts." *Neue Zeitschrift Für Systematische Theologie Und Religionsphilosophie*, 57 (1), pp. 110–128. https://doi.org/10.1515/nzsth-2015-0006.

Reckwitz, Andreas (2003): "Grundelemente Einer Theorie Sozialer Praktiken. Eine Sozialtheoretische Perspektive." *Zeitschrift Für Soziologie*, 32 (4), pp. 282–301. http://www.zfs-online.org/index.php/zfs/article/view/1137.

Rosenthal, Gabriele/ Bogner, Arthur (eds.) (2009): *Ethnicity, Belonging and Biography: Ethnographical and Biographical Perspectives.* Berlin: LIT Verlag.

Senders, Stefan (1996): "Laws of Belonging: Legal Dimensions of National Inclusion in Germany." *New German Critique*, no. 67 (147), pp. 1–56. https://www.jstor.org/stable/827773.

Stahl, Garth/ Habib, Sadia (2017): "Moving Beyond the Confines of the Local: Working-Class Students. Conceptualizations of Belonging and Respectability." *YOUNG*, 25 (3), pp. 268–85. https://doi.org/10.1177/1103308816669451.

Torre, M. E./ Cahill, C./ Fox, M. (2015): "Participatory Action Research in Social Research". In: wright, J. D. (ed.) *International Encyclopedia of the Social and Behavioral Sciences.*, 2nd ed., Oxford: Elsevier, pp. 540–544.

Vertovec, Steven (2007): "Super-Diversity and Its Implications". *Ethnic and Racial Studies*, 30 (6), pp. 1024–54. https://doi.org/10.1080/01419870701599465.

Voss Roberts, Michelle (2010): "Religious Belonging and the Multiple." *Journal of Feminist Studies in Religion*, 26 (1), pp. 43–62. https://doi.org/10.2979/fsr.2010.26.1.43.

Wargo, Jon M (2017): "#donttagyourhate: Reading Collecting and Curating as Genres of Participation in LGBT Youth Activism on Tumblr." *Digital Culture & Education*, 9 (1), pp. 14–31.

Wimmer, Andreas (2013): *Ethnic Boundary Making: Institutions, Power, Networks.* Oxford: Oxford University Press.

Youkhana, Eva (2015): "A Conceptual Shift in Studies of Belonging and the Politics of Belonging". *Social Inclusion*, 3 (4), pp.10–24. https://doi.org/10.17645/si.v3i4.150.

Yuval-Davis, Nira (2006):"Belonging and the Politics of Belonging." *Patterns of Prejudice*, 40 (3), pp. 197–214. https://doi.org/10.1080/00313220600769331.

Yuval-Davis, Nira (2011): *The Politics of Belonging: Intersectional Contestations.* London: Sage.

Giulia Evolvi

#NousSommesUnis: Muslim Youth, Hypermediated Internet Spaces, and European Islam

Abstract

In the aftermath of the November 2015 terrorist attacks in Paris, the French youth interfaith association *Coexister* created the hashtag #NousSommesUnis (We Are United) to show solidarity and promote social cohesion. The hashtag assumes a particular meaning for young Muslims, such as the members of the association *Étudiants Musulmans de France* (EMF, French Muslim Students), who use it not only to mourn victims, but also to distance themselves from religious-inspired violence and counteract Islamophobia. This chapter explores the diffusion of #NousSommesUnis to show that digital media are a relevant tool to understand the religious engagement of young people, who tend to rely on Internet communications more heavily than previous generations. By means of a qualitative analysis, the chapter explores discourses created in three digital venues: 1) Twitter messages containing the hashtag #NousSommesUnis sent by members and sympathizers of *Coexister* and EMF; 2) videos about #NousSommesUnis created and uploaded on YouTube by EMF members and other young users; and 3) the website of the collective of associations #NousSommesUnis, founded by *Coexister* to promote campaigns in digital as well as physical venues. The analysis suggests that #NousSommesUnis helps to create a hypermediated religious space. The theory of hypermediation is useful to understand how young Muslims connect everyday actions and experiences on various digital media, articulate discourses that are re-mediated by other users, and aim at attracting the attention of national and international media. They create hypermediated spaces because they are able to connect online and offline activities through different media strategies, and establish venues to negotiate their religious identities in a society that tends to frame Islam as incompatible with Western values. In conclusion, the chapter argues that a focus on hypermediated spaces created by young Muslims can open up new perspectives on relationships between religion, race, age, communities, and social actions.

"We know it very well," says a veiled Muslim student in an interview with the channel CNEWS, "That today everything works on social networks. A video will have a greater impact than writing a text or marching in the streets" [YouTube, 16 November 2015, translated by the author]. The woman is a member of *Étudiants Musulmans de France* (EMF, French Muslim Students). EMF is an association that gained national and international media attention after producing the YouTube video "#NousSommesUnis" (We Are United) in response to the Paris terrorist attacks of the 13th of November 2015. The video reached more than 200.000 views in 24 hours and is inspired by the Twitter hashtag #NousSommesUnis, created by the interfaith French association *Coexister* (Coexist). #NousSommesUnis also became a collective of associations, launched by *Coexister* and supported by EMF, whose aim is to improve social cohesion.

In the aftermath of the November terrorist attacks in Paris, as well as other similar attacks in various European countries, many people worldwide created messages of peace and solidarity. These narratives may assume a particular relevance for Muslims. Terrorist attacks claimed by Islamic fundamentalists, indeed, seem to confirm existing media and political representations of Islam as incompatible with Western secularism and democracies (Betz / Meret 2009; Roy 2013). While the Muslim population in Europe is steadily growing (Hackett 2016), some discourses show anxieties about Islam and frame it as being "other" to Western values (Asad 2003). Therefore, some Muslims may express solidarity after terrorist attacks not only to mourn the victims, but also to distance themselves from religious-inspired violence and counteract Islamophobic allegations.

Young Muslims, such as those who are members of EMF and *Coexister*, may feel a particular need to participate in online discourses about Islam. Indeed, Muslim youth born or raised in Europe often believes in Islam while endorsing European secular values, even when the two are deemed as incompatible. These young Muslim Europeans risk being overlooked by superficial media representations of Islam, which tend to portray Muslims only as recent migrants or terrorists (el-Aswad 2013; Behloul / et al. 2014). Therefore, in order to counteract such stereotypes and avoid becoming an "invisible category" (Zinn 2011), many young Muslims employ the Internet. When they are familiar with digital technologies, they may be able to create a "great impact" and attract media attention, as the EMF member says in the CNEWS interview.

By exploring discourses produced by young Muslims in connection with the #NousSommesUnis hashtag, videos, and website, this chapter argues that digital media are a relevant tool to understand the religious engagement of young people in migration society. This chapter shall, first, talk about methods to study the digital engagement of Muslim youth in a migration society. It proceeds with a review of relevant literature about young people and the media, exploring the theory of *hypermediated religious spaces* in relation to Muslim youth. Then, the chapter shall analyse the networks of actions and actors created around the hashtag #NousSommesUnis, including the video produced by EMF and the website of the collective with the same name. In the conclusion, the chapter discusses how the theory of hypermediation can provide a framework to analyse the digital engagement of young Muslims and other minority groups that use the Internet to counteract stereotypes and become actively involved in public debates.

Exploring Young Muslims' Digital Discourses

Social networks represent strategic venues to articulate individual and collective narratives. As the quote at the beginning of this chapter exemplifies, young people are often aware that their participation in the public sphere depends also on their ability to navigate digital media logics. The president of EMF explains that the members use the Internet to interact with mainstream media, and they hope to establish the association as the main interlocutor for Muslim youth in France (personal communication, 22 June 2017). Young Muslims, in this case, create Twitter exchanges, videos, and websites to attract the attention of society on positive representations of Islam and to talk about their experiences as European Muslims. Studying these media discourses allows gaining a picture of how these young Muslims – specifically, members of EMF and *Coexister* – want to be described and perceived in the public sphere.

The Internet can offer creative and discursive opportunities for members of minorities to express agency in telling their own narratives. Anna Piela (2017), in studying online interactions of women wearing the Muslim full-face veil *niqab*, observes that the Internet may help people that have difficulties to connect with society to portray their everyday experiences. Piela conducts online ethnography because minorities might express themselves more freely online, compared to when they are interviewed by a researcher. While I had contacts with EMF and *Coexister* members via email and telephone, I follow in this case Piela's methodology: I focus on the Internet self-representations of young Muslims rather than directly asking them questions. As a non-Muslim, I prefer to position myself outside of the studied groups and refrain from establishing a relationship with my subjects, to avoid imposing my own narratives on them. Even if there is always a certain degree of subjectivity in data analysis (Patton 2014), I employ unobtrusive methods in order to let young Muslims' perspectives emerge and shape my exploration of data.

Assuming a qualitative approach, I collect my data through a "social media ethnography" (Postill / Pink 2012) that looks at the interplay between online and offline actions, as well as various media technologies that characterize the engagement of young people with the Internet. I conduct an online observation of the tweets, videos, and posts connected with the #NousSommesUnis hashtag. Expressed through the symbol "#", hashtags are ways to highlight keywords and create networked discourses on social media. I explore the most popular tweets that mention #NousSommesUnis as collected with Twitter search API. In addition, I look at videos on YouTube that mention #NousSommesUnis. Lastly, I analyse the website of the collective #NousSommesUnis and its campaigns on social networks. In so doing, I focus on narratives created by the associations *Coexister* and EMF.

I employ a multimethod approach that takes into account textual narratives and images, because they can both emotionally frame discourse (Vaisman 2016). To explore narratives connected with #NousSommesUnis, I perform a Critical Discourse Analysis (CDA), which allows looking at interconnections between texts and other semiotic forms, and at entanglements with sociocultural practices (Fairclough 1995). Applied to media texts, this approach helps to analyse the meaning of narratives in relation to power relationships and social practices (Wodak / Bush, 2004). In relation to Internet discourses, CDA can prove useful in understanding the nuances of written narratives that often mirror spoken conversations, and in capturing the different forms of interactions between digital communities (Weir 2005). I apply CDA also to the analysis of videos and images, putting visual semiosis in relation with written texts, exploring dominant representing patterns, and attempting to capture the ideologies embedded in visual objects (Wang 2014).

The analysis focuses on Muslim actors mainly based in France. Looking primarily at narratives created by the two youth associations EMF and *Coexister*, it explores young people's negotiations of Islam within society. Because of the global and interactive character of social media exchanges, many of the narratives go beyond national borders. While I mostly analyse exchanges in French, I also found many tweets and comments in other languages, and I consider those written in English. At the same time, there are discourses that involve non-Muslim actors (as is the case of some members of the association *Coexister*), who discuss and define the terms of European Islam by interacting with Muslims. While focusing on people that self-identify as Muslims, I also take into account their exchanges with non-Muslims, especially in case of videos and tweets created by *Coexister*. Because digital media practices require skills and access, my research does not claim to explore discourses that apply to all young European Muslims. Rather, it captures narratives of some digitally literate Muslims that have the economic and intellectual means, as well as the motivation, to intervene in Internet debates. In so doing, this chapter explores how certain young Muslims create Internet-based descriptions of European Islam for their self-representation.

Digital Engagement of Young Muslims

The creation of Internet narratives after terrorist attacks helps people to articulate their emotions and opinions. After the July 2005 bombings in London, for example, the "We are not afraid" website allowed people posting pictures and messages. In so doing, it helped to create collective representations in a context of shared trauma, and also offered Muslims a platform to express their feelings (Mitchell 2006). In order to mourn the killing of journalists from the magazine *Charlie Hebdo,* accused of ridiculing the Prophet Mohammed, people employed the hashtag #JeSuisCharlie (I am Charlie). At the same time, #JeNeSuisPasCharlie (I am not Charlie) was also used to challenge mainstream discourses, discuss freedom of speech, and criticize Islamophobia (Giglietto / Lee 2016; 2017). As a reaction to the 2015 Paris attacks, when #NousSommesUnis was created, people worldwide employed Twitter to both blame and support Muslims (Magdy / et al. 2015).

Digital texts and images are arguably created by people from different age groups, provided that they have access to digital technologies. However, people born after 1983, the so-called "digital natives," have an Internet behaviour that is different from that of older generations because they have been exposed to digital media since an early age (Page / et al. 2010). For example, the typical Twitter user is between 18 and 34 years old (Fuchs 2017). Digital natives are familiar with the creation and diffusion of digital narratives and often employ the Internet as one of the primary means of socialization. According to the president of *Coexister* (personal communication, 12 July 2018), Facebook was the main tool to recruit people when the association was founded in 2009, because it was the most popular social media at the time and almost exclusively used by young people.

Young people's engagement with the Internet includes also Muslims in non-Muslim countries. For example, some young Muslim women create fashion blogs or YouTube videos to describe religious-related stylistic practices, and also to negotiate the visibility of the *hijab* (Kavakci / Kraeplin 2016; Peterson 2016). The use of humour on Twitter allows Muslims to create spaces of socialization, as in the case of the hashtag #Muslimcandyheartreject employed to ironically talk about romantic relationships between Muslims living in the West (Wills / Fecteau 2016). When Dutch politician Geert Wilders produced an anti-Islam video, Muslims worldwide responded by posting their own videos on YouTube to challenge stereotypes (Zoonen / et al. 2011). Through blogging, young Muslims can employ their everyday experiences and opinions to counteract superficial representations of Islam and negotiate their religiosity, as happens with the blogs *Muslimah Media Watch* (Echchaibi 2013) and *Yalla Italia* (Evolvi 2017).

These Internet-based discourses often aim at showing the compatibility of Muslims identities with Western values, and challenging the idea that Islam is "other" to European culture. In negotiating the terms of European Islam, they help to articulate "hybrid" identities – a term Homi Bhabha (2004) employs in relation to post-colonial settings – that are situated between different cultures and traditions. For example, young people may discuss hybrid identities by displaying visible marks of religious and ethnic diversities that normalize the presence of Muslims in the public sphere. Muslim women may show and discuss their *hijab* online to connote it as unthreatening, especially in countries, such as France, where policies against religious symbols are in place (Ardizzoni 2004). In so doing, they articulate hybrid identities because they describe themselves as both Muslims and Europeans, and create Internet spaces to negotiate their belonging to Islam in a non-Muslim society.

I define these hybrid Internet spaces where people discuss religious meanings and values as *hypermediated religious spaces*. The theory of hypermediation explores interpersonal communication in the digital age. In particular, it looks at how people's Internet exchanges put in connection different media venues and contents. Because of the diffusion of the Internet, today's communication is faster and connects multiple physical and virtual venues (Scolari 2015). *Hypermediated religious spaces* are Internet-based venues that seek to have an impact on society by showing and negotiating material forms of religion, targeting the discourses of national and international media institutions, and embedding various media content through the use of digital technologies (Evolvi 2018). Young Muslims create *hypermediated religious spaces* when they connect their everyday actions and experiences on various digital media, create discourses that are re-mediated by other users, and aim at attracting the attention of national and international media. In so doing, these *hypermediated religious spaces* help to establish a "Muslim" voice in the European public sphere through different physical and media venues.

#NousSommesUnis: Tweets, Videos, Website

Hours after the Paris terrorist attacks, the interfaith association *Coexister* created the hashtag #NousSommesUnis. The president of *Coexister* (personal communication, 12 July 2018) explained that the associations' members wanted to create a keyword to contrast social hate and Islamophobia. They tweeted the entire weekend until it became the most used hashtag in the aftermath of the attacks. For this reason, *Coexister* also received an official recognition from Twitter as a positive influencer. *Coexister* is a French youth organization that, since 2009, gathers people from various religious faiths, including non-believers. The association's goal, as described by its president (personal communication, 12 July 2018), is to help people to live together despite their different religious backgrounds. *Coexister*'s website also explains that the association counts 3000 members in 45 local groups working with French youth, which it defines as the "most *métissée* (mixed) and interconnected generation."

The association *Étudiants Musulmans de France* (EMF) employed the hashtag #NousSommesUnis to create a video two days after the attacks, on the 15th of November 2015. While *Coexister* has members from various religious backgrounds, EMF is primarily involved with Muslim youth. Founded in 1989 and divided into local chapters, EMF aims at organizing activities for university students and challenging Islamophobia. According to its president (personal communication, 22 June 2017), the association, which counts thousands of members and sympathizers, gained considerable national and international media attention because of the video #NousSommesUnis.

Coexister and EMF also sustain mutual collaborations, as in the case of the collective of associations #NousSommesUnis. The collective is not only a response to the Paris terrorist attacks, but also supports various campaigns in online and offline spaces. It started with a petition that involved eighty individual supporters, mostly religious leaders and people engaged with multiculturalism and interfaith dialogue, and almost thirty religious and youth associations. The petition had the purpose of gathering the signatures of people that share the message of #NousSommesUnis and are interested in social cohesion.

While it is not the only hashtag used in connection to terrorist attacks, #NousSommesUnis gained national and international media attention: it was displayed on the Eiffel Tower and employed by prominent political characters, such as Paris mayor Anne Hidalgo in a tweet from 16th October 2016. In addition, people write the hashtag on signs and pins, and display it during demonstration and marches.

These various actions, all connected to the hashtag #NousSommesUnis, form a hypermediated religious space because they create narratives and circulate them in different media venues. While this movement is not based in a physical location, it puts in conversation different actors and seeks to have an impact on French and European society. In this chapter, I focus on Islam-related narratives connected with #NousSommesUnis and mainly produced by Muslims, and I analyse three interconnected venues: Twitter, YouTube, and the website of #NousSommesUnis.

Twitter

#NousSommesUnis was first established as a Twitter hashtag to show solidarity after the Paris attacks and reiterate the importance of social unity. For example, the Twitter account of the *Coexister* section in Montpellier uses the hashtag to share some photos of young people mourning the attacks. Published on the 21st of November 2015, a tweet shows members of *Coexister* and EMF writing messages for the families of the victims and distributing candles. In one of the pictures, there is a white candle with a handwritten *Coexister* logo. In another, four young people, who seem to have different ethnic backgrounds and wear *Coexister* t-shirts, smile at the camera. In the third, two women, who appear to be a young mother and her daughter, hug each other while holding a pen and writing a message of solidarity. The text says: "Accomplished together with EMF. Distribution of candles, and writing a word to the families of the victims" [translated by the author]. There is no explicit reference to Islam, but the pictures probably aim at giving a positive image of the associations *Coexister* and EMF. They also show the emotional connections between people from different religions, including Muslims.

Some Muslims seem to employ the hashtag with the additional aim of discussing Islam in non-Muslim countries. For example, a tweet written on the 26th of July 2016 in French says: "I'm Muslim and I'd risk my life to save the victims of these barbarians. They're not Muslims #NousSommesUnis" [translated by the author]. The author of the tweet symbolically reiterates the sense of belonging to French culture through the hashtag #NousSommesUnis. The tweet also distinguishes between Muslims and terrorists, implying that terrorism – and not Islam – is the dangerous "other" to European culture. Taking into account the context in which the tweet was written, this sentence can be analysed as a counter-narrative against dominant media and social discourses on Islam.

Muslims sometimes use Twitter to challenge Islamophobia. As an article in the English newspaper *The Telegraph* (17 November 2015) explains, Muslims fear the rise of Islamophobia after terrorist attacks. The article's title – "As French Muslim in *hijab*, I feel people's fear" – is quoted in a tweet written on the 18th of November 2015. Together with the article's link, the tweet includes the same picture of the article, a veiled young woman smiling. On the picture, the quote "The way they look at you sometimes, you can feel they are afraid. They're connecting you with Isis and terrorism. For them, I'm responsible for what happened" is added. The tweet does not openly condemn terrorism, but arguably implies that the majority of Muslims are not violent, and employs #NousSommesUnis to condemn prejudices and intolerance within society. *The Telegraph* article is about a female member of EMF, who claims to avoid the hashtag #NotInMyName, used by some Muslims to distance themselves from terrorism. Instead, she prefers to employ #NousSommesUnis, because it helps to show unity and solidarity.

Furthermore, people use #NousSommesUnis both in relation to other terrorist attacks after Paris, and in connection to debates not directly referring to terrorism. This is the case of a tweet, written on the 12th of December 2015, which sponsors a lecture about Sufism and a multicultural event organized by *Coexister* and EMF in Strasbourg. In this case, the use of #NousSommesUnis probably indicates the importance of an interfaith dialogue that continues beyond the mourning of attacks and promotes the knowledge of Islam in everyday life. Also, a tweet in French, published on the 26th of July 2016, says: "Black, White, Yellow, Red, Green, Blue, Jews, Christians, Muslims, Buddhists, Atheists...#NousSommesUnis #IlsNeNousDiviseronPas" [translated by the author]. The tweet employs #NousSommesUnis together with the hashtag #IlsNeNousDiviseronPas (They Will Not Divide Us). It does not specifically refer to a terrorist attack, but advocates for the coexistence of different ethnicities and religions. By so doing, the tweet shows that the message of *Coexister* and EMF went beyond the associations' activities and people adopted it to spread tolerance for all religions, including Islam.

The hashtag, therefore, has different uses: showing solidarity after terrorist attacks, helping Muslims to express their feelings and condemn Islamophobia, and stressing the importance of interfaith dialogue and multicultural collaborations. #NousSommesUnis assumes different nuances probably because it rapidly spread within and outside the Internet. For example, some YouTube videos employ the hashtag #NousSommesUnis to create various narratives, thus amplifying its Twitter impact.

YouTube

The rapid diffusion of the #NousSommesUnis hashtag made it popular on other media, as the YouTube video created by EMF two days after the attacks exemplifies. The video, which lasts two minutes and a half, starts with a speech of French President Francois Hollande in response to the terrorist attacks, and shows some images of Paris on the 13th of November. It then turns to a black screen, with the words in French: "After the attacks, EMF expresses its emotion" [translated by the author]. The video proceeds by showing some young people (EMF members) looking at the ground. The images of EMF members alternate with excerpts from news reporting the attacks, and showing ambulances, commemorative candles, and people mourning. As the video continues, the young EMF members start looking at the camera. They show black paper signs with the hashtag #NousSommesUnis and the logo of EMF printed on. They appear serious and sad, an effect that is enhanced by the plain white background and the dim lights used in filming the video. They are from different ethnicities, and almost all the women – except one – wear a *hijab*. The video ends with a quote from the Quran, which says "if anyone slays a person, it would be as if he slew the whole people" [translated by the author].

During the video, the Muslim students do not talk, but a dramatic music and a poem, read in French, complete the images. Together with the images and the #NousSommesUnis sign, the poem's words create an emotional effect and express the profound sorrow of young Muslims after the attacks. They reiterate that Islam condemns violence, with a line of the poem saying "They invoke the Quran and its verses/ but there is no law that allows spilling the blood of an innocent." At the same time, the poem shows that young Muslims suffer also because of the symbolic impact of the attacks on France. A part of the poem recites "'I have pain in my France' screams by heart with loud voice/ and the way chosen by my heart hangs on my faith." It continues by saying: "They wanted to weaken France. They strengthened the hearts of the French" [translated by the author]. These words in combination with the video suggest how EMF members mourn the attacks not only as Muslims, but also as French citizens. In presenting their sorrow as a collective mourning, they indirectly refuse to choose between Islam and European values and frame their identity as both Muslim and French.

Many media talk about and circulate the video. For example, the aforementioned *The Telegraph* article, and the online page of the French national newspaper *Le Monde* (16 November 2015), reproduce the video. Arguably, media show interest in the video because of its emotional character and its portrayal of Muslims as peaceful students rather than violent terrorists, which offers an alternative story about Islam. At the same time, some YouTube users upload videos inspired by #NousSommesUnis. As it happens with Twitter exchanges, both public characters and private users embed the hashtag #NousSommesUnis in videos to share opinions and express solidarity. This includes Muslims and non-Muslims, members of EMF and *Coexister*, and YouTube users from France and a number of other countries.

For example, members of the local sections of *Coexister* and EMF in the city of Caen also created a video, which is about two minutes long and was uploaded on the 22nd of November 2015. The concept of the video is similar to the one created by EMF, because it shows images of the Paris attacks and images of young people holding signs with the #NousSommesUnis hashtag. This time, however, the signs also display the *Coexister* logo; the participants are not all Muslims and some of them wear *Coexister* and EMF t-shirts. The images are accompanied by an instrumental version of the French anthem. At a certain point, the music stops and the young people start talking in French. By describing themselves, they counteract stereotypes: "I'm black, but my name isn't Mamadou"; "I'm atheist, but I have beliefs"; "I'm Catholic, but I'm for homosexual marriage" [translated by the author]. The images of the young people are briefly interrupted by a black screen with a quote from Jean-Jacques Rousseau: "Reason and judgment come slow; prejudices come in crowds" [translated by the author].

Muslim students in the video focus on some commonplaces against Islam. By saying "I'm Arab, but I'm not a thief" and "I'm Muslim, but I'm a social actor and a French citizen," a young member of EMF reiterates the compatibility of Islam with French society. Similarly, a veiled student says "I'm a woman and I practice boxing" and "I'm Muslim and I'm an independent woman" [translated by the author], going against the stereotype that veiled Muslim women are weak and submitted. At the end of the video, all the eleven young participants stand one next to the other and display a banner with the hashtag #NousSommesUnis. The video arguably employs #NousSommesUnis to show that social identities are nuanced: while prejudices often focus on a single aspect of an individual, people cannot be reduced uniquely to their ethnicity or religion. In addition, many prejudices establish false associations because they are based on generalizations and stereotypes. Muslims, as members of any other social group, are complex individuals who can simultaneously believe in Islam and be French citizens, wear a veil and be a strong person, without being violent or submitted.

Similar to Twitter, videos can help to frame Islam as compatible with European values and offer young Muslims a platform to express their feelings. They allow people to directly speak their mind, show their bodies and display various ethnicities and religious garments. Videos also permit to create emotional narratives through music and poems. While tweets and videos often directly respond to the terrorist attacks, #NousSommesUnis also leads to campaigns that aim at engaging people in the long-term.

Website

After its success on Twitter and YouTube, #NousSommesUnis became the name of a collective, which *Coexister* launched together with EMF and other religious and non-religious associations. It was created after the 2015 Paris attacks, but it also responds to other terrorist incidents. The home page of the website, indeed, mentions Nice, the city where a truck driver, who claimed affiliation with ISIS, drove into people on the 14th of July 2016. The #NousSommesUnis website explains that it was created because: "Every time we blame or point the finger hastily to a community in its whole seen as guilty we are falling into the trap of a planned and orchestrated division." The collective does not only involve Muslim actors, having also Christian, Jews, and atheist members. However, as the quote suggests, it aims at promoting social unity with Muslims after terrorist attacks. While many media and political discourses tend to "blame or point the finger hastily" to all Muslims and target them as scapegoats for social issues, #NousSommesUnis articulates narratives and actions to show how Muslims can be – and are – an integral part of French and European society.

The website includes some pictures of young people mourning together in public squares and streets, deposing flowers and commemorative candles. It also offers quotes from intellectuals and religious leaders. Among the quotes, there are the words of Gandhi, Martin Luther King, Fyodor Dostoevsky, as well as passages from the Bible and the Quran. An example is the sentence "If anyone slays a person, it would be as if he slew the whole people," which EMF also used in the #NousSommesUnis video. These quotes show how website users probably see themselves as connected to a greater struggle for social cohesion, and combine various ideas in the creation of their discourses.

In addition, the website includes some testimonies of people describing their experiences and feelings after the Paris attacks. A testimony in French titled "they felt my sadness" tells the story of a young Muslim woman wearing a *hijab.* The day of the Paris attacks, the woman fears harassments because of her headscarf. However, the majority of the people show kindness and support, because they "feel her sadness." Meeting friendly people helps the Muslim woman to face Islamophobia, and the testimony concludes with the words "because love creates love I could, I believe, diffuse a little bit of love around me" [translated by the author]. The testimony does not deny Islamophobia, but suggests that showing support for Muslims and treating them kindly is an important step to improve society, especially in the aftermath of terrorist attacks.

The website also promotes various campaigns, which are listed on the website together with their matching hashtags. The initiative #DonDuSang (Blood Donation), for example, exhorts people to donate blood as a "simple and universal act of solidarity." The hashtag #ParlerUnis (Speak Together) is used to promote the creation of safe spaces for people to share their experiences after the attacks. #VoyageAvecMoi (Travel With Me) helps people that do not feel safe to find somebody walking or traveling with them. The campaign #KiffTaFrance (Love Your France, where "kiff" is a slang expression generally used by young people) aims at protecting and expressing attachment for places that are symbolically important and meaningful for France, including schools, city halls, churches, and mosques. These various actions do not openly mention Islam, but one of their aims may be to engage Muslims (together with members of other religions) in various social activities, such as blood donation. Furthermore, initiatives such as #VoyageAvecMoi probably aim at supporting Muslims, women in particular, that are harassed on public transportation because of the way they look, and #KiffTaFrance might be used to counteract acts of vandalism against mosques.

The #NousSommesUnis website promotes Internet narratives and actions that are often based on physical spaces: pictures of squares where people mourn are displayed online; the website is a platform for Muslims to share everyday experiences; campaigns such as #VoyageAvecMoi and #KiffTaFrance are diffused on Twitter but they imply offline actions. The #NousSommesUnis website probably employs these narratives to articulate a social movement that continues beyond the immediate reactions to terrorist attacks, and to create online and offline communities to promote inclusivity and tolerance.

#NousSommesUnis also attracts criticism. For example, *Coexister*'s president was defined an "Islamist" on Twitter for including in the collective some conservative Muslims (*L'Obs*, 28 February 2016). As the president of *Coexister* explained (personal communication, 12 July 2018), the collective #NousSommesUnis ended its activities in three months because of this criticism. However, the webpage remains active and some associations, *Coexister* included, created the organization *Labo de la Fraternité* (Fraternity Lab), which has similar aims. Despite criticism, #NousSommesUnis became part of some mainstream discourses about Islam, and helped to connect some youth groups with society at large by diffusing narratives on multiple media venues. While it is difficult to assess the impact of the #NousSommesUnis hashtag, it arguably reached many people in France and Europe, because of its resonance in mainstream media (e.g. news coverage of the video), support from various associations, and people connecting it to a number of different discourses.

Discussing #NousSommesUnis Hypermediated Space

The hashtag #NousSommesUnis allows people to express solidarity and emotions on social media after terrorist attacks. It does not specifically refer to a religious group, but aims at promoting social unity. In focusing on discourses created by young Muslims, the analysis of Twitter, YouTube, and the website of #NousSommesUnis suggests that the hashtag is frequently used to condemn terrorism and challenge Islamophobia. Young Muslims often do so by emphasizing the compatibility of Islam with French and European values, and describing the complexity of Muslim European identities. Young Muslims and non-Muslims use the hashtag to establish online and offline collaborations, and collectively negotiate the meaning of Islam in Europe. Because of its different nuances, #NousSommesUnis continues to have a meaning and to promote the activities of interfaith groups beyond the immediate mourning of terrorist attacks.

The concept of *hypermediated religious space* can be useful to understand the complex network of actions created by #NousSommesUnis. The hashtag, indeed, exists in different venues – Twitter, YouTube, and websites – that allow for the same issue to be framed from various viewpoints, using textual and/or visual elements. Online images and exchanges often refer to physical spaces, as in the case of tweets that use pictures of people commemorating the attacks' victims in Paris. At the same time, offline spaces are influenced by Internet culture, for example, when people wear #NousSommesUnis t-shirts and pins. These actions connect specific locations – such as Paris – with the global space of the Internet, where people create communities and organize actions. It is the Internet that makes the diffusion of #NousSommesUnis possible, and that allows people using it to negotiate religious and national identities. The network of venues connected with #NousSommesUnis constitutes a *hypermediated religious space* because people use the Internet to interact with each other and to create discourses about European Islam in a way that is not dissimilar to traditional physical spaces. These people are not based in the same location, but use digital media as a space to virtually gather and promote a multifaith society.

#NousSommesUnis has a hypermediated character because it is mainly based on Internet communications, which foster interactions that are fast and emotional. The #NousSommesUnis hashtag constitutes a fast way for people to respond to the Paris terrorist attacks. *Coexister* and EMF members can intervene in public debates and attract the attention of other associations and groups because they can rapidly create tweets and YouTube videos. The hashtag quickly diffused not only on Twitter, but also on YouTube and other Internet venues. The logic of social media, indeed, is precisely that of diffusing ideas among the highest number of actors in a short time. The rapid diffusion of #NousSommesUnis, however, does not mean that the hashtag has a short lifespan. On the contrary, it continues to be used in various narratives. #NousSommesUnis can be seen as an example of how media exchanges are "spreadable" (Jenkins / et al. 2013) because they quickly reach various media and social spaces.

The Internet also allows for the articulation of emotions. The diffusion of certain images and texts helps to frame a news story from an emotional angle and to connect with the audience in a more personal way. For example, people reading narratives or watching videos of young Muslims expressing their feelings are more likely to empathize with their stories. The display of Muslim bodies (often wearing religious garments) in pictures and videos may be a way to normalize their presence in society, and to perceive them as individuals rather than members of a threatening group. The Internet amplifies these emotions because it offers a public platform to describe intimate experiences and feelings to a potentially high number of users. People from different religious backgrounds can use texts and images as a common ground to focus on their similarities, and create a "digital affect culture" through the use of shared solidarity symbols (Döveling / et al. 2018). Fast and emotional narratives characterize *hypermediated religious spaces* as venues where people find new strategies to discuss their religious identities.

Hypermediated religious spaces also have some additional features. For example, they combine material forms that exist offline with the Internet. The #NousSommesUnis hashtag started on Twitter but it was soon "materialized" on paper signs, and once again displayed online in videos. Furthermore, hypermediated spaces may serve the purpose to reach other media: the #NousSommesUnis hashtag gives a voice to young Muslims, a group that mainstream media generally overlook or misrepresent, and allow some of them emerging in public debates. In addition, hypermediated spaces blur the boundaries between different media technologies, as Twitter narratives connected with #NousSommesUnis often embed videos and pictures together with links to other websites.

Hypermediated religious spaces, therefore, help to re-think the concept of space through Internet-based religious discourses. Having focused on young Muslims, it appears that they are able to connect online and offline activities through different media strategies. They also create venues to negotiate their religious identities in a society that tends to frame Islam as incompatible with secular democracy. It is for this reason that the concept of *hypermediated religious spaces* can help to understand certain aspects of digital youth exchanges, here discussed with the example of French Muslim youth in mind.

Hypermediated Religious Spaces and Muslim Youth

This chapter began with a quote from a young Muslim woman who said that "today everything works on social networks." Indeed, the Internet constitutes a venue that young people can use to offer their opinion in public debates, especially when they are part of a minority and might be overlooked by mainstream media. Exploring young Muslims' online narratives helps to understand how they wish to be represented, and gives insights in the type of discourses used to describe European Islam in their own terms. In using various digital media, young Muslims often negotiate identities that show the compatibility of Islam with European values. #NousSommesUnis is an example of how young Muslims – in this case, members of the youth associations *Coexister* and EMF – can use the Internet to attract attention and to establish collaborations. Even if "today everything works on social networks," Internet-based actions are arguably more successful if they are able to create networks of digital spaces connected with offline activities and other media.

The theory of *hypermediated religious spaces* helps to understand some peculiar characteristics of these networks and the religious engagement of the people who create them. Young Muslims, for example, employ #NousSommesUnis to create fast and emotional responses to social inputs, thus establishing an alternative model of social participation. While this chapter focuses on Muslims and Islam-related discourses, the theory can arguably be applied also to other religious groups, especially those that have difficulties in intervening in social debates. The theory of hypermediation may prove useful to understand young people's religious engagement in migration society for three main reasons.

First, *hypermediated religious spaces* offer venues to creatively negotiate the terms of national citizenship by blending religion with race, ethnicity, and other social identities. By focusing on Internet spaces where young people from different backgrounds interact and promote multiculturalism, it is possible to explore complex identities that go beyond religious participation. #NousSommesUnis, for example, connotes religion as an element that can kindle collaborations and activism. The hashtag is likely not meant to talk about religious practices and beliefs, but to situate religion in a larger effort to create a multicultural society that celebrates ethnic and religious differences. They do so thanks to the creative potential of the Internet, that allows producing emotional videos where young Muslims explain that they feel French and European citizens. As a result, they try to express agency in defining European Islam in terms of complex religious and ethnic identities.

Secondly, the articulation of identities in *hypermediated religious spaces* is often collective and based on intergroup exchanges. The Internet, in certain circumstances, can enhance the communicative potential of young people by offering them tools to express themselves. Because young people tend to build relationships on the Internet more than previous generations, digital spaces arguably constitute venues where they enter in contact with other members of their age group and discuss the characteristics of their own generation. Young Muslims that employ #NousSommesUnis, for example, frequently refer to French and European youth as having the potential to bridge social differences. In this way, they help to describe their generation as the "most *métissée* (mixed) and interconnected," as for the aforementioned definition of *Coexister.*

Thirdly, *hypermediated religious spaces* show how complex religious identities exist in a broader context that blends local and global discourses. The Internet, indeed, shrinks time and space by allowing people to connect with a variety of social discourses and actors. This may be particularly relevant for minority groups in Europe, that often feel they are not fully accepted in their national or local contexts. Analysing hypermediated spaces allows understanding how young people use the Internet to frame their religious engagement beyond their immediate religious community of belonging. In the case of #NousSommesUnis, the Internet promotes exchanges not based solely in physical locations, but in a virtual space connected to larger social discourses about multiculturalism. The hashtag #NousSommesUnis exemplifies how young people engage in religious-related discourses by creating *hypermediated religious spaces*, and how studying those spaces can open up new perspectives to understand the relationships between religion, race, age, communities, and social actions.

References

Ardizzoni, Michela (2004): "Unveiling the Veil: Gendered Discourses and the (In)Visibility of the Female Body in France." *Women's Studies*, 33 (5), pp. 629–49. https://doi.org/10.1080/00497870490464440.

Asad, Talal (2003): *Formations of the Secular: Christianity, Islam, Modernity.* 1 edition. Stanford: Stanford University Press.

Aswad, el-Sayed el- (2013): "Images of Muslims in Western Scholarship and Media after 9/11." *Digest of Middle East Studies*, 22 (1), pp. 39–56. https://doi.org/10.1111/dome.12010.

Behloul, Samuel M. / Leuenberger, Susanne / Tunger-Zanetti, Andreas, eds (2014): *Debating Islam: Negotiating Religion, Europe, and the Self.* Bielefeld: Transcript-Verlag.

Betz, Hans-Georg / Susi Meret (2009): "Revisiting Lepanto: The Political Mobilization against Islam in Contemporary Western Europe." *Patterns of Prejudice*, 43 (3–4), pp. 313–34. https://doi.org/10.1080/00313220903109235.

Bhabha, Homi K. (2004): *The Location of Culture.* 2 edition. London, New York: Routledge.

Döveling, Katrin / Harju, Anu A. / Sommer, Denise (2018): "From Mediatized Emotion to Digital Affect Cultures: New Technologies and Global Flows of Emotion." *Social Media + Society*, 4 (1), https://doi.org/10.1177/2056305117743141.

Echchaibi, Nabil (2013): "Muslimah Media Watch: Media Activism and Muslim Choreographies of Social Change." *Journalism*, (March), https://doi.org/10.1177/1464884913478360.

Evolvi, Giulia (2017): "Hybrid Muslim Identities in Digital Space: The Italian Blog Yalla." *Social Compass*, (April), https://doi.org/10.1177/0037768617697911.

– (2018): *Blogging My Religion: Secular, Muslim, and Catholic Media Spaces in Europe.* 1 edition. Abingdon: Routledge.

Fairclough, Norman (1995): *Critical Discourse Analysis: The Critical Study of Language.* Boston: Addison Wesley Publishing Company.

Fuchs, Christian (2017): *Social Media: A Critical Introduction.* 2 Revised edition. Thousand Oaks: Sage.

Giglietto, Fabio / Lee, Yann (2016): "To be or not to be Charlie: Twitter Hashtags and Counter-discourse in the Aftermath of the 2015 Charlie Hebdo Shooting in France" *AoIR Selected Papers of Internet Research*, 5 (0), https://spir.aoir.org/index.php/spir/article/view/1078.

– (2017): "A Hashtag Worth a Thousand Words: Discursive Strategies Around #JeNeSuisPasCharlie After the 2015 Charlie Hebdo Shooting." *Social Media + Society*, 3 (1), https://doi.org/10.1177/2056305116686992.

Jenkins, Henry / Ford, Sam / Green, Joshua (2013): *Spreadable Media: Creating Value and Meaning in a Networked Culture.* New York; London: NYU Press.

Kavakci, Elif / Kraeplin, Camille R (2016): "Religious Beings in Fashionable Bodies: The Online Identity Construction of Hijabi Social Media Personalities." *Media, Culture & Society*, November, https://doi.org/10.1177/0163443716679031.

Magdy, Walid / Darwish, Kareem / Abokhodair, Norah (2015): "Quantifying Public Response towards Islam on Twitter after Paris Attacks." *ArXiv*:1512.04570 [Cs], http://arxiv.org/abs/1512.04570.

Mitchell, Jolyon (2006): "Posting Images on the Web: The Creative Viewer and Non-Violent Resistance against Terrorism." Material Religion, 2 (2), pp. 146–73. https://doi.org/10.2752/174322006778053726.

Page, Kelly / DK / Mapstone, Mark (2010): "How Does the Web Make Youth Feel? Exploring the Positive Digital Native Rhetoric." *Journal of Marketing Management*, 26 (13–14): 1345–66. https://doi.org/10.1080/0267257X.2010.523709.

Patton, Michael Quinn (2014): *Qualitative Research & Evaluation Methods: Integrating Theory and Practice.* 4 edition. Thousand Oaks, California: SAGE Publications, Inc.

Peterson, Kristin M (2016): "Beyond Fashion Tips and Hijab Tutorials: The Aesthetic Style of Islamic Lifestyle Videos." *Film Criticism*, 40 (2): http://dx.doi.org/10.3998/fc.13761232.0040.203.

Piela, Anna (2017): "How Do Muslim Women Who Wear the Niqab Interact with Others Online? A Case Study of a Profile on a Photo-Sharing Website." *New Media & Society*, 19 (1): 67–80. https://doi.org/10.1177/1461444816649919.

Postill, John / Pink, Sarah (2012): "Social Media Ethnography: The Digital Researcher in a Messy Web." *Media International Australia*, 145 (1), pp. 123–34. https://doi.org/10.1177/1329878X1214500114.

Roy, Olivier (2013): "Secularism and Islam: The Theological Predicament." *The International Spectator*, 48 (1), pp. 5–19. https://doi.org/10.1080/03932729.2013.759365.

Scolari, Carlos A (2015): "From (New)Media to (Hyper)Mediations. Recovering Jesús Martín-Barbero's Mediation Theory in the Age of Digital Communication and Cultural Convergence." *Information, Communication & Society*, 18 (9), pp. 1092–1107. https://doi.org/10.1080/1369118X.2015.1018299.

Vaisman, Carmel L (2016): "Pretty in Pink vs Pretty in Black: Blogs as Gendered Avatars." *Visual Communication*, 15 (3), pp. 293–315. https://doi.org/10.1177/1470357216643909.

Wang, Jiayu (2014): "Criticising Images: Critical Discourse Analysis of Visual Semiosis in Picture News." *Critical Arts*, 28 (2), pp. 264–86. https://doi.org/10.1080/02560046.2014.906344.

Weir, Katie (2005): "Critical Discourse Analysis and Internet Research." *Melbourne Studies in Education*, 46 (2), pp. 67–86. https://doi.org/10.1080/17508480509556425.

Wills, Emily Regan / Fecteau, André (2016): "Humor and Identity on Twitter: #muslimcandyheartrejects as a Digital Space for Identity Construction." *Journal of Muslim Minority Affairs*, 36 (1), pp. 32–45. https://doi.org/10.1080/13602004.2016.1153825.

Wodak, Ruth / Bush, Brigitta (2004): "Approaches to Media Texts." In: Downing, John D. H. / Wartella, Ellen / McQuail, Denis / Schlesinger, Philip (eds): *The Sage Handbook of Media Studies.* Thousand Oaks: Sage.

Zinn, Dorothy Louise (2011): "'Loud and Clear': The G2 Second Generations Network in Italy." *Journal of Modern Italian Studies*, 16 (3), pp. 373–85. https://doi.org/10.1080/1354571X.2011.565640.

van Zoonen, Liesbet / Vis, Farida / Mihelj, Sabina (2011): "YouTube Interactions between Agonism, Antagonism and Dialogue: Video Responses to the Anti-Islam Film Fitna." *New Media & Society*, 13 (8), pp. 1283–1300. https://doi.org/10.1177/1461444811405020.

Webpages, online videos and online newspapers:

Buratti, Laura (2015): "'Nous sommes unis', la vidéo de solidarité des étudiants musulmans." *Le Monde* [newspaper, online] 16. 11. 2017, available http://www.lemonde.fr/attaques-a-paris/article/2015/11/16/nous-sommes-unis-la-video-de-solidarite-des-etudiants-musulmans_4811017_4809495.html#kSZfmLsvFTrXJPYe.99 [10. 05. 2018].

CNEWS (2015): "'Nous Sommes Unis,' le message d'espoir d'étudiants Musulmans." [video stream] *Youtube.com*, available: https://www.youtube.com/watch?v=RmgSKb450_c&t=7s [28. 04. 2018].

Coexister [organizational website] available: www.coexister.fr [05. 05. 2018].

EMF Asso (2015): "Nous Sommes Unis, Etudiants Musulman de France EMF." [video stream] *Youtube.com*, available: https://www.youtube.com/watch?v=WVUCMBuAQNs [27. 04. 2018].

EMF Caen (2015): "Nous Sommes Unis contre le prejudges." [video stream] *Youtube.com*, available: https://www.youtube.com/watch?v=jetdYXFmscQ&t=7 s [01. 05. 2018].

Etudiantes Musulman de France [organizational website], available: www.emf-asso.com [23. 04. 2018].

Kefi, Ramses (2016): "Samuel Grzybowski, victime collatérale de la guerre des laïcités." L'Obs, [newspaper, online] 28. 02. 2016, available: https://www.nouvelobs.com/rue89/rue89-nos-vies-connectees/20160228.RUE2303/samuel-grzybowski-victime-collaterale-de-la-guerre-des-laicites.html [15. 04. 2018].

Labo de la Fraternité [organizational website] available: www.labodelafraternite.fr [23. 10. 2018].

#NousSommesUnis [organizational website] available: www.noussommesunis.com [01. 05. 2018].

Sanghani, Radhika (2015): "Paris attacks: 'As a French Muslim woman in a hijab, I can feel people's fear'." *The Telegraph*, [newspaper, online] 17. 11. 2017, available: https://www.telegraph.co.uk/women/life/paris-attacks-as-a-french-muslim-woman-in-a-hijab-i-can-feel-peo/ [12. 03. 2018].

Interviews

Semi-structured interview on Skype, 22. 06. 2017, Bochum-Paris, Giulia Evolvi, President of the *Etudiants Musulman de France.*

Semi-structured interview on Skype, 12. 07. 2018, Bochum-Paris, Giulia Evolvi, President of *Coexister.*

Rüdiger Lohlker

Emerging Alternatives and Participatory Action Research: Report on the Video Project "Jamal al-Khatib"

Abstract
Attempts in countering violence extremism are facing a problem: usually, initiatives start from the assumption that there is an object to be enlightened about the evilness of violence. This article discusses the video project "Jamal al-Khatib", which constitutes an innovative approach to countering violent extremism strategies and serves an example for 'academia meets activism'. Carried by young Muslim men of different ethnical and national backgrounds, often considered as marginalized youth, the video project was accompanied by academic advisors as well as social workers and realized with the help of a professional film crew. This form of "participatory action research" allowed developing authentic alternative narrations to Jihadi-narratives. Its wide resonance among young viewers suggests, that the collaboration of young people, academics and media professionals allows limiting problems of credibility, other attempts in countering violence usually see.

Introductory remarks

The video project "Jamal al-Khatib" started as "Magomed al-Shishani", referring to a person who was part of the nucleus this project emerged from. The project team decided to avoid the risk of using a real person's name in the title of the project and an ethnicized identification – Magomed al-Shishani means "Magomed the Chechen", since a fictitious person like "Jamal al-Khatib" would open up a space allowing for inclusion and functions as a point possible viewers can dock on. Due to the character of the project, the following remarks should be read as a narrative text, not as an academic study. Any transgressions of conventional academic writing are intentional.

The project "Jamal al-Khatib" consists of a group of young men, part of marginalized youth communities in the city of Vienna with a self-perception as Muslims, youth workers who were in contact with them, technical support by a film producer, a professional social media promoter, and some Islamic Studies scholars from the University of Vienna, complemented by some refugees from Arab countries. The lead in this project was held by the group of young males with regards to producing of the content and the performing of the videos. The focus on young males is caused by the reflection on Jihadi propaganda focusing mainly on young males.[1] The present writer has to be understood as a symbolic representative of the group in academia, producing an academic representation of this project, not the 'maker' of the project. The project may therefore be described as 'academia meets activism' or more academic from the point of view of the writer: "participatoryt action research".

The project emerged from a longer process of interaction of young men from Chechen, Albanian, and from other families with a Muslim background usually described as marginalized, vulnerable, and other terms evoking a weak position and inability to act, with youth workers, academic Islamic studies scholars from a non-religious perspective, and video producers, including refugees from Iraq. The possibility of producing a non-Jihadi position in Islam (Lohlker 2016a and 2016b) was influenced by many years of collaboration with Indonesian Islamic scholars and the University of Vienna research group on Islamic Studies.

As the people who would be regarded as participants in other methodological settings are activists who shape the ongoing research and the people who are in these settings are usually perceived as researchers and specialists are participants, many of the questions arising in mainstream or so-called critical research projects do not arise in our specific case. A conscious attitude of learning from the experience of the activist youngsters by the researchers/experts is the prerequisite for the successful realization of such a project. Respecting the abilities of all members of the project is essential for it.

Some thoughts on methodology

As said above, the project may be described in an academic perspective as participatory action research. For the young people involved, the perspective may be different seeing it as an opportunity to be active – not passive – and leaving the subdued position of young, marginalized people and being in a defective state. For the youth workers, their perspective may be seen as the logical consequence of their day-to-day work with these young people, broadening their approach of social work respecting their clients and developing a way of interaction that helps to empower their clients. For the 'technical' members of the project staff, their experience may be the enriching participation in non-conventional media production with persons who are usually not part of media productions. For the refugees involved it may offer the perspective of being part

1 The inclusion of religious aspects of youth culture is quite recent (cf. Tertilt 1996 for field research in a non-religious context).

of Austrian society, not mainstream society, but another part of the Austrian society equally important as mainstream society. The project is a way of creating a relation beyond the common distinctions, new plays of 'string figures' as Donna Haraway (Haraway 2018) wrote.

For the sake of brevity and the context of an academic edited volume, we will focus on the academic view. As said above, for the Islamic studies members of the project the starting was the practical experience of orientalist and colonialist prejudice (cf. Attia 2007) and stereotyping hindering a real understanding of "the other" without othering. The resulting distorted worldview without any self-understanding of the occidentalist position (for a critique see Dietze/ et al. 2009) of white European scholars created the need of developing new approaches. In this context, this means trying to stay in contact with and learn from people that are constructed as non-whites, e.g., Indonesian scholars at different levels trying to translate their vision into European contexts. The opportunity to expand such contacts through collaboration with youth workers in Vienna and marginalized young people plus refugees the project discussed here emerged. We do not expect the theological results to be in line with an idea of homogenous 'true' Islam. The assumption of this project is – following recent research in Islamic Studies – to pay attention to "prolific scale and definitive import of the phenomenon of internal contradiction to the constitution of the human and historical phenomenon of Islam" (Ahmed 2016, p.72).

From a practical point of view, the role of the academic members is to provide a kind of academic credibility towards possible funding agencies, to translate the experience into academic discourse, access to sources of funding – and doing the administrative work related to a project.

The theoretical framework has been called "participatory action research" in the introduction (cf., e.g., Ngwenya 2018). To avoid lengthy theoretical discussions on this approach and presenting it to readers who may be familiar with it, we refer to the concept as described by McTaggart et al.:

"Action research is associated with many approaches to change and inquiry into social practices. Recently [...] and in the past [...], we referred to critical participatory action research as a spiral of individual and collective self-reflective cycles of:
- planning a change,
- acting and observing the process and consequences of the change,
- reflecting on these processes and consequences, and then,
- re-planning,
- acting and observing,
- reflecting, and so on.

Critical participatory action research is rarely as neat as this spiral of self-contained cycles suggests. Many aspects of practices are involved. Kemmis [...] argued that a significant aspect of this spiral with respect to critical participatory action research is that outside researchers and practitioners are working side by side in highly participatory ways rather than the outside researcher facilitating or managing the change process. Also, participants getting together to address a legitimate concern of mutual importance as the impetus of the change process is a central feature. What the spiral does not capture is that critical participatory action research is more than a 'method' of change; instead, participants are committed to engaging in a broad social analysis of their situation (exploring the conditions that prefigure their practices) and a collective self-study of their practices to determine what to do to improve their situation." (2017, p.21f.)

The project fits well into the critical view proposed in the International Handbook of Action Resarch, claiming that, "(1) the emergence and proliferation of networks and how this is transforming both theory and practice in action research, while retaining the philosophical roots of action research in social justice; (2) acknowledgment of the link between the diverse global contexts within which action research theory and practice has been, and is being, developed and the importance of knowledge democracy in creating an alternative globalization; and (3) the necessity for a reflective cross-cultural and cross-case comparative perspective within the global action research community to show respect for the diversity of epistemologies within which action research emerges." (Rowell/Bruce/Shosh/Riel 2017, p. Xvf.)

We are also subscribing to the view of the editors of the above-cited handbook. "We avoid declaring all things 'relative,' which seems both unsustainable and irresponsible, and instead make the case that an 'ecology of knowledges' [...] that addresses the relation between action research and social change on the one hand and action research and knowledge production on the other is not only healthy but necessary." (Rowell/Bruce/Shosh/Riel 2017, p. XV) This kind of research may be necessary (and healthy) to help research to integrate into the society as a – different – but maybe a helpful part of our societies as global ecologies. The main lacunae are the lack of female members, at an academic and non-academic level, a situation we hope to be able to change in the next step of the project.

The alternative narrations (not counter-narratives)

The widely accepted need to produce counter-narratives against, e.g., Jihadi narratives has to be scrutinized. Starting from empirical network analysis, we may question the proclaimed effects of these counter-narratives (see Lohlker 2017). It needs to be stated that the anti-Jihadi counter-narratives do not reach the audience they are aiming at. The main reason is the lack of credibility due to three major deficits, namely a) political or security institutions trying to convince an audience that is marginalized by these institutions, b) the lack of knowledge about the – Islamic – contexts that are appropriated by Jihadis, c) the lack of professional ways of producing videos compared to the high-end Jihadi videos.

These reasons caused the project team to reflect on possible alternative ways of thinking and practicing. The alternative narrations developed during the project are

1) Jihadi style: two homogenous ways, tawhid (understood as homogeneity, not allowing any difference) and kufr (understood as unbelief)
a) Alternative style: a variety of individual and collective ways

2) Jihadi style: "Neo-Umma" as unitarian, totalitarian community
a) Alternative style: pluralistic Umma, a variantology of communities

3) Jihadi style: military, violent Jihad
a) Alternative style: nuanced idea of Jihad, esp., non-violent one

4) Jihadi style: violence as the only way to confront injustice
a) Alternative style: highly nuanced forms to confront injustice

5) Jihadi style: fundamental opposition against a world system perceived as capitalist/imperialist
a) Alternative style: criticism based on a nuanced understanding of reality

6) Jihadi style: obedience
a) Alternative style: critical scrutiny

7) Jihadi style: 'the West' as unifying enemy
a) Alternative style: differentiated worldview

8) Jihadi style: "association and dissociation" (al-wala' wa'l-bara') as guiding principle, i. e., having contact to the in-group only and avoiding contact with all people not part of it
a) Alternative style: god is close to everybody doing good deeds

9) Jihadi style: worshiping something other than god (shirk), theological principle legitimizing an authoritarian way of living and thinking
a) Alternative style: non-authoritarian ways of living and thinking

10) Jihadi style: constructing permanent threat to provoke fear
a) Alternative style: facing the real problems and criticizing

The first part of the project helped to produce four videos that were put online. We would like to recommend to view the videos online since images will not help to understand the experience of visual, audio, and textual aspects of the videos. The titles of the videos are
- Part 1: "Mein Weg – Jamal al-Khatib" (My way – Jamal al-Khatib)
- Part 2: "Heimat – Mein Weg: Jamal al-Khatib" (Home – My Way: Jamal al-Khatib)
- Part 3: "Jihad an-nafs – Mein Weg: Jamal al-Khatib" (Jihad an-nafs – My Way: Jamal al-Khatib)
- Part 4: "Mein Bruder – Mein Weg: Jamal al-Khatib" (My brother – My Way: Jamal al-Khatib)

The video channel on YouTube[2] was supplemented with a Facebook page "Jamal al-Khatib,"[3] and a Twitter account called "Jamal al-Khatib"[4]. The intention was to cover several accessible platforms with alternative narrations and to build a network to spread the message in a cross-platform manner. The videos may be summarized as the story of a young man turning away from Jihadism and reflecting upon his former ideas. The story is told in a style palatable to young people in European societies; the visual structure is adapted to the viewing habits of a younger audience being part of the marginalized part of youth culture in Austria as stated by years of doing youth work with this audience. An important element is the reflection on religious issues deconstructing the Jihadi appropriation of common Islamic ideas.[5]

One technical problem occurred: For some time the Facebook account was blocked due to it being perceived as Jihadi propaganda. This resulted in a drop of views, likes, etc. after Video 2. To some extent, this may be understood as a success of the project aiming at creating alternatives for young people in a Jihadi subculture, since Facebook has become aware of the videos and posting. The problem was solved in negotiations with the Internet companies.

Leaving these technical problems due to the Internet companies need to control the online activities of Jihadi subcultures aside, the crucial problem was the creation of online credibility resulting from a message that can be identified as Islamic, as visual language that is well embedded in contemporary youth

2 Jamal al-Khatib (2017): "Mein Weg: Jamal al-Khatib (Teil 1 von 4)", *youtube.com*, available: https://www.youtube.com/channel/UCKmWuKvMLGHQ4Z0VaVjwYVQ [10.05.2018].
3 https://de-de.facebook.com/jamalalkhatibmeinweg/ [10.05.2018].
4 https://twitter.com/jamal_al_khatib?lang=de [10.05.2018].
5 For a detailed description of the content of the videos see below.

(sub-)culture, and a deep knowledge of Jihadi discourses. All of these elements are lacking in conventional counter-narratives.

Video Content

The following remarks try to give an idea of the content of the videos produced. We limit the discussion to a textual mode, as an illustration by some screengrabs will not give an idea of the flow of images, music, text, and storytelling.

Video 1: "Mein Weg – Jamal al-Khatib" (My way – Jamal al-Khatib)[6]

Introduction with images from Vienna, 'Jamal' telling he is for 16 years in Vienna because in his homeland there was war. Cut to teenagers attacking each other in the street, Jamals commenting he did it himself, disliked it and turned away from such behaviour. Young males smoking shishas mixed with images form war in Syria. Jamal telling some of the people he knows went to war, some of them were killed. He himself pondered on joining IS. Being told by the media that still people are joining IS, killing and being killed he decided to turn away from this path, choosing his own path. He had spent some time in prison reflecting on what he has thought before. He announced that in the videos he will tell his experience – with the help of some friends. 'Jamal' is shown in all videos with a hoodie, an 'Islamic' shirt, no face visible, simply black, walking around in Vienna.

Video 2: "Heimat – Mein Weg: Jamal al-Khatib" (Home – My Way: Jamal al-Khatib)[7]

Telling that he lived in a situation of war in his homeland mixed with images of destruction and warfare, he mentions that his mother and father took him away to Vienna to live in peace, he spent some words on their flight. The first time when he felt being secure when he entered an accomodation for refugees, mixed with some tourist views of Vienna. Vienna became home for him, but there was a break when people looked at him as Muslim coming from a region of war as if he was a terrorist. And as if Islam was a violent religion. He says for him Islam is a

6 Jamal al-Khatib (2017): " Mein Weg: Jamal al-Khatib (Teil 1 von 4) ", *youtube.com*, available: https://www.youtube.com/watch?v=Hay8UKHLywM [10.05.2018].

7 Jamal al-Khatib (2017): " Heimat – Mein Weg: Jamal al-Khatib (Teil 2 von 4)", *youtube.com*, available: https://www.youtube.com/watch?v=sJkBZRn82kY [10.05.2018].

religion of peace and mercy quoting a verse of the Qur'an that is cut in the video with a reproduction of the same verse in Arabic. He is mentioning racism and enmity he and others had to face but mentions, however, there are other people helping refugees and Muslim. This leads to stress the need to stick to mercy as a guideline of life.

Part 3: "Jihad an-nafs – Mein Weg: Jamal al-Khatib" (Jihad an-nafs – My Way: Jamal al-Khatib)[8]

Starting with a martial arts fighting situation, illustrating the text, the video changes to Jamal and his friends watching videos from Syria, changing back to the martial arts situation, mixed with the urge he felt to fight against the regime of the Syrian president Bashshar al-Asad. He talked to an elderly man about these issues after Friday prayer. The elderly man tells him it is better fight against the negative feeling in himself (called jihad al-nafs in Islamic traditions), shooting at someone can be done by everyone. Jamal defines this concept as "effort to become a better human". Changing again to the martial arts situation, this time to young males fighting, he is telling daily life examples of how to do this jihad al-nafs. Cut: Telling about the Iranian diplomat at the embassy in Paris during Nazi occupation and his support for Jewish people issuing Iranian passports for them and saving lives by doing this. Jamal calls to follow this example to help people in need in Austria, in the background there are images from the recent refugee movement. Again martial arts ending with the two fighters merging into one, having successfully fought the negative feelings.

Part 4: "Mein Bruder – Mein Weg: Jamal al-Khatib" (My brother – My Way: Jamal al-Khatib)[9]

The video tells a story about a kind of gang and of one of the friends of Jamal who went to Syria committing acts of crimes. The video ends with a call to care for other persons to make them think in another way.

For offline work, especially in youth centers, the team developed a media package including the videos but other material, too.[10] A technical challenge was

8 Jamal al-Khatib (2017): "Jihad an-Nafs – Mein Weg: Jamal al-Khatib (Teil 3 von 4)", *youtube.com*, available: https://www.youtube.com/watch?v=AqRbiHqPwvQ [10.05.2018].

9 Jamal al-Khatib (2017): "Mein Bruder – Mein Weg: Jamal al-Khatib (Teil 4 von 4)", *youtube.com*, available: https://www.youtube.com/watch?v=cDDDqwTlTs0 [10.05.2018].

10 The media package has been used for public viewing in youth centres and schools followed by

to find actors/speakers who have the accent expected by the audience not producing the effect of counter-narrative videos with young middle-class people teaching marginalized youths the right way to behave. This is a practical critique of the homogenized view of migration communities by the majority and the self-homogeneous presentation of these communities by communicators.

An important part of the project was a moderated form of comments limited in time. Some of the results may be seen in the appendix. The majority of the team acted as moderators to cover at least for a short period 24 hours a day, 7 days a week. This was necessary to avoid Jihadi sympathizers taking over the comments section. But Jihadi positions were less visible then expected. We may read this as a first success of the project since it seems not to be interesting and promising for Jihadi sympathizers to attempt such a take-over.

Credibility

The problem of (street) credibility as a central element of any part of academic encounter with contemporary youth and street culture was solved by bringing together a group of nine young men, four of them may be called former IS-sympathizers or members of the Jihadi milieu with youth workers who engage with these young men (and some young women) in a discourse on Jihadi matters for years now, and Islamic Studies researchers doing research on Jihadism for many years, too. This group is represented by the present writer with some discomfort.

Conclusion

The project is understood as a combination of a content producing and acting team of young men from marginalized communities in Vienna, Austria, and a supporting team consisting of predominantly white males who intentionally were expected to bring in their expertise when needed, e.g., the film producer who produced in a painstaking process the final videos to put online. Continuously a process of feedback loops between all members of the Jamal al-Khatib team helped to create the videos as the common product of all members. We have to acknowledge an imbalance between white and non-white males but are confident that putting the white males second line and holding up the idea of an anonymous person called "Jamal al-Khatib" helped to minimize the effects of

---

discussions. The package may be downloaded from http://www.boja.at/projekte/flucht/jamal-al-khatib-paedagogisches-paket/.

this still distorted structure. We have to stress: the lead was to the non-white group.

Due to the structure of the project team and the lead by the non-white group of members creating and expressing their own brand of Islam the relation of religion we may state the experimental setting of the project meant a reconfiguration of authority in religious matters as the only way to exclude any recruitment by authoritarian religious groups like Jihadis. As seen in one video, the elder generation is understood by the team as a resource to support their process of creating their idea of Islam. In other contexts, the youth only approach is dominant. We might say the project means opening up a space of action, interaction, and common action creating a new approach of dealing with religious issues. Community related questions are not put on the agenda.

The project deals with non-community marginalized young people, male and – in the future – female being empowered to create their own way of living in a migration society. The main problem of the project was how to face the attitudes of the white male members of the group and their understanding of religion not vice versa, a problem that could almost be solved by referring to the previous experience and reflection of these members.

The first part of the project was funded by the Zukunftsfonds der Republik Österreich[11], the City of Vienna[12], and the Beratungsstelle Extremismus[13] The second step of the video project will include female youths as actors/producers and refugees, the majority coming from Iraq to Austria, adding female and refugee perspectives and aiming at the construction of a more diversified view of the Austrian society.[14]

References

Ahmed, Shahab (2016): *What is Islam? The Importance of Being Islamic.* Princeton, Oxford: Oxford University Press.

Attia, Iman (ed.) (2007): *Orient- und Islambilder. Interdisziplinäre Beiträge zu Orientalismus und antimuslimischem Rassismus.* Münster: Unrast.

11 http://www.zukunftsfonds-austria.at/index.php?suche=magomed [10.05.2018] for s short description of the Magomed-part of the project.

12 The city of Vienna organized a "Network on Culture of Democracy and Prevention", acting as an internal network to create an anti-extremist culture in the administration of the city of Vienna directed against social and individual devaluation (https://kja.at/site/praevention/netzwerk-deradikalisierung-praevention/) [10.05.2018].

13 https://www.beratungsstelleextremismus.at/uber-uns/, an Austrian-wide network acting as a consulting agency for families [10.05.2018].

14 Since this means a reconfiguration of the group of members any attempt to conceptualize the future of the process called project would be premature.

Bennett, Delancy / Diamond, William (2012): "Street Credibility: What Is It? Who Has It? Why Is It So Appealing to Diverse Consumer Groups?"*Advances in Consumer Research 40*, pp. 1017–1018.

Dietze, Gabriele/ Brunner, Claudia/ Wenzel, Edith (eds.) (2009): *Kritik des Okzidentalismus. Transdisziplinäre Beiträge zu (Neo-)Orientalismus und Geschlecht.* Bielefeld: transcript.

Haraway, Donna (2018): *Unruhig bleiben. Die Verwandschaft der Arten im Chthuluzän.* Frankfurt a. M./ New York: Campus.

Lohlker, Rüdiger (2016a): "The 'I' of ISIS: Why Theology matters." In: *Interventionen* 7, pp. 4–15.

– (2016b): "Theology matters: The case of jihadi Islam." In: *Strategic Review* available: http://sr-indonesia.com/in-the-journal/view/europe-s-misunderstanding-of-islam-and-isis [18.10.2018].

– (2017): "Rewiring the Islamc Net: Creating an Alternative to the Online Propaganda of IS (Islamic State)". In Hofkirchner, Walter/Burgin, Mark (eds.): *The Future Information Society: Social and Technological Problems.* Singapore et al.: World Scientific, pp. 307–313.

McTaggart, Robin/ Nixon, Rhonda/ Kemmis, Stephen (2017): "Critical Participatory Action Research". In: Rowell, Lonnie L./ Bruce, Catherine D./ Shosh, Joseph M./ Margaret M. Riel (eds.): *The Palgrave International Handbook of Action Research*, New York: Palgrave MacMillan, pp. 21–35.

Ngwenya, Dumisani (2018): *Healing the Wounds of Gukarahundi in Zimbabwe: A Participatory Action Project.* Cham: Springer International.

Rowell, Lonnie L./ Bruce, Catherine D./ Shosh, Joseph M./ Margaret M. Riel (Hg.) (2017): *The Palgrave International Handbook of Action Research*, New York: Palgrave MacMillan.

Tertilt, Hermann (1996): *Turkish Power Boys. Ethnographie einer Jugendbande.* Frankfurt a. M.: Suhrkamp.

Appendix: Social Media Report (October 2017)[15]

Facebook

Facebook Demography (Views)

Country

DE	168.814
AT	60.793

15 Social Media Report, Jamal al-Khatib, internal project report. There has also been an impact of the videos offline being discussed in groups of young people.

Gender

male	94 %
female	6 %

Age

13–17	21 %
18–24	56 %
25–34	22 %

Facebook Demography (Fans)

Cities

Vienna	348
Berlin	73
Munich	50

Gender

male	89 %
female	10 %

Age

13–17	23 %
18–24	53 %
25–34	12 %

Facebook (Reach)

Video 1:	106.759
Video 2:	191.590
Video 3:	106.785
Video 4:	115.997

Facebook (Interactions)

Video 1

shares	87
comments	164

Video 2

shares	291
comments	283

Video 3

shares	104
comments	248

Video 4

shares	106
comments	176

YouTube

average playtime	02:16 min
subscribers	157
likes	197
dislikes	70
playlist	25

Twitter

reach	345.597
media advertisement	643
interactions	14.697
level of interaction	4,25 %

Part III –
Negotiating Religious Belonging in Migration Society

Katharina Limacher

Bhangra, Bhajan, Bollywood – Religious Knowledge among Hindu Youth in Switzerland and Austria

Abstract

Religious knowledge and its transmission are important aspects of processes of identifications and therefore have an impact on religious communities. When we conceptualise religious knowledge as the things we know, both implicitly and explicitly, it becomes clear that every person holds a broad range of knowledge, required for example in the context of a common religious practice. Starting from the observation that young Hindus in Switzerland and Austria express a lack of knowledge about their respective religious tradition, I am interested in the circumstances that influence their conception as well as the transmission of religious knowledge. My paper aims at showing how different institutional arrangements add up to create a setting within which Hindu religious youth experiences ambivalences in the evaluation of their own religious knowledge. To do so I will firstly present methodological reflections on doing research in Hindu temples in Zurich and Vienna. Secondly, I will focus on a broad concept of religious knowledge and the processes of its transmission in Hindu traditions in Europe. Finally, I will link the question of transmission of knowledge to Pierre Bourdieus distinction of different forms of capital and show, how the analysis of access to and distribution of cultural capital helps to see institutionalised inequalities that frame the processes of transmission of religious knowledge and therefore influence the processes of identification of young people.

Introduction

> "And when I visit the temple I really feel like, like really at home. You know, I feel (…) you know I was born here. But I know somehow in my heart that I do not fully belong here. You know, my skin colour already shows that I do not fully belong here" (IJK, Z120–124).

What Jahnavi Karunanithi tells me when asked about her visits to the Hindu[1] temple in Glattbrugg, at the outskirts of the city of Zurich, generally touches upon the processes of identifications of young people and the ambivalences and

1 The use of the terms Hinduism and Hindu generally refers to a wide variety of religious practices and beliefs that originate in the Indian subcontinent (Malinar 2009).

boundaries that shape them. On the one hand, Jahnavi Karunanithi clearly states the importance of religious belonging. Yet she cannot do so without touching upon the general challenges of processes of identifications in a society, where migration is the norm, not the exception, but that nevertheless still constructs itself as predominantly white and Christian.

While conflicting aspects of belonging as expressed in the quote of Jahnavi Karunanithi are important for the understanding of religious youth in migration society, it is also widely known that concepts of belonging and identity are, as Anthias (Anthias 2006, 19) puts it, "overused and under-theorised". Hence, to approach processes of identifications of young Hindus in Switzerland and Austria I will focus one specific aspect: the aspect of religious knowledge. Knowledge is the key ingredient to understand and take part in society in general and in different societal domains – Berger and Luckmann speak of so-called sub-worlds (Berger/ Luckmann 1966, 158ff.) – such as, for example, religious communities. In addition, knowledge is closely linked to questions of legitimacy and predominance, because not all forms of knowledge in a plural society are judged equally valuable and powerful. For example, there are different evaluations of the knowledge of a burglar and of a teacher in terms of legitimacy. This makes religious knowledge an important starting point to assess processes of identifications of religious youth.

Religious knowledge or knowledge about religion is an important topic of research in the area of religious education. While lots of research has been conducted on secular and religious education about religion in the Christian traditions (for example Frank 2014, 2015), the different aspects of transmission of religious knowledge of Hindu religious youth in Switzerland or Austria has not been researched thoroughly so far. Of course, the specific aspects of the transmission of religious knowledge in Hindu traditions have been closely examined. Other than in most Christian traditions the transmission of religious knowledge is seldom institutionalised and more often than not takes place in the private setting of one's family home (Suthren Hirst 2011). Whereas the family home is the primary place where young Hindus acquire and negotiate religious knowledge, it is by far not the only one. Peer groups, school and workplaces as well as digital spaces are important places where different forms of knowledge are acquired, challenged or validated. How religious knowledge is appropriated and what kind of challenges young people face doing so therefore deserves our attention. Not only does it provide important insights into the lives of young self-identified religious people in a society shaped by religious and cultural diversity, it also points us toward the place religious youth will eventually in their respective religious communities.

Research Setting and Methodological Reflections

The data I present here stem from my ethnographic research in Hindu temples in Vienna and Zurich that I conducted for my PhD project in 2013 and 2014 and occasionally thereafter (Limacher 2018).[2] The body of data I draw on consists of observation protocols and episodic interviews as well as notes on informal conversations with devotees I encountered during my visits in various temples. I visited weekly gatherings celebrating *pūjā*[3] or *ārati*, regular temple rituals, and the celebration of different religious festivals, such as the celebration of *Durgāpūjā*. While the focus of my PhD research was not limited to religious youth, young people were part of the research field, as they were regular visitors at the different temple sites and thus part of the people I engaged in conversations with or asked for interviews. I analysed my data in different steps, using open coding to find recursive issues (Strauss and Corbin 1996) but also the documentary method (Bohnsack 1989, 2010, 2013) to reconstruct the documentary meaning in an interview. Eventually, I reconstructed specific temple practices in a thick description from my diverse materials and different analytical steps (Geertz 1983).

Doing fieldwork in Hindu temples in Zurich and Vienna, I became aware of the particular challenges of this research setting and its implications repeatedly. As participant observer I was often the only person perceived as white and at the same time the one observing the doings of a group of predominantly people of colour. In interview settings I invited my partners to speak about their experiences in Hindu temples and therefore to speak about their religious identifications which, in the case of Hinduism has a long tradition as an exotic and orientalist trope of the European intellectual history (Inden 2000). And when I visited religious festivals, young women were ordered by the temple board to lend me their support, accompany me and answer potential questions I could have. This special treatment – without doubt a thoughtful gesture of the temple board – contributed to shape my relationship to these younger women in a hierarchical way.

As discussed by Christoph Novak in this volume, privileges of race, religion and age also affected my research process. I tried to deal with these aspects in two ways. Firstly, I opted for a strictly praxeological approach in my methodological foundation thereby focussing on situations and their people rather than on people and their situations, to paraphrase Erving Goffman (Goffman et al. 1986,

2 The research was part of the research project "Civic Engagement of immigrant religious communities in Switzerland and Austria: a comparative analysis of Hindu, Buddhist and Muslim associations in Zurich and Vienna" funded by the Swiss National Science Foundation.

3 Transliteration of Sanscrit-Terminology according to I.A.S.T. Transliteration guidelines.

p. 9). Praxeology or practice theory as a methodological perspective places *the social in practices* (*Praktiken*) and not in discourses or interactions (Reckwitz 2002). This is not to say that people and their (inter-)actions are not a significant part of the social world but rather that in a praxeological perspective the emphasis lies on practice as “a routinized type of behaviour which consists of several elements, interconnected to one another: forms of bodily activities, forms of mental activities, ‘things’ and their use, a background knowledge in the form of understanding, know-how, states of emotion and motivational knowledge” (Reckwitz 2002, 249). Practice theory therefore wants to understand how the repeated celebrating of a *pūjā* is done rather than *who* is doing it and for what reasons. In conceptualising practices as the focal point, a praxeology consequently has to reflect upon its empirical research practice as well (Bohnsack 2017, 11). This can be achieved through the continuous self-reflection of one’s own position as a (white, female, academic, non-religious) researcher. Secondly, I reflected my position as a researcher at different moments of the research process (fieldwork, data analysis, writing up) following ethical guidelines[4] in ethnographic research and trying to avoid generalisations about Hindus as the other, rather looking at practices that constitute Hindu temples in a specific societal and spatial context instead.

In both Switzerland and Austria the history of Hindu temples, and by association the history of an institutionalised Hindu religious practice on a larger scale, although quite different, began in the 1980ies (Hutter 2010, Eulberg 2008).[5] The history of migration of Hindus from South Asia to Switzerland is strongly marked by the civil war in Sri Lanka that officially lasted from 1983 to 2009. The war broke out as a result of a long period of ethnic polarisation between the Singhalese majority and the Tamil minority, cultivated under British rule and intensified after the independence from the British Commonwealth in 1948. Subsequently almost 800’000 Tamils have fled Sri Lanka and are displaced all over the world (Eulberg 2014, 113). Since the early 1980s some 45000 Tamils, over 90 % of them Hindus, have sought refuge in Switzerland and most of them have been granted asylum under a new Asylum Act that became law in 1981, yet only after some tedious waiting periods that were shaped by a high precariousness of their residence status (Moret et al. 2007, 30ff.). As a result, Sri Lankan Tamil Hindus make up the largest part of Hindus in Switzerland. Even though there are a number of people of Indian descent living in Switzerland, the institutions of

4 Interestingly, the ethics codex of the German Sociological Association doesn’t touch upon the topic of privileges and representation at all: https://www.soziologie.de/de/die-dgs/ethik/ethik-kodex.html, last accessed 03.10.2018.

5 However, both countries have a history of neo-Hinduist practice dating back at least to the 70ies and there are different instances of contact with spiritual ideas originating in India even before this (Eulberg 2008).

Hindu religious practice such as the over 25 temples are maintained by Hindus of mainly Sri Lankan Tamil descent. Sri Lankan Tamil Hinduism isn't a homogenous religious tradition; yet Hindu temple practices in Switzerland bear traces of Sri Lankan Tamil *Śaivaism* which most Sri Lankan Tamil Hindus follow. One such feature is the centrality of the god *Kārttikeya* (tam. *murukaṉ*), son of *Śiva*, that is a central part of the Sri Lankan Tamil temple practice. Another feature is the importance of *Tai Ponkal* (tam. *taipponkal*), the Tamil harvest festival, one of the most important festivals in the Sri Lankan Tamil Hindu year (Jagannathan 2005, 139ff.).

In comparison, Hindu temple practice in Austria reflects the history of migration from South Asia. It is important to note that Austria has not seen a similarly significant and uniform migration movement from South Asia as has Switzerland. Instead, migration from South Asia to Austria is a rather heterogeneous phenomenon (Hintermann 1997). Moreover, not all of the migrants from India and neighbouring states can be counted as mainly affiliated with Hinduism. Vienna has a large community of Sikhs, most of whom migrated from the Indian federal state of Punjab. Recent statistical data on Hindus in Austria do not exist. Yet it is safe to say that the numbers of Hindus in Austria rank between the 3629 compiled during the last census in 2001 (Hutter 2015) and the rather generous estimates of 10000 to 12000 Hindus presented within an issue of "Hinduism Today" in 2014 (Himalayan Academy 2014, S.23).

Vienna Hindu life reflects the history of these migration patterns. The Austrian Hindus come from such different places as Punjab, West-Bengal, Gujarat, Kerala or Tamil Nadu but also Bangladesh, Nepal or Afghanistan. As there tend to be more people from northern India, the temples and association emphasize the traditions of this region. This becomes visible in the festivities of the *Durgāpūjā*, a festival that marks an important moment of the religious year for most Hindus in West-Bengal and Bangladesh. Several celebrations of *Durgāpūjā* are hosted every autumn by different associations and temples in Vienna. Another link to migration patterns can be found in the religious folks songs, *bhajans*, that are sung on the occasion of the weekly temple gatherings and that differ in language and style according to region of provenance of the people performing it.

While the history of migration of Hindus from South Asia to Switzerland and Austria as well as the size of these established communities are very different (Limacher 2018, 57ff.), the stories and current challenges of the temples in these two settings bear striking resemblances. Both in Zurich and Vienna the devotees expressed concern about the future of their temples because both, the necessary funds and the volunteers to keep the temples up and running are scarce. Yet they view temples as important institutions to pass on Hindu religious culture.

In both countries, the temples grew out of small weekly gatherings of committed devotees held in private flats, restaurants and basements and developed into associations that managed to keep up these weekly gatherings (Limacher 2018), but furthermore organise public celebrations of special holidays (Limacher and Rückamp 2016). In Switzerland, these communities managed employing a priest, buying buildings or land, and starting or even successfully finishing the constructing of a temple (Baumann/ Tunger-Zanetti 2014). Even though partly very big, functioning associations developed, the devotees are doubtful that younger people will want or be able to carry on. Moreover, younger devotees voice concern that they do not have enough knowledge or resources to do so. It is against this backdrop that I examine the role of religious knowledge for young Hindus in Switzerland and Austria, starting with some conceptual considerations.

Conceptions of (Religious) Knowledge

In my paper, I draw upon a broad understanding of knowledge. Thus, I do understand knowledge as on the one hand theoretical, explicit knowledge i.e. as knowledge about the creation myth of a specific religious belief or knowledge about different religious traditions. On the other hand, I want to think of knowledge as practical, implicit knowledge i.e. as a form of know-how or understanding and therefore as something that involves a material dimension in the form of bodies as well as artefacts (Reckwitz 2002). Accordingly, a Hindu ritual such as *āratī,* the presentation of light to the image of god, reveals different aspects of knowledge. As an interviewer asking a religious expert, I might learn the significance of *āratī,* as a devotional ritual in a Vedic tradition. As an observer in the situation of *āratī* it is possible to distinguish different forms of implicit knowledge of the right bodily postures of different devotees in front of the image of god, the handling of involved objects. Sociology of knowledge can provide us with an understanding of the link between knowledge, the individual person, and society. Following the ideas of Peter L. Berger and Thomas Luckmann (1966) we find the useful distinction between "common-sense knowledge (…) I share with others in the normal, self-evident routines of everyday life" (Berger/ Luckmann 1966, 37) and different forms of specialised knowledge of so called 'sub-worlds'. This second form of knowledge I only acquire selectively (ibid. 158), for example as a practising member of a Christian congregation or as a Hindu who regularly performs *pūjā* at his or her home shrine. Whereas the knowledge about the existence of public transport is common knowledge that is accessible to everyone, the theoretical but also practical knowledge about Hindu temple rituals, Muslim prayer or Christian mass most certainly is not. Rather, it is part of the knowledge of a person growing up Hindu, Muslim or Christian or engaging in either religious practice at some point in his/her life.

Knowledge therefore is inherently linked to processes of identification and belonging and it has to be understood as a relational category. "To retain confidence that he is indeed who he thinks he is, the individual requires not only the implicit confirmation of this identity that even casual everyday contacts will supply, but the explicit and emotionally charged confirmation that his significant others bestow on him" (Berger/ Luckmann 1966, 170). Thus, for Berger and Luckmann the social interactions of our everyday lives with our families, friends and colleagues reassure the different aspects of our identity through the confirmation of shared knowledge in the situation of face-to-face interaction. And, we might want to take into account other forms than those of face-to-face interaction as well and look at processes of digital identifications as Astrid Mattes convincingly argues in this volume.

Of course, it is also in these everyday interactions that specific aspects of this process are called into question. In a religiously plural society, as sketched in the introduction of this book, the interactions with one's social environment are diverse. Thus, encounters with different religiously or non-religiously identified people often invite comparison between one's own religious identifications and that of others (Frank 2014, 8). Furthermore, religious knowledge does exist in different forms (Frank 2015, 48). Whereas religious experts or adherents of a certain religious tradition transfer *religious* knowledge about religion in the context of religious practices or through explanations, there also exists a *secular* knowledge about religion that is taught in ethics or philosophy classes in public schools.

It is against this concept of knowledge that we ought to look at how young Hindus evaluate their respective religious knowledge. In the following, I argue that by analysing the explicit and implicit religious knowledge of young Hindus and their own claim of a lack of knowledge we can critically assess societal factors that influence processes of religious identification and belonging in migration society.

Transmission of Religious Knowledge in Hindu Traditions in Vienna and Zurich

In her study on young Hindus of Sri Lankan Tamil descent in Germany, Sandhya Marla-Küsters (2015) identifies four major lines of transformation in the religiosity of the second generation.[6] She designates one of these transformations a

6 I refer to the notion of the 'second generation' because it is used in the research on religious youth that I quote. However, it needs to be emphasised that the concept itself is not unproblematic as it reflects a general attitude that still sees migration processes as an anomaly

"transformation in the culture of questioning" (*Transformation der Fragekultur*, ibid. 408). Marla-Küsters shows that young Hindus frequently turn to their parents and ask them questions about religious beliefs and practices but that the answers do not suffice to satisfy their curiosity. While the transmission of religious knowledge in Hinduism is by tradition the responsibility of the parents or rather the women of the family, the parents in Marla-Küsters study express surprise about the constant questioning of their children. Marla-Küsters explains this surprise with cultural differences that manifest themselves in the shift from a first to a second generation. She calls attention to South Asian cultures where it is deemed highly disrespectful to scrutinise religious or other authorities, and that parents therefore do not encourage this behaviour. Yet German public schools do incite this way of critical reflection (ibid. 147). She adds that parental confusion can be explained with regard to Hindu religious tradition itself and its reliance on orthopraxy where it is generally deemed more important to follow certain rituals through then to grasp their distinct meaning (ibid. 148). However, the young self-identified Hindus I talked to seemed still more concerned with what they perceived to be a lack of religious knowledge. In Vienna, a young woman, Nitnam Chana, told me about her perceived lack of religious education:

> "When I went to school we didn't have this religious education. Or / but I / I don't know (…) probably it's just not possible because we are not enough [people] in Vienna and that's why we cannot have this instruction / you know?"

Moreover, she goes on to relate this lack of institutionalised religious education to a general lack of representation of her mother tongue:

> "(…) or for example we do not have any books in Hindi in the library, you see. I've seen some in Arabic, even some / quite a lot actually, in Turkish and even some Chinese books but I think in Hindi there is no single book" (INC, Z365–371).

When asked to whom she turns with religious questions she answered:

> "Well, to my parents. But uh when I'm not really satisfied with their answer then I research on my own on the Internet or we do have books at home. Or, there is / there is enough on the Internet though there is YouTube there are so many religious men that talk about it, so, well, it is a huge source" (INC, Z224–226).[7]

A young woman in Zurich, Neruthaya Palli, told me that she always turns to Tamil movies for advice on religion and culture because her parents did not teach her:

instead of a societal normalcy and therefore aids the construction of migrants and their children as 'the other'.

7 The Interview was originally conducted in German.

> "You know, actually, truthfully, it is not my parents who taught me about our culture, but Tamil movies did. Because there you always learn, ok, I see, that's how our religion could actually look, how about our culture, uh-huh, ok (...)" (INP, Z88–91).[8]

These and similar quotes from young Hindus in Zurich and Vienna show that they feel they lack knowledge about their own religious tradition and, consequently, tackle it by consulting different sources such as their parents, books, Tamil Bollywood movies or instructional YouTube videos. Though, when we understand knowledge to encompass both, explicit and implicit forms, and therefore not only focus on discourses but take practices into account, we see that young Hindus in Zurich and Vienna frequently are part of religious and other practices that exhibit a great variety of knowledge about Hindu religious culture. Furthermore, young people often attend some form of language and cultural education. So for example, Neruthaya Palli attended Tamil language school in Switzerland every Wednesday afternoon for nine years, where Hindu religious culture is an important topic besides mastering the language and learning about the history of Sri Lanka (Somalingam 2017, 182). Accordingly, Marla-Küsters attests these Tamil language schools an important role for the processes of religious identification (Marla 2013, p. 182). Nitnam Chana, the other young woman I quoted, does lead *bhajan* sessions in the temple and knows a great number of theses religious folk songs by heart. Both women are regular temple visitors and even help at major festivals in Zurich and Vienna, respectively. And, of course, they follow ritual practice in the temple. As participant observer in diverse religious celebrations in the temple, I witnessed young people's involvement in a very broad range of activities. They were part of preparatory activities such as cleaning and decorating temple spaces for upcoming celebrations, they participated in and even led *bhajan* sessions, they prayed in front of the temple community, and younger adolescents and children even presented plays of religious stories. In Vienna, on the occasion of the public celebration of Diwali, young people present different dances such as *bhāratanāṭyam,* one of the classical Indian religious dances but also cultural dances such as the popular Punjabi folk dance Bhangra that appears (mostly for the sake of the alliteration) in the title of this paper. They helped prepare religious festivities or served *prasāda*, the food offered to god during worship and afterwards distributed to the visitors of the temple.

Yet despite all these diverse manifest forms of knowledge, my young interlocutors expressed, that they lacked knowledge about their respective religious tradition.

While I agree with Marla-Küsters analysis that there seems to be a trans-

8 The interview was originally conducted in Swiss German.

formation that is linked to knowledge, I would not necessarily link it to a shift between a first and a second generation. Especially since in my own data, the lack of knowledge seems to preoccupy young people independently of their generational belonging. Rather, I suggest looking at the societal surroundings of young Hindus for an explanation. The environment of young Hindus in Switzerland and Austria is indeed religiously plural: most of my interview partners mention friends belonging to diverse religious traditions. In addition, their own religious practice generally is not exclusive, as is common in the South-Asian context. Of course, this does not change much outside of South Asia as most Hindus – my interlocutors among them – visit churches as well as gurdwaras and other religious places (Lüthi 2003).

At the same time, the societal environment is marked by its historic dominance of Christianity that is reflected in the privileged position Christian churches hold both in Switzerland and Austria. Whereas Austria, with its past in the multi-ethnic Danube Monarchy, recognised Muslims, besides Catholics, Protestants Orthodox Christians and Jews, already in 1912 under public law, Switzerland only grants this recognition to the Catholic and Protestant Church, the Old-Catholic Church and some Jewish communities. In both countries Hindus are not recognised under public law although in Austria the *Hinduistisch-Österreichische Religionsgesellschaft* (HRÖ, Hindu Religious Organisation Austria) is registered as a *Religiöse Bekenntnisgemeinschaft* (religious confessional community), "a very vague wording coined as an umbrella term covering rather diverse religious communities" (Hutter 2015, p. 91). This registration grants the HRÖ a secondary and limited form of recognition with no specific privileges but the prospect to attain the status of the full recognition under public law after a waiting period of at least ten years and the fulfilment of the corresponding requirements, such as the necessary amount of 17000 registered members. Nonetheless, with regard to the relationship of church and state, Switzerland and Austria are comparable. Richard Potz argues that both are systems of *coordination*, where the institutional separation of church and state was accomplished, yet the state takes the activities of the religious communities into account (Potz 2007, p. 346).[9] These activities encompass religious education that religious communities under public law are allowed to organise in Austria and some Cantons of Switzerland in public schools. However, in both countries Hindu religious communities are not granted this privilege so far. Yet, it is this

9 As the relation of religion and state is organised on the level of cantons, the coordinative model does not apply everywhere in Switzerland. Especially the canton of Geneva is influenced by the laicité of neighbouring France.

institutionalised transmission of religious knowledge that Nitnam Chana and other young Hindus feel to lack.[10]

(Religious) Knowledge as Cultural Capital

While these young adults do exhibit a significant amount of implicit and explicit knowledge, their expressed lack thereof should be analysed against the backdrop of a societal surrounding where certain forms of knowledge are more legitimate and powerful than others. To grasp these differences analytically I will make use of Pierre Bourdieu's concept of capital. Even though Bourdieu himself reproaches Berger and Luckmann for being oblivious to the analysis of power, Dreher (2016) shows convincingly that both traditions are comparable in their understanding of how societal power structures emerge: "Society as objective reality with its institutions and symbolic universes is characterized by established power structures [in the theory of Berger and Luckmann, K.L.]. (…) And it is specifically Pierre Bourdieu who (…) develops a quite similar theoretical conception with reference to the objective and the subjective dimension of society (…)" (Dreher 2016, 61).

Conveniently, it was in his research on the link between social background and scholastic achievement that Pierre Bourdieu first came up with the idea of different forms of capital. His expansion of capital by two basic forms besides economic capital wants to "grasp capital and profit in all their forms and to establish the laws whereby the different types of capital (or power, which amounts to the same thing) change into one another" (Bourdieu 1986, 16). Bourdieu differentiates three forms in which capital does present itself: "as economic capital, which is immediately and directly convertible into money and may be institutionalized in the form of property rights; as cultural capital, which is convertible, in certain conditions, into economic capital and may be institutionalized in the form of educational qualifications; and as social capital, made up of social obligations ("connections"), which is convertible, in certain conditions, into economic capital and may be institutionalized in the form of a title of nobility" (ibid.)

I argue that the institutionalised transmission of religious knowledge is part of

10 In this context, it is important to note that for some years until its closure one temple in Vienna provided religious education for children in the form of classes organised by a volunteer, a German woman married to the Hindu priest of the temple. The classes – even though open to all children – were visited by the children of the families of Bangladeshi descent that visited this temple. As it was a new and short-lived offer, the young people I spoke to had not participated in or known about it.

the second form, of the so-called cultural capital.[11] In Bourdieu's concept, cultural capital is tripartite. In its embodied state it contains the things we learn as part of the culture we live in or the education we pass through during our lifetime. Therefore, cultural capital is highly context specific. Not all people share the same cultural capital, because it depends on the time and place in society that you are born into. So when Marla-Küsters observes that the parents of her interview partners do not understand why their children constantly question the authority of parents, teachers or priests it can be explained with reference to the different contexts within which they each earned their respective cultural capital (Marla-Küsters 2015, 147ff.).

Cultural capital in its embodied form is limited to the individual and can be passed on or traded only indirectly, as it consists of accumulated labor on oneself. An academic title could be bought more or less legally but the work accumulating the knowledge associated with it cannot. Qualifications such as the knowledge that allows to obtain a university diploma or to master vocational training then are forms of embodied cultural capital.

The second form of cultural capital in its objectified state describes cultural goods that can be appropriated materially and symbolically. In its material appropriation, cultural capital comprises cultural goods such as works of art, books, instruments and the like. These cultural goods can be passed on much like economic capital itself. There is however an aspect to them, that makes them not only materially significant but also symbolically. To consume a painting, play an instrument or enjoy a book, we need embodied cultural capital that cannot be transmitted directly from one person to another. Of course, not everyone has the economic capital to buy these forms of cultural capital. But there are ways to appropriate it symbolically, for example by reading the book, lent from a public library – unless there are no such books in your mother tongue to be found, as Nitnam Chana observes.

Finally, the third form of cultural capital is the capital in its institutionalised state. Here, Bourdieu addresses the significance of academic or other scholarly qualifications. The institutionalisation in the form of certificates or titles ob-

11 Of course, religion itself has already been operationalised as a form of capital in different theoretical contexts. The works of economist Laurence Iannaccone (1998) defined "religious capital" in the tradition of rational choice as one form of human capital and laid the foundation for the analysis of religious diversity as a market situation where different religious traditions and denominations compete for the attention of potential members. Another way of linking religion to the idea of capital was done in the wake of Pierre Bourdieu's classification of capital. Bradford Verter (2003) coined the term "spiritual capital" to describe religion in accordance with Bourdieus conceptualisation of cultural capital. While I think that the attempt of Verter is a very useful way to talk about religion, I will use Bourdieu's original distinction of capitals and think of religious knowledge as one part of cultural capital.

jectifies cultural capital. The certificate attests its bearer a cultural competence so she or he does not have to prove it constantly, as would an autodidact. Bourdieu calls this the "power of instituting": "In this case, one sees clearly the performative magic of the power of instituting, the power to show forth and secure belief or, in a word, to impose recognition" (Bourdieu 1986, p. 21). As a critic of societal power structures, Bourdieu takes great interest in the relationship and possibilities of conversion among these different versions of capital. In his view, it is an interplay of different forms of capital that manages to produce powerful and lasting differences between individuals. For example, to acquire institutionalised cultural capital in the form of academic qualifications or certificates, one needs time but also economic capital to be able to invest this time otherwise spent working. Yet these interplays are themselves objects of constant change. One process of change that Bourdieu mentions is the growing number of positions in the labour market where an educational qualification is the condition for legitimate access to it. No longer is it sufficient to actually have the qualifications that a position demands but they need to be institutionalised in the form of certificates that an educational system provides. That young people who are in the process of education are much more concerned with questions of institutionalised knowledge is therefore only natural. However, it has repercussions on the domestic sphere that are important in the context of religious knowledge: "(….) the educational system tends increasingly to dispossess the domestic group of the monopoly of the transmission of power and privileges" (ibid. 26). This general shift toward institutionalised cultural capital together with privileges of some religious communities under public law shape the societal environment within which young Hindus navigate processes of religious Identifications. They grow up learning about the importance of institutionalised knowledge yet do not have access to institutionalised knowledge about their own religious tradition as do their Christian peers.

Young Hindus in Switzerland and Austria locate themselves within a context that they see on the one hand shaped through a high demand for institutionalised cultural capital. This demand is linked to the general themes that the stage of life as adolescent or young adult comprises. Successful graduations and subsequent application to schools, universities or apprenticeship preoccupy most young people. Not surprisingly, Monika Müller (Müller 2013, 233 ff.) shows in her research on young Muslim and Hindu men in Switzerland that the preoccupancy with questions of education are among the most important subject these young men are concerned with. Müller indicates that the belief in meritocracy is a central aspect of how they navigate within the system of education, even though it has been established for a long time, that schools do not necessarily eradicate socio-economic inequalities by merit but rather tend to reproduce them (ibid. 238). This belief in meritocracy is not just a misconception on the part of somewhat naïve young people. After all, the educational system still claims to hold responsibility for the transmission of power and privileges through the handing out of certificates for certain accomplishments. This is further backed by the access to jobs or further educational possibilities a person gets through institutionalised cultural capital. It is therefore only reasonable for adolescents and young adults to seek different forms of institutionalised cultural capital – even more so when it touches upon important aspects of processes of identification.

It is also in this setting that the privileges of (mainly) Christian communities to take part in this educational system are perceived by (mainly) non-Christian religious youth. In Switzerland and Austria where there is a separation of religion and state but certain religious communities enjoy the privilege to organize religious education in public schools, young people who identify as religious but are part of religious traditions considered a minority feel that they fail to gain institutionalised cultural capital with regard to their own religious tradition. This situation where a certain form of religious knowledge is institutionalised through curricula and transmitted in public schools, also underlines the distinction between forms of knowledge that are legitimate and powerful and forms that seemingly are not. Consequently, young Hindus comparing themselves to their Christian peers will feel a lack of legitimate knowledge about religion. From this follows that non-Christian religious youth has to make an effort to come to terms with the content and the legitimacy of their own religious knowledge. This, finally, is the context where challenges for Hindu religious communities can arise and/or where the agency of young people can stir change.

Conclusion

With my analysis I showed, that research on processes of religious identifications of young people have to consider the societal context. The transmission of religious knowledge is a good example to see the ambivalence of a religiously plural society on the one hand and institutional privileges of some religious communities and their influence on self-identified religious youth on the other hand. While it is true that contemporary society is ever more diverse – religiously and otherwise – it is, in the case of Switzerland and Austria, still shaped by its Christian history that results in certain privileges, among them the handling of religious education in public schools. It is important to see, that the cooperative systems between church and state in Switzerland and Austria managed to create a situation of institutionalised transmission that grants its participants access to institutionalised cultural capital in the form of legitimate (religious) knowledge about religion. Looking at the situation from a Bourdieuan perspective one can see that the lack of institutionalised cultural capital does challenge processes of identification of Hindu religious youth – which contrasts with the diverse forms of religious knowledge young people actually have.

Institutionalised cultural capital as well as questions of identification are important in the time of adolescence and young adulthood, and probably even more so in a plural society where encounters with religious people from different faiths as well as non-religious people challenge own religious identifications. Therefore, the absence of institutionalised religious education carries weight. In a situation where young people experience marginalisation owing to different aspects of their identity as Jahnavi Karunanithi reports at the outset of this article, the quest for legitimate forms of religious knowledge can be seen as a quest for assurance – one that is provided, among others, by the stories of Bollywood cinema.

It is against the backdrop of this interplay of the societal environment, the different forms and sources of religious knowledge and claims for institutionalised cultural capital that we should analyse future developments of Hindu religious communities in Switzerland and Austria.

Resarch Data

IJK: Episodic Interview, 09.07.2014, Zurich, Jahnavi Karunanithi, Katharina Limacher
INC: Episodic Interview, 08.03.2014, Vienna, Nitnam Chana, Katharina Limacher
INP: Episodic Interview, 18.08.2014, Zurich, Neruthaya Palli, Katharina Limacher

References

Anthias, Floya (2006): "Belongings in a Globalising and Unequal World. Rethinking Translocations." In: Nira Yuval-Davis, Kalpana Kannabiran, Ulrike Vieten (Eds.): *The Situated Politics of Belonging.* London: SAGE Publications Ltd, pp. 17–31.

Baumann, Martin; Tunger-Zanetti, Andreas (2014): *Der Hindutempel in Trimbach. Von der Idee bis zur Einweihung.* With assistance of Rafaela Eulberg, Elsbeth Iten, Beatrice Mahrer und Naomi Ruef. Luzern: Universität Luzern, Zentrum Religionsforschung.

Berger, Peter L.; Luckmann, Thomas (1966): *The social Construction of Reality. A Treatise in the Sociology of Knowledge.* London: Penguin Books.

Bohnsack, Ralf (1989): *Generation, Milieu und Geschlecht. Ergebnisse aus Gruppendiskussionen mit Jugendlichen.* Opladen: Leske + Budrich.

Bohnsack, Ralf (2010): *Rekonstruktive Sozialforschung. Einführung in qualitative Methoden.* Opladen & Farmington Hills MI: Barbara Budrich.

Bohnsack, Ralf (2013): *Die dokumentarische Methode und ihre Forschungspraxis. Grundlagen qualitativer Sozialforschung.* Wiesbaden: Springer VS.

Bohnsack, Ralf (2017): *Praxeologische Wissenssoziologie.* Opladen, Toronto: Verlag Barbara Budrich.

Bourdieu, Pierre (1986): "The forms of social capital." In John G. Richardson (Ed.): *Handbook of theory and research for the sociology of education.* New York: Greenwood Pr, pp. 15–29.

Dreher, Jochen (2016): "The Social Construction of Power. Reflections Beyond Berger/Luckmann and Bourdieu." *Cultural Sociology* 10 (1), pp. 53–68. https://doi.org/10.1177/1749975515615623.

Eulberg, Rafaela (2008): VII – 24 Hindu-Traditionen in der Schweiz. In Michael Klöckner, Udo Tworuschka (Eds.): Handbuch der Religionen. 19. Ergänzungslieferung. München: Olzog Verlag, pp. 1–28.

Eulberg, Rafaela (2014): "Temple Publics as Interplace of Multiple Public Spheres: Public Faces of Sri Lankan Tamil Hindu Life in Switzerland." In: Ester Gallo (Ed.): *Migration and Religion in Europe. Comparative Perspectives on South Asian Experiences.* Farnham: Ashgate, pp. 111–130.

Frank, Katharina (2014): "Die Konstruktion von religiösem und säkularem Wissen im schulischen Religionsunterricht." Universität Zürich, Zürich. Religionswissenschaftliches Seminar. https://doi.org/10.5167/uzh-94176.

Frank, Katharina (2015): "Vermittlung und Rezeption von religiösem und säkularem Wissen im schulischen Religionsunterricht." Universität Zürich, Zürich. https://doi.org/10.5167/uzh-122182.

Geertz, Clifford (1983): *Dichte Beschreibung. Beiträge zum Verstehen kultureller Systeme.* Frankfurt a.M: Suhrkamp.

Goffman, Erving; Bergsträsser, Renate; Riemer, Sabine (eds.)(1986): *Interaktionsrituale. Über Verhalten in direkter Kommunikation.* Frankfurt am Main: Suhrkamp.

Hintermann, Christiane (1997): "InderInnen in Wien – zur Rekonstruktion der Zuwanderung einer 'exotischen' Migrantengruppe." In: Hartmut Häussermann, Stephan Beetz (Eds.): *Zuwanderung und Stadtentwicklung.* Opladen: Westdeutscher Verlag (Leviathan. Sonderheft, 17), pp. 192–214.

Himalayan Academy (Eds.) (2014): *Hinduism Today: Feature: The Hindu Diaspora within Continental Europe.* Kapaa.

Hutter, Manfred (2010): "VII – 25 Hindus asiatischer Herkunft in Österreich." In: Michael Klöcker, Udo Tworuschka (Eds.): *Handbuch der Religionen. Kirchen und andere Glaubensgemeinschaften in Deutschland/deutschsprachigen Raum.* München: Olzog Verlag, pp. 2–13.

Hutter, Manfred (2015): "Austria." In Knut A. Jacobsen (Ed.): *Brill's encyclopedia of Hinduism.* With assistance of Helene Basu, Angelika Malinar, Vasudha Narayanan. Leiden: Brill (Handbook of oriental studies India Brill's encyclopedia of Hinduism, Vol. VI), pp. 91–94.

Iannaccone, Laurence R. (1998): "Introduction to the Economics of Religion." In *Journal of Economic Literature* 36 (3), pp. 1465–1495.

Inden, Ronald (2000): *Imagining India.* Bloomington, Ind.: Indiana University Press.

Jagannathan, Maithily (2005): *South Indian Hindu festivals and traditions.* New Delhi: Abhinav Publications.

Limacher, Katharina (2018): *doing mandir, doing kōvil. Eine empirische Rekonstruktion hinduistischer Tempelpraktiken in der Schweiz und in Österreich.* Unveröffentlichte Dissertationsschrift. Universität Luzern, Luzern. Religionswissenschaftliches Seminar.

Limacher, Katharina; Rückamp, Veronika (2016): "'Entrance Free – we are Looking Forward to your Visit!': Public Events as Strategies of Legitimisation in Immigrant Religious Organisations." In: *Journal of Religion in Europe* 9 (4), pp. 369–401. https://doi.org/10.1163/18748929-00904004.

Lüthi, Damaris (2003): "Heimatliche Konventionen im Exil bewahren: Hinduistische und christliche Religiosität tamilischer Flüchtlinge in Bern." In: Martin Baumann, Brigitte Luchesi, Annette Wilke (Eds.): *Tempel und Tamilen in zweiter Heimat. Hindus aus Sri Lanka im deutschsprachigen und skandinavischen Raum.* Würzburg: Ergon-Verl (Religion in der Gesellschaft, Bd. 15), pp. 295–322.

Malinar, Angelika (2009): *Hinduismus. Studium Religionen.* Göttingen: Vandenhoeck & Ruprecht.

Marla, Sandhya (2013): "Diaspora-Hinduismus 2.0: Christlich-hinduistische Kontaktmomente bei jungen Tamilen in Deutschland." In: Alexander-Kenneth Nagel (Ed.): *Diesseits der Parallelgesellschaft. Religiöse Migrantengemeinden als soziale Netzwerke.* Bielefeld: Transcript, pp. 175–205.

Marla-Küsters, Sandhya (2015): *Diaspora-Religiosität im Generationenverlauf.* Würzburg: Eron Verlag (Religion in der Gesellschaft, Band 38).

Moret, Joëlle; Efionayi, Denise; Stants, Fabienne (2007): *Die srilankische Diaspora in der Schweiz.* Edited by Bundesamts für Migration BFM. Redaktion und Realisation: Schweizerisches Forum für Migrations- und. Bern.

Müller, Monika (2013): *Migration und Religion. Junge hinduistische und muslimische Männer in der Schweiz.* Wiesbaden: Springer VS (Research).

Potz, Richard (2007): "14 Islam, Migration und Integration." In: Heinz Fassmann (Ed.): *2. Österreichischer Migrations- und Integrationsbericht. Rechtliche Rahmenbedingungen, demographische Entwicklungen, sozioökonomische Strukturen.* Klagenfurt/Celovec: Drava Verlag, pp. 337–351.

Reckwitz, Andreas (2002): "Toward a Theory of Social Practices." In *European Journal of Social Theory* 5 (2), pp. 243–263. https://doi.org/10.1177/13684310222225432.

Somalingam, Thusinta (2017): *Doing Diaspora. Ethnonationale Homogenisierung im transnationalen Bildungsraum der Tamil Diaspora.* Wiesbaden: Springer VS.

Strauss, Anselm L.; Corbin, Juliet M. (1996): *Grounded theory: Grundlagen qualitativer Sozialforschung.* Weinheim: Beltz Psychologie Verlags Union.

Suthren Hirst, Jacqueline (2011): "Transmission of Knowledge." In: Knut A. Jacobsen (Ed.): *Brill's encyclopedia of Hinduism.* Leiden, Boston: Brill (Volume III), pp. 194–202.

Verter, Bradford (2003): "Spiritual Capital. Theorizing Religion with Bourdieu against Bourdieu." In *Sociological Theory* 21 (2), pp. 150–174. https://doi.org/10.1177/1749975515615623.

Andreas Tunger-Zanetti / Silvia Martens / Jürgen Endres

Der Tradition verbunden und doch selbständig. Muslimische Jugendliche und junge Erwachsene in der Schweiz auf der Suche nach religiöser Orientierung*

Abstract
Committed to Tradition and Yet Independent
In this book chapter, we scrutinize the relation of young Muslims in Switzerland towards Islamic authority. We draw on our empirical research in which we asked which religious authorities are meaningful to this age group (15–30 years) who have spent all or most of their life in Switzerland, how they make use of those authorities and to what extent this influences their ways to position themselves within and towards Swiss society. Addressing one of the guiding questions of this book, we rely on the narrations of the Muslim youths themselves to compare the young generation with that of their parents.
An important result of our study is that there is a certain ambivalence in the relationship between the young generation and the generation of their parents. On the one hand, parents and other older persons are among what we call ‚near authorities'. As such, they are individuals mostly without a higher formal religious formation but trustworthy on a personal basis and equipped with some religious knowledge and personal experience of living Islam in a strongly-secular environment. On the other hand, young Muslims perceive their parents' generation as shaped by their own upbringing in a country of the Western Balkans, Turkey or elsewhere. Therefore, most of the young refuse to imitate what they call the ‚cultural Islam' of their parents and try to find their own way. Advice on religious practice by the older generation as well as by other ‚authorities' is heard and sometimes actively sought for by the young. Yet, the young generation clearly reserves itself the ultimate autonomous decision based on their own assessment as to what fits their individual situation.
On a conceptual level, our research connects to the debate about authority in Islam. So far, empirical research among Muslims in Western Europe has highlighted the trends of individualization, pluralization and fragmentation, but has not yet explained how such trends relate to the Islamic tradition. Our study confirms that these three phenomena are indeed strong in Switzerland. At the same time, our findings suggest that the Islamic tradition is not in conflict with these trends, and that young Muslims in Switzerland can still connect to it.

* Die Autorin und die Autoren danken Prof. Rüdiger Lohlker und Prof. Martin Baumann für ihre hilfreichen Kommentare zu einer vorläufigen Version dieses Beitrages.

Einleitung

Forschung zu Immigrantinnen und Immigranten sowie ihren Nachkommen hat in der Schweiz wie in anderen Ländern Westeuropas in den letzten Jahren zunehmend den Faktor Religion in den Blick genommen. Die Religionswissenschaft schließt dazu bei sozialwissenschaftlichen Debatten und Methoden an; sie fragt sowohl nach den Merkmalen und dem Wandel von religiösen Vorstellungen und Praktiken unter Zugewanderten wie auch nach dem Wandel der einheimischen Religionslandschaft insgesamt und der Weise, wie die gesellschaftlichen Akteure diesen Wandel wahrnehmen und dabei den Platz von Religion in der Gesellschaft neu verhandeln. Sie hat dabei gelernt, wie stark Befunde vom Kontext geprägt sind und demnach variieren können.

Während die Forschung in anderen westlichen Ländern längst auch die Religiosität von Kindern und Enkeln der Eingewanderten in den Blick genommen hat, sind Untersuchungen hierzu in der Schweiz noch rar (Morgenthaler et al. 2011, Schlieter et al. 2014). Uns interessieren besonders muslimische Jugendliche und junge Erwachsene, die ihr Leben ganz oder größtenteils in der Schweiz verbracht haben. In dem Forschungsprojekt, aus dem wir hier berichten, wollten wir wissen, welche religiösen ‚Autoritäten' für diese Generation bedeutsam sind und was dies für ihre Positionierung in der Gesellschaft bedeutet. Im Folgenden geht es spezieller um die Frage: Wie orientieren sich junge Musliminnen und Muslime in der Schweiz heute bezüglich Religion und wie positionieren sie sich dabei im Verhältnis zu ihren Eltern? Dabei geht es uns primär nicht darum, Generationeneffekte zu beschreiben oder ‚Generationen' zu definieren und zu typisieren, sondern um die subjektiven Erfahrungen und Einschätzungen der Interviewpartnerinnen und -partner.

Zunächst sei dazu der gesellschaftliche wie der wissenschaftliche Kontext unserer Forschung umrissen und der konzeptionelle Rahmen des vorliegenden Beitrags abgesteckt. Sodann schildern wir empirische Befunde mit Bezug zur Fragestellung und erörtern in einem weiteren Kapitel mögliche Erklärungen. Der Beitrag ordnet die empirischen Befunde in den Begriffen der Forschungsdebatte um die allgemein angenommenen Trends der Individualisierung sowie der Pluralisierung und Fragmentierung von Autorität. Dabei zeigt sich, dass die genannten Trends im konkreten Forschungsfeld feststellbar sind, jedoch nicht zur Auflösung islamischer Tradition führen.

Forschungskontext

Unsere Frage, wie sich junge Musliminnen und Muslime in der Schweiz heute bezüglich Religion orientieren, ergab sich aus dem Vorgängerprojekt zu muslimischen Jugendgruppen: 2011–2013 hatte unser Team erforscht, welche Einstellungen bezüglich Religion und Gesellschaft in muslimischen Jugendgruppen in der Altersstufe nach dem traditionellen Koranunterricht der Moscheen zu finden sind und inwieweit solche Gruppen zur Integration ihrer Mitglieder in die Schweizer Gesellschaft beitragen oder diese behindern. Unumstritten ist, dass nur eine Minderheit derjenigen jungen Menschen, die sich als Muslime verstehen, regelmäßig in Gruppenaktivitäten unter religiösen Vorzeichen engagiert ist. Andere nehmen aber selektiv zumindest ab und zu teil, wenn schon nicht am Vortrag über islamische Geschichte, so doch etwa an einem Hobbyfußballturnier oder an einem Grillfest. Diese vielfältigen Aktivitäten der Jugendgruppen, inner- und außerhalb der Moscheen, halten die Kernmitglieder ebenso wenig wie die gelegentlichen Teilnehmerinnen und Teilnehmer davon ab, mit beiden Beinen in der Schweizer Gesellschaft zu stehen. Der Forschungsbericht *Jung, muslimisch, schweizerisch* zeigt dies differenziert auf (Endres et al. 2013).

Zunehmend interessierte uns in der Folge die Frage, an welchen ‚Autoritäten' sich die jungen Menschen orientieren. Dass der typische Imam oder Hoca bei ihnen keineswegs ein Monopol innehat, hatte uns der bisherige Feldkontakt deutlich gezeigt, auch wenn öffentliche Debatten um ‚Hassprediger' und ‚Imam-Ausbildung' ihm genau ein solches Monopol zuschreiben. Das Gleiche gilt für öffentlich bekannte Persönlichkeiten wie etwa einen Tariq Ramadan, selbst wenn sie bisweilen Säle füllen können. Was also gab es sonst noch an ‚Autoritäten'? Was macht diese überhaupt erst zu ‚Autoritäten'? Vor allem aber: Wie gingen die jungen Menschen bei ihrer Suche vor und was machten sie aus den verfügbaren Angeboten für sich und im Blick auf ihren Platz in der Gesellschaft?

Mit diesen Fragen setzten wir ab 2014, gefördert von der Stiftung Mercator Schweiz und wiederum unter der Projektleitung von Martin Baumann, unsere Forschung fort. Mit dem Projekttitel „Imame, Rapper, Cybermuftis" versuchten wir bereits anzudeuten, dass wir mit einem breiten Spektrum an ‚Autoritäten' rechneten. Auch der Gehalt des Begriffs ‚Autorität' verlangte für unseren Kontext noch nach Präzisierung.

Wie beim Vorgängerprojekt folgten wir einem qualitativen Forschungsdesign. In 61 stark narrativen, von einem Leitfaden lose strukturierten Einzelinterviews versuchten wir unsere Gesprächspartnerinnen und -partner zum Erzählen zu bringen. Das Altersspektrum reichte von 15 bis 30 Jahre. Die Interviews waren umso ergiebiger, je älter und je religiös aktiver die Interviewten waren. Wir führen dies darauf zurück, dass junge Musliminnen und Muslime im Alter von 15 oder 16 Jahren, selbst wenn sie sich regelmäßig in der Moschee aufhalten, noch keine Übung darin haben, ihre beginnende eigenständige religiöse Entwicklung zu reflektieren und gegenüber Dritten zu erläutern. Ebenso haben religiös nur schwach oder selektiv aktive Personen, auch wenn sie schon älter sind, nicht unbedingt viele Bezugspunkte in der religiösen Tradition, die sie mit ihrer eigenen Biografie verknüpfen können. Dennoch interviewten wir bewusst auch solche auf den ersten Blick ‚unergiebigen' Personen.

Unvermeidlich sind in unserer Auswahl jedoch die religiös Aktiven zahlreicher, als es ihrem Anteil an der gesamten muslimischen Bevölkerung entspricht. Dies ist vertretbar, weil es sich um eine qualitative Studie handelte, die das Feld erst einmal explorativ entdecken, beschreiben und verstehen wollte. Um das Feld nicht künstlich auf die religiös Aktiven zu reduzieren, achteten wir darauf, auch Interviewpartnerinnen und -partner zu gewinnen, von denen wir absehen konnten, dass religiöses Handeln und Selbstverständnis in ihrem Alltag keine große Rolle spielen. Weiter achteten wir bei der Auswahl darauf, der Vielfalt der ethnischen Herkunft der Schweizer Musliminnen und Muslime wenigstens annähernd ebenso gerecht zu werden wie weiteren Merkmalen (Alter, Geschlecht, Bildungsgrad, religiöse Traditionslinie, Wohnregion; genauer führt dies der Forschungsbericht *Hallo, es geht um meine Religion* aus: Baumann / et al. 2017, S. 8f.).

Gravierender als das Übergewicht der religiös Aktiven erscheint demgegenüber das unvermeidliche *framing* des gesamten Projekts. Im Projekttitel, in der Ausbildung der Forschenden, ihrer institutionellen Anbindung und den angekündigten Themenfeldern des Interviews – überall tauchte der Bezug zu Religion oder Islam auf. Auch unabhängig von dieser Forschung sieht sich ein junger Mensch aus einer muslimischen Familie in Schule, Medien und manchmal auch Freizeit ohne eigenes Zutun mit seinem Muslimsein konfrontiert. So konnte es nicht ausbleiben, dass Interviewpartnerinnen und -partner früher als vom Leitfaden vorgesehen von sich aus das Thema Religion ansprachen. In manchen Fällen mögen sie gehofft haben, damit eine Erwartung auf unserer Seite zu erfüllen. In anderen drückten sie jedoch am Ende des Gesprächs spontan aus, wie zufrieden sie waren, über ihre Religion endlich einmal zu jemandem sprechen zu können, der sich für ihre Sicht wirklich interessierte.

Das starke *framing* auf Religion war es auch, das fast alle Interviewten beim Punkt ‚Spielt Religion für Sie persönlich eine Rolle?' bekunden ließ, Religion sei für sie wichtig. Wenn jedoch zugleich die ansonsten geschilderten Umstände nur eine sehr sporadische religiöse Aktivität bezeugen, wirft dies Fragen auf. Verschiedene Erklärungen sind denkbar: soziale Erwünschtheit, persönliches Wunschdenken, divergierende Empfindungen von ‚Wichtigkeit'. In jedem Fall mahnt es zur Vorsicht dabei, analoge Antworten in anderen Studien zum Nennwert zu nehmen und womöglich in quantitativen Vergleichen auf einen markant höheren Anteil hochreligiöser Personen unter Muslimen als unter Angehörigen anderer Traditionen zu schließen.

Was hingegen ebenfalls in unseren Interviews ungefragt immer wieder hereindrang, war die öffentliche Islam-Debatte, wie im Kapitel über unsere Befunde deutlich werden wird. Zwar schildern unsere Befragten ganz unterschiedliche Strategien im Umgang mit dieser Debatte. Sie ist jedoch allgegenwärtig. Ein junger Mensch mit muslimischem Hintergrund in der Schweiz, unabhängig davon, ob und wie er sich als muslimisch versteht, kann ihr unmöglich entgehen. Er sieht sich zumindest sporadisch gezwungen, das eigene Muslimsein zu erläutern.

Trotz der geschilderten Einschränkungen ergaben die Interviews reichhaltiges Material, das wir in der Folge codierten und analysierten und dem vorliegenden Beitrag zugrunde legen. Im Folgenden sehen wir die Dinge also gleichsam durch die Brille der jungen Interviewten, auch dann, wenn es um die Generation ihrer Eltern geht; wir verzichten im vorliegenden Beitrag darauf, kritisch und anhand anderer Untersuchungen zu fragen, in welchen Punkten die Sicht unserer Interviewpartnerinnen und -partner allenfalls Wichtiges weglässt oder unzulässig deutet. Es geht uns darum, welche Rolle die junge Generation der älteren zuschreibt und wo sie in ihrer Darstellung beide Generationen innerhalb der Gesellschaft platziert.

In der ursprünglichen Abfolge unseres Interviewleitfadens sollte die Rolle der Elterngeneration erst dort ins Spiel kommen, wo es darum ging, die Entwicklung des eigenen Verhältnisses zur Religion darzustellen und Personen zu benennen, die dabei eine Rolle gespielt haben. Bewusst hatten wir im ersten Gesprächsteil ganz allgemein um einen Abriss der wichtigen Etappen der Biographie gebeten, dabei auch nach den für das eigene Leben wichtigen Personen gefragt und Religion explizit auf einen späteren Teil des Gesprächs verschoben. Wie oben angedeutet, brachten die Interviewpartnerinnen und -partner Religion jedoch oft von sich aus schon im allgemein biographischen Teil zur Sprache und dann sehr oft im Zusammenhang mit den Eltern und der erweiterten Verwandtschaft.

Bevor wir die Aussagen der Interviewpartnerinnen und -partner schildern, gilt es aber im folgenden Abschnitt den Rahmen zu erläutern, den wir für die Analyse des Materials gewählt haben.

Konzeptioneller Rahmen: Autoritäten und Vergleichsebenen

Wie offen auch immer wir für Überraschungen in der Feldforschung und bei der Analyse des Materials sein wollen, wir benötigen einen zumindest vorläufigen Begriff für das, wonach wir Ausschau halten. Wie vorläufig und schwer zu fassen in unserem Fall der Begriff ‚Autorität' ist, war uns aufgrund unserer Beobachtungen in muslimischen Jugendgruppen während des Vorgängerprojekts von Anfang an bewusst. Zum andern hatte schon der grundlegende Forschungsüberblick von Frank Peter (2006) die Ausgangslage ähnlicher Forschung mit ihren unterschiedlichen Ansätzen konzeptionell geordnet.

Demnach ist sich die Forschung weitgehend einig darin, dass das Feld des Islams im Westen gekennzeichnet ist von mehreren großen Trends: Traditionelle Autoritäten, allen voran die Imame, verlieren an Gewicht und Einfluss in dem Maß, wie neue Modelle auftreten, insbesondere reisende oder via Internet wirkende Prediger und öffentliche Intellektuelle. Laut Peter dominierte in den Studien bis dahin eine akteurzentrierte Perspektive, die religiöse Autorität überdies meist mit *leadership* gleichsetze; Peter fragt, ob nicht „a more resolutely supra-individual perspective" zusätzliche Einsichten verspreche (Peter 2006, S. 111). So regt er etwa an zu fragen, ob und wie die Organisation und die Strukturen bestimmter Gemeinschaften mit ihrer religiösen Lehre zusammenhängen oder wie sich innermuslimische Beziehungen auf die Ausgestaltung von Autoritätsstrukturen auswirken (ebd., S. 112). Zudem bedürfe das Schlagwort von der Individualisierung weiterer Differenzierung, denn zumindest in Olivier Roys Terminologie „[it] refers primarily and almost exclusively to a democratization of the religious sphere and not to any significant changes in dogma" (ebd., S. 108).[1]

Peter identifiziert in seinem Forschungsüberblick bereits einen alternativen Ansatz: Schirin Amir-Moazami und Armando Salvatore fassen das Problem in den Begriffen der diskursiven Tradition nach Talal Asad und deren Transformation durch *‚internal interventions'*. Sie hätten jedoch noch nicht ausgearbeitet, über welche konkreten Strukturen und Akteure die islamische Tradition weitergegeben werde (ebd., S. 109–110).[2]

Bezogen auf das Forschungsfeld der jungen Musliminnen und Muslime in der Schweiz müssen wir unsere Befunde also zunächst in Bezug setzen zu den soeben genannten Stichwörtern: Inwiefern finden wir Individualisierung? Beobachten

1 Damit ist keineswegs ausgeschlossen, ja, es ist gar zu erwarten, dass sich islamische Lehre im Westen dennoch in kleinen Schritten verändert, indem die Akteure Akzente der überkommenen Gewissheiten verschieben, womöglich ohne sich dessen bewusst zu sein.

2 Strukturen und Akteure, die sich bemühen, ‚den Islam' kohärent zu fassen und zu tradieren, sind durchaus von der Forschung schon dargestellt und das Problem der Autorität erkannt worden, für den nahöstlichen und weltweiten Islam etwa von Schulze (1990), Krämer und Schmidtke (2006), Ahmed (2016), für den Islam in Westeuropa z. B. von Caeiro (2010). Selten hat die Forschung jedoch gefragt, was die Empfänger für sich daraus machen. Petra Bleisch hat dies anhand von Konvertitinnen in der Schweiz unternommen und ein „Modell der Aneignung und Produktion islamischer Normen und normativer Ordnungen" (Bleisch Bouzar 2016, S. 220) vorgeschlagen. Das Modell erscheint insgesamt geeignet, um die Interaktionen zwischen der einzelnen Frau und ihrem muslimischen Umfeld zu fassen. Das Modell blendet aber das Generationenverhältnis aus, um das es uns hier geht, da es im Blick auf Konvertitinnen konzipiert ist.

auch wir die Pluralisierung des Angebots und die Fragmentierung religiöser Autorität? Unter „Pluralisierung religiöser Autorität“ verstehen wir hierbei in Übereinstimmung mit Krämer die Erweiterung sowohl des Angebots als auch der Zugangsmöglichkeiten zu „alternativen Islamauffassungen, konkurrierenden Autoritäten und eigenständigen Möglichkeiten der Information und Meinungsbildung“ (Krämer 2011, S. 137). Im Unterschied dazu beziehen wir „Fragmentierung religiöser Autorität“ auf den Umstand, dass religiösen Autoritäten nur für spezifische Teilbereiche Autorität zugesprochen wird, für andere Bereiche wiederum andere religiöse Autoritäten als relevant erachtet werden (so etwa Bleisch Bouzar 2016, S. 107).[3] Unter „Individualisierung“ wiederum verstehen wir den Vorgang, dass Individuen ihr Verhalten, ihre Wahl und ihre Entscheidungen zunehmend autonom gestalten. Dabei spielen Traditionen und soziale Normen eine abnehmende Rolle, nicht nur, aber gerade auch in religiösen Fragen. Wir gehen im Übrigen nicht davon aus, dass ‚die Vergangenheit‘ oder der Islam in seiner Geschichte durch absolute Homogenität, Uneingeschränktheit und Abhängigkeit von religiöser Autorität gekennzeichnet war. Ganz im Gegenteil: Pluralität der (Gelehrten-)Meinungen, Spezialistentum und eigenes Urteil waren stets vorhanden, und islamische Traditionen selber entwickelten gegenüber der Pluralität der Stimmen in religiösen Belangen früh einen pragmatischen, teils gar wertschätzenden Umgang.[4] Allerdings – und dies gilt es zu betonen – haben es junge Musliminnen und Muslime heute im Westen mit ganz anderen Größenordnungen der Angebotsauswahl zu tun: In Nachbarschaft, Volksschule, Berufswelt und durch die Medien kommen sie mit wesentlich mehr und wesentlich unterschiedlicheren Lebenswelten und -entwürfen in Kontakt als frühere Generationen. Dies wirkt sich unweigerlich auch auf den Bereich der Religion aus (Joas 2012, Charim 2018, v. a. Kap. 3), wie – das bleibt zunächst unübersichtlich.

Die soeben gestellten Fragen nach dem Vorkommen und der Art von Individualisierung, Pluralisierung und Fragmentierung lassen sich mit unseren empirisch erhobenen Daten eindeutig und differenziert beantworten (s. Abschnitt „Empirische Befunde“).

Die Resultate gilt es anschließend zu erklären, indem sie kontextualisiert und in Vergleich zu Resultaten anderer Forschung gesetzt werden. Von Interesse ist dabei ein vergleichender Blick auf die zweite Generation anderer Religionsgemeinschaften, der in den Studien über Muslime im Westen oft unterbleibt. Als

3 Einzelne andere Autoren wie etwa Zaman 2009 bezeichnen mit „fragmentation of religious authority“ die Tatsache, dass unterschiedliche Segmente der muslimischen Öffentlichkeit sich an unterschiedlichen Autoritäten orientieren.

4 Prägnantester Ausdruck dafür ist das angebliche Prophetenwort „Die Meinungsunterschiede meiner Gemeinde [oder „unter meinen Gefährten“] sind eine Gnade“, der allerdings als fingiert gilt.

einer von wenigen hat etwa Eriksen (2015) am Beispiel Norwegens gezeigt, dass Muslime im Bereich der Religion im Wesentlichen denselben allgemeinen Entwicklungen unterworfen sind wie Nicht-Muslime mit Migrationshintergrund. Beim Übergang von der ersten zur zweiten Generation verschiebt sich demnach der Begriff von Personalität *(personhood)* deutlich, „while the ‚cultural stuff' may be variously subcontinental [im Falle eines Paares mit pakistanischem Hintergrund], Norwegian, mixed, or something else“ (2015, S. 15).

Bezieht sich dies auf die Individualebene, so haben mit Blick auf die Meso-Ebene die US-amerikanischen Forscher Fred Kniss und Paul D. Numrich ein analytisch aufschlussreiches Vergleichsraster entwickelt. Sie haben im Großraum Chicago am Vergleich von 16 religiösen Gemeinschaften herausgearbeitet, wie unterschiedlich stark diese das Kollektiv und das Individuum gewichten. Sie unterscheiden dabei die Dimension des Ortes von Autorität *(locus of authority)* vom sinnstiftenden Ziel *(moral project)* und nehmen sie als Achsen eines Koordinatensystems, der *Moral Order Map* (s. Grafik 1).

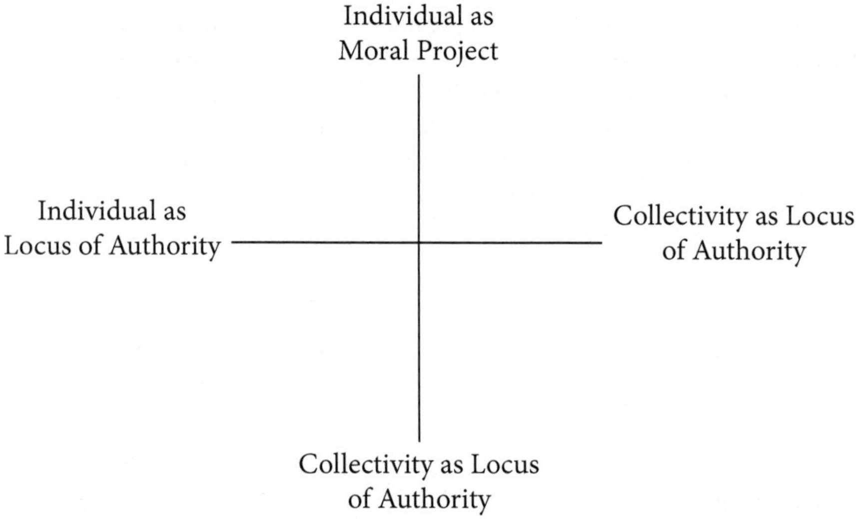

Grafik 1: Moral Order Map, vereinfacht nach Kniss/Numrich (2007, S. 39)

Kniss und Numrich entwickeln zwar selber Kriterien, die begründen, warum sie eine Gemeinschaft innerhalb eines bestimmten Quadranten und dort näher oder weiter entfernt vom Achsenschnittpunkt lokalisieren. Sie verstehen die *Moral Order Map* jedoch nicht als exaktes Messinstrument, sondern als heuristisches Mittel (Kniss / Numrich 2007, S. 38–47).

Das Konzept von Kniss und Numrich hat Martin Baumann (2017) aufgegriffen und erweitert, indem er das Schema sowohl auf religiöse Gruppen und Organisationen als auch annäherungsweise auf Personen der ersten und zweiten

Generation der religiösen Traditionen bezogen hat. Unter anderem hat er dafür auch die Daten des mit uns durchgeführten Projekts verwendet.

Ähnlich wie Baumann und Eriksen suchen auch wir im vorliegenden Beitrag einerseits nach Gründen, *warum* die zweite Generation offensichtlich den Ort der Autorität und womöglich noch andere Parameter markant in die Richtung des Individuums verschiebt. Noch vorgelagert ist anderseits im Sinn unseres Forschungsdesigns die Frage, *wie* die Individuen mit Autorität(en) umgehen. Mit diesem Fokus verbinden wir die von Peter skizzierten Problembereiche und können uns eine Antwort erhoffen auf die Frage, über welche Mechanismen die Individualisierung von Religiosität und die Pluralisierung und Fragmentierung von Autorität zusammenhängen.

Im Projekt haben wir zunächst darauf verzichtet, eine Definition von Autorität, etwa im Sinne Max Webers, zugrunde zu legen, die den Blick schon eingeengt hätte. Übernommen haben wir aus früheren Definitionsversuchen lediglich die Einsicht, dass Autorität in keinem Fall ohne eine Form der Zuschreibung auskommt (so etwa bei Paris 2005, S. 77). Unter den Bedingungen einer offenen, demokratischen Gesellschaft, in der die Religionsfreiheit im Wesentlichen gegeben ist, erscheint es uns plausibel, die Situation rund um das Zuschreiben von Autorität im Vokabular des Marktes auszudrücken: Wir haben uns zunächst nicht die ‚Anbieter' von Autorität bzw. Religion angesehen, also etwa Prediger oder Musiker, sondern die ‚Kunden' und ihre Art der ‚Nachfrage', demnach muslimische Jugendliche und junge Erwachsene.[5] Sie sehen sich einer großen Auswahl an ‚Angeboten' gegenüber, die sich zwar alle auf die islamische Tradition beziehen, die dabei aber kaum unterschiedlicher sein könnten. So führt forschungspraktisch der Arbeitsbegriff des ‚Orientierungsangebots' deutlich weiter als derjenige der ‚Autorität', deren Überzeugungs- und Durchsetzungskraft unter den Bedingungen der modernen westlichen Gesellschaft von Beginn an prekär erscheint. Selbst beim Begriff des ‚Angebots' ist uns weniger der konkrete Inhalt wichtig, als vielmehr dessen allgemeiner Charakter.

Erst nach der Analyse des Materials gelangten wir zu einem nunmehr sehr weichen Autoritätsbegriff. ‚Autorität' ist demnach im vorliegenden Kontext jede Person, Organisation oder Instanz, deren Position vom Interviewpartner ernsthaft in Betracht gezogen wird bei der Suche nach für ihn bedeutsamen Auskünften, Erklärungen oder Handlungsempfehlungen. Mit ‚Instanz' sind dabei abstrakte Konzepte oder textliche Quellen gemeint, die die Interviewpartnerinnen und -partner uns bisweilen als bedeutsam nannten, wie z. B. Gott, der Koran und der Prophet.

5 Nach den Interviews mit den Jugendlichen und jungen Erwachsenen führten wir auch 18 Interviews mit ‚Autoritäten' unterschiedlichen Typs. Dieses Material bleibt für den vorliegenden Beitrag ausser Betracht.

Die gesamte Definition mag extrem weit erscheinen, so dass sie beinahe Beliebiges umfassen könnte. Nimmt man die ‚Kundenperspektive' ernst, ist dies aber die einzige Möglichkeit, um den Befunden, wie wir sie im Folgenden schildern, gerecht zu werden. Stärker als die meisten Definitionen von Autorität, nimmt sie den individuellen Umgang mit Orientierungsangeboten in den Blick. Da das Gesamtangebot dank der heutigen Technik zumindest theoretisch unendlich groß ist, wird von besonderem Interesse sein, mit welchem Vorgehen und nach welchen Kriterien die Jugendlichen und jungen Erwachsenen ihre Auswahl treffen und was sie mit dieser Auswahl anfangen, sprich, welche Konsequenzen diese hat.

Empirische Befunde: Auslöser, Angebote und der Umgang damit

Religiöse Ratgebung – sowohl in einer institutionalisierten, offiziellen als auch in einer informellen, privaten Form – ist in der islamischen Tradition fest verankert (Motzki 1994). In mehrheitlich muslimischen Gesellschaften hat besonders die religionsrechtliche Ratgebung durch Gelehrte in Form von Fatwas („Auskünften", Rechtsgutachten) seit der Frühzeit des Islams eine wichtige Rolle gespielt. Dabei hat nur schon das Fatwa-Wesen in den verschiedenen Epochen, Gesellschaften und politischen Systemen der vormodernen Zeit höchst unterschiedliche Formen angenommen (Powers 2017) und wandelte sich ab dem 19. Jahrhundert nochmals in mehreren Hinsichten grundlegend (Messick 2017). Wie aber funktioniert das religiöse Rat-Suchen und Rat-Geben in der muslimischen Gemeinschaft in der Schweiz, wo traditionelle islamische Autoritäten keine staatlich legitimierte Funktion ausüben oder gar nicht zur Verfügung stehen? Welche Bedeutung haben traditionelle Autoritäten im Vergleich zu neuen Autoritäten wie z. B. Internet-Predigern für junge Musliminnen und Muslime?

Die öffentliche Islam-Debatte thematisiert vor allem Imame und einige stark in sozialen Medien (Blogs und Foren, Video-Portalen, sozialen Netzwerken u. a.) präsente Prediger und mutmasst über ihre Rolle bei der ‚Radikalisierung' muslimischer Jugendlicher. Die Angebote zur religiösen Orientierung und Ratgebung sind in der Schweiz heute jedoch wesentlich vielfältiger, sowohl im Hinblick auf ihre theologische und politische Verortung als auch auf die von ihnen genutzten Ausdrucksformen und Medien: Es finden sich stärker traditionell-konservative ebenso wie eher liberale und radikal innovative Positionen, Anbieter mit religiöser und weltlicher Expertise in unterschiedlicher Mischung. Teilweise begegnen sie jungen Musliminnen und Muslimen direkt (z. B. in der Moschee, bei Vorträgen, Seminaren, spezifischen Events), teils wirken sie aber über klassische Medien (Buch, TV) und in besonderem Maße gegenwärtig über soziale Medien. Welche dieser Quellen nutzen muslimische Jugendliche und junge Erwachsene in der Schweiz nun und wie tun sie dies? Wir nähern uns der Antwort, wenn wir uns zunächst den Ausgangssituationen für die Suche nach solchen Quellen zuwenden.

Auf dem Weg zur Identitätsfindung setzen sich Jugendliche und junge Erwachsene allgemein alterstypisch neben vielen anderen Themenfeldern auch mit Religion auseinander. Die Situation junger Musliminnen und Muslime ist allerdings im Vergleich zu ihren nicht-muslimischen Altersgenossen besonders: Die öffentliche Islam-Debatte nötigt sie, sich zu dem in den Medien präsentierten Islambild zu positionieren. Etliche möchten sich in der Folge unabhängig von den Publikumsmedien eigenes Wissen über den Islam aneignen. Die Suche nach Informationen und Rat dient dabei einerseits der Bestimmung der eigenen, wenn auch vorläufigen Position. Anderseits unterstellt ihnen ihre nicht-muslimische Umgebung oft schlicht und einfach aufgrund ihrer Religionszugehörigkeit eine Expertise in Sachen Islam, die sie oft zunächst einmal nicht haben. So erwarten etwa bisweilen Lehrpersonen, Arbeitskollegen oder Zufallsbekannte von ihnen nicht nur eine persönliche Position zu einer bestimmten Frage, sondern Auskunft darüber, wie die Position ‚des Islams' dazu ist. Obwohl sich die Beschäftigung mit dem Islam somit regelrecht aufdrängt, gehen die in unserer Studie befragten jungen Frauen und Männer bei ihrer Suche und beim Umgang mit den gefundenen Informationen schließlich stark von ihren eigenen Bedürfnissen aus. Wie bei Nicht-Muslimen gehören im Übrigen auch biographische Ereignisse (Tod eines nahestehenden Menschen, eindrückliche Begegnungen) oder eine allgemeine Sinnsuche zu den Auslösern einer Auseinandersetzung mit dem Islam.

Spektrum islamischer Autoritäten

So vielfältig die Auslöser und Motive für das Fragen, so verschieden sind auch die Angebote, die junge Musliminnen und Muslime in der Schweiz dafür nutzen. Teils geht es ihnen darum, sich Sachwissen über den Islam anzueignen. Teils suchen sie aber auch nach religiöser Orientierung, d. h. nach islamischer Ratgebung und Ermutigung, um persönliche Entscheidungen ggf. ‚islamgerecht' abzustützen oder schlicht, um sich als Teil einer muslimischen Gemeinschaft sicherer und weniger marginalisiert zu fühlen. Die vielen in den Interviews genannten religiösen Autoritätspersonen und anderen Autoritätsquellen lassen sich den vier in Tabelle 1 beschriebenen Kategorien „Person", „personale Instanz", „Organisation" und „abstrakte Instanz" zuordnen.

Tabelle 1: Typen von Autorität

Form	Merkmale	Beispiele
Person	Einzelperson, als Individuum gefragt oder aufgesucht	Elternteil, guter Freund, Vertrauensperson in der Moschee oder im muslimischen Bekanntenkreis
Personale Instanz	Person mit Bedeutung qua Amt, Funktion oder innermuslimisches Ansehen	Imam, Frau des Imams, Prediger, Privatlehrer, Religionslehrer, Intellektuelle, spiritueller Führer, Bloggerin
Organisation	formell oder informell verfasster dauerhafter Personenverband, u. U. mit eigenem Informations- und Beratungsangebot und mit wechselnden Bezugspersonen	Diyanet, Islamologisches Institut, Schweizerische Islamische Gemeinschaft, Ahl al Bayt, Islamischer Zentralrat Schweiz
Abstrakte Instanz	religiöses Kernkonzept, u. U. mit Textkorpus identisch oder verbunden (vermittelt durch personale Autoritäten)	Gott, Koran, *as-salaf aṣ-ṣāliḥ*, Sunna, *ʿulamāʾ*, Prophet Muhammad, Klassikertexte

Die Mehrheit unserer Interviewpartnerinnen und -partner nutzt dabei jeweils mehrere religiöse Autoritäten gleichzeitig – oder verschiedene je nach Frage und Bedürfnis. Einzelne hingegen konsultieren gezielt Material einer bestimmten Person oder Organisation, der sie vertrauen. Rund jede zehnte namentlich genannte personale Instanz ist eine Frau.

Als unmittelbares Wort Gottes genießt der Koran in der islamischen Glaubenslehre einen hohen Stellenwert. So überraschte es uns nicht, dass er in rund der Hälfte der Interviews prominent als Autoritätsquelle genannt wurde. Obwohl der liturgische Gebrauch des Korans (Koranrezitation auf Arabisch) im Alltag klar im Vordergrund steht, greifen junge Musliminnen und Muslime immer wieder auf Koranübersetzungen zurück. Bei der Suche nach Informationen zum Islam und als Grundlage für persönliche religiöse Entscheidungen schlagen einige von ihnen demnach zunächst einmal den Koran auf und lesen relevante Passagen nach. Während ein Teil den Text nach eigenem Ermessen selbst deutet, betonen andere, dass sie sich bei der Textdeutung an Personen orientieren, denen sie aufgrund ihres vertieften Wissens über den Islam in religiösen Fragen Autorität zuschreiben. Denn der Korantext sei sprachlich schwer zu verstehen und müsse in die heutige Zeit übersetzt werden, um daraus wichtige Handlungsempfehlungen ableiten zu können.

Es können offizielle und öffentlich sichtbare Personen sein, deren Auslegungen des Korans und anderer klassischer islamischer Texte den Jugendlichen und jungen Erwachsenen Orientierung bieten. Zu diesen „personalen Instanzen“ gehört der lokale Imam und seine Frau ebenso wie die Religionslehrerin, deren Islamunterricht sich didaktisch zum Teil stark vom typischen Islamunterricht des Imams in der Moschee unterscheidet. Der klassische „Koranunterricht" in den Moscheen soll die Schülerinnen und Schüler im Wesentlichen befähigen, den arabischen Koran lesen bzw. rezitieren zu können und die religiösen Pflichten korrekt zu verrichten. Er vermittelt i. d. R. wenig vertiefte Sachkenntnis über den Islam, und weil er oft stark auf Sünde und Bestrafung fokussiert, trägt er wenig zu einer positiven Beziehung der Schülerinnen und Schüler zum Glauben bei. Ferida unterscheidet bei ihrer Suche Prediger in diesem Sinne wie folgt:

> Es gibt mehrere Arten von Predigern, aber ich teile sie immer in zwei Gruppen auf. Diejenigen, die nur sagen: „Von dem sollst du dich fernhalten, von dem [sc. auch]." Also immer nur mahnen, immer nur deine Sünden erwähnen und wie schlimm es ist und wie Sünden dein Herz verderben. […] Und dann gibt es eben noch die anderen […], die dann sagen: „Bereue." […] Gewisse Redner haben so diese Art, die dir eigentlich auch […] die Leichtigkeit des Islam zeigt, wie einfach es ist, es umzusetzen. (Ferida, w, 19)

Diese positive Haltung und die an der jugendlichen Lebenswelt anknüpfende Orientierung machen etwa das Seminarangebot des Sozialpädagogen und Theologen Mohammed Naved Johari[6] beliebt bei der jungen Generation. Für vertiefendes theologisches und religionsrechtliches Wissen mit Bezug zur Schweiz und in deutscher Sprache schätzen viele junge Frauen und Männer auch den seit Jahren immer wieder durchgeführten ‚Islamologie'-Kurs des gebürtigen Syrers Amir Zaidan.[7] Auch ein türkischer Diyanet-Imam kann die Jugend fesseln, wie Dominik Müller (2017) in der Studie eines Ausnahmefalls schön gezeigt hat.

Für die Jugendlichen und jungen Erwachsenen, die heute immer und überall online sind, ist die erste Adresse aber oft das Internet. Dort stoßen sie auf eine breite Auswahl an Informationsquellen. Sie nutzen Suchmaschinen wie Google, um erste schnelle Antworten auf ihre Fragen zu finden, lesen in islamischen Internetforen und finden auf Videoplattformen wie YouTube Videos von einer Vielzahl islamischer Prediger und Intellektueller zu den gesuchten Themen. Auf welchen Prediger die jungen Musliminnen und Muslime bei einer ersten Suche stoßen oder welchen Prediger sie dann ggf. gezielt immer wieder anhören, hängt zu einem Teil vom sprachlichen Zugang ab: Dass sehr viele unserer Interviewpartnerinnen und -partner bei ihrer Auseinandersetzung mit dem Islam zu-

6 Vgl. seine eigene Webseite www.monajo.de [17.12.2018].

7 Zaidan, geboren 1964, kam 1983 als Stipendiat nach Deutschland, engagierte sich religiös und interreligiös, belegte später islamische Studiengänge im Ausland, erteilte zunächst in Hessen, seit 2003 von Wien aus Islamkurse und publiziert ausgiebig. Für die in seinen Kursen am eigenen privaten Institut vermittelte Form islamischer Bildung in deutscher Sprache prägte er den Ausdruck ‚Islamologie' (vgl. Islamologisches Institut).

mindest irgendwann einmal Videos des salafistischen Predigers Pierre Vogel gehört haben, hängt stark damit zusammen, dass man bei der Suche nach deutschsprachigen Videos fast zwangsläufig auf sie stößt. Diejenigen Jugendlichen, die weitere Sprachen ausreichend gut verstehen, konsultieren auch eher noch Videos und Webseiten in ihrer Muttersprache bzw. der Sprache ihrer Eltern (z. B. die albanischen Prediger Ahmed Kalaja und Shefqet Krasniqi) oder auch auf Englisch und Französisch (z. B. Nouman Ali Khan, Tariq Ramadan[8] und Zakir Naik) und nutzen Material in verschiedenen Sprachen. Dabei geht es nicht in jedem Fall um die Vermittlung theologischen Wissens. Bloggerinnen wie die Juristin Betül Ulusoy und die Politikwissenschaftlerin Kübra Gümüşay, aber auch muslimische Sportler wie Zinédine Zidane oder Musiker wie der Rapper Ammar 114 können für junge Musliminnen und Muslime als Vorbilder und ‚Ermutiger' zu wichtigen Figuren werden.[9]

Umgang mit den Orientierungsangeboten

Große Vorteile des Internets sind aus Sicht der Jugendlichen und jungen Erwachsenen die Anonymität und unmittelbare Verfügbarkeit einer Vielzahl an Informationen und islamischen Meinungen. Gerade sehr persönliche Themen, insbesondere zu Sexualität und Intimität, möchten sie eher nicht mit der Mutter oder dem Imam besprechen und sich zumindest erst einmal selbst – anonym – einen ersten Überblick verschaffen. Über das Internet lassen sich zudem rasch erste Antworten finden, ohne dass man den Weg zur Moschee auf sich nehmen oder bis zur nächsten Begegnung mit der Religionslehrerin warten müsste. Den Jugendlichen und jungen Erwachsenen ist aber auch ein entscheidender Nachteil des Internets bewusst: Bei der Breite an Materialien und Meinungen, die dort zu finden sind, ist es schwer, die Qualität und Vertrauenswürdigkeit dieser Informationen zu beurteilen. Demgegenüber ist die Vertrauenswürdigkeit im Allgemeinen bei Personen aus dem direkten sozialen Umfeld wie z. B. Verwandten oder Freunden, aber auch Bekannten aus der muslimischen Gemeinde vor Ort eher gegeben. Manche jungen Musliminnen und Muslime betrachten sie auch als eine Art Korrektiv, um einerseits eigene Haltungen und Verhaltensweisen zu

8 Unsere Feldforschung war abgeschlossen, als ab Oktober 2017 mehrere Frauen Anschuldigungen gegen Tariq Ramadan wegen Vergewaltigung erhoben und die französische Staatsanwaltschaft ihn am 2. Februar 2018 in Untersuchungshaft nahm.

9 Die genannten Namen machen nur einen kleinen Teil des in den Interviews genannten Spektrums aus. Betül Ulusoy bloggt auf https://betuelulusoy.com/ [17. 12. 2018]; über sie: u. a. Focus Online (2016). – Über Kübra Gümüşay: Winkler (2013). – Über den Fussballstar Zinédine Zidane, der seine Religion öffentlich praktisch nie kommentierte: Dauncey und Morrey (2008). – Über den Rapper Ammar 114: ufuq.de (2008).

überprüfen. Andererseits dienen sie ihnen auch als Kompass bei der Beurteilung verschiedener Autoritäten hinsichtlich der Tauglichkeit ihrer Positionen für das muslimische Leben in der Schweiz.

In den Interviews nennen die muslimischen Jugendlichen und jungen Erwachsenen insbesondere folgende Kriterien, anhand deren sie für sich persönlich die Glaubwürdigkeit einer islamischen Autorität beurteilen:

- Eine Person, deren religiöse Auskünfte und Ratschläge ernsthaft in Betracht gezogen werden, muss die Lebensumstände der Jugendlichen und jungen Erwachsenen in der Schweiz/Europa kennen. Viele Imame, insbesondere, wenn sie nur für kurze Zeit in der Schweiz leben, erfüllen dieses Kriterium nicht und können deshalb die Erwartungen und Wünsche der jungen Generation nicht erfüllen.
- Die ‚Autorität' muss ihre Aussagen mit islamischen Quellen (Koran und Hadithe) belegen und ihre Positionen auch logisch nachvollziehbar begründen.
- Die ‚Autorität' sollte sich um die Darstellung verschiedener islamischer Perspektiven auf eine Frage bemühen oder die Berechtigung verschiedener islamischer Positionen zu einem Thema zumindest grundsätzlich akzeptieren.
- Die Person gilt auch bei anderen aufgrund ihrer (religiösen und weltlichen) Ausbildung, aber auch der eigenen Lebensführung als kompetent und glaubwürdig.
- Der Präsentationsstil soll ansprechend und nicht aufdringlich sein.

Gemäß diesen Kriterien kritisierten etliche unserer Interviewpartnerinnen und -partner den häufig genannten Pierre Vogel in verschiedener Hinsicht: Sein Redestil spreche zwar Jugendliche, die über den Islam noch nicht viel wissen, zunächst an, weil er ‚cool' und locker auftrete und theologische Inhalte in sehr einfacher Sprache zusammenfasse. Auch gebe er sunnitische Positionen durchaus zutreffend wieder. Aber er blende abweichende Beurteilungen vorschnell aus oder mache sie lächerlich, trete in der Tonlage zu offensiv auf und pflege einen Stil, der schmuddeligem Geschenkpapier gleiche, wie es ein Interviewpartner in ein Bild fasst:

> Die Sprache ist ja auch ein Paket sozusagen. Oder wie ein Geschenkpapier. Wenn ich Ihnen z. B. ein Geschenk mache – mein Handy – dann kann ich es natürlich schmuddelig verpacken, […] einfach so fast wie kaputt mit kaputtem Geschenkpapier mit ein paar Löchern. […] Oder ich kann es schön verpacken so mit schönen Schnürchen in Goldpapier und so. […] Und ich denke, Pierre Vogel macht das nicht in einer so schönen Art und Weise. (Clirim, m, 25)

Aufgrund solcher Mängel verliert Vogel für viele junge Zuhörerinnen und Zuhörer rasch an Reiz und bietet auf Dauer intellektuell zu wenig.

Die Suche junger Musliminnen und Muslime in der Schweiz nach religiöser

Orientierung können wir anhand der geführten Interviews grundsätzlich als einen iterativen Prozess beschreiben. Bei einer ersten vertieften Auseinandersetzung mit dem Islam stösst ein junger Mensch auf eine religiöse ‚Autorität', deren Auskünfte und Ratschläge er anhand eigener Bedürfnisse und Kenntnisse beurteilt und eventuell als hilfreich für die eigene Positionierung und eigene Entscheidungsprozesse bewertet oder aber verwirft. Bei dieser Evaluation spielt der Vergleich mit gezielt gesuchten oder zufällig angetroffenen Alternativangeboten sowie der Austausch mit Vertrauenspersonen (Familie, Freunde) eine wichtige Rolle. Bei zukünftigen Suchgängen wird die junge Frau oder der junge Mann zielgerichteter, ist sich ihrer bzw. seiner Kriterien und eigenen Bedürfnisse zunehmend bewusster. Unserer Beobachtung nach ist die religiös interessierte junge muslimische Generation in der Schweiz in der Beurteilung der zur Auswahl stehenden islamischen Orientierungsangebote mehrheitlich kritisch-reflektiert und selbstbestimmt. So beschreibt Sedat seinen Umgang mit religiösen Fragen als sehr eigenständig:

> Erstens lasse ich meinen gesunden Menschenverstand walten. Weil eben, eigentlich ist unsere Religion so konzipiert, dass man mit dem gesunden Menschenverstand agieren kann, ohne Bedenken. Von dem her habe ich das Vertrauen an mich selbst, dass ich meinen Lebensweg so gestalte, der eben nach dem Islam gerichtet ist. (Sedat, m, 28)

Muslimische Jugendliche und junge Erwachsene messen die Angebote stark daran, ob die gefundene Information oder Handlungsempfehlung zu ihrer persönlichen Lebenssituation passt und sie es für sich verantworten können, der Empfehlung zu folgen. In diesem Prozess werden mitunter verschiedene islamische Positionen ‚ausprobiert', um sich über diese eigenen Erfahrungen schließlich dem anzunähern, mit dem man sich wohl fühlt.

> Die Religion ist vor über tausend Jahren entstanden, 1400, man kann nicht jede Antwort eins zu eins übernehmen auch heute. Es funktioniert einfach nicht und da muss man halt denken, ja was die Grundsätze hinter der Frage ist [sind] […] Das finde ich vor allem, selber überlegen, selber schauen. Ja, auch überlegen, ist es okay für mich? Denn Religion ist schlussendlich für mich zumindest persönlich, es muss für jeden stimmen, was man macht. Also für jeden selber stimmen, was man macht. (Ismeta, w, 18)

Unterschiede zur Elterngeneration

Für viele unserer Interviewpartner sind die Eltern Vertrauenspersonen, die auch in religiösen Fragen konsultiert werden und den Jugendlichen bei ihrer Suche nach religiöser Orientierung als Referenzpunkt dienen. Vor allem dort, wo in der Familie der Islam praktiziert wurde, sind Mütter und Väter auch in der Jugendphase und für die jungen Erwachsenen bei Unsicherheiten in religiösen

Fragen gleichsam als ‚nahe Autoritäten' bedeutsam und ihre Einschätzung wird zumindest ergänzend zu Auskünften und Ratschlägen ‚ferner Autoritäten', die nicht im direkten Vertrauensverhältnis mit den jungen Musliminnen und Muslimen stehen, beigezogen. Gleichwohl grenzen sich viele der interviewten Jugendlichen und jungen Erwachsenen auch von ihren Eltern ab und hinterfragen deren religiös begründete Aussagen und Praktiken. So konstatieren sie, dass der Islam der eigenen Eltern oder der Elterngeneration allgemein stark kulturell geprägt sei und diese Generation nicht immer bewusst zwischen kulturellen Praktiken und islamischen Normen zu unterscheiden wisse. Besonders häufig äußern diese Kritik junge Frauen, die sich für eine islamische Lebensgestaltung entscheiden und sich zu negativen Stereotypen über Geschlechterrollen im Islam positionieren müssen: Sie argumentieren meist, dass bestimmte Vorstellungen über das ‚islamisch-korrekte' Verhalten von Mädchen und Frauen sowie die damit z. T. einhergehende fehlende Gleichberechtigung in Partnerschaften und bei der Behandlung von Geschwistern kulturell verwurzelt und im Kern nicht ‚islamisch' seien. An einem Beispiel beschreibt Yllzana, wie solche Diskussionen mit ihrer Mutter verlaufen können:

> Und bei ihr [meiner Mutter] ist einfach das Problem, sie kann Kultur und Religion nicht voneinander trennen. […] Genau wie zum Beispiel übers Heiraten. Sie sagt mir, sie möchte gerne einen Muslim, das ist am wichtigsten. Aber er muss Albaner sein, oder. Und dann habe ich mit ihr mal diskutiert. Ich sage: „Ja aber das ist schon recht so, wenn du das so möchtest, aber laut dem Koran ist es eigentlich nur das wichtigste, dass er Muslim ist. Also egal woher er kommt, er muss Muslim sein." Also nein, das geht nicht ja (lacht). Also sie vermischt das gerne ein bisschen, aber ich sage ihr dann immer, ja es ist anders. Sie kann mir viel über Kultur beibringen, aber ich ihr vom Islam mehr (Yllzana, w, 21)

Während die jungen Musliminnen und Muslime in unserer Studie Ratschläge der Eltern also durchaus ernst nehmen, ist es ihnen auch hier wichtig, sich eine eigene, unabhängige Position zu erarbeiten, die für sie stimmt und einerseits ihrem Islamverständnis und andererseits dem Leben in der Schweizer Gesellschaft entspricht. Dabei verschiebt sich der inhaltliche Schwerpunkt der Religiosität: Während die jungen Musliminnen und Muslime die intellektuelle Dimension der Religiosität (also das Wissen und Nachdenken über Religionsinhalte) stark aufwerten, verliert die Dimension der religiösen Praxis im Allgemeinen an Gewicht oder verschiebt sich jedenfalls von einer kollektiven Praxis in eine individuell sehr unterschiedlich gelebte private Form der Religionsausübung.

Erklärungsansätze

Wie lassen sich nun diese hier knapp zusammengefassten Resultate einordnen und ihre Ausprägungen erklären? Welche gesellschaftlichen Entwicklungen und welche biographischen Rahmenbedingungen, gerade im Vergleich zur Elterngeneration, vermögen zu erklären, warum muslimische Jugendliche und junge Erwachsene in der Schweiz so ihre Religiosität und Glaubenspraxis individueller und autonomer gestalten als ihre Eltern, warum sie ein so breites Spektrum an ‚Autoritäten' nutzen und Autorität so außerordentlich fragmentiert erscheint? Sicherlich lassen sich diese Tendenzen nicht monokausal erklären, sondern vielmehr durch ein Bündel an unterschiedlichen, teilweise miteinander verwobenen Ursachenkomplexen sowohl auf Mikro- als auch auf Makroebene. In einem nachfolgenden Schritt ist dann aber auch nach islamspezifischen Faktoren zu fragen.

Gesellschaftliche Trends

Religion, ihre Interpretation, ihre Praxis wie auch die Bedeutung, die ihr individuell oder gesellschaftlich zugeschrieben wird, steht immer im Kontext von Staat und Gesellschaft und damit im Kontext von ‚abstrakten' gesellschaftlichen und ‚konkreten' biographischen Veränderungsprozessen. Wenn unsere Befunde, im Einklang mit vielen Studien in anderen Ländern Westeuropas, den individuellen Umgang der jungen Musliminnen und Muslime mit ihrer Religion bestätigen, so fügt sich dies ohne weiteres ein in den für alle „modernen Staaten" feststellbaren „Megatrend" (Stolz / Ballif 2010, S. 36) der „Individualisierung". Die moderne Gesellschaft ist die individualisierte Gesellschaft, oder in den Worten von Uwe Schimank:

> Die Person in der modernen Gesellschaft begreift sich als Individuum. Individualität ist eine tragende Säule der Identitätskonstruktion des modernen Menschen. (Schimank 2000, S. 107)

Im Sinne von Ulrich Beck und Elisabeth Beck-Gernsheim meint „Individualisierung" einen tiefgreifenden Prozess, der dazu beiträgt, dass das Individuum mehr und mehr Entscheidungsverantwortung für seine Biographie übernehmen muss:

> Die Biographie der Menschen wird aus traditionellen Vorgaben und Sicherheiten, aus fremden Kontrollen und überregionalen Sittengesetzen herausgelöst, offen, entscheidungsabhängig und als Aufgabe in das Handeln jedes einzelnen gelegt. Die Anteile der prinzipiell entscheidungsverschlossenen Lebensmöglichkeiten nehmen ab, und die

Anteile der entscheidungsoffenen, selbst herzustellenden Biographie nehmen zu. (Beck / Beck-Gernsheim 1990, S. 12f.)

Was für das Leben in heutigen westlichen Gesellschaften allgemein gilt, zeigt sich in unserer Studie auch im Umgang mit Religion. Was der Islam ist, wie er verstanden werden soll, welche Bedeutung ihm für das konkrete Leben zugeschrieben wird, entscheidet das Individuum eigenverantwortlich und laufend neu für sich selbst. Dies führt auf Basis divergierender Interpretationen von religiösen Traditionen zu äußerst individuellen Religionsentwürfen und Islamverständnissen in unserem Datenmaterial. Das Spektrum reicht von Religionsentwürfen, in denen konkrete Glaubensvorstellungen, Glaubenspraktiken sowie Gebote und Verbote dominieren, über Entwürfe, in denen Religion lediglich der Ursprung vager moralischer Vorstellungen für das ‚gute Leben' ist, bis hin zu Religionsverständnissen, in denen die kollektive Zuschreibung – nicht unbedingt aber ein Zugehörigkeitsgefühl – zu einer Gruppe im Vordergrund steht. Muslim oder Muslimin sein ist in diesem Fall ein eher unbestimmtes Gefühl der Zugehörigkeit, das nicht mit spezifischen Glaubensüberzeugungen oder einer tatsächlichen Glaubenspraxis einhergeht.

In einen weiteren, wenn nicht gar *den* Megatrend schlechthin – nämlich den, der Globalisierung – ist auch die in unserer Studie empirisch festgestellte Fragmentierung religiöser Autorität und die damit unweigerlich einhergehende Pluralisierung religiöser Autorität(en) einzubetten. In Anlehnung an Anthony Giddens soll Globalisierung hier als zumindest zwei Dimensionen umfassender Prozess verstanden werden: nämlich als „Zunahme weltweiter Vernetzung" wie auch als „Intensivierung weltweiter sozialer Beziehungen, durch die entfernte Orte in solcher Weise miteinander verbunden werden, dass Ereignisse an einem Ort durch Vorgänge geprägt werden, die sich an einem viele Kilometer entfernten Ort abspielen, und umgekehrt" (Giddens 1996, S. 85).

Der Prozess der Globalisierung zeigt sich in unserer Studie auch am Spektrum jener religiösen Autoritäten, die für die jungen Musliminnen und Muslime in der Schweiz relevant sind. Wie dargestellt, sind darunter zum einen lokale und regionale, also in der Schweiz oder in den Nachbarländern lebende und wirkende Autoritäten. Zahlreich sind aber auch religiöse Autoritäten (Personen und Institutionen) aus den Herkunftsländern der Schweizer Musliminnen und Muslime oder ‚internationale' Akteure wie etwa Yusuf al-Qaradawi oder Nouman Ali Khan und viele andere mehr, deren Wirkkraft regionale und kulturelle Grenzen weit überschreitet.[10]

Im wahrsten Sinne des Wortes ‚bahnbrechend' für die beobachtete Frag-

10 Zu Qaradawi etwa Gräf / Skovgaard-Petersen 2009. Nouman Ali Khan ist ein US-Prediger und Direktor des Instituts Bayyinah (http://bayyinah.com [17.12.2018]), über das er via YouTube und einen eigenen Online-TV-Kanal Kurse gibt.

mentierung und Pluralisierung religiöser Autorität ist zudem eine jener Dynamiken, die Giddens als spezifisch für die Moderne ansieht, nämlich die so genannte „Entbettung", also das „,Herausheben' sozialer Beziehungen aus ortsgebundenen Interaktionszusammenhängen und ihre unbegrenzte Raum-Zeit-Spannen übergreifende Umstrukturierung" (Giddens 1996, S. 33).

Die von Giddens für die Moderne konstatierte zunehmende „raumzeitliche Abstandsvergrößerung" (1996, S. 34) wird heute insbesondere durch das Internet (YouTube, Facebook, Twitter, Instagram, etc.) und den damit verbundenen Möglichkeiten der Kommunikation über Zeit und Raum hinweg ermöglicht.

Anders als der Großteil der Elterngeneration, sind die jungen, in der Schweiz lebenden Musliminnen und Muslime in und mit der digitalen Welt aufgewachsen und bewegen sich mit aller Selbstverständlichkeit in ihr. Dies gilt – wie oben aufgezeigt – auch für den Bereich des religiösen Lebens. Dabei ist das Internet allerding nicht nur, wie El Tahawi feststellte, „the new mosque" (2008, S. 11). Vielmehr ist es der digitale Marktplatz unzähliger und zugleich unterschiedlichster religiöser Interpretationen und Angebote oder, um im Bild von El Tahawi zu bleiben, der Platz, an dem unzählige Moscheen mit den unterschiedlichsten Imamen und Islaminterpretationen stehen und täglich neu gebaut werden.[11]

Deutlich wird dies insbesondere dadurch, dass junge Musliminnen und Muslime das Internet nicht nur als Zeiten und Räume übergreifende Zugangsmöglichkeit zu religiösen Autoritäten nutzen, sondern auch als Möglichkeit, die Vielzahl der Angebote auf dem Markt der islamischen Interpretationen miteinander zu vergleichen und vor diesem Hintergrund das ‚richtige' oder das ‚passende' Angebot selbstbestimmt auszuwählen. Dass dabei oftmals ‚Scheich Google', also dem Suchalgorithmus von Google eine besondere Bedeutung zukommt, mag in Sachen Religion besonders verwundern, lässt sich als Trend jedoch nicht von der Hand weisen.

Der teilweise äußerst kritische Umgang mit religiösen Interpretationen und Handlungsempfehlungen, das Hinterfragen dessen, was religiöse Autorität eigentlich ausmacht, und das Beharren der jungen Musliminnen und Muslime auf kritischer Distanz zu ihnen und auf der eigenen Entscheidungsmacht ist auch als Konsequenz des breiten Angebotes zu erklären. Wer die Wahl hat, hat die Qual der Entscheidung. Verstärkt wird dieser Prozess, wie Martin Baumann (2017, S. 131) herausarbeitet, auch durch das Schweizer Bildungssystem, in dem kritisches und eigenständiges Denken, Eigenverantwortlichkeit und Individualität von zentraler Bedeutung sind. Dies führt dann unter anderem dazu, dass der Anspruch des Imams der lokalen Moschee, auch von der jungen Generation als religiöse Autorität wahrgenommen und akzeptiert zu werden, immer wieder in

11 Schaffar und Friesinger (2013) zeigen, dass und warum nicht alle jungen Menschen in Bezug auf den Umgang mit digitalen Medien die gleichen Fähigkeiten entwickeln.

Leere läuft. Autorität, auch religiöse Autorität besitzt man nicht einfach, sondern sie wird einem, wie Rainer Paris zu Recht feststellt, zugeschrieben:

> Im Zentrum des Autoritätsbegriffs steht das Merkmal der *Anerkennung*. Autorität ist jemand dann, wenn er geachtet und anerkannt ist, wenn andere ihm aus freien Stücken eine Überlegenheit attestieren, an die sie selbst nicht heranreichen. (Paris 2005, S. 77)

Wenn also viele junge Musliminnen und Muslime gerade die Autorität des Imams in der Moschee immer wieder in Frage stellen, ist gerade auch das gesellschaftliche Selbstverständnis der jungen Generation im Vergleich zur Elterngeneration von erklärender Bedeutung. Verstehen sich ihre Eltern in vielen Fällen auch nach Jahrzehnten in der Schweiz immer noch als Gäste, so verstehen sich fast alle unserer muslimischen Interviewpartnerinnen und -partner als „muslimische Schweizer" oder „Schweizer Muslime". Das heisst nicht, dass man sich des eigenen Migrationshintergrunds nicht bewusst wäre. Im Gegenteil. Dieser wird in den Interviews stets thematisiert. Auch das Bewusstsein, dass die Zugehörigkeit von Teilen der Schweizer Mehrheitsgesellschaft und Politik in Frage gestellt wird und mit jedem weiteren Attentat militanter Islamisten weitere Vorbehalte gegenüber Muslimen in der Schweiz geschürt werden, ist stark ausgeprägt. In diesem Sinne zählen junge, in der Schweiz lebende Musliminnen und Muslime gleich wie diejenigen in Norwegen zu einem „kulturellen Prekariat" (Eriksen 2015, S. 3), das bei jedem sie betreffenden Diskursereignis befürchten muss, zwar nicht das Bürgerrecht, aber die soziale Anerkennung wieder zu verlieren.

Nichtsdestotrotz sehen aber beinahe alle der von uns interviewten Musliminnen und Muslime ihre Zukunft in der Schweiz. Dieses (neue) Selbstverständnis wirkt sich auch auf die Auswahl und Anerkennung religiöser Autoritäten aus. Nach wie vor bedeutsam sind traditionell hochgehaltene Kriterien wie die Ausbildung einer ‚Autorität', ihre Lebensweise, die Nachvollziehbarkeit eines Arguments und die Belege aus den einschlägigen islamischen Quellen. Daneben aber wird das Kriterium der Aussagekraft für die Schweizer Verhältnisse, der Praktikabilität in der Schweiz immer wichtiger. Gefragt sind dementsprechend religiöse Autoritäten, die in einer Schweizer Landessprache predigen, die in der westlichen Welt aufgewachsen sind und damit die gleichen oder zumindest vergleichbare Prägungen und Erfahrungen aufweisen wie die jungen Musliminnen und Muslime in der Schweiz. Wenig oder thematisch eingeschränkte Autorität erkennt dieses ‚Kundensegment' hingegen jenen Imamen zu, die von den religiösen Institutionen mancher Herkunftsländer entsandt werden, oftmals nur über rudimentäre Kenntnisse einer Landessprache verfügen und auch wenig über die konkreten Lebenswelten muslimischer Jugendlicher und junger Erwachsener in der Schweiz wissen.

Islamspezifische Aspekte

Die allermeisten der bis hierher erwogenen Faktoren treffen nicht nur auf junge Musliminnen und Muslime zu, sondern ebenso bspw. auf junge Orthodoxe aus den Balkanländern oder Tamilinnen und Tamilen, die sich einer Hindu-Tradition zurechnen (Baumann 2017). Dass der öffentliche Diskurs den Musliminnen und Muslimen deutlich rauer ins Gesicht bläst als allen andern Religionsgruppen, mag bei Hinwendungsprozessen eine Rolle spielen, erklärt aber nicht die Vielfalt an Orientierungsangeboten und die Fragmentierung islamischer Autorität. Wirksam sind in unseren Augen hingegen zwei islamspezifische Merkmale.

Zum einen ist das Verhältnis unter Muslimen im religiösen Kontext ausgesprochen egalitär. Dies drückt sich etwa darin aus, dass jeder unbescholtene Gläubige als Vorbeter beim Pflichtgebet fungieren kann, sofern er den Ablauf beherrscht. Die islamischen Traditionen kennen kein Amt wie etwa das des römisch-katholischen Priesters, der durch die Priesterweihe erst autorisiert wird, bestimmte für das Heil notwendige Sakramente zu verwalten (vgl. Gellner 1992, S. 8). Wohl verfügen manche Personen über größere Kenntnisse von Praxis und Inhalten der Religion als andere und erwerben dadurch individuelles Prestige. Das Umfeld mag ihnen Sachkompetenz oder auch vorbildlichen Lebenswandel attestieren und dadurch eine bestimmte Autorität zuerkennen. Aber sie können den Zugang der anderen Gläubigen zum Heil nicht kontrollieren, da sie keinerlei weitere Sakramente verwalten, die sich als Druckmittel einsetzen ließen (Warner / Wenner 2006, S. 461). In der Praxis haben sich zwar Formen herausgebildet, die manchen Spezialistinnen und Spezialisten große soziale Macht verleihen: unter Sufis dem Scheich, dessen Führung sich der einzelne Adept völlig überlassen soll; unter Schiiten der Pyramide der Geistlichen bis hinauf zur ‚Quelle der Nachahmung'. Aber beide Formen sind in westlichen Ländern unter Muslimen wenig anzutreffen und ohne Einfluss auf die übergroße sunnitische Mehrheit. Explizite dogmatische Monopole hat es geschichtlich jeweils nur in vergleichsweise kurzen Phasen gegeben, während die Gelehrten sonst stets die Pluralität der Meinungen hinnahmen, oft gar begrüßten. In einer sehr ‚protestantischen' Art und Weise ist somit der einzelne Muslim und nicht minder die einzelne Muslimin in eine Beziehung zu Gott gestellt und selber für sein bzw. ihr Heil verantwortlich.

Zum andern – als Folge der Sakramentlosigkeit – verlangt diese Eigenverantwortlichkeit dem Muslim wie der Muslimin theoretisch laufend Entscheidungen für das eigene Verhalten ab. In den gängigen Fragen des Alltags haben die islamischen Rechtsschulen und die muslimischen Gesellschaften in den unterschiedlichen Kulturen den gängigen Weg längst formuliert. Als diffuses ‚Wissen' sind diese Lösungen in einer muslimisch geprägten Gesellschaft vorhanden und entfalten normative Kraft: ‚Im Islam ist das so' oder ‚Das ist einfach so'. Die

Lösungen sind jedoch für konkrete Situationen gefunden worden. Sie sind aber weder verbindlich kodifiziert, noch ‚heilig', noch prinzipiell unhinterfragbar. In neuen Kontexten ist deshalb auch nach traditioneller islamischer Rechtsauffassung neu zu entscheiden, ob die überkommenen Antworten dem Sachverhalt noch gerecht werden. Gerade wenn Autoritäten fehlen, denen das Umfeld die nötige Kompetenz zubilligt, ist der Einzelne regelrecht gezwungen, sich nach einschlägigen Einschätzungen umzusehen, und zum eigenverantwortlichen Urteil aufgerufen. Die islamische Tradition setzt hier keineswegs eine Barriere, sondern stellt dem Individuum Instrumente und Grundsätze zur Verfügung, die dieses Vorgehen legitimieren, gewisse Kriterien an die Hand geben und die Folgen von Fehlentscheiden nachsichtig beurteilen.

Fazit

In der Summe lässt sich Folgendes festhalten: Junge, in der Schweiz lebende Musliminnen und Muslime leben ihre Religion ähnlich individuell, wie es andere Untersuchungen zuvor in anderen Ländern Westeuropas beschrieben haben. Die an der ‚Nachfrageseite' orientierte Untersuchung hat gezeigt, dass sie dafür eine unerwartete Vielfalt an Orientierungsangeboten nutzen, unter denen die von uns so genannten ‚nahen' Autoritäten des persönlichen Umfelds einen wichtigen Platz einnehmen. Mit dieser Pluralität der Autoritäten geht eine zunehmende Fragmentierung einher. Da viele Quellen sehr rasch verfügbar sind, kann das Individuum, das die technischen Mittel zu nutzen weiß, mehrere Angebote gegeneinander abwägen, bevor es einer bestimmten Quelle für ein konkretes Thema die gewünschte Autorität zuerkennt. Für ein anderes Thema wendet es sich aber womöglich bereits einer anderen Autorität zu. Das Fehlen heilsnotwendiger Sakramente und die im islamischen Dogma zentral verankerte Eigenverantwortlichkeit des Einzelnen vor Gott verstärken die Wirkung des gesellschaftlichen Megatrends der Individualisierung eher, als ihn zu bremsen.

All dies erlaubt die Aussage, dass sich auf der Ebene des Einzelnen, um es in der Terminologie von Fred Kniss und Paul D. Numrich (2007) zu fassen, der ‚Ort von Autorität' weg vom Kollektiv hin zum Individuum verschoben hat.[12] Dies ist jedenfalls klar für die Individuen der jungen Generation von Musliminnen und Muslimen in der Schweiz und vermutlich auch in ähnlich geprägten Gesellschaften Westeuropas (vgl. Baumann 2017, S. 127).

12 Kniss und Numrich fragen in ihrer eigenen Studie primär danach, warum sich bestimmte religiöse Gemeinschaften zivilgesellschaftlich engagieren und andere nicht. Sie rechnen jedoch auch damit, dass sich historisch und gegenwärtig auf der Ebene von Gemeinschaften oder ganzen Gesellschaften der Schwerpunkt deutlich verschieben kann (2007, 52f., 63).

Die geschilderten Entwicklungen bedeuten anderseits nicht, dass muslimische Religiosität oder religiöse Autorität sich auflöst in Beliebigkeit. Was wir beobachten können, ist nicht ihre Auflösung, sondern lediglich der Wandel ihrer Form wie auch der Bedeutung, die ihnen zugeschrieben wird. Womöglich liegt darin ein Teil der Antwort im Streit um die Frage, ob sich ‚der Islam in Europa' liberalisiere oder nicht. Während sich die Praxis und der Umgang mit Autorität individualisiert und dabei durchaus verändert, sind die Glaubensinhalte und die Geltung von Normen davon nicht betroffen: Auch wer selbst grundlegende Normen nicht einmal annähernd umsetzt, nämlich die große Mehrheit der Musliminnen und Muslime, anerkennt, dass diese ‚im Prinzip' gelten, behält sich aber die individuelle Entscheidung darüber womöglich bewusster vor, als dies in eher geschlossenen Gesellschaften der Fall ist.[13] In bestimmten Grundsätzen der Tradition findet er dafür sogar starke Anknüpfungspunkte, so dass er sich mit guten Gründen dieser Tradition weiter verbunden fühlen kann.

Zwischen den Generationen der Erstimmigranten und ihren Kindern und Enkeln besteht also kein scharfer Bruch, was die religiöse Kernpraxis und die Glaubensinhalte betrifft (so auch Diehl / Koenig 2009): Auch Junge beten, fasten, spenden für soziale Zwecke und pilgern teils jünger als ihre Eltern zu *ḥağğ* oder *ʿumra* nach Mekka. Und auch unter den Jungen ist es eine Minderheit, die den Islam mehr oder weniger umfassend praktiziert (vgl. de Flaugergues 2016). Was die junge Generation von der älteren unterscheidet, ist ihre Ausrüstung und ihr soziales Umfeld: Vom Kindergarten an erleben sie gemischt-religiöse *peer groups.* Praktisch ausnahmslos durchlaufen sie die neunjährige Volksschule, da es bisher keine muslimischen Privatschulen gibt. Sie erleben danach, gleich wie ihre Eltern, den rauen öffentlichen Islam-Diskurs, der viel dazu beiträgt, dass sie bei der Suche nach einer Lehr- oder Arbeitsstelle öfter als andere Gleichaltrige Absagen bekommen. Doch letztlich kommen sie bestens ausgerüstet im Arbeitsmarkt unter, wie die sehr tiefe Jugendarbeitslosigkeit zeigt.[14] In praktisch allen Belangen sind sie im Durchschnitt besser vorbereitet als die Generation ihrer Eltern, können mit den Ansprüchen wie den Widersprüchen der Schweizer Gesellschaft umgehen und fühlen sich ihr wesentlich mehr zugehörig als die Eltern. Der Islam ist dabei für sie keineswegs ein Hindernis.

---

13 In diesem Sinn etwa Abdellah Hammoudi: „Ich war zwar an die Rituale gebunden, mit denen im Islam Gott verehrt wird (Gebet, Fasten, Glaubensbekenntnis usw.), aber nicht an ihre regelmässige Verrichtung. Die Frage der Regelmässigkeit war mir bei weitem nicht so wichtig wie das Mysterium des Gebots […]." *Saison in Mekka. Geschichte einer Pilgerfahrt,* München: Beck, 2007, S. 178.

14 Siehe https://www.seco.admin.ch/ > Arbeit > Arbeitslosenversicherung > Arbeitslosenzahlen.

Quellen und Literatur

Interviews

Ferida: Narratives Interview, 21.01.2016, Weinfelden, Silvia Martens.
Clirim: Narratives Interview, 06.11.2015, Bern, Jürgen Endres.
Sedat: Narrative Interview, 05.08.2015, Zürich, Jürgen Endres.
Ismeta: Narratives Interview, 14.08.2015, Luzern, Silvia Martens.
Yllzana: Narratives Interview, 08.05.2015, Luzern, Silvia Martens.

Literatur

Ahmed, Shahab (2016): *What Is Islam? The importance of being Islamic.* Princeton: Princeton University Press.

Baumann, Martin (2017): „Religiös selbstbestimmt, reflektiert und integriert. Analyse religiöser Neuinterpretationen bei jungen Erwachsenen mit Migrationshintergrund". In: Arens, Edmund / Baumann, Martin / Liedhegener, Antonius / Müller, Wolfgang W. / Ries, Markus (Hg.): *Religiöse Identitäten und gesellschaftliche Integration.* Baden-Baden: Nomos (Religion – Wirtschaft – Politik, 18), S. 107–138.

Baumann, Martin / Endres, Jürgen / Martens, Silvia / Tunger-Zanetti, Andreas (2017): *„Hallo, es geht um meine Religion!" Muslimische Jugendliche in der Schweiz auf der Suche nach ihrer Identität.* Verfügbar: https://www.unilu.ch/fileadmin/fakultaeten/ksf/institute/zrf/dok/Forschungsbericht_Hallo_es_geht_um_meine_Religion.pdf [17.12.2018] Luzern: Universität Luzern, Zentrum Religionsforschung.

Beck, Ulrich / Beck-Gernsheim, Elisabeth (1990): *Das ganz normale Chaos der Liebe.* Erstausg., [3. Aufl.]. Frankfurt am Main: Suhrkamp (Suhrkamp-Taschenbuch, 1725).

Bleisch Bouzar, Petra (2016): *Gelebte und erzählte Scharia in der Schweiz. Empirische Studien zur Aneignung religiöser Normen durch zum Islam konvertierte Frauen.* Zürich: Schulthess (Freiburger Veröffentlichungen zum Religionsrecht, 33).

Caeiro, Alexandre (2010): „The power of European fatwas. The Minority Fiqh Project and the making of an Islamic counterpublic." In: *International Journal of Middle East Studies,* 42 (03), S. 435–449.

Charim, Isolde (2018): *Ich und die Anderen. Wie die neue Pluralisierung uns alle verändert.* Wien: Zsolnay.

Dauncey, Hugh / Morrey, Douglas (2008): „Quiet contradictions of celebrity." In: *International Journal of Cultural Studies,* 11 (3), S. 301–320. DOI: 10.1177/1367877908092587.

de Flaugergues, Amélie (2016): *Religiöse und spirituelle Praktiken und Glaubensformen in der Schweiz. Erste Ergebnisse der Erhebung zur Sprache, Religion und Kultur 2014.* Verfügbar: https://www.bfs.admin.ch/bfsstatic/dam/assets/350455/master [17.12.2018] Neuchâtel: Bundesamt für Statistik.

Diehl, Claudia / Koenig, Matthias (2009): „Religiosität türkischer Migranten im Generationenverlauf. Ein Befund und einige Erklärungsversuche." In: *Zeitschrift für Soziologie,* 38 (4), S. 300–319.

El-Tahawy, Abdallah (2008): „The Internet is the New Mosque. Fatwa at the Click of a Mouse." In: *Arab Insight,* 188, S. 11–19.

Endres, Jürgen / Tunger-Zanetti, Andreas / Behloul, Samuel-Martin / Baumann, Martin (2013): *Jung, muslimisch, schweizerisch. Muslimische Jugendgruppen, islamische Lebensführung und Schweizer Gesellschaft. Ein Forschungsbericht.* Luzern: Universität Luzern, Zentrum Religionsforschung.

Eriksen, Thomas Hylland (2015): „Rebuilding the ship at sea: super-diversity, person and conduct in eastern Oslo." In: *Global Networks,* 15 (1), S. 1–20.

Focus Online (2016): Kopftuch-Juristin Betül Ulusoy droht Rauswurf aus der Jungen Union. Verfügbar: https://www.focus.de/politik/deutschland/betuel-ulusoy-kopftuch-juristin-droht-rauswurf-aus-der-jungen-union_id_5744677.html, zuletzt aktualisiert am 20.07.2016 [17.12.2018].

Gellner, Ernest (1992): *Postmodernism, reason and religion.* London et al.: Routledge.

Giddens, Anthony (1996): *Konsequenzen der Moderne.* Frankfurt am Main: Suhrkamp (Suhrkamp-Taschenbuch Wissenschaft, 1295).

Gräf, Bettina / Skovgaard-Petersen, Jakob (Hg.) (2009): *Global mufti. The phenomenon of Yūsuf al-Qaraḍāwī.* New York: Columbia University Press.

Islamologisches Institut: Prof. Dr. Amir Zaidan. Institutsleiter & Dozent. Islamologisches Institut. Wien. Verfügbar: https://islamologie.info/das-institut/dozenten/ [17.12.2018].

Joas, Hans (2012): *Glaube als Option. Zukunftsmöglichkeiten des Christentums.* Freiburg i. Br.: Herder.

Kniss, Fred / Numrich, Paul David (2007): *Sacred assemblies and civic engagement. How religion matters for America's newest immigrants.* New Brunswick N. J.: Rutgers University Press.

Krämer, Gudrun (2011): „Zum Verhältnis von Religion, Recht und Politik: Säkularisierung im Islam." In: Elke Ariëns (Hg.): *Glaubensfragen in Europa. Religion und Politik im Konflikt.* Bielefeld: transcript (Europäische Horizonte, 7), S. 127–147.

Krämer, Gudrun / Schmidtke, Sabine (Hg.) (2006): *Speaking for Islam. Religious authorities in Muslim societies.* Leiden et al.: Brill (Social, economic, and political studies of the Middle East and Asia, v. 100).

Messick, Brinkley (2017): „Fatwā, modern." In: Fleet, Kate / Krämer, Gudrun / Matringe, Denis / Nawas, John / Rowson, Everett K. / Allen, Roger (Hg.): *The encyclopaedia of Islam three.* [3rd edition]. Leiden et al.: Brill.

Morgenthaler, Christoph / Zehnder, Sabine / Peng, Aristide / Brodbeck, Kathrin / Christl, Taylor / Käppler, Christoph (2011): „Wertorientierungen und Religiosität. Ihre Bedeutung für die Identitätsentwicklung und psychische Gesundheit Adoleszenter / The VROID-MHAP-Study: Values, Religious Orientations, Identity Development and Mental Health Adolescents' Perspectives." Verfügbar: http://www.snf.ch/SiteCollectionDocuments/nfp/nfp58/NFP58_Schlussbericht_Morgenthaler_Kaeppler.pdf [17.12.2018] Bern/Dortmund: Universität Bern, Technische Universität Dortmund.

Motzki, Harald (1994): „Religiöse Ratgebung im Islam: Entstehung, Bedeutung und Praxis des muftī und der fatwā." In: *Zeitschrift für Religionswissenschaft,* 2 (1).

Müller, Dominik (2017): „‚Aber Hocam…': Imame und die Aushandlung islamischer Autorität im Alltag von Schweizer Moscheen", in: Zeitschrift für Ethnologie 142, H.1, S. 67–92.

Paris, Rainer (2005): „Autorität – Führung – Elite“. In: Paris, Rainer: *Normale Macht. Soziologische Essays.* Konstanz: UVK, S. 75–96.

Peter, Frank (2006): „Individualization and religious authority in Western European Islam.“ In: *Islam and Christian-Muslim Relations,* 17 (1), S. 105–118.

Powers, David S. (2017): „Fatwā, premodern.“ In: Fleet, Kate / Krämer, Gudrun / Matringe, Denis / Nawas, John / Rowson, Everett K. / Allen, Roger (Hg.): The encyclopaedia of Islam three. [3rd edition]. Leiden et al.: Brill.

Schaffar, Andrea / Friesinger, Claudia (2013): „Digital natives: myth busted: Digitale Kompetenzen und habituelle Verstrickungen“. In: Medienimpulse, 4. Verfügbar: https://www.medienimpulse.at/articles/view/613 [24. 2. 2019].

Schimank, Uwe (2000): „Die individualisierte Gesellschaft – differenzierungs- und akteurtheoretisch betrachtet.“ In: Kron, Thomas (Hg.): *Individualisierung und soziologische Theorie.* Opladen: Leske + Budrich (Lehrtexte Soziologie), S. 107–128.

Schlieter, Jens / Kind, Marietta / Lauer, Tina (Hg.) (2014): Die zweite Generation der Tibeter in der Schweiz. Identitätsaushandlungen und Formen buddhistischer Religiosität. Zürich: Seismo (Sozialer Zusammenhalt und kultureller Pluralismus).

Schulze, Reinhard (1990): *Islamischer Internationalismus im 20. Jahrhundert. Untersuchungen zur Geschichte der islamischen Weltliga.* Leiden et al.: Brill (Social, economic and political studies of the Middle East, 41).

Stolz, Jörg / Ballif, Edmée: *Die Zukunft der Reformierten. Gesellschaftliche Megatrends – kirchliche Reaktionen.* Zürich: TVZ.

ufuq.de (2008): „Ammar 114. Gegen Ehrenmorde, Jugendgewalt und Terror.“ In: *Newsletter Jugendkultur, Islam und Demokratie* (01.06.2008). Verfügbar: http://www.bpb.de/system/files/pdf_pdflib/pdflib-65078.pdf [17.12.2018] Berlin: Bundeszentrale für politische Bildung.

Warner, Carolyn M. / Wenner, Manfred W. (2006): „Religion and the Political Organization of Muslims in Europe.“ In: *Perspectives on Politics,* 4 (03), S. 457–479.

Winkler, Claudia (2013): „Kübra Gümüşay's Blog ein fremdwoerterbuch. Re-Presenting the ‚Silent Muslima' in the Public Sphere.“ In: *Women in German Yearbook,* 29, S. 1–20.

Zaman, Muhammad Qasim (2009): „The ulama and contestations of religious authority.“ In: Masud, Muhammad Khalid / Salvatore, Armando / van Bruinessen, Martin (Hg.): *Islam and modernity. Key issues and debates.* Edinburgh : Edinburgh University Press, S. 206–236.

Rebekka Christine Khaliefi

Karma, Konfuzius und K-Pop: Die Bedeutung des Buddhismus bei der Identitätsaushandlung junger Erwachsener mit vietnamesischen Wurzeln in der Schweiz und in Deutschland

Abstract

Karma, Confucius, K-Pop: Buddhism's Role in Negotiations of Identity Among Young Adults of Vietnamese Origin in Switzerland and Germany

The contribution analyses how young adults with Vietnamese roots deal with the ethno-religious heritage of their parents. The "2.0 generation", "post immigrant generation" (Rumbaut 2006), are brought up in a religious pluralized or secular society. Unlike their parents or older siblings, they have no experience of migration because they were born in Switzerland or Germany. They are socialized in western countries and grow up with Vietnamese parenting. Sometimes they are categorized as "Asians" in the migration society and on the other hand, they have difficulties with the Vietnamese language and culture or feel more western. The article assumes that religion can help young adults developing their identity and negotiating their position between the migration society and the cultural context of their parents. For the methodological approach, the biographical research according to Rosenthal (2005) is used. Through two case studies, the paper shows the process of creating an individual religiosity. It is shown how questions of identity and religiousness arise during the adolescence and how the social context influences questions of religious identification. Referring to the case studies and the concept of "religiousness dimensions" of Hervieu-Légers (2004), the article analyses ways of being religious in Switzerland and in Germany. In both countries, young adults deal with their religiousness in a self-determined way. Unlike the parents' generation, they are more interested in an intellectualized approach to religion. They integrate their religiosity into their biographies and thus position themselves vis-à-vis the Christian and secular Swiss and German society as well as the parent generation. In summary, they reflect the ethno-religious heritage of the parent generation and adapt it to their environment.

Aufwachsen zwischen zwei Bezugssystemen – Die „2.0 Generation"

Sowohl in der Schweiz als auch in Deutschland bleiben VietnamesInnen im öffentlichen Diskurs weitgehend „unsichtbar" (Kocatürk-Schuster et al. 2017). Die Kinder vietnamesischer EinwandererInnen werden in den Medien als „leise

Musterschüler" (Michna 2016), „Integrationswunder" (Beglinger 2017) und „Bildungswunder" (Lenz 2016) positiv stereotypisiert. Häufig wird in solchen Darstellungen die konfuzianische Prägung des vietnamesischen Buddhismus als Erklärung für den Bildungserfolg der jungen Generation herangezogen. Über die Religiosität und die intergenerationellen Veränderungsprozesse in der Einwanderungsgesellschaft ist jedoch kaum etwas bekannt. Akteurszentrierte Forschung zu jungen Erwachsenen mit vietnamesischen Wurzeln und ihrer Religiosität stellt somit bislang ein Forschungsdesiderat in der Schweiz und in Deutschland dar.

Der Beitrag widmet sich daher den folgenden Fragen: Welche Praktiken und Konzepte des ethno-religiösen Erbes der Elterngeneration übernehmen die jungen Erwachsenen in den beiden Ländern? Welche intergenerationalen Veränderungen folgen dadurch im Verlauf der religiösen Biografie?

In der Forschung werden die Kinder von EinwanderInnen häufig mittels des Konzeptes der „Mehrfachzugehörigkeit" (Mecheril 2003) und der „transnationalen Identität" (Levitt / Waters 2002) beschrieben. Sie handeln ihre Identität zwischen der Herkunftskultur der Eltern und ihrer Sozialisation in der Einwanderungsgesellschaft aus (Beth / Tuckermann 2008; Barber 2015; Müller 2017).[1] Unter den Befragten befinden sich junge Erwachsene, die sich in der Schweiz und in Deutschland verorten und zugleich eine an Asien angelehnte Jugendkultur, bestehend unter anderem aus Asia-Parties und Korean Pop, so genannter K-Pop, pflegen. Teilweise wächst diese Generation in einem Spannungsverhältnis auf, das von Kulturkonflikten zwischen den Generationen geprägt ist (Zhou / Bhankston 1998, S. 160f.; Ho 2003, S. 102). Eine Ursache für dieses Spannungsverhältnis kann das Selbstverständnis der jungen Erwachsenen sein. Je nach Grad der Migrationserfahrung zeigen sich Unterschiede im Selbstverständnis der Kinder von EinwanderInnen (Rumbaut 2006, S. 48f.). Kinder von vietnamesischen EinwanderInnen, die selbst aus Vietnam migriert sind, verstehen sich häufig selbst als VietnamesInnen. Kinder, die außerhalb von Vietnam geboren wurden, bezeichnen Vietnam hingegen oftmals als das Herkunftsland ihrer Eltern. Die Folge können Entfremdungen zwischen den Generationen sein (Röttger-Rössler 2017, S. 274).[2]

Diese Beobachtung spiegelt sich auch in meinen Daten wieder, da die Be-

1 Beth / Tuckermann (2008) geben mittels eines Interviewbandes einen Einblick in die Lebenswelt und die Mehrfachzugehörigkeiten junger VietnamesInnen in Deutschland. Müller (2017) zeigt anhand junger Erwachsener mit vietnamesischen Wurzeln in Berlin transnationale Identitätskonstruktionen auf. Barber (2015) untersucht Identitätskonstruktionen und das Zugehörigkeitsgefühl junger Erwachsener mit vietnamesischen Wurzeln in London.

2 In dem Projekt „Gefühlsbildungen im vietnamesischen Berlin" untersuchen Forschende der Freien Universität Berlin unter Röttger-Rösslers Leitung die emotionalen und affektiven Herausforderungen der Sozialisation „zwischen zwei Welten".

fragten sich mehrheitlich als SchweizerInnen oder Deutsche mit vietnamesischem Aussehen beschreiben. Im Alltag werden sie dennoch teilweise mit Fremdkategorisierungen als „Asiaten" konfrontiert. Innerhalb der Familie ergeben sich aufgrund ihrer westlichen Prägung teilweise Schwierigkeiten mit dem vietnamesischen Erziehungsmodell der Eltern (Pham 2012).[3] In den Pagoden, buddhistischen Tempeln, zeigt sich diese Entfremdung insbesondere im Umgang mit Ordinierten. Häufig verfügen die Befragten über nur sehr geringe Vietnamesisch Kenntnisse und fühlen sich deshalb in dem religiösen Kontext und bei der Kommunikation mit den Ordinierten unsicher.

Eine Differenzierung bei der Beschreibung der Zweitgeneration erscheint aufgrund dieser Beobachtungen sinnvoll. Ausgangspunkt dieses von Rumbaut (2006) vertretenen Ansatzes ist eine Binnenperspektive, die „Eltern-Kind Beziehung" (Röttger-Rössler 2017, S. 277). Für die biografische Fallrekonstruktion im Folgenden eignet sich dieser Ansatz, da er vom Selbstverständnis der Akteure ausgeht. Als junge Erwachsene mit vietnamesischen Wurzeln werden daher in diesem Beitrag die Kinder vietnamesischer EinwanderInnen verstanden, die in der Schweiz oder in Deutschland geboren und aufgewachsen sind. Wichtigstes Kriterium der sogenannten „post immigrant-generation", der „2.0 Generation", ist, dass sie nicht im Herkunftsland der Eltern aufwächst, sondern in einem anderen Land sozialisiert wird (Rumbaut 2006, S. 49ff.).

Insgesamt kann davon ausgegangen werden, dass neben einer abnehmenden Sprachkompetenz auch der kulturelle Kontext und die Religion der Elterngeneration für die junge Generation an Bedeutung verliert (Rumbaut 2006, S. 90). Ho (2003) beobachtet für die zweite und dritte Generation von Kindern vietnamesischer EinwanderInnen in den USA ein nachlassendes Interesse an religiösen Gemeinschaften. Zugleich konstatiert er jedoch eine religiöse Hinwendung zu den Institutionen während der Jugendphase (2003, S. 228f.). Auch Gidoin (2014) beobachtet im Rahmen seiner Forschung im Großraum von Paris ein nachlassendes Interesse der jüngeren Generation, das ethno-religiöse Erbe der Elterngeneration fortzuführen. Zugleich stellt er fest, dass junge Erwachsene die Auseinandersetzung mit dem Buddhismus mit der vietnamesischen Herkunft verknüpfen und die Institutionen somit zu einem Ort der ethno-religiösen Rückbesinnung auf den vietnamesischen Herkunftskontext werden (2014, S. 56).

Obgleich davon auszugehen ist, dass unter jungen Erwachsenen mit vietnamesischen Wurzeln, wie unter anderen Angehörigen der „2.0 Generation", nur eine Minderheit religiös ist (Allenbach et al. 2010, S. 2), ist zu vermuten, dass Religion in der Phase der Identitätsfindung für Einzelne an Bedeutung gewinnt

3 Die Journalistin Khue Pham beschreibt dieses Spannungsverhältnis autobiografisch in dem Buch „Wir neuen Deutschen".

und in Form von Orientierung eine unterstützende Funktion für die Selbstpositionierung gegenüber unterschiedlichen Bezugssystemen übernimmt (Kögler / Dammayer 2015, S. 172). In meiner bisherigen Forschung zeigt sich, dass die von mir befragten jungen Erwachsenen mit zunehmendem Alter weniger Interesse daran haben Pagoden zu besuchen. Zugleich orientieren sie sich in Form von Konzepten wie Karma oder mittels Praktiken wie der Meditation, in ihrer Lebensführung am Buddhismus.

Dem Beitrag liegt zudem die These zugrunde, dass die befragten jungen Erwachsenen – anders als die Elterngeneration – ihre Religiosität individuell aushandeln. Mittels ihrer Religiosität positionieren sie sich zugleich gegenüber der christlich und säkular geprägten Schweizer und Deutschen Gesellschaft sowie der Elterngeneration.

In Anlehnung an Hurrelmann (2007) ist die Altersgruppe der befragten jungen Erwachsenen sehr breit gefasst und reicht von 17 bis 30 Jahren (2007, S. 41). Für die Forschung ist diese Jugendphase von besonderem Interesse, da junge Erwachsene in dieser Lebensphase Muster der späteren Lebensführung vorbereiten und in ihrer Biografie anlegen (King 2013). Biografisch-narrative Interviews (Rosenthal 2005) und teilnehmende Beobachtungen stellen eine geeignete Methode dar, um Einblick in den Generationenwandel, das Selbstverständnis der jungen Erwachsenen und ihre Lebenswelt, zu erhalten. Mittels der Rekonstruktion der Biografie wird im Folgenden versucht, die biografische Entwicklung einer individualisierten Religiosität nachvollziehbar darzustellen.

Zunächst gebe ich einen kurzen Einblick in das Sample und die Methoden der Datenerhebung und -auswertung. Darauf folgt die Auseinandersetzung mit der Lebensphase Jugend. Mittels des Konzeptes der *Identifikationswege* von Hervieu-Léger (2004) zeige ich individuelle Formen von religiöser Identitätsbildung anhand zweier Fallbeispiele auf. Danach werden Gemeinsamkeiten und Unterschiede der Fallbeispiele benannt. Den Abschluss bildet ein Fazit.

Migrationsbedingungen von VietnamesInnen und das Untersuchungsdesign

Die in diesem Beitrag präsentierten Fallbeispiele stellen Teilergebnisse meines laufenden Dissertationsprojektes am religionswissenschaftlichen Seminar der Universität Luzern dar.[4] Die Studie fokussiert auf Formen von Um- und Neuinterpretation vietnamesisch-buddhistischer Religiosität in der Schweiz und in

4 Die Promotion erfolgt im Rahmen des SNF- Forschungsprojektes: „Biographische Prozesse von religiöser Um- und Neuinterpretation: Vietnamesisch-buddhistische junge Erwachsene in der Schweiz und in Deutschland" unter der Leitung von Prof. Martin Baumann.

Deutschland. In diesem Beitrag stehen hingegen die biografischen Verläufe der jungen Erwachsenen im Vordergrund. Um diese Biografien besser verstehen zu können, gebe ich einen kurzen Einblick in die Migrationsgeschichte der Elterngeneration: In der Schweiz leben heute etwa 15.000[5] Menschen mit vietnamesischen Wurzeln. Insbesondere in den 1970er und 1980er Jahren immigrierten VietnamesInnen als Folge des Vietnamkrieges als Flüchtlinge in die Schweiz. Zuvor waren bereits in den 1960er Jahren VietnamesInnen zu Studienzwecken in die Westschweiz gekommen. Aufgrund des Krieges blieb ein Großteil von ihnen dauerhaft in der Schweiz.[6] Auch in Deutschland finden sich unterschiedliche vietnamesische Einwanderungsgruppen. In den 1950er Jahren entsandte die vietnamesische Regierung VietnamesInnen zu Ausbildungszwecken und ab den 1980er Jahren als VertragsarbeiterInnen nach Ostdeutschland (DDR). Ein Teil der VertragsarbeiterInnen blieb nach dem Systemzusammenbruch in Deutschland. In Westdeutschland (BRD) fanden VietnamesInnen vermehrt Ende der 1970er Jahre als Flüchtlinge[7] Aufnahme. Heute leben schätzungsweise 165.000 (Schaland/Schmiz 2016, S. 13) Menschen mit vietnamesischen Wurzeln in Deutschland. Sie stellen die größte asiatische MigrantInnengruppe in Deutschland dar sowie BuddhistInnen aus Vietnam die größte asiatisch-buddhistische Gruppierung in Europa (Baumann 2015, S. 41).

Wie die kurze Skizzierung der Einwanderungsgeschichte in den beiden Ländern zeigt, sind die Migrationsbedingungen von Menschen aus Vietnam sehr heterogen.[8] Ebenso verhält es sich bezüglich des ethnischen und sozio-ökonomischen Hintergrundes (Schaland/Schmiz 2016, S. 8; Weigelt 2013, S. 107). Etwa 50 % aller vietnamesischen MigrantInnen in den beiden Ländern gehören dem buddhistischen Glauben an.[9] Aufgrund zahlreicher Pagoden und der Pagode Vien Giac[10] in Hannover im Speziellen, sind VietnamesInnen in Deutschland öffentlich deutlich präsenter als in der Schweiz. In der Schweiz gibt es insgesamt

5 Die Zahlen umfassen Personen, die das Schweizer Bürgerrecht erhielten. Zwischen 1974 und 2017 waren dies 9951 Personen sowie Personen mit vietnamesischer Nationalität; 2018 waren dies 4307. (Angaben des Bundesamtes für Migration auf Nachfrage). VertreterInnen vietnamesischer Organisationen gehen von 15.000 Menschen mit vietnamesischen Wurzeln in der Schweiz aus.

6 Für eine ausführliche Darstellung der vietnamesischen Migrationsgeschichte in die Schweiz und nach Deutschland siehe u. a.: Wicker (1984), Weiss (2005), Weigelt (2013), Lê (2011), Hillmann (2005).

7 Für einen Überblick über die historische Entwicklung der VietnamesInnen in Deutschland: Schaland et al. (2016).

8 Auf die diesbezügliche Gefahr des „methodologischen Ethnizismus" weist unter anderem auch Schmiz (2014, S. 34) hin.

9 Zu berücksichtigen gilt es, dass die Zugehörigkeit zum Buddhismus häufig nicht exklusiv verstanden wird (Weigelt 2012, S. 92).

10 Die Pagode Vien Giac in Hannover gilt, neben der Pagode Khanh-Anh bei Paris, als eine der größten vietnamesisch-buddhistischen Pagoden Europas.

drei Pagoden. In Deutschland finden sich etwa 20 Pagoden.[11] Auch wenn auf den Ländervergleich in diesem Artikel nicht ausführlich eingegangen werden kann, werden länderspezifische Besonderheiten in den Fallanalysen berücksichtigt.

Wer sind nun die befragten jungen Erwachsenen? Insgesamt habe ich zwischen 2015 und 2017 rund 22 Interviews in der Schweiz und in Deutschland geführt.[12] Unter den Befragten befinden sich Personen, die stark in vietnamesisch-buddhistische Institutionen eingebunden sind und Personen, die sich als religiös distanziert positionieren.[13] Das Durchschnittsalter der Befragten liegt bei 23 Jahren. Bis auf zwei Personen besitzen alle InterviewpartnerInnen keine eigene Migrationserfahrung. Die Mehrheit stammt aus Flüchtlingsfamilien.[14] Mehrheitlich besitzen sie die Schweizer oder deutsche Staatsangehörigkeit. Der Großteil der befragten jungen Erwachsenen befindet sich im Studium.[15]

Für die Befragungen wurde die Form des biografisch narrativen Interviews gewählt. Für die akteurszentrierte Forschung eignet sich diese Erhebungsform, um „Prozessstrukturen des Lebenslaufs" (Schütze 1983) zu untersuchen. Mittels eines Erzählstimulus wird dem Gegenüber Raum für die selbstbestimmte Strukturierung der Lebensgeschichte gegeben. Der Vorteil dieser Interviewform liegt darin begründet, dass die Erzählpersonen in ihre Erzählung, im besten Falle, „Handlungsmotive" und „prozessuale Zusammenhänge" einfließen lassen. Somit wird es möglich, einen Einblick in die „Orientierungen" und „Ordnungsstrukturen" der Erzählpersonen zu erhalten (Strübing 2013, S. 100). Zudem zeigen sich in den Biografien gesellschaftliche Gegebenheiten:

11 Die Zahl beruht auf einer Schätzung von VertreterInnen der vietnamesisch-buddhistischen Gemeinschaften auf Nachfrage.

12 In die Auswertung fließen zudem Daten aus teilnehmenden Beobachtungen in religiösen Institutionen in der Schweiz, Deutschland und Frankreich ein sowie bei jugendspezifischen Anlässen. Ein weiteres Erhebungsinstrument stellen im Dissertationsprojekt Ego-zentrierte Netzwerkkarten dar.

13 Die Rekrutierung der InterviewpartnerInnen erfolgte über das *Schneeballverfahren*, religiöse Institutionen, Social Media, jugendspezifische Anlässe und Personen, die sich von sich aus als InterviewpartnerInnen meldeten.

14 Die Etablierung der vietnamesisch-buddhistischen Infrastruktur in der Schweiz und in Deutschland erfolgte vorwiegend auf Initiative der sogenannten Boat-People. Die Religiosität und Einbindung der ehemaligen VertragsarbeiterInnen wird häufig in Zusammenhang mit der religiösen Revitalisierung in Vietnam gesehen. Erst 2008 entstand, initiiert von ehemaligen Vertragsarbeiterinnen, die erste größere Pagode Lien Tri in Ostdeutschland (Mundt 2012, S. 26).

15 Kinder vietnamesischer EinwanderInnen gelten als überdurchschnittlich bildungserfolgreich (siehe für Deutschland El-Mafaalani / Kemper 2017). Das Sample spiegelt somit Tendenzen im Feld. Aus eigener Erfahrung gitl es jedoch zu bedenken, dass sich dieser Personenkreis eher bereit erklärt, an Befragungen teilzunehmen.

> „Die Rekonstruktion des Einzelfalls in seiner Einbettung in soziale Kontexte ermöglicht es, die Wechselbeziehung zwischen Individuellem und Allgemeinem, zwischen Individuum und Gesellschaft aufspüren zu können" (Rosenthal 2015, S. 50).

Die Auswertung der beiden Fallbeispiele erfolgt in Anlehnung an das rekonstruktive Verfahren der Biografieforschung. Für die Auswertung verwendet Rosenthal eine Verbindung aus Textanalyse strukturaler, objektiver Hermeneutik und thematischer Feldanalyse. Einzelne Sequenzen der Narration werden bei der Analyse in den Zusammenhang der Gesamterzählung gestellt. Rosenthal unterscheidet zwischen der „erlebten" und der „erzählten" Lebensgeschichte. Die Erzählung wird daher mittels „objektiver Daten", wie den Kontextbedingungen und spezifischer Daten des Lebenslaufs kontrastiert. Dieses Vorgehen soll es ermöglichen, zwischen der Selbstpräsentation des Befragten und seiner tatsächlichen Lebensgeschichte zu differenzieren. Für die beiden Fallbeispiele bedeutet dies in der Analyse zu berücksichtigen, wie sich die zwei jungen Erwachsenen im Gespräch präsentieren und die Bedeutung dieser Präsentation und des in der Vergangenheit erlebten für die jeweilige Lebensgeschichte zu rekonstruieren (Rosenthal 2005, S. 202ff.).

Die Jugendphase und die Bedeutung der eigenen Religiosität

Die Jugendphase ist für das Generationenverhältnis markant, da „über Jugend (…) der Generationenwechsel einerseits vorbereitet, andererseits aufgeschoben wird" (King 2013, S. 25). In diese Lebensphase fällt die „Entwicklung der intellektuellen und sozialen Kompetenzen", die „Entwicklung der Körper- und Geschlechtsidentität und der Bindungsfähigkeit", die „Entwicklung von sozialen Kontakten und Entlastungsstrategien" sowie die „Entwicklung eines individuellen Werte- und Normensystems" (Hurrelmann / Quenzel 2016, S. 26f.). Jugendliche und junge Erwachsene reflektieren und verarbeiten die bisher vermittelten Werte und Erfahrungen. In der Folge entscheiden sie sich, Traditionen und religiöse sowie kulturelle Praktiken fortzuführen oder sie umzuinterpretieren bzw. nicht zu übernehmen. Bestimmt wird diese Entwicklung von dem zur Verfügung stehenden *Möglichkeitsraum* (vgl. King 2013, S. 39), d.h. den gesellschaftlichen und sozialen Bedingungen der Sozialisation.

Sowohl in der Schweiz als auch in Deutschland wachsen junge Erwachsene heute in individualisierten, religiös pluralisierten und säkularisierten Gesellschaften auf. Die heutige Jugendphase ist geprägt von Wahl- und Individualisierungsmöglichkeiten und zugleich bestimmt durch sozialen Druck zur Individualisierung (Hurrelmann / Quenzel 2016, S. 59f.). Auch makrostrukturelle Bedingungen prägen die Sozialisation. Ein Beispiel hierfür sind die Aufnahme-bedingungen von VietnamesInnen in der Schweiz und in Deutschland. Das „Inkorporationsregime“ (Soysal 1994) der beiden Länder unterscheidet sich deutlich. Dieser Umstand hat auch einen Einfluss auf die religiöse Infrastruktur: Im Vergleich zur Schweiz kam es in Deutschland zu einer verstärkten Gemeinschaftsbildung, die sich in der kulturellen, religiösen und ökonomischen Infrastruktur wiederspiegelt. Zudem entstand teilweise eine hohe räumliche Konzentration von VietnamesInnen (Schaland/Schmiz 2016, S. 15), was ebenfalls einen Einfluss auf die Sozialisation der jungen Erwachsenen hat.

Neben diesen makrostrukturellen Gegebenheiten und den sozio-ökonomischen Sozialisationsbedingungen prägen auch individuelle Erfahrungen die Identitätsbildung junger Erwachsener. Bei Kindern von MigrantInnen kommt es häufig in der Jugendphase durch die Auseinandersetzung mit ihren Eltern gleichsam auch zu der Auseinandersetzung mit ihren kulturellen Wurzeln und der Mehrheitsgesellschaft, in der sie sozialisiert wurden (Tressat 2011, S. 40). Angehörige einer religiösen Minderheit, wie die des Islams, reflektieren teilweise in der Jugendphase ihre Religiosität aufgrund des Minderheitenstatus (Baumann et al. 2017, S. 11).[16] Diese Feststellung lässt sich auch auf die befragten jungen Erwachsenen in meinem Sample übertragen.

Die Ausbildung der eigenen Identifikationen umfasst somit die Reflexion der eigenen Persönlichkeit und die Selbstpositionierung gegenüber unterschiedlichen Bezugssystemen wie des Elternhauses, des Schul- und Ausbildungssystems und des bis dahin vermittelten Werte- und Glaubenssystems.

Gärtner (2013) konstatiert eine „Individuierung“ von Religion. In ihrer Studie untersucht sie junge Erwachsene mit sowie ohne zugewanderte Eltern in Deutschland. Ihr Fazit lautet, dass die jungen Erwachsenen ihre Religiosität individuell ausbilden und biografisch deuten (2013, S. 229). Zwischen den Generationen lassen sich dadurch Verschiebungen feststellen. So benennt Baumann (2017) ein individuelleres Religionsverständnis unter jungen MuslimInnen und tibetischen BuddhistInnen in der Schweiz als noch in der Elterngeneration. Als Gründe hierfür nennt er den ‚Megatrend‘ der Individualisierung, „die Sozialisation im Schweizer Bildungssystem“ und „das gesellschaftliche Bild von Religion als individuell und privatisiert“ (Baumann 2017, S. 133). Zu dieser Verschiebung gehört, dass unter der „Zweitgeneration“ eine Fragenkultur entsteht (Marla-Küsters 2015, S. 409; Schlieter / et al 2014, S. 198).[17] Teilweise kommt es zudem bei der „Zweitgeneration“ zu einer Entkopplung von Religion und Ethnizität. Damit einher gehen Abgrenzungs- und Zugehörigkeitsformen bezüglich der eigenen Identität (Dahinden et al. 2010). Dies ist auch in meinem

16 Siehe auch den Beitrag von Andreas Tunger et al. in diesem Band

17 Auch der Beitrag von Katharina Limacher in diesem Band zeigt den Einfluss der Sozialisationsbedingungen deutlich auf.

Sample der Fall. Ein Teil der Befragten beruft sich in seinem Selbstverständnis als BuddhistInnen auf die vietnamesischen Wurzeln, ein anderer Teil der Befragten differenziert zwischen Ethnie und Religionszugehörigkeit.

Die individuelle Auseinandersetzung hat zur Folge, dass junge Erwachsene häufig weniger in religiösen Institutionen aktiv sind und geringes Interesse am Vollzug von religiösen Ritualen zeigen. Stattdessen setzen sie sich stärker intellektuell mit ihrer Religiosität auseinander (vgl. Schlieter et. al 2011, S. 8f.). Trotz des individuellen Zugangs zeigen junge Erwachsene weiterhin Interesse an Vergemeinschaftungsformen. Es kann somit nicht grundsätzlich von einer Distanzierung von religiösen Institutionen ausgegangen werden. Kögler / Dammayr (2015) stellen in ihrer Studie zu Jugendlichen in Österreich fest: „Der gemeinschaftsstiftende Charakter von Religion ist nach wie vor ein zentrales Kriterium, das von Jugendlichen positiv konnotiert und geschätzt wird." (2015, S. 172). Die Zugehörigkeit zu religiösen Gemeinschaften erfolgt jedoch stärker als individuelle Wahl und ohne eine Verpflichtung einzugehen. Gebhardt spricht daher von Formen des *belonging without obeying* und *belonging without commitment* (Gebhardt 2013, S. 299ff.). Diese Zugehörigkeitsformen finden sich auch bei den befragten jungen Erwachsenen.

Um Formen von individueller Religiosität genauer herauszuarbeiten, beziehe ich mich im Folgenden auf Hervieu-Légers Konzept von Religion. Die Grundlage dieses Konzeptes ist die Annahme, dass Religion mittels kollektiv geteilter Erinnerung von Generation zu Generation weitergegeben wird (Hervieu-Léger 2004, S. 11, vgl. auch 1993). In der Moderne erfolgt die Aneignung von Religion mittels individueller *Identifikationswege* (2004, S. 45). Trotz der „Entkopplung von Glaubensvorstellung und Religionspraxis" haben Individuen weiterhin das Bedürfnis aufgrund von Gruppenzugehörigkeiten, eine Bestätigung der eigenen Religiosität zu erfahren (ebd. 32). Die Identifikation mit Religion vollzieht sich aufgrund von unterschiedlichen *Identifikationsdimensionen*, die die Gläubigen individuell ausbilden und zu unterschiedlichen Typen von Religiosität kombinieren.

Eine dieser Dimensionen stellt die *Gruppendimension* dar. Hierunter fällt die formale Zugehörigkeit zu einer Gruppe und die damit einhergehende Abgrenzung gegenüber anderen Gruppen. In den geführten Interviews erklären die Befragten immer wieder, dass sie aufgrund der „Zufluchtnahme zu den Drei Juwelen", dem Ritual zur Aufnahme in die buddhistische Religionsgemeinschaft, BuddhistInnen sind. Sie berufen sich, ähnlich wie ChristInnen aufgrund der Taufe, auf ihre formale Mitgliedschaft in der buddhistischen Religionsgemeinschaft. Auch ohne den regelmäßigen Vollzug von religiösen Ritualen identifizieren sich die Befragten aufgrund dieser Initiierung mit der Gruppe der BuddhistInnen (ebd. S. 47).

Eine weitere Dimension stellt die *ethische Dimension* dar. Ohne die Mitgliedschaft in einer religiösen Gemeinschaft werden Werte einer Religion übernommen. Ein Beispiel hierfür ist, wenn Befragte erklären, dass sich ihre Religiosität mittels der Orientierung am Buddhismus als *way of life* ausdrückt (ebd.).

Die *kulturelle Dimension* umfasst „die Gesamtheit der kognitiven, symbolischen und praktischen Elemente, aus denen das Erbe einer einzelnen Tradition besteht." Ein Teil der Befragten versteht seine Religiosität als ethno-religiöses Erbe oder verbindet die eigene Religiosität mit der buddhistischen Religiosität der Eltern (ebd. 47f.).

Die *emotionale Dimension* umfasst Erfahrungen, die zu einem „Wir-Gefühl" führen. Ein Beispiel hierfür ist das gemeinsame Erleben während der Teilnahme an einer Pilgerreise. Das außeralltägliche Erlebnis verstärkt die Verbundenheit mit anderen Teilnehmenden dieser Reise (ebd. 48).

Diese religiösen *Identifikationsdimensionen* werden aufgrund unterschiedlicher Erfahrungen und Kontexte ausgebildet und schließen auch gelebte Einstellungen und die Religionspraxis mit ein (ebd. 45).

Religiöse Identitätsbildung durch individuelle „Identifikationswege"

Im Folgenden wird der *Identifikationsweg* von individueller Religiosität anhand zweier Biografien rekonstruiert. Die religiösen Biografien veranschaulichen, welchen Einfluss vietnamesisch-buddhistische Institutionen, die vietnamesisch-buddhistische Erziehung und die Sozialisation in der Schweiz bzw. in Deutschland auf die religiöse Identitätsbildung haben können. Nathalie[18] ist zum Erhebungszeitpunkt 25 Jahre alt und in der Schweiz aufgewachsen. Mike stammt aus Deutschland und ist zum Erhebungszeitpunkt 18 Jahre alt.

Nathalie: Die Buddhistische Gemeinschaft als Rückbindung an die Herkunftsfamilie

Ende der 1980er Jahre kommt Nathalie in der deutschsprachigen Schweiz zur Welt. Regelmäßig besuchen die Eltern eine der drei Pagoden in der Schweiz oder

18 Markant im Sample ist der Umgang der Elterngeneration mit Vornamen. So haben die Befragten teilweise vietnamesische Namen oder/und internationale Namen, wie die beiden Personen in den Fallbeispielen. Hinzu kommen teilweise noch Dharma Namen, buddhistische Namen, für die vietnamesisch-buddhistische Gemeinschaft. Für die Veröffentlichung wurden alle Namen anonymisiert.

fahren zu religiösen Anlässen nach Deutschland. Nathalie kommt so mit anderen Kindern in Kontakt und lernt die buddhistischen Zeremonien in der Pagode kennen. Dort besucht sie auch den Vietnamesisch-Unterricht, den ältere Mitglieder der Gemeinschaft anbieten. Die Familie ist folglich zunächst sehr stark in die vietnamesisch-buddhistische Gemeinschaft eingebunden. Im Alltag nimmt die Religion hingegen eine geringere Rolle ein. Ein festes Ritual ist lediglich die jährliche Ahnenverehrung für die verstorbenen Großeltern am Hausaltar.

Als Nathalie in die Schule kommt, lernt sie durch ihre MitschülerInnen christliche Glaubensinhalte kennen und besucht mit ihnen hin und wieder die Jungschar. Jetzt reflektiert sie das erste Mal ihre eigene Religiosität:

> „Als Kind denkt man ja: Du bist doch Buddhistin und du musst doch an die Wiedergeburt glauben, und ans Karma. Also, mir war das wie zu weit weg. Ich konnte es mir auch nicht wirklich vorstellen, ich konnte mir das mit Himmel und Hölle besser vorstellen. Vielleicht, weil das meine Mitmenschen mehr beschäftigt, weil das viel präsenter war" (IN, Z573–577).

Zunächst führt der Kontakt mit den christlichen MitschülerInnen zu einer Ambivalenz gegenüber der eigenen Religiosität. Nathalie positioniert sich als Buddhistin. Zugleich empfindet sie die christliche Religion als „viel präsenter" und kann sich „Himmel und Hölle" besser als Konzepte wie die „Wiedergeburt" vorstellen.

Im Verlauf der Biografie entfremdet sich Nathalie von der vietnamesisch-buddhistischen Gemeinschaft. Zudem wird der Kontakt der Familie zu den buddhistischen Institutionen in der Folgezeit geringer. Um ihre schulischen Leistungen nicht zu gefährden, entscheiden die Eltern, sie nicht weiter in den Vietnamesisch-Unterricht zu schicken. In der Jugend kommt es zunehmend zu Konflikten mit den Eltern. Die Religion hat für sie während dieser Zeit keine große Bedeutung:

> „Ich war sowieso mit mir selbst beschäftigt. Da hatte die Religionsfrage noch gar keinen Platz für mich oder ich habe den Kontakt gar nicht gesucht" (IN, Z190–192).

Die Auseinandersetzung mit dem von der Mutter vorgelebten Frauenbild wird zu einem wichtigen Thema in der Adoleszenz und führt zu Ablehnung sowie der Entwicklung eigener Geschlechterbilder (vgl. King 2013, 80f.). Sie empfindet ihre Mutter als „konservativ" und geprägt durch das „alte Gedankengut der Vietnamesen". Da sie sich an ihrem Schweizer Umfeld orientiert, fordert sie den Lebensstil Schweizer Jugendlicher ein, einen Freund zu haben und auszugehen. In ihrem Selbstverständnis positioniert sie sich als Schweizerin:

> „Ich würde auch sagen, ich bin ziemlich westlich. Also auch wenn ich vietnamesisch aussehe, ist schon mehr Schweizer Blut drin (lacht) als Vietnamesisches (...). Ich fühle

mich ehrlich gesagt in der vietnamesischen Gesellschaft ein bisschen eingeengt" (IN, Z977–981).

In dieser Sequenz wird das Spannungsverhältnis zwischen den beiden Bezugssystemen deutlich. Markant ist Nathalies Betonung der Gegensätzlichkeit von „westlich" und „vietnamesisch" In der Schweizer Mehrheitsgesellschaft ist sie mit dem „vietnamesischem Aussehen" konfrontiert, in der vietnamesischen Gemeinschaft mit dem „Schweizer Blut", das sie von der Elterngeneration unterscheidet. In der „vietnamesischen Gemeinschaft" fühlt sie sich eingeengt, möglicherweise aufgrund von Erwartungshaltungen, während sie in der Schweizer Gesellschaft eine gewisse Freiheit empfindet.

Erst aufgrund ihrer Ausbildung zur Lehrerin kommt es wieder zu einer Annäherung an die vietnamesisch-buddhistische Gemeinschaft, in der sie nun aufgrund ihres Bildungsstandes Anerkennung genießt:

> „Also, man schätzt, dass ich wie eine Verbindung bin zwischen diesen zwei Welten, also ich bin im Schulsystem drinnen, habe noch die vietnamesische Kultur, aber kenne auch das Schweizerische und das schätzen sie glaube ich noch" (IN, Z1198–1201).

Sie engagiert sich nun in der Nachwuchsarbeit der vietnamesisch-buddhistischen Gemeinschaft. Auch die Auseinandersetzung mit der eigenen Religiosität gewinnt an Bedeutung. In ihrem Selbstverständnis ist der Buddhismus als *kulturelle Identifikationsdimension* eng mit ihren Wurzeln verknüpft, wie in der folgenden Interviewsequenz zum Ausdruck kommt:

> „Durch das Studium (…) bin ich in Kontakt gekommen mit verschiedenen Religionen wie dem Islam und dem Christentum und es gab Diskussionen und die haben mich wahrscheinlich wie angeregt und deshalb habe ich dann wahrscheinlich schnell gemerkt, dass der Buddhismus schon die Religion ist, die mir am nächsten steht, obwohl ich es gar nicht möchte. Und aus diesem Grund heraus hab ich dann angefangen, Bücher zu lesen auf Deutsch und die habe ich mir bewusst gesucht, weil vorher war es immer auf Vietnamesisch und ich konnte kein Vietnamesisch und das war sicher ein Hindernis, dass ich keinen Zugang hatte " (IN, Z234–242).

In dieser Passage zeigt sich die *kulturelle Identifikationsdimension.* In der Aussage „obwohl ich es nicht möchte" drückt sich aus, dass sie den Zugang nicht wählt, sondern bereits Buddhistin ist. Zusätzlich zu dieser „vererbten" Zugehörigkeit beginnt sie sich aktiv mit dem Buddhismus auseinanderzusetzen. Der Impuls hierfür entsteht durch die Ausbildung. Markant ist, dass sie nun aufgrund von Lektüre bewusst einen Zugang sucht, um Glaubensinhalte verstehen zu können. Während die vietnamesische Sprache in den Institutionen eine Barriere darstellt, ermöglicht die deutschsprachige Literatur einen Zugang.

Dieser Zugang erfolgt weniger wie bei der Elterngeneration über Rituale als vielmehr durch die Lektüre deutschsprachiger Bücher des vietnamesischen Zen Meisters Thich Nhat Hanh. Durch diese individuelle Auseinandersetzung mit dem Buddhismus entwickelt sie ein Religionsverständnis, das die Religion von der Ethnie entkoppelt:

> „Im Nachhinein muss ich sagen, es ist nicht die Religion, die mich damals gestört hat, sondern die Tradition oder die Werte und die Normen, die die Vietnamesen haben. Also das Konservative das hat mich glaube, ich gestört, und erst im Nachhinein, wenn ich jetzt die Bücher lese, kann ich langsam wie die Trennung sehen, aber vorher war das für mich ein Ganzes und deshalb so schwierig dann zu verstehen. Und indem ich nur die Lehre lese, und für mich das durchgehe und mir meine eigenen Gedanken dazu mache, kann ich es wie besser trennen. Es ist ja klar, es geht ja nur um die Lehre, und nicht um die Kultur, aber ich kann das mir dann vorstellen, wo dann die Grenze anfängt" (IN, Z293–303).

Der Textausschnitt zeigt die selbstbestimmte Auseinandersetzung mit der eigenen Religiosität, die Reflektion und die starke Intellektualisierung des Zugangs auf. Nathalie beruft sich nicht auf Autoritäten wie Ordinierte, sondern mittels Lektüre auf ihre eigene Auseinandersetzung mit buddhistischen Inhalten. Sie interpretiert die „Lehre" und macht sich „ihre eigenen Gedanken dazu." Kulturelle Elemente und die buddhistischen Rituale in der Pagode lehnt sie als etwas „Konservatives" ab. So gelingt ihr die Vereinbarung des selbstbestimmten „Schweizer" „Lebensstils" und der Zugehörigkeit zur vietnamesisch-buddhistischen Gemeinschaft. Sie identifiziert sich mittels der *ethischen Dimension* mit dem Buddhismus:

> „Es ist eher für mich ein Gedankengut eine Lebenseinstellung der Buddhismus, eine Weltansicht, wie man sein Leben lebt ja, eine Art Philosophie" (IN, Z553–555).

Deutlich wird hier die *ethische Dimension* der Identifikation mit Religion. Zudem zeigt sich das individuelle Verständnis von Buddhismus. Hinzu kommt eine selbstbestimmte Einbindung in die vietnamesisch-buddhistischen Institutionen:

> „Zum Beispiel die buddhistische Zeremonie am Morgen: Dort bin ich nicht anwesend. Ich komme immer extra später, aber es ist nicht so, dass der Buddhismus mir nicht wichtig ist, aber ich praktiziere ihn lieber für mich selbst oder lese lieber selbst für mich buddhistische Bücher und eigne mir so das Wissen oder die Gedanken selber an" (IN, Z43–47).

Statt der buddhistischen Zeremonie am Morgen bevorzugt sie es „für sich selbst" zu praktizieren. Worin diese Praxis besteht, wird nicht erwähnt. Stattdessen verweist sie darauf, „für sich selbst buddhistische Bücher" zu lesen oder sich „das Wissen oder die Gedanken selber" anzueignen. Gleichzeitig zeigt sich eine Form der Zugehörigkeit zur vietnamesisch-buddhistischen Institution, die auf keinerlei Verpflichtung gemäß des von Gebhardt (2013) konstatierten *belonging without obeying / commitment* beruht, sondern aufgrund der selbstbestimmten Form von Zugehörigkeit.

Zudem besucht Nathalie die vietnamesisch-buddhistische Gemeinschaft nicht aufgrund des religiösen Interesses, sondern aufgrund der Möglichkeit, sich in diesem Raum mit ihrer ethnischen Herkunft auseinandersetzen zu können:

> „Weil klar der Buddhismus ist der Kern, deshalb trifft man sich, man tauscht sich über die buddhistische Lehre aus und das ist so wie das Setting. Es zieht dann die vietnamesischen Leute an und das ist dann die Community und ich schätze diesen Austausch einfach noch das Vietnamesische, weil ich das sonst verlieren würde und das ist eigentlich die Hauptmotivation, dass ich meine Wurzeln nicht verliere, dass ich überhaupt in diesen Verein gehe" (IN, Z155–160).

Die Entkopplung von Ethnie und Religion zeigt sich hier deutlich. Zwar ist „das Setting" ein Religiöses, die Motivation für die Einbindung in die vietnamesisch-buddhistische Gemeinschaft sind jedoch die ethnischen Wurzeln. Anders als bei anderen befragten jungen Erwachsenen erfolgt diese Rückbindung nicht über Elemente der Jugendkultur oder einer Peergroup, sondern über die Einbindung in die buddhistische Gemeinschaft. Es muss jedoch berücksichtigt werden, dass sich in der deutschsprachigen Schweiz kaum solche Vergemeinschaftungsformen finden lassen und der zur Verfügung stehende *Möglichkeitsraum* in dieser Hinsicht beschränkt ist.

Abschließend lässt sich festhalten, dass die Religion für Nathalie eine Möglichkeit darstellt, sich nicht von den Eltern zu entfremden. Ihre berufliche Position im Bildungsbereich verschafft ihr Anerkennung und ermöglicht es ihr selbstbestimmt, ihre Zugehörigkeit und den Vollzug von Ritualen in der Gemeinschaft auszuüben. Sie positioniert sich als bildungserfolgreich und Vermittlerin zwischen dem Schweizer Schulsystem und dem Herkunftskontext ihrer Eltern. Die Einbindung in den Tempel sucht sie nach eigener Aussage, um ihre Wurzeln nicht zu verlieren. Es lässt sich annehmen, dass die Einbindung in die vietnamesisch-buddhistische Gemeinschaft auch eine Möglichkeit darstellt, mit dem Spannungsverhältnis der unterschiedlichen Bezugssysteme umzugehen. Der „Typus" ihrer religiösen Identifikation beinhaltet die *ethische Dimension*, da sie den Buddhismus bspw. als Philosophie versteht. Trotz der Entkopplung von Religion und Ethnie versteht sie sich aufgrund ihrer vietnamesischen Wurzeln als Buddhistin. Weniger Bedeutung kommt der *emotionalen Dimension* zu, da sie sich mit ihrer Religiosität in Form von Lektüre auseinandersetzt. Der *Gruppendimension* kommt ebenfalls eine geringe Bedeutung zu, da sie sich aufgrund der *ethischen* und *kulturellen Dimension* als Buddhistin definiert.

Mike: Identitätsbildung mittels vietnamesisch-buddhistischer Peergroup

Mike wird Ende der 1990er Jahre in Deutschland geboren. Mit seinen Eltern besucht er als Kind häufig die Pagode Vien Giac in Hannover. Im Elternhaus prägen die Kindheit Rituale wie die Ahnenverehrung oder die vegetarische Ernährung an Vollmondtagen. In der Grundschulzeit besucht er den evangelischen Religionsunterricht und beginnt nun seine eigene Religionszugehörigkeit zu reflektieren:

> „Es war dadurch, dass ich ja immer an den Buddhismus geglaubt habe und Buddha, wars dann halt ein bisschen komisch, dass ich dann irgendwie in der Schule dann über nen Gott gelernt hab und dass es einen Jesus gab und der uns ja von den Sünden erlöst und das kam mir alles so suspekt vor, weil ich kam noch nie mit den Werten klar dass irgendjemand eine Person oder ein Gott sich geopfert hat, damit wir unsere Sünden nicht mehr büßen müssen. Also, das habe ich nicht verstanden (...). Ich musste dann auch in den Gottesdienst gehen (...) und ich habe mir irgendwann gedacht: Okay wir singen jetzt Lieder aber irgendwie wird nicht richtig irgendwas praktiziert, also du machst dich halt nie irgendwann davon überzeugt, ein besserer Mensch zu sein. Wir essen vegetarisch, um eben keine Tiere zu töten (...). Ich habe auch nicht verstanden okay warum die Bibel? Warum glaubt man an so ein Buch? Und das war mir alles so suspekt" (IM, Z321–338).

Mike positioniert sich hier als Buddhist. Markant an der Interviewsequenz ist die Gegenüberstellung des Buddhismus und des Christentums und die Ablehnung des Christentums, da es ihn nicht „überzeugt." In Mikes Verständnis übernimmt im Buddhismus das Individuum die Verantwortung für sein Handeln, während im Christentum die Verantwortung an „einen Gott, der sich geopfert hat" oder an ein „Buch" abgegeben wird.

Zudem gibt es in dem Unterricht keinen Raum für die eigene religiöse Prägung, was dazu führt, dass Mike mit Eintritt in das Gymnasium den Besuch des Religionsunterrichts ablehnt. Stattdessen besucht er nun den Ethikunterricht.

> „Also ich war dann eher so Referent (lachend) dann also im Unterricht, dass ich eben gefragt wurde: „Ja okay passt das so?" Oder als irgendwelche Beispiele kamen, ob das irgendwie dem Buddhismus entspricht und dann konnte ich halt antworten. Ich war dann eher so der Experte im Bereich Buddhismus, statt, dass ich da wirklich was Neues über den Buddhismus gelernt habe" (IM, Z394–399).

Seine Religionszugehörigkeit wird nun im Bildungssystem thematisiert und er findet als „Experte" Anerkennung. In der Familie gewinnt die Religion zu dieser Zeit ebenfalls an Bedeutung, da die Eltern einen Gebetsraum einrichten und beginnen, sich vegetarisch zu ernähren. Die Familie besucht nun auch häufiger die Pagode.

Während dieser Zeit setzt sich Mike verstärkt mit seinem Glauben auseinander, um bei Fragen Dritter antworten zu können:

> „Ich habe mich immer durch meine Eltern als Buddhist identifiziert. Hab dann immer gesagt: „Okay ich bin Buddhist." Falls irgendjemand fragt, was ich glaube und dann wurde immer gesagt: „Ja okay, an was glaubt ihr denn genau?" Das Einzige, was ich sagen konnte, war halt eben: „Ja okay ich bin halt Buddhist, glaube an Buddha und Karma und Wiedergeburt." Aber warum genau konnte ich halt nie beantworten. Und eigentlich war es anfangs so dementsprechend halt auch, dass ich mich an die Mönche gewendet habe, um diese Fragen beantwortet zu kriegen, so dass ich eben solche Fragen beantworten kann. Und letzten Endes haben mich die Antworten dann auch überzeugt, dass ich dann eben auch überzeugter Buddhist sein kann" (IM, Z288–298).

In der Schule gerät Mike durch sein Bekenntnis zum Buddhismus in einen Positionierungszwang und setzt sich daraufhin mit dem Buddhismus auseinander, um als „Experte" Auskunft geben zu können. Markant ist, dass er dies zunächst nicht individuell versucht, sondern sich an religiöse Autoritäten in den Pagoden wendet. Durch die Erklärungen der Ordinierten findet er einen individuellen Zugang zum Buddhismus und setzt sich kritisch mit der eigenen Religiosität auseinander. Nachdem er sich zunächst mittels der *kulturellen Dimension* in Form von: „Ich habe mich immer durch meine Eltern als Buddhist identifiziert" als Buddhist positioniert hat, kommt nun die *ethische Dimension* in Form von „Antworten" hinzu, die ihn „überzeugen". Zudem entwickelt er in der Folge eine individuelle Religiosität, die sich von der Elterngeneration abgrenzt:

> „Was mir nicht wichtig ist im Buddhismus, ist so dieser Aberglaube, also vor allem die Geschichte des Buddhas, also nicht, dass sie dann irgendwie Mist ist oder so, sondern das ist dann eher so, dass es nicht mein Leben beeinflusst. Also, dass ich sozusagen die Grundgedanken also, dass man eben gutes Karma sammeln muss also, dass man gute Taten vollbringen sollte und dass man keinen Schaden oder kein Leid anrichten soll, das sehe ich so als mein Lebenspart an. Also eben als Philosophie." (IM, Z418–425).

Diese Interviewsequenz verdeutlicht das individualisierte Verständnis von Religion. Bestandteil des eigenen Religionsverständnisses sind keine jenseits gerichteten Praktiken, die Mike als „Aberglauben" bezeichnet. Die eigene Religiosität dient in erster Linie als eine Hilfestellung für den Alltag und das jetzige Leben. Hier drückt sich Mikes *ethische Dimension* von Identifikation mit Religion aus. Die Abgrenzung von der Elterngeneration zeigt auch deutlich den individualisierten und intellektualisierten Zugang von Mike auf.

Von großer Bedeutung wird für Mike die Peergroup in der Pagode. Sie ist für ihn identitätsstiftend. Die Pagode bietet folglich einen *Möglichkeitsraum*, mit anderen Jugendlichen in Kontakt zu kommen:

> „Ja also was halt vor allem gut ist, wenn ich Freunde habe, die auch Vietnamesen sind, eben auch mit vietnamesischer Erziehung groß geworden sind, ist es halt einfacher mit seinen Problemen klar zu kommen, weil viele Deutsche Freunde von mir z. B. können nicht verstehen, was das Problem sozusagen bei meinen Eltern ist. Es ist einfach einfacher mit Menschen zu reden, die dieselben Situationen durchleben, die eben den

> Buddhismus auch pflegen, die auch vietnamesisch erzogen worden sind. Ist einfacher mit denen einfach über Probleme zu reden, weil sie eben diese auch nachvollziehen können, das kann man bei Deutschen nicht unbedingt erwarten, dass die es nachvollziehen können" (IM, Z1098–1107).

Die religiöse Einbindung hilft in der Jugendphase durch Peers, die den gleichen ethnischen Hintergrund haben, die eigene Identität zu entwickeln. Zu der religiösen Grenzziehung gegenüber Christen lässt sich auch eine Abgrenzung gegenüber „Deutschen" und eine *emotionale Dimension* der Identifikation mit „Vietnamesen" feststellen. Die Peergroup in der Pagode bietet Unterstützung in der Jugendphase, da Mike hier auf andere junge Erwachsene trifft, die ihre Identität ebenfalls zwischen unterschiedlichen Bezugssystemen aushandeln.

Mit 16 Jahren nimmt Mike mit seinen Freunden aus der Pagode an einer Pilgerreise nach Indien teil. Ein Ordinierter, der als Bezugsperson der jungen Erwachsenen fungiert, pilgert mit ihnen durch Indien, um ihnen den Buddhismus vor Ort näher zu bringen.

> „Also, wir sind dann zweieinhalb Wochen rumgereist und sind an alle möglichen Denkmäler des Buddhismus gepilgert und haben auch allgemein den Buddhismus praktiziert, eben auch körperlich, sind dann auch den Berg hoch gepilgert sozusagen, immer alle drei Schritte dann die Niederwerfungen. Das war so ja durch diese Pilgerfahrt habe ich vor allem verschiedene Wege der Meditation gelernt und den inneren Frieden sozusagen" (IM, Z465–471).

Anhand der Pilgerreise zeigt sich ebenfalls die *emotionale Dimension*, da die Reise zusammen mit den Freunden erlebt wird. Das außeralltägliche Erlebnis in der Gemeinschaft führt zu einer Stärkung der eigenen Religiosität. Während Mike den Vollzug von Ritualen in der Pagode ablehnt, stellen die religiösen Niederwerfungen in Indien für ihn eine Besonderheit dar.

Markant an Mikes Selbstpräsentation ist, dass er sich klar von dem Christentum abgrenzt und somit ein sehr exklusives Religionsverständnis vertritt. Von dem „Aberglauben" der Elterngeneration grenzt er sich ebenfalls deutlich ab. Vielmehr präsentiert er sich als Vertreter einer Ethik, die es individuell im Alltag umzusetzen gilt. Es lässt sich annehmen, dass die Einbindung in die religiöse Gemeinschaft ihm mit Beginn der Adoleszenz einen Distinktionsgewinn ermöglicht. Die vietnamesisch-buddhistische Gemeinschaft gibt ihm Orientierung, da er hier auf andere Jugendliche trifft, die ähnlich wie er aufwachsen und sich in ihrem Empfinden von der deutschen Mehrheitsgesellschaft unterscheiden. Die Selbstpräsentationen als „Vietnamese" und als „Buddhist" dienen ihm dazu, sich klar zwischen den unterschiedlichen Bezugssystemen zu verorten. Diese klare Verortung markiert auch die ethnisch-religiöse Abgrenzung gegenüber Vertretern der Mehrheitsgesellschaft.

Der „Typus" seiner religiösen Identifikation beinhaltet die *ethische Dimen-*

sion, da er sich an den Werten des Buddhismus orientiert und ihn als eine Philosophie versteht. Auch die *kulturelle Dimension* der religiösen Identifikation findet sich bei Mike. Aufgrund seiner vietnamesischen Wurzeln definiert er sich als Buddhist. Die *emotionale Dimension* von Religion findet sich bei ihm in Form des „Wir-Gefühls“ gegenüber der vietnamesisch-buddhistischen Peergroup.

Gemeinsamkeiten und Unterschiede zwischen Nathalie und Mike

Die Fallbeispiele zeigen in verdichteter Form unterschiedliche Prozesse hin zu einer individuellen Religiosität auf. Sowohl Nathalie als auch Mike werden in einem religiös pluralen Umfeld sozialisiert. Nathalies *Möglichkeitsraum* ist bezüglich vietnamesisch-buddhistischer Anbindungen begrenzt. In der Kindheit besucht sie mit den Eltern verschiedene Pagoden, doch es ergibt sich keine Einbindung in eine vietnamesisch-buddhistische Peergroup oder der Kontakt zu Ordinierten als Bezugspersonen. Stattdessen stellt sie einer traditionellen „vietnamesischen“ Erziehung und Sozialisation im vietnamesischen Buddhismus eine offenere „Schweizerische“ Erziehung entgegen, die dann wiederum eine individuelle und intellektualisierte Annährung an den Buddhismus erlaubt. An ihrem Beispiel zeigt sich deutlich die Charakteristik der 2.0 Generation: Sie verortet sich nicht im Herkunftskontext der Eltern, sondern in dem Land, in dem sie aufwächst (Röttger-Rössler 2017, 274ff.). Mikes *Möglichkeitsraum* umfasst die Einbindung in die vietnamesisch-buddhistische Gemeinschaft der renommierten Pagode Vien Giac. Zudem trifft er in der Pagode auf Ordinierte, die ihm Orientierung geben. Eine weitere Form der Einbindung stellt die vietnamesisch-buddhistische Peergroup dar. Dennoch wählt auch er einen individuellen Umgang mit seiner Religiosität und lehnt Elemente wie die Rezitation als „Aberglauben“ ab.

Neben der Heranführung durch die Eltern an die vietnamesisch-buddhistische Religion prägen beide das Schulsystem und die Orientierung an Gleichaltrigen. Mit ihren *Identifikationswegen* einher geht die Abgrenzung und Selbstpositionierung gegenüber den unterschiedlichen Bezugssystemen. Während sich Nathalie gegenüber ihren Eltern und den vietnamesisch-buddhistischen Institutionen als „Schweizerin“ positioniert, positioniert sich Mike stärker gegenüber der Mehrheitsgesellschaft als „Vietnamese“ und „Buddhist.“ Markant ist weiterhin, dass für beide das Christentum eine Vergleichsfolie für die eigene Religionszugehörigkeit darstellt. Auffallend ist zudem, dass beide nach Vergemeinschaftungsformen suchen. Nathalie sucht den Kontakt zur vietnamesisch-buddhistischen Gemeinschaft, um ihre „Wurzeln nicht zu verlieren.“ Ihre religiöse Identifikation erfolgt aufgrund der *kulturellen Dimension.* Um sich mit der „Lehre“ und ihrer Religiosität individuell auseinanderzusetzen, bevorzugt sie die Lektüre. Mike sucht stärker Vergemeinschaftungsformen, um unter „Gleichgesinnten“ zu sein. Anders als bei Nathalie steht für ihn weniger die Wissensaneignung mittels Lektüre im Vordergrund, sondern der Austausch mit Ordinierten und der Peergroup. Seine religiöse Identifikation erfolgt ebenfalls aufgrund der *kulturellen Dimension* sowie der *emotionalen Dimension.*

Trotz der Unterschiede in den beiden Biografien passen beide das ethnoreligiöse Erbe der Elterngeneration an ihre Biografie an. Beide wählen eine *ethische Dimension* von religiöser Identifikation und eine selbstbestimmte Einbindung in vietnamesisch-buddhistische Gemeinschaften.

Fazit

Die Biografien von Nathalie und Mike geben einen Einblick in die religiöse Identitätsbildung junger Erwachsener mit vietnamesischen Wurzeln in der Schweiz und in Deutschland. Zudem fokussieren die Fallbeispiele auf Angehörige einer Religionsgemeinschaft, die in der Forschung bislang kaum beachtet wurden.

Der Beitrag hat gezeigt, dass die Jugendphase eine für die Religionsforschung relevante Lebensphase darstellt, da sich hier intergenerationale Veränderungsprozesse vollziehen. Die Religion kann in dieser Lebensphase an Bedeutung gewinnen und den Individualisierungs- und Selbstfindungsprozess unterstützen. Mittels der beiden Fallbeispiele habe ich aufgezeigt, dass die Religion auch dabei helfen kann, sich gegenüber unterschiedlichen Bezugssystemen zu positionieren. Anhand der Biografien wird auch deutlich, dass junge Erwachsene, die einer religiösen Minderheit angehören, teilweise in einen Positionierungszwang geraten. Hervieu-Légers (2004) Konzept der *religiösen Identifikationswege* erwies sich für die Analyse der Daten als geeignet, da es, wie die biografische Fallrekonstruktion, vom Akteur ausgeht. Es wird auf die Erzählperson und ihre Handlungsstrategien bezüglich der eigenen Religiosität fokussiert.

Das Ziel des Beitrages war es nicht, eine verallgemeinerte Aussage bezüglich der Religiosität junger Erwachsener mit vietnamesischen Wurzeln in den beiden Ländern zu treffen, sondern vielmehr – im Sinne der interpretativen Sozialforschung – die Entwicklung der individuellen Religiosität anhand zweier junger Erwachsener aufzuzeigen. An Nathalies und Mikes religiösen Biografien lassen sich dennoch Tendenzen bezüglich der Religiosität junger Erwachsener mit vietnamesischen Wurzeln für die beiden Länder ableiten. In den beiden Biografien spiegeln sich beispielsweise makrostrukturelle Bedingungen wider. Sie stellen einen Bestandteil des *Möglichkeitsraums* dar, in dem junge Erwachsene mit vietnamesischen Wurzeln ihre religiöse Identität aushandeln. Die Untersuchung von Biografien kann dabei helfen, für solche Bedingungen zu sensibilisieren.

Interviews

IN: Biografisch narratives Interview, 13.04.2017, Deutschschweiz, Nathalie
IM: Biografisch narratives Interview, 08.03.2017, Bayern, Mike

Literatur

Allenbach, Brigit / Herzig, Pascale / Monika Müller (2010): *Schlussbericht Migration und Religion: Perspektiven von Kindern und Jugendlichen in der Schweiz.* verfügbar: http://www.snf.ch/SiteCollectionDocuments/nfp/nfp58/NFP58_Schlussbericht_Giordano.pdf [22.10.2018]. Bern: Nationales Forschungsprogramm NFP 58.

Barber, Tamsin (2015): *Oriental identities in super-diverse Britain: Young Vietnamese in London.* London: Palgrave Macmillan.

Baumann, Martin (2000): *Migration, Religion, Integration: buddhistische Vietnamesen und Hinduistische Tamilen in Deutschland.* Marburg: Diagonal-Verlag.

– (2015): „Buddhismus in Europa -Geschichte und die zweite Immigrantengeneration." *Migration und Soziale Arbeit,* 37 (1), S. 38–44

– (2017): „Religiös selbstbestimmt, reflektiert und integriert. Analyse religiöser Neuinterpretationen bei jungen Erwachsenen mit Migrationshintergrund." In: Arens, Edmund / Baumann, Martin / Liedhegener, Antonius / Müller, Wolfgang W. / Ries, Markus (Hg.): *Religiöse Identitäten und gesellschaftliche Integration.* Baden-Baden: Nomos, S. 107–138.

Baumann, Martin / Endres, Jürgen / Martens, Silvia / Tunger-Zanetti, Andreas (2017): *„Hallo, es geht um meine Religion!" Muslimische Jugendliche in der Schweiz auf der Suche nach ihrer Identität.* verfügbar: https://www.unilu.ch/fileadmin/fakultaeten/ksf/institute/zrf/dok/Forschungsbericht_Hallo_es_geht_um_meine_Religion.pdf [22.10.2018]. Luzern: Zentrum Religionsforschung.

Beglinger, Martin (2017): „Warum sich Vietnamesen im Westen so gut zurechtfinden und als Integrationswunder gelten." *Neue Zürcher Zeitung,* [Zeitung, Onlineausgabe] 18. August 2017, verfügbar: https://www.nzz.ch/gesellschaft/vietnamesen-integrations wunder-ld.1311265 [17.12.2018].

Beth, Uta / Tuckermann, Anja (2008): *Heimat ist da, wo man verstanden wird. Junge VietnamesInnen in Deutschland.* Berlin: Archiv der Jugendkulturen Verlag.

Dahinden, Janine / Duemmler, Kerstin / Moret, Joëlle (2010): *Schlussbericht Religion und Ethnizität: Welche Praktiken, Identitäten und Grenzziehungen? Eine Untersuchung mit jungen Erwachsenen.* verfügbar: http://www.snf.ch/SiteCollectionDocuments/nfp/nfp58/NFP58_Schlussbericht_DahindenJanine.pdf [17.12.2018] Bern: Nationales Forschungsprogramm NFP 58.

El-Mafaalani, Aladin / Kemper, Thomas (2017): „Bildungserfolgreich trotz ungünstiger Rahmenbedingungen. Empirische Ergebnisse und theoretische Überlegungen zum Bildungserfolg von vietnamesischen Kindern und Jugendlichen im deutschen Schulsystem" In: Kocatürk-Schuster, Bengü / Kolb, Arnd / Long, Than / Schultze, Günther / Wölck, Sascha (Hg): *Unsichtbar. Vietnamesisch-Deutsche Wirklichkeiten.* Köthen: druckhaus köthen, S. 217–229.

Gärtner, Christel (2013): „Religiöse Identität und Wertbindungen von Jugendlichen in Deutschland.“ *Kölner Zeitschrift für Soziologie und Sozialpsychologie,* (65), S. 211–233.

Gebhardt, Winfried (2013): „Believing without belonging? Religiöse Individualisierung und neue Formen religiöser Vergemeinschaftung“ In: Kreutzer, Ansgar / Gruber, Franz (Hg.): *Im Dialog. Systematische Theologie und Religionssoziologie.* Freiburg im Breisgau: Herder, S. 297–317.

Gidoin, Jerome (2014) : „La réactualisation du lien de filiation chez les Vietnamiens de France à partir du bouddhisme.“ *Revue Enfances Familles Générations,* (20), S. 45–57.

Hervieu-Léger, Danièle (1993) : *La religion pour mémoire.* Paris: Cerf.

– (2004) : *Pilger und Konvertiten. Religion in Bewegung.* Würzburg: Ergon Verlag.

Hillmann, Felicitas (2005): „Riders on the storm: Vietnamese in Germany's two migration systems“ In: Spaan, Ernst / Hillmann, Felicitas / van Naerssen, Ton (Hg.): *Asian Migrants and European Labour Markets.* London, New York: Routledge, S. 80–100.

Ho, Loc (2003): *Der vietnamesische Buddhismus in den USA. Der Stellenwert des Glaubens in der neuen Heimat.* Dissertation: Universität Hannover.

Hurrelmann, Klaus (2007): *Lebensphase Jugend. Eine Einführung in die sozialwissenschaftliche Jugendforschung.* Weinheim München: Juventa Verlag.

Hurrelmann, Klaus / Quenzel, Gudrun (2016): *Lebensphase Jugend. Eine Einführung in die sozialwissenschaftliche Jugendforschung.* Weinheim München: Juventa Verlag.

King, Vera (2013): *Die Entstehung des Neuen in der Adoleszenz. Individuation, Generativität und Geschlecht in modernisierten Gesellschaften.* Opladen: Leske + Budrich.

Kocatürk-Schuster, Bengü / Kolb, Arnd / Long, Than / Schultze, Günther, Wölck, Sascha (2017) (Hg.): *Unsichtbar. Vietnamesisch-Deutsche Wirklichkeit.* o.O.: Edition DOMiD.

Kögler, Ilse / Dammayer, Maria (2015): „Jugend und Religion in Österreich.“ *Interdisciplinary Journal for Religion and Transformation in Contemporary Society,* 1(1), S. 152–176. https://doi.org/10.14220/jrat.2015.1.1.15 [17. 12. 2018].

Lê, Sébastian (2011) : *Des Étudiants Aux ViêtKiêu. La communauté Vietnamienne de Lausanne de 1960 à 2008.* Bureau lausannois pour l'intégration des immigrés, Ville de Lausanne.

Lenz, Susanne (2016): „Das vietnamesische Bildungswunder.“ *Berliner Zeitung.* [Zeitung, Onlineausgabe] 27. 08. 2016, verfügbar: https://www.berliner-zeitung.de/berlin/wahl/lichtenberg-das-vietnamesische-bildungswunder-24654152 [17. 12. 2018].

Levitt, Peggy / Waters, Mary C. (2002): *The Changing Face of Home. The transnational Lives of the Second Generation.* New York: Russel Sage.

Marla -Küsters, Sandhya (2015): *Diaspora Religiosität im Generationenverlauf. Die zweite Generation srilankisch-tamilischer Hindus in NRW.* Würzburg: Ergon Verlag.

Mecheril, Paul (2003): *Prekäre Verhältnisse. Über natio-ethno-kulturelle (Mehrfach-)Zugehörigkeit.* Münster: Waxmann.

Müller, Max (2017): „Die vietnamesische Diaspora in Berlin -transnationale Identitätskonstruktion im Spannungsfeld zwischen Viet kieu und Bindestrich-Deutscher.“ *GISCA Occasional Papers,* (11), Gottingen: Institute for Social and Cultural Anthropology. https://doi.org/10.3249/2363-894X-gisca-11 [17. 12. 2018].

Mundt, Karin (2012): *Vom Delegierten der sozialistischen Moderne zum gläubigen Zuwanderer? Religiöser Wandel vietnamesischer Migranten in der DDR und Ostdeutschland.* Berlin: LIT Verlag.

Pham, Khue (2012): „Mein vietnamesisches Ich." In: Bota, Alice / Pham, Khue / Topcu, Özlem (Hg.): *Wir neuen Deutschen. Wer wir sind, was wir wollen.* Reinbek bei Hamburg: Rowohlt. S. 80–88.

Rosenthal, Gabriele (2005): „Die Biographie im Kontext der Familien- und Gesellschaftsgeschichte." In: Völter, Bettina/Dausien, Bettina/Lutz, Helma/Rosenthal, Gabriele (Hg.): *Biographieforschung im Diskurs.* Wiesbaden: Springer Fachmedien. S. 46–64.

– (2015): *Interpretative Sozialforschung. Eine Einführung.* Weinheim und München: Juventa.

Röttger-Rössler, Birgitt (2016): „Multiple Zugehörigkeiten. Eine emotionstheoretische Perspektive auf Migration". *Working Paper SFB 1171 Affective Societies – Dynamiken des Zusammenlebens in bewegten Welten,* (4). Berlin: SFB 1171 Affective Societies. https://refubium.fu-berlin.de/bitstream/handle/fub188/19021/MultiplexZugehxriglei ten_Workingxpapers_final.pdf?sequence=1&isAllowed=y [17.12.2018].

– (2017): „Deutsche mit Eltern aus Vietnam. Affektive Dimensionen der Eltern-Kind-Beziehungen im vietnamesischen Berlin." In: Kocatürk-Schuster, Bengü / Kolb, Arnd / Long, Than / Schultze, Günther, Wölck, Sascha (Hg.): *Unsichtbar. Vietnamesisch-Deutsche Wirklichkeit.* o.O.: Edition DOMiD, S. 274–287.

Rumbaut, Rubén (2006): „Severed or Sustained Attachments? Language, Identity, and Imagined Communities in the Post-Immigrant Generation." In: Levitt, Peggy / Waters, Mary (Hg.): *The Changing Face of Home: The Transnational Lives of the Second Generation.* New York: Russel Sage Foundation, S. 43–96.

Schaland, Ann-Julia / Schmiz, Antonie (2016): *Die vietnamesische Diaspora in Deutschland.* Bonn, Eschborn: GIZ. https://www.giz.de/fachexpertise/downloads/giz2016-de-diasporastudie-vietnam.pdf [17.12.2018].

Schlieter, Jens / Kind, Marietta / Lauer, Tina (2014): *Die zweite Generation der Tibeter in der Schweiz. Identitätsaushandlungen und Formen buddhistischer Religiosität.* Zürich: Seismo

Schmiz, Antonie (2011): *Transnationalität als Ressource? Netzwerke vietnamesischer Migranten und Migrantinnen zwischen Berlin und Vietnam.* Bielefeld: Transcript.

Schütze, Fritz (1983): „Biographieforschung und narratives Interview." *Neue Praxis,* (13)3, S. 283–293.

Soysal, Yasemin Nuhoglu (1994): *Limits of Citizenship: Migrants and Postnational Membership in Europe.* Chicago: University of Chicago Press.

Strübing, Jörg (2013): *Qualitative Sozialforschung: Eine Einführung.* Berlin / Boston: De Gruyter Oldenbourg.

Tressat, Michael (2011): *Muslimische Adoleszenz? Zur Bedeutung muslimischer Religiosität bei jungen Migranten. Biografieanalytische Fallstudien.* Frankfurt am Main: Lang.

Weigelt, Frank (2013): *Die vietnamesisch-buddhistische Diaspora in der Schweiz: über Organisationsstrukturen und Dynamiken buddhistischer Praxis.* Hamburg: Kovac.

Weiss, Karin / Dennis, Mike (2005): *Erfolg in der Nische? Die Vietnamesen in der DDR und in Ostdeutschland.* Münster: LIT Verlag.

Wicker, Hans-Rudolf (1984): „Flüchtlinge aus Vietnam: Elemente ihrer traditionellen Kultur und neueren Geschichte" In: Wicker, Hans-Rudolf (Hg.): *Asiatische Flüchtlinge in der Schweiz: Fragen zur Integration.* Freiburg: Universitätsverlag, S. 41–95.

Michna, Joanna, (2016): „Die leisen Musterschüler-Little Hanoi in Berlin.“ *ZDF* [TV-Sender, Onlinepräsenz], verfügbar: https://www.zdf.de/dokumentation/mein-land-dein-land/vietnamesen-die-leisen-musterschueler-little-hanoi-in-berlin-100.html [17. 12. 2018].

Zhou, Min / Bhankston, Carl (1998): *Growing up American: How Vietnamese children Adapt to life in the United States.* New York: Russel Sage.

Jana Wetzel

Es kommt auf die Rahmung an: Dekoloniale Perspektiven auf die Religiosität der Anderen am Beispiel muslimischer Religiosität

Abstract

It Depends on the Frame. Postcolonial and Decolonial Perspectives of Others Using the Example of Muslim Religiosity

The paper explores the role of framing in research processes and scientific knowledge production focusing on religious minorities. It aims to avoid othering and re-marginalization of subaltern and postcolonial knowledge. The paper is written from a white non-Muslim position and focuses on research on Muslims by authors who do not identify themselves as Muslim. Current German research about Muslims is often based on Eurocentric concepts and is deductively used as universal knowledge, applicable to any context. Implying decolonial analyses as well as the interviewees' knowledge, the paper highlights the functions of mosques and asks which spaces for actions and possibilities are provided to its members?

Through the analysis of qualitative interviews, it can be seen that religion and the practice of religion are highly relevant for young interviewees who describe themselves as Muslims. The mosque, understood as a social space, has a particular relevance because members share the same understanding of religiousness and of religious practice. This includes classical worshipping like praying and receiving sacred texts, as well as social activities like „doing good", socializing, providing social support, and spending leisure time together with activities like playing soccer or video games.

At the same time the youth concept of religion and its aspects, which the interviewees perceive as important for their positioning themselves as Muslims, are ignored by the non-Muslim majority population. On the contrary, the non-Muslim majority tends to conflate specific symbols or practices with a certain understanding of religion. Wearing a headscarf, for example, is equated with being deeply religious and having a political understanding of Islam. Because of this, the interviewees rarely find acknowledgement for their self-perception by members of the non-Muslim majority population.

Following the analysis, I neither plead for disregarding religion or perceiving religion merely as relevant for analyzing social inequality, nor do I want to overemphasize young people's religious affiliation. Instead, I want to highlight the importance of acknowledging marginalized concepts of religion. This should include a critical view on one's own (Eurocentric) conceptual frameworks, as well as opening up research for decolonial and marginalized perspectives.

Einleitung

Die Religionen der Anderen, dabei insbesondere „der Islam“, sind in öffentlichen, dominanzgesellschaftlichen Diskursen oftmals Ziel von problematisierenden Darstellungen (vgl. Attia 2009; Hafez 2018; Shooman 2012). In diesen Diskursen wird an Bilder angeknüpft, welche „den Islam“ als „Quelle der Gewalt“ (Asad 2017, S. 17) und Intoleranz stilisieren (z. B. in 10 Thesen für ein weltoffenes Deutschland veröffentlicht am 14. Oktober 2017 auf welt.de von Richard Schröder, Eva Quistorp und Gunter Weißgerber). Gewalt und Unterdrückung werden zu etwas wesenhaft Islamischen erklärt[1] (vgl. Asad 2017, S. 17; Said 1981) und von nicht-muslimischen „Islamexpert_innen“ zum „Beweis“ von den heiligen Schriften des Islams abgeleitet (vgl. Asad 2017, S. 17). Dahinter verbirgt sich die dominanzgesellschaftliche Annahme, dass Nicht-Muslim_innen islamisch-religiöse Texte „objektiver“ und „unvoreingenommener“ deuten können als Muslim_innen selbst (vgl. Asad 2017, S. 18 f.). Im Gegensatz zu den interpretationsfähigen Dominanzeuropäer_innen werden Muslim_innen dabei als passive Objekte konstruiert, welche nicht in der Lage sind, eigene Interpretationen zu erstellen, sondern mit dem Lesen der heiligen islamischen Schriften quasi schon zu Gewalttaten animiert werden (vgl. ebd.). Diese beschriebenen Darstellungen sind Teil weit verbreiteter Deutungsmuster anti-muslimischer, rassistischer Diskurse (vgl. Attia 2009) und nehmen in öffentlichen Diskursen über „die Muslim_innen“ oftmals die Deutungshoheit in Anspruch. Die Wirkmächtigkeit dieser anti-muslimischen Diskurse trägt dazu bei, eigene Verständnisse von Religiosität von sich selbst als Muslim_innen positionierenden Personen zu missachten und zu ignorieren sowie eine Objektivierung und Homogenisierung von Menschen voranzutreiben.

Nicht nur im öffentlichen Diskurs, auch in sozialwissenschaftlichen Forschungen sind Muslim_innen einem teilweise einseitigen Blick ausgesetzt (vgl. u. a. Hafez 2018; Amir-Moazami 2017). Betrachtet man qualitative Studien die zu Beginn des Jahrtausends veröffentlicht wurden, so wird deutlich, dass diese eine muslimische Religiosität oder eine (vermeintliche) Religionszugehörigkeit als hauptidentitätsstiftenden Faktor in den Mittelpunkt der wissenschaftlichen Auseinandersetzung rücken. So befasst sich Nikola Tietze (2001) mit „muslimischen Identitäten“, Claudia Dantschke (2007) mit der „muslimische(n) Jugendszene“, Sigrid Nökel (2002) mit „Neo-Muslimas“, Julia Gerlach (2006, 2010) mit den „Pop-Muslimas“ oder aber es werden „Jugendphasen junger Muslime“ (Wensierski 2012) und „Jugendkulturen junger Muslime“ (von Wensierski / Lübcke 2007) von Hans Jürgen von Wensierski und Claudia Lübcke analysiert. Trotz des Verdienstes dieser Arbeiten, ein differenzierteres Bild von Mus-

1 Auch in besagten „10 Thesen für ein weltoffenes Deutschland“ zu finden.

lim_innen in wissenschaftlichen und öffentlichen Debatten zu etablieren[2], bergen solche Beschreibungen die Problematik, den Islam als einen möglichen Teil von Identitätsentwürfen sehr dominant erscheinen zu lassen. Der_dem Leser_in wird suggeriert, die religiöse Dimension des Islams sei die bedeutsamste oder auch ausschließliche Dimension mit der sich die Interviewten identifizieren. Gleichzeitig gehen Teile dieser Studien davon aus, dass junge Menschen, die als zweite oder dritte Einwanderungsgeneration beschrieben werden, ein „moderneres" Verständnis der Religion haben als ihre Eltern. Bacem Dziri (2011) verweist in diesem Zusammenhang auf die Problematiken, die solche binär gegenübergestellten Bezeichnungen wie „zwischen Pop und Dschihad" (Gerlach 2006) oder „zwischen Kopftuch und Minirock" (Ostermann 1996) bergen. „Zwischenentwürfe (werden demnach als) entweder spannungsgeladene Ausnahmen, individuelle Glücksfälle oder vorbildliche Prozesse der Massenerscheinung" (Dziri 2011, S. 186) gewertet. Dadurch werden Vielschichtigkeiten der Identitätsentwürfe ausgelassen (vgl. ebd.) und es kommt zu einer Präferenzsetzung. D.h. „die Neo-Muslima", die beschrieben wird als Meisterin des Spagats zwischen traditionellem Elternhaus und moderner deutscher Gesellschaft, wird als „Integrationsvorbild" für junge Muslim_innen dargestellt. Das europäische Verständnis von Moderne wird damit unhinterfragt als universell anzustrebend dargestellt und es kommt durch die Gegenüberstellung „moderner Westen" versus „traditioneller Islam" zur Reproduktion von Vorstellungen unterschiedlicher „Zivilisationsgrade" und damit verbunden zu Hierarchisierungen und Überlegenheitsdenken des „Westens" (vgl. Said 1981; vgl. Asad 2017). Neuere Forschungen haben diese Kritik oftmals schon aufgegriffen und analysieren in ethnographischer Forschungsweise Aufbau und Funktionsweisen von Verbänden oder Vereinen (vgl. Beilschmidt 2015; Schiffauer 2010) oder Beleuchten die diskursive Herstellung und die Schwierigkeit von „muslimischen Jugendliche" zu sprechen (vgl. Franz 2015). Trotz dieses Perspektivwechsels steht eine kritische Auseinandersetzung mit dem eigenen Standpunkt, dem eigenen Wissen sowie dem theoretischen Überbau, dem sich der_die Forschende bedient, bis auf wenige Ausnahmen (z.B. Beiträge des Sammelbandes von Amir-Moazami 2017) noch aus.

Der Beitrag möchte sich im Folgenden kritisch mit Forschungsarbeiten zu „den Muslim_innen" auseinandersetzen und möchte, anhand eines theoretischen Bezugs zum Dekolonialismus sowie Zitaten von sich selbst als religiös

2 Die bis dato geläufigen Interkulturellen Studien befassten sich vor allem mit der vermeintlichen Verschiedenheit (nationaler) Kulturen und mit der Frage wie ein Zusammenleben möglich ist. Dabei standen Metaphern wie „zwischen den Stühlen sitzen" und eine Zerrissenheit zwischen zwei Kulturen im Vordergrund der Betrachtungsweise, welche uneindeutige und heterogene Positionierungen vor allem problematisierten (vgl. u.a. Foroutan / Schäffer 2009).

verstehenden jungen Muslim_innen, aufzeigen, inwieweit Grossteile der derzeitigen deutschsprachigen Forschung zu „Muslim_innen", und damit schließe ich auch meine eigene Forschung ein, gefangen ist in ihren eurozentristischen Konzepten (von Religion) und damit die Deutung bestimmter Praktiken und Verständnisse verunmöglicht. Im Anschluss daran möchte ich fragen, welche Bedingungen erfüllt sein müssen, um Bezüge zu Religiosität und Religion herzustellen ohne in die Fallstricke zu geraten und erneut minorisierte Wissensbestände lediglich anhand eines eurozentristischen Referenzrahmen zu lesen und damit *Othering*-, Objektivierungs- und Markierungsprozess zu (re)produzieren.

Im Folgenden soll zunächst eine Selbstverortung und damit der Standpunkt der Analyse, die sich mit den Ambivalenzen einer *weißen*[3] Forschung über Angehörige von als „anders" markierten und minorisierten Religionen auseinandersetzt, erfolgen, und anhand derer Hinleitung zum Entstehen dieses Beitrags veranschaulicht werden. Im dritten Kapitel erfolgt die theoretische Auseinandersetzung mit einer dekolonialen Perspektive. Anschließend präsentiere ich im vierten Kapitel die empirischen Ergebnisse meiner Studie, bevor im abschließenden Kapitel ein Fazit und ein weiterführender Ausblick erfolgen.

Straucheln im Forschungsprozess

In diesem Kapitel möchte ich meine eigene *weiße* Position im Forschungsprozess thematisieren, sowie diskutieren, inwiefern die Forschung über Angehörige einer Religion, die in öffentlichen Debatten als „die Religion der Anderen" (Mecheril / Thomas-Olalde 2011) markiert ist, als *Weiße* legitim ist. Mein Straucheln, das mich bedingt durch meine *weiße* Positionierung und mein Selbstverständnis als Nicht-Muslimin während des ganzen Forschungsprozesses begleitete und auch weiterhin meine Forschung prägt, diente als Grundlage zur Verfassung dieses Beitrags.

Mein Weißsein und meine Beschränkung auf hegemoniale „Wissensbestände" wurden mir im Forschungsprozess vor allem bewusst, als ich meine Inter-

3 Bei der Verwendung des Wortes *weiß* handelt es sich um einen politischen Begriff mit dem der Konstruktionscharakter und die verschiedenen Machtverhältnisse im Rassismus in den Fokus der Auseinandersetzung gerückt werden sollen. *Weiß* stellt damit keinen biologischen Begriff dar, durch den die Hautfarbe von Menschen beschrieben werden soll, sondern es geht vielmehr um die Herausstellung der „ideologische(n) Konstruktion von ‚Hautfarben'" (Arndt 2005). Als *weiße* Positionen werden damit diejenigen bezeichnet die keine Rassismuserfahrungen machen und sich in dominanten Kontexten automatisch und stillschweigend nicht positionieren müssen, als unmarkierte Norm gelten und Privilegien innehaben (vgl. Marmer 2018).

views in transkribierter Form gelesen und interpretiert habe. Durch die Analyse der Interviews und damit auch der Analyse und Interpretation meiner Sprecher_innenrolle, sowie der von mir gesetzten Inhalte, wurde mir deutlich, mit wie vielen Vorurteilen und Vorannahmen ich in meine Forschung gegangen bin und wie sehr sie *weiße*, u. a. medial geprägte Vorannahmen repräsentieren.

Besonders bewusst wurde mir das anhand der Wahl meines Forschungsgegenstandes, „junge Muslim_innen", und meinem Anliegen, etwas über „Muslim_innen" aussagen zu wollen. Meine implizite Vorannahme bestand darin, etwas Allgemeines und gleichzeitig „Besonderes" über „junge Muslim_innen" aussagen zu können. Über diese Vorannahme homogenisierte und „anderte" ich die Interviewten auf Grundlage ihrer Religionszugehörigkeit. Zwar habe ich anhand der Fragen versucht offen zu halten, ob und inwiefern die interviewten Jugendlichen und jungen Erwachsenen dem Islam eine Bedeutung zuschreiben oder nicht, aber schon alleine die Tatsache, dass alle Gruppendiskussionen im Raum Moschee erhoben wurden, verunmöglichte eine Nicht-Markierung. Mein Forschungsanliegen, Muslim_innen als vermeintlich „besondere" und „andere" Gruppe von jungen Menschen zu untersuchen, wurde mir von den Interviewten als unzutreffend zurückgespiegelt. Dies wurde mir vor allem daran deutlich, dass Rückfragen dazu gestellt wurden, warum und wie ich auf die Idee gekommen bin, Forschung über Muslim_innen zu machen oder auch in Erzählungen über schmerzhafte Erfahrungen mit Überislamisierungen durch Angehörige der Dominanzgesellschaft (ausführlich im weiteren Verlauf des Beitrags). Überhaupt erschien mir das Unterfangen, eine Forschung durchzuführen, die auf einer Kennzeichnung bzw. Auswahl von jungen Menschen auf Grund ihrer Religionszugehörigkeit oder einer Migrationsgeschichte basiert, im Verlauf des Forschungsprozesses immer absurder. Dieser verstärkte Wunsch der Dominanzgesellschaft, Menschen auf Grundlage von familiären Migrationszusammenhängen zu bezeichnen und dafür immer neue Wortschöpfungen zu erfinden, um dabei politisch korrekt zu bleiben, macht Tuba Isik (2015) in ihrem Aufsatz „Dispositiv Muslim in Deutschland – Ein nie endendes Unterfangen" sehr deutlich. Muslim_in ist, so Isik, nicht „nur" eine Bezeichnung für die Religionszugehörigkeit von Menschen, sondern kann als Weiterführung und damit Synonym zu Begriffen wie „Ausländer_in" oder „Migrant_in" verstanden werden und beinhaltet damit auch immer eine Positionierung der Nicht-Zugehörigkeit zur Dominanzgesellschaft (vgl. auch Mecheril / Thomas-Olalde 2011).

Mein Gefühl der Absurdität analysierte ich damit im Forschungsprozess als die sich im Forschungsprozess einstellende Erkenntnis, dass es sinnlos ist, eine von mir selbst bzw. auf der Basis von dominanzgesellschaftlichen Diskursen konstituierte Gruppe der „muslimischen Jugendlichen" als vermeintlich homogene Gruppe zu untersuchen.[4] Gleichzeitig wurde mir dabei immer klarer, wie eine Forschung über „muslimische Jugendliche" zur Reproduktion von *Othering* und Fremdpositionierungen beiträgt.[5] Entgegen meines ersten Impulses Religiosität als Ausweg von *Othering*-Prozessen zu dethematisieren, wurde mir in Gesprächen mit und Feedbacks von sich selbst als Muslim_innen positionierenden Menschen deutlich, dass eine solche Auslassung und Negierung dem Selbstverständnis der Interviewten auch nicht gerecht werden würde.

Im Anschluss an diese Reflexionen stellte sich mir die Frage, ob es überhaupt möglich ist, mit denjenigen Konzepten und Theorien, die ich mir im Laufe meines Studiums und wissenschaftlichen Werdegangs angeeignet hatte, das Selbstverständnis der Jugendlichen als „Muslim_in" angemessen zu repräsentieren. Mit Rückbezug auf die Schriften von Talal Asad und anderen Vertreter_innen postkolonialer und dekolonialer Theorie, kann diese Frage nur mit „Nein" beantwortet werden (vgl. dazu genauer Kapitel 3). In der Folge ist es notwendig, auf einen erweiterten Wissenskanon zurückzugreifen, sowie andere Formen der Wissensgenerierung und eine verstärkte Reflexion des eigenen Standpunktes zu forcieren. Folglich entwickelte sich die Frage, wie eine von dekolonialen Perspektiven inspirierte Forschung mit „muslimischen Jugendlichen" aussehen könnte. Besonders zwei Aspekte scheinen mir dabei notwendig kritisch zu hinterfragen: Erstens, inwiefern benötigen Interviewte und Interviewer_in zumindest ansatzweise einen geteilten Erfahrungsraum, damit die_der Interpret_in überhaupt auf bestimmte Konzepte, die den Aussagen der Befragten zugrunde liegen, kommen können (vgl. dazu Okcu 2018)? Ist es als Nicht-Muslim_in also überhaupt möglich, etwas über das Religionsverständnis von Muslim_innen auszusagen ohne dass dies lediglich ein Spiegelbild der eigenen Positioniertheit und Annahmen darstellt? Zweitens, inwiefern ist *weiße* Forschung über „muslimische Jugendliche" legitim? Denn auch weiterhin ist der Blick auf geanderte Erfahrungen und Konzepte gerichtet. Dieses Dilemma einer *weißen* Forschung, die im Spannungsfeld zwischen einer fortlaufenden Reproduktion der Anderen und einer Kritik an derzeitigen migrationsgesellschaftlichen und eurozentristischen Verhältnissen verortet ist, lässt sich nicht auflösen. Ob eine fortwährende, kritische Auseinandersetzung mit der eigenen Forschung sowie der eigenen *weißen* Positioniertheit in rassistischen gesellschaftlichen Verhältnissen ausreichend ist (vgl. auch Linnemann / Ronacher 2018), sei dahingestellt und kann von mir nicht abschließend beantwortet werden.

4 Siehe zur diskursiven Verwendung des Terminus „muslimische Jugendliche" auch Julia Franz (2013, 2015).

5 Zum *Othering* von Menschen die als Muslim_innen markiert werden Edward Said (1981) und seine Theorie des Orientalismus sowie Iman Attia (2009).

Dekoloniale Perspektiven – Verdrängtes Wissen sichtbar machen

Postkolonialismus und Dekolonialismus sind Perspektiven, die sich mit weltweiten kolonialen Folgen auseinandersetzten. Wichtiger Bezugspunkt ist eine Neuschreibung der Geschichte, die marginalisierte und subalterne Perspektiven sichtbar macht (vgl. u. a. Exo 2017). Dahinter verbirgt sich die Annahme, dass europäische und „westliche" Konzepte und Geschichte keineswegs den Anspruch auf Allgemeingültigkeit und Objektivität besitzen, sondern einer spezifischen eurozentristischen Perspektive entsprungen sind (vgl. Asad 2017). Damit sagt ein wissenschaftlicher Text nichts über die „Realität" oder Korrektheit bestimmter Sachverhalte aus, sondern stellt primär das Spiegelbild der Position der Autor_in dar (vgl. Exo 2017, S. 18). Said (1981) entlarvt in diesem Zusammenhang vor allem auch den Mechanismus der Wissenschaft, marginalisierte Narrative in ihrer Unsichtbarkeit zu belassen und demgegenüber eurozentristische Perspektiven zu bestätigen, zu reproduzieren und diesen einen universal-gültigen Status zuzusprechen. Westliche Wissenschaft, die sich ebendiesem monokulturellen, eurozentristischen „Wissen" bedient, wird dabei als „machtvollstes Verfahren" verstanden, um die Nichtexistenz von weltweiten sozialen Erfahrungen zu (re)produzieren (vgl. Sousa Santos 2004, zit. n. Exo 2017, S. 18). Infolgedessen ist eine *weiße* Deprivilegierung ein wichtiges Ziel von postkolonialen und dekolonialen Ansätzen. Diese Deprivilegierung hat es zum Ziel der Privilegierung ihre „Natürlichkeit" zu rauben und stattdessen machtvolle und ausbeutende Praktiken zu entlarven (vgl. u. a. Ahmed 2012, zit. n. https://www.zhdk.ch/forschung/iae/glossar-972/post-koloniale-theorie-und-dekoloniale-perspektiven-3836).

Insbesondere der Dekolonialismus, welcher postkolonialen Theorien entsprungen ist und als Weiterführung, teilweise sogar in Abgrenzung von diesen, verstanden wird, treibt dieses Anliegen voran (vgl. Castro Varela / Dhawan 2015, S. 318). Vertreter_innen des Dekolonialismus fordern einen Bezug auf andere, nicht-eurozentristische Theoriezugänge (vgl. ebd.) und, wie Mechthild Exo (2017) mit Bezug auf Sousa Santos (2004) deutlich macht, eine gleichwertige Anerkennung nichtwissenschaftlichen Wissens (vgl. S. 18). Im Anschluss an die obigen Ausführungen möchte ich eurozentristische Konzepte von Religion in derzeitigen Forschungen zu Muslim_innen infrage stellen und auf ihre Hierarchiereproduktion befragen. Zudem sollen Konzepte und Wissen der Befragten in den Vordergrund der Analyse gerückt werden.

Empirische Beispiele

Die im Folgenden vorgestellten Beispiele entstammen drei Gruppendiskussionen, die zwischen 2013 und 2016 stattgefunden haben.[6] Die Teilnehmer_innen der Gruppendiskussionen waren zum Zeitpunkt des Interviews zwischen 14 und 26 Jahren alt. Alle Gruppendiskussionen haben in Räumlichkeiten von sich selbst als sunnitisch verstehenden Moscheen in Kontexten von Jugendgruppen stattgefunden.

Im Anschluss der Erhebungen wurden die Gruppendiskussionen nach der Dokumentarischen Methode nach Ralf Bohnsack et al. (2013) transkribiert und ausgewertet und damit auf den geteilten, konjunktiven Erfahrungsraum der Befragten hin analysiert.[7] Der Analyse eines konjunktiven Erfahrungsraums liegt die Annahme zugrunde, dass Menschen auf Grund ihrer Positionierung im Raum unterschiedliche Erfahrungen machen. In Gruppendiskussionen mit „natürlichen" Gruppen, d.h. Menschen, die sich nicht nur zum Zweck des Interviews zusammenfinden und bestimmte Merkmale teilen, wird davon ausgegangen, dass es einen geteilten Erfahrungsraum der Interviewten gibt, der sich aus den Gruppendiskussionen rekonstruieren lässt.

Im Folgenden möchte ich ausgewählte Beispiele darstellen, die aufzeigen sollen, wie die Jugendlichen und jungen Erwachsenen muslimische Praktiken beschreiben, was ihnen für ihr religiöses Selbstverständnis wichtig ist und welche Strategien sie verwenden, um das den Angehörigen der Dominanzgesellschaft zu erklären.

Dem folgenden Zitat der Gruppendiskussionsteilnehmerin Befragte 2 (Bf2) geht die Frage voraus, welche Räume, Personen und Dinge für die Interviewten bedeutsam sind.

> Bf2: Ja, ich habe einmal hier die Moschee als Raum und dann noch den dazugehörigen Gebetsteppich. Wegen dem fünfmaligen Gebet am Tag, was ja auch Priorität hat[8] (Gruppe Heterogenität).[9]

---

6 Insgesamt wurden acht Gruppendiskussionen im Zuge der Dissertation der Autorin erhoben.

7 Durch den begrenzten Umfang des Beitrags kann an dieser Stelle nicht näher auf das Interpretationsverfahren der Dokumentarischen Methode eingegangen werden. Für einen Überblick siehe u.a. Bohnsack et al. (2013).

8 Zur besseren Lesbarkeit wurden die Zitate für den Beitrag orthographisch an die übliche deutsche Rechtschreibung angepasst.

9 Im Folgenden werden die Gruppen anhand von bestimmten, der Interpretin markant erscheinenden Begriffe, die dem transkribierten Text der Gruppendiskussion entsprungen sind, benannt und anonymisiert. Die einzelnen Gesprächspartner_innen werden in geschlechtshomogenen Gruppen mit Gp1, Gp2, Gp3… für Gesprächspartner_in 1, Gesprächspartner_in 2, Gesprächspartner_in 3 abgekürzt. In der geschlechtsheterogenen Gruppe Heterogenität werden die weiblichen Gesprächsteilnehmerinnen mit Bf1, Bf2… abgekürzt, während die männlichen Teilnehmer die Abkürzung Bm1, Bm2… erhalten.

In diesem Zitat wird deutlich, dass die Moschee und die Praktik des Betens für Bf2 von großer Bedeutung sind. Für Bf2 stehen Objekte wie das Moscheegebäude oder der Gebetsteppich symbolisch für die Ausübung von muslimischen Praktiken, wie dem fünfmaligen Gebet am Tag. Dem Raum Moschee mitsamt Gebetsteppich kommt dabei als spiritueller Raum eine besondere Bedeutung und dem Gebet *„Priorität"* zu.

Im Gegensatz dazu wird der Alltag von Bf2 als „stressig" wahrgenommen, in dem es schwierig ist, Zeit für den Islam zu finden:

> Bf2: Ich finde auch die Atmosphäre an sich macht es wirklich aus. Das ist ein Ort der Ruhe und ähm des Gebets und das merk ich auch immer wieder besonders im Ramadan wenn nachts halt die langen Gebete sind, die Tarawih Gebete ähm wieviel man da wieviel man da mitbekommt einfach und äh gerade jetzt in äh angesichts des stressigen Alltags das wir alle haben. Wir haben ja immer wenig Zeit für den Islam (.) man will immer was machen aber man kommt einfach nicht dazu/ (Gruppe Heterogenität)

Damit wird gleichzeitig deutlich, dass Bf2 grundsätzlich den Anspruch hat, etwas für den Islam auch außerhalb ihrer Moscheebesuche zu tun. Moscheebesuche, bei denen sie sowohl zeitlich lange anwesend ist und die dem intensiven Gebet gewidmet werden, kompensieren für Bf2 Zeiten, in denen der Religion weniger Aufmerksamkeit zukommt.

Neben der hohen Bedeutung des Gebets, wird in den Interviews deutlich, dass das Verständnis von Religion über Gebete und Praktiken, hinausgeht. Bf2 expliziert in diesem Sinne unterschiedliche Aktivitäten, der sie in der Moschee nachgeht, als Gottesdienste und verortet muslimische Praktiken im alltäglichen Handeln:

> Bf2: Es ist so als ob ich in die Moschee komme (.) meinen Gottesdienst verrichte aber gleichzeitig ist mein Gottesdienst auch, mich mit meinen Brüdern und Schwestern zu unterhalten und mit meiner Familie Zeit zu verbringen (.) das ist ebenfalls für mich ein Gottesdienst den ich dann vollbringe (Gruppe Heterogenität)

Ebenso beschreibt auch die Gruppe Tankstelle muslimische Praktiken im Kontext des alltäglichen Tuns und hebt die Relevanz, die die Gemeinschaft dabei spielt, hervor. Dabei betonen die Mitglieder der Gruppe Tankstelle die Relevanz „Gutes zu Tun".

> Gp2: Natürlich wollen wir auch Gutes tun, ne (Lachen) weil wenn wir uns versammeln, wollen wir natürlich Gutes tun (2 sec.) wir ham auch coole Projekte hier am Laufen
> Int: Ja?
> Gp4: Ja. Wir helfen Menschen gerne
> Gp2: Ja, wir ham zum Beispiel Blutspende, also ähm/ (Gruppe Tankstelle)

Beispielhaft für gute Taten wird eine Blut-Spende-Aktion genannt oder die Organisation von Veranstaltungen. Dieses Verständnis von muslimischen Praktiken, das bei den Interviewten zu finden ist, schließt an die Ergebnisse von Theresa Beilschmidt (2015) an. Sie rekonstruiert bei den von ihr Interviewten ein Islam-Verständnis, welches Gottesdienste in den alltäglichen Handlungen der Einzelnen verortet und die Religion nicht lediglich auf eine einzelne Sphäre des Lebens beschränkt (vgl. dazu auch Amir-Moazami 2017; Daniel 2017).

Dabei steht ähnlich wie bei der Gruppe Tankstelle das Helfen im Vordergrund und ganz allgemein Taten mit einer guten Absicht (vgl. Beilschmidt 2017, S. 129–132).

Die gemeinnützigen Aktionen werden von Gp2 als „coole Projekte" bezeichnet und die Gruppe, die sich in der Moschee trifft, als „auch coole Leute hier drinne" (Gruppe Tankstelle). Damit positioniert sie sich explizit gegen ein Verständnis von muslimischer Religiosität als uncool oder unmodern und scheint Personen der Dominanzgesellschaft, hier die Interviewerin, explizit darauf hinweisen zu müssen, dass sich als gläubige_r Muslim_in zu verstehen nichts damit zu tun hat, uncool zu sein. Die Notwendigkeit, dieses explizieren zu müssen, könnte das Resultat bereits gemachter Erfahrungen mit Zuschreibungen von Seiten der Dominanzgesellschaft sein, als gläubige_r Muslim_in automatisch als altmodisch und traditionell angesehen zu werden (vgl. Asad 2017; Attia 2009; Said 1981). Muslimische Religiosität wird in solchen, von Orientalismus und antimuslimischem Rassismus geprägten Diskursen als etwas verstanden, was es zugunsten eines als modern dargestellten Säkularismus zu überwinden oder zumindest in ein bestimmtes Verständnis zu verwandelt gilt (vgl. Asad 2017, S. 23f.). Im Gegenteil dazu verortet Gp2 Modernität (oder Jugendkultur) im Religiösen selbst und lässt „Zwischen"-Metaphern damit hinfällig werden. Bei ihr wird Muslimisch-Sein zu etwas „Coolem", anstatt dass Jugendkultur und Religiosität als zwei Identifikationsfaktoren verstanden werden, die unverbunden nebeneinander bestehen, wie in Forschungen häufig angenommen wird.

Im folgenden Zitat wird deutlich, dass ein Religionsverständnis, welches muslimische Praktiken im Alltäglichen verortet keineswegs etwas „Neues" darstellt, welches von jungen, „modernen" Muslim_innen praktiziert wird (welches Wortschöpfungen wie Neo-Muslima suggerieren). Im Gegenteil, die Organisation von Playstation-Turnieren oder die Umfunktionierung des Gebetsraums wird beispielsweise von allen Gemeindemitgliedern getragen:

> Bf1: Hat (Imam der Moschee) das erlaubt? Das die / früher durften die hier immer komplett Fussball spielen aber jetzt wo wir den neuen Teppich haben ist das nicht mehr erlaubt (lachen) (Gruppe Heterogenität)

Durch die Akzeptanz der Umnutzung des Gebetsraums als Fussballfeld wird deutlich, dass auch ältere Moscheemitglieder und geistliche Autoritäten muslimische Praktiken als vielschichtig verstehen und die Moschee als Raum in dem diese stattfinden können.

Im folgenden Zitat stellt Gp2 der Gruppe Tankstelle das eigene Gefühl in den Mittelpunkt ihrer Auseinandersetzungen:

> Gp2: Das motiviert ja einen auch. Ich mein, wenn man dann die Resultate sieht, die man dann von irgendeiner Veranstaltung mit sich nehmen kann, dann is das natürlich immer äh, eine Bereicherung für sich selbst und da hat man auch ein gutes Gewissen und sagt: Okay, ich hab jetzt was für mich getan, für meine Religion, für meine Freunde und alles mögliche und joah (3 sec.) (Gruppe Tankstelle)

So ist die Ausübung von muslimischen Praktiken keine Pflicht für Gp2, sondern wird als „Bereicherung“ verstanden, da für sie Resultate sichtbar werden. Auch wird deutlich, dass Gp2 die Durchführung von Veranstaltungen nicht nur als Dienst an Gott versteht, sondern den Dienst an Gott auch als Mehrwert für sich selbst und für ihre Freunde.

Neben muslimischen Praktiken, die im Alltäglichen verortet werden, versehen die Jugendlichen alltägliche Praktiken auch mit spirituellen Inhalten. So widmen sich die Jugendlichen der Gruppe Musik Pop-Songs mit dezidiert religiösen Inhalten. Dem folgenden Zitat ging eine informelle Unterhaltung voraus, die nicht als Audio-Datei dokumentiert wurde, in der die Jugendlichen der Gruppe Musik der Interviewerin von Musiktiteln berichteten, die sie vom Kurdischen oder Türkischen ins Deutsche übersetzen und im Anschluss auf offiziellen Feiern vorsingen, wie z. B. an interreligiösen Dialogveranstaltungen:

> Gp2: Äh meistens Türkisch auf Deutsch übersetzen (achso) und dann singen wir das vor (.) meistens und
> Int: Aber macht ihr so Pop-Musik (.) oder
> Gp1: Alle (.) also von allen Arten
> Gp2: Also das (.)
> Gp1: Nur über Islam
> Gp2: Wie Pop aber da singen wir
> Gp1: Über Islam
> GP2: Da singen wir über (den) Islam für unseren Propheten und so (.) Lieder (…)
> Gp1: Zum Bespiel (.) das ist aber englisch
> Gp2: Das ist aber/ das ist aber über Islam
> Gp3: Ja egal (.) das ist aber über
> Gp2: Also jeder (Musik an)
> Int: Ach so es gibt auch englische Lieder?
> Mehrere: Ja
> Gp1: Ja es gibt alle Sprachen
> Gp3: Englische
> Gp1: Persisch Arabisch Syrisch

Int: Und die englische Musik ist die dann trotzdem aus der Türkei oder (.) auch USA
Mehrere: Ne
Gp3: Ne der der das jetzt singt kommt aus äh Schweden oder
Gp1: Ja
Gp2: Ja der kommt aus Schweden
Gp3: Der ist Moslem (5 Sekunden nur Musik)
Gp3: Das ist die Moderne sozusagen (Gruppe Musik)

Hier werden religiöse Lieder erstens popkulturell interpretiert und zweitens kommen transnationale Bezüge zum Vorschein, indem die Lieder sowohl vom Kurdischen und Türkischem ins Deutsche übersetzt werden, als auch Lieder in weiteren Sprachen gehört werden, wie im Beispiel englische Lieder eines schwedischen Interpreten. Die transnationalen Bezüge gehen hier also nicht nur in die Herkunftsländer der Eltern, sondern bestehen weltweit. Die Jugendlichen unterscheiden zwischen Liedern, die „mehr so für Ältere" gedacht sind und jugendlichere Popsongs („Moderne sozusagen").

Gleichzeitig haben die Lieder dezidiert islamische Inhalte („Da singen wir über (den) Islam für unseren Propheten") und die Praktik des Singens ist eng mit Aufenthalten in der Moschee verbunden. Deutlich wird hier also, dass sowohl Lokalität als auch Transnationalität wichtige Bezugspunkte und Referenzen für die Religionsausübung der Jugendlichen darstellen.

Die Vorstellung davon, dass die Ausübung des Islams nicht nur auf bestimmte gesellschaftliche Sphären zu reduzieren ist, sondern unterschiedliche Bereiche der Lebenswelt durchdringt, verdeutlicht Bm2 durch die Verwendung des Wortes „Lebensstil":

Bm2: Ja ich wollt noch sagen die Aktivitäten hier auch sind auch ein bisschen ein Grund weil (1) äh Moscheen müssen ja auch immer aktiv sein so und auch das man gefüttert wird sozusagen da gibts viele Unterrichte dann gibts immer mal Seminare oder (1) viele Sachen wirklich und ich denke das ist auch ein Grund weil wenn man z. B. nur beten kommt und Islam ist ja eigentlich ein ganzer Lebensstil //mhh// und deswegen muss das auch so sein dass wir wirklich Sport machen zusammen dass wir zusammen Koran lernen (.) dass wir über Probleme reden also wie das Bf1 vorhin gesagt hat z.B das ist wie eine Familie hier sozusagen (1) diese Aktivitäten sind auch ein wichtiger Grund dafür (Gruppe Heterogenität)

Das Bekenntnis zum Islam stellt für Bm2 damit nicht nur einen gesonderten Aspekt in seinem Leben dar, sondern zieht sich durch Aktivitäten, Praktiken sowie die allgemeine Lebensgestaltung. Die Moschee stellt dabei für Bm2 den Raum dar, in dem dieser Lebensstil Anerkennung findet, und an dem es möglich ist, das eigene Verständnis von Religion zu leben.

Die vorgestellten Fallbeispiele sind anschlussfähig an Überlegungen von Talal

Asad (2017) zum Verhältnis von Säkularem und Religiösem.[10] In seinem vielbeachteten Buch *Ordnungen des Säkularen* rekonstruiert er die historische Entwicklung des Säkularen in Europa, die eine Vereinheitlichung der Vorstellungen von religiöser Sprache und Erfahrungen zur Folge hatte (vgl. S. 34). Das Säkulare geht laut Asad (2017) über eine formale Trennung von Religion und Staat hinaus; es trägt dazu bei, wie Ariane Sadjed im Anschluss an Armando Salvadore formuliert, „Religion auf eine bestimmte Art zu formen" (2013, S. 17). Dieses beinhaltete u. a. Verständnisse davon, was als heilig angesehen wurde und wird, in welchen Praktiken sich Heiliges widerspiegelt, sowie in welchen Räumen das Religiöse Platz findet. Dieses religiöse Verständnis wird gleichzeitig nicht als eine mögliche Form unter anderen angesehen, sondern von Europa zum universellen Maßstab erhoben, an dem andere Religionen dann in den Blick genommen werden (vgl. Amir-Moazami 2017; Asad 2017; Daniel 2017). Das wird u. a. an den vielen Schwierigkeiten deutlich, mit denen islamische Verbände zu kämpfen haben, um in einem vermeintlich säkularen Staat eine rechtliche Gleichstellung zu christlichen Kirchen und Verbänden zu erlangen. Hauptargument gegen eine Gleichstellung ist dabei immer wieder die Organisationsform der in Deutschland ansässigen Verbände, die von der Organisationsform der anerkannten christlichen Konfessionen abweicht. In dieser Argumentationsweise wird der (post)koloniale Charakter der Säkularisierung deutlich. Indem das christliche Verständnis von religiösen Organisationsformen kurzum zur universellen Größe erklärt wird, müssen sich minorisierte Religionsgemeinschaften dieser entweder anpassen oder ihnen werden gleiche Rechte abgesprochen.

Im Anschluss an die Ausführungen Asads könnten Moscheen im Kontext der Migrationsgesellschaft in der obige Aussage von Bm2 folglich als Räume interpretiert werden, in denen religiöse Erfahrungen, religiöse Praktiken und religiöse Verständnisse die von dominanzgesellschaftlichen Setzungen abweichen, anerkannt werden. Damit fungieren Moscheen als Räume, in denen sich muslimische Praktiken nicht den Vorstellungen von Religiös-Sein des säkularen Europas und der Dominanzgesellschaft unterwerfen müssen.

10 Er vertritt die Annahme, dass Religionen keinesfalls als „das Andere" des Säkularen zu verstehen sind oder ausschließlich der privaten Sphäre zugeordnet werden können, der gegenüber ein religiös neutraler säkularer Staat steht (vgl. S. 33). Talal Asad entlarvt den Säkularismus selbst als Ideologie die in Abhängigkeit zum Religiösen steht (vgl. S. 35) und nicht als „Überwindung" des religiösen Alltags, Werten und Lebensführung zu verstehen ist (vgl. S. 33). Im Gegenteil stellt er sich gegen die Essentialisiung des Religiösen und die Vereinheitlichung des Glaubens.

Fazit

Die vorgestellten Fallbeispiele zeigen, dass die Identifizierung mit dem Islam und muslimische Praktiken für die Befragten einen hohen Stellenwert aufweisen. Die religiöse Überzeugung stellt für die Jugendlichen und jungen Erwachsenen eine handlungsleitende Funktion dar, welche sich in einem Verständnis von muslimischen Praktiken widerspiegelt, das über eurozentristische Verständnisse von als religiöse Riten gedeutete Handlungen hinausgeht.

So zeigen die Interviews, dass im Sozialraum Moschee unterschiedlichste Praktiken von sowohl, im Alltagsgebrauch, als jugend-kulturelle Praktiken verstandene Praktiken, wie Fußball spielen, Playstation spielen oder Pop-Songs singen, als auch dezidiert religiöse Pflichten, wie das Gebet, als Teil eines muslimischen Selbstverständnisses, gelebt werden können. Bm2 der Gruppe Heterogenität beschreibt sein Religionsverständnis als „Lebensstil“ und die Moschee als Raum der diesen anerkennt. Entgegen der Vorstellung vieler Forschungen zu Muslim_innen, die Verbindung von Religiosität und sozialen und kulturellen Praktiken sei ein jugendspezifisches Phänomen (wie z. B. durch den Begriff der Neo-Muslima suggeriert), lässt sich aus den Aussagen der Gesprächspartner_innen rekonstruieren, dass die Integration von muslimischer Religiosität in die alltägliche Lebensführung von weiten Teilen der Mitglieder geteilt wird.

Talal Asad zeichnet in diesem Zusammenhang die Entstehungsgeschichte der Vorstellung einer Trennung von religiös und profan nach. Diese Vorstellung ist eng mit der europäischen nationalstaatlichen Entstehungsgeschichte verflochten und weist dem Heiligen bestimmte Orte, Zeiten und Gegenstände zu, in deren Folge Religion auf die private Sphäre beschränkt wurde und somit eine Homogenisierung der Bevölkerung zur Folge hatte (2017, S. 42f.)

Weiter wurde in den Rekonstruktionen deutlich, dass Praktiken, in Abhängigkeit von Raum und Personen religiöse Bedeutung erlangen können oder auch nicht. Die Idee, die die Autorin und auch viele andere nicht-muslimische Autor_innen haben,[11] dass „muslimische Jugendliche“ oftmals Pop und Religiosität kombinieren[12], verweist auf ein von eurozentristischen Annahmen geprägtes Verständnis von Religion, welches von den Autor_innen vorausgesetzt und als Rahmung für Aussagen der Befragten dient. Dabei wird oftmals nicht reflektiert,

11 Dies zeigt sich beispielsweise in den Forschungen von Julia Gerlach (2010) oder Sigrid Nökel (2002). Julia Gerlach beschreibt eine Bewegung der Pop-Muslim_innen ab Ende der 90er Jahre in Deutschland sowie in Ägypten. Charakteristisch für die Bewegung sei eine Identifikation mit einem sowohl pop-kulturellen als auch frommen, gläubigen Lebensstil, so Gerlach.

12 Wie schon in der Einleitung an Begriffen wie Pop-Muslima oder Neo-Muslima deutlich gemacht wurde.

inwiefern diese Rahmung, d.h. das eigene Verständnis von einer säkularen Religiosität, überhaupt universalistisch anwendbar ist und welche Hierarchisierungen in solchen Annahmen stecken. Die Analysen von Talal Asad sowie meine Forschungen zeigen einmal mehr, wie bedeutsam es ist, das Wissen postkolonialer und minorisierter Autor_innen heranzuziehen. Damit können als selbstverständlich erachtete Konzepte hinterfragt und gegebenenfalls als eurozentristisch und herrschaftssichernd enttarnt werden, so dass schliesslich mit ihnen gebrochen werden kann. Deutlich wird in meiner Forschung, dass dominanzgesellschaftliche Räume oftmals eben nicht offen sind für Selbstverständnisse und Selbstpositionierungen Marginalisierter, da es einen schon fixen Rahmen gibt, innerhalb dessen eine Positionierung nur möglich ist (siehe auch zur Rahmung: Soliman 2018).

Diese Rahmung wird auch im Zitat der Gruppe Musik, in den Erzählungen von Gp2 über ihre Erfahrungen als kopftuchtragende Muslimin sichtbar. Auch in diesem Zitat wird deutlich, dass es die Dominanzgesellschaft ist, die bestimmte muslimische Merkmale, wie in diesem Beispiel das Kopftuch, erstens in den Mittelpunkt der religiösen Auseinandersetzungen rückt und zweitens die Bedeutung, die das Kopftuch für die Jugendlichen hat, bereits zu „kennen" meint. Damit wird eine Deutungshoheit über muslimische Praktiken in Anspruch genommen. Dass die Fremdzuschreibung nicht mit der Selbstpositionierung der Jugendlichen übereinstimmt, scheint für Angehörige der Dominanzgesellschaft sekundär und wird ignoriert:

> Gp2: Also viele Menschen äh denken nur weil wir ein Kopftuch tragen sind wir immer anders
> Gp3: Du sollst dich erklären (Lachen)
> Gp2. Ja warte (Lachen) ich werde dazu kommen (...)
> Gp2: Ja und hmm eigentlich ist das nicht so (1) jeder (.) wir sind alle gleich (.) meine hmm also ich hab mit meinen meisten deutschen Freunden (.) also wir haben den gleichen Meinung (.) also gleichen Hobbys und so also ähm ich find nichts hmm also ich finds nichts ob ich anders bin nur weil ich ein Kopftuch trage (...)
> Gp3: Vorgeschriebenen Dinge einfach auch nur einhalten dazu zählt auch Kopftuch (.) breite Sachen //hmmhmm// ja und so ich glaub dass manche Leute das einfach zu viel (2) wahrnehmen naja und das dann auch (.) das die dann auch sagen ok was sind das denn für Leute und so weiter ja (Gruppe Musik)

Im Gegensatz dazu scheint es in innerhalb der Gruppe ein geteiltes Verständnis über die Individualität der Gestaltung sowie die Bedeutung von Religion zu geben, das nicht erklärungsbedürftig erscheint. Im Anschluss an die vorgestellten Analysen und Reflexionen möchte ich dafür plädieren, unterschiedliche Selbstverständnisse von Religiosität ernst zu nehmen.

Es gilt, Jugendliche, die sich mit dem Islam identifizieren, nicht weiterhin auf ihre Religionszugehörigkeit zu reduzieren und zu besonderen, sondern genauso wie alle anderen Jugendlichen auch, vor allem anhand ihrer Selbstidentifizierungen und Selbstpositionierungen als heterogene Persönlichkeiten wahrzunehmen, deren Identitäten als fluide und vielschichtig zu verstehen sind. Dies beinhaltet eine Vermeidung von Überislamisierung (vgl. Hafez 2018), u.a. anhand von Symbolen, die die/der Forscher_in als Ausdruck eines bestimmten Religionsverständnisses versteht, z.B. das Tragen eines Kopftuches als Kennzeichen besonders tiefer Religiosität. Ebenso wenig entspricht es der Selbstpositionierung der interviewten Jugendlichen und jungen Erwachsenen muslimische Religiosität lediglich als Differenzmarker und Platzhalter für bereits überholte Begriffe, wie „Ausländer_in", des rassistischen Diskurses zu verstehen. Denn trotz dieser wichtigen Hinweise auf die diskursive Austauschbarkeit der Begriffe ist eine Zugehörigkeit zum Islam für diejenigen, die sich davon angesprochen fühlen, mehr als „nur" ein Element im rassistischen Diskurs und sollte deshalb auch nicht darauf reduziert werden.

Literatur

Amir-Moazami, Schirin (Hg.) (2017): *Der inspizierte Muslim. Wissensproduktion und Machtreproduktion im Forschungsfeld Islam in Europa.* Bielefeld: transcript.

– (2017): „Epistemologien der ‚muslimischen Frage' in Europa." In: (ebd.) (Hg.): *Der inspizierte Muslim. Wissensproduktion und Machtreproduktion im Forschungsfeld Islam in Europa.* Bielefeld: transcript, S. 91–123.

Asad, Talal (2017): *Ordnungen des Säkularen. Christentum, Islam und Moderne.* Konstanz: Konstanz University Press.

Attia, Iman (2009): *Die „westliche Kultur" und ihr Anderes. Zur Dekonstruktion von Orien talismus und antimuslimischem Rassismus.* Bielefeld: transcript.

Arndt, Susan (2005): „Weißsein und kritische Weißseinsforschung. Zusammengestellt aus: Arndt, Susan: Weißsein. Die verkannte Strukturkategorie Europas und Deutschlands und Arndt, Susan: Mythen des weißen Subjekts: Verleugnung und Hierarchisierung von Rassismus." In: Eggers, Maureen Maisha / Kilomba, Grada / Piesche, Peggy / Arndt, Susan (Hg.): *Mythen, Masken und Subjekte. Kritische Weißseinsfor schung in Deutschland* . Münster: Unrast Verlag.

Becker-Schmidt, Regina (2003): Zur doppelten Vergesellschaftung von Frauen. Soziologische Grundlegung, empirische Rekonstruktion. In: *gender...politik...online. Sozialwissenschaftliches Gender-Portal der FU Berlin,* S. 1–18, verfügbar:

https://www.fu-berlin.de/sites/gpo/soz_eth/Geschlecht_als_Kategorie/Die_doppelte_Vergesellschaftung_von_Frauen/becker_schmidt_ohne.pdf [15.09.2018].

Beilschmidt, Theresa (2015): *Gelebter Islam. Eine empirische Studie zu DITIB-Moscheegemeinden in Deutschland.* Bielefeld: transcript.

Bohnsack, Ralf / Nentwig-Gesemann, Iris / Nohl, Arnd-Michael (2013): *Die Dokumentarische Methode und ihre Forschungspraxis. Grundlagen qualitativer Sozialforschung.* Wiesbaden: Springer VS.

Castro Varela, María do Mar / Dhawan, Nikita (2015): *Postkoloniale Theorie. Eine kritische Einführung.* Bielefeld: transcript.

Daniel, Anna (2017): „Welche Religion gilt als modern?" In: Amir-Moazami, Schirin (Hg.): *Der inspizierte Muslim. Wissensproduktion und Machtreproduktion im Forschungsfeld Islam in Europa.* Bielefeld, transcript, S. 36–60.

Dantschke, Claudia (2007): Die muslimische Jugendszene. *bpb*

Dziri, Bacem (2011): „Chancen muslimischer Jugendarbeit gegen Radikalisierung". In: Borchard, Michael / Ceylan, Rauf (Hg.): *Imame und Frauen in Moscheen im Integrationsprozess: Gemeindepädagogische Perspektiven.* Fachkonferenz der Reihe „Religiöse Bildung von Muslimen in Deutschland". Konrad-Adenauer-Stiftung/Zentrum für Interkulturelle Islam-Studien der Universität Osnabrück.

Exo, Mechthild (2017): *Das übergangene Wissen. Eine dekoloniale Kritik des liberalen Peacebuilding durch basispolitische Organisationen in Afghanistan.* Bielefeld: transcript.

Foroutan, Naika / Schäfer, Isabel (2009): Hybride Identitäten – muslimische Migrantinnen und Migranten in Deutschland und Europa. In: *Aus Politik und Zeitgeschichte* (5) 2009, Lebenswelt von Migrantinnen und Migranten, S. 11–18.

Franz, Julia (2013): *Muslimische Jugendliche. Eine empirisch-rekonstruktive Studie zu kollektiver Zugehörigkeit.* Opladen/Berlin/Toronto: Verlag Barbara Budrich.

– (2015): Bilder, die wir uns von jungen MuslimInnen machen. Zur Konstruktion einer Zielgruppe. In: *TELEVIZION*, 28/2015/1, S. 45–48.

Gerlach, Julia (2006): *Zwischen Pop und Dschihad. Muslimische Jugendliche in Deutschland.* Berlin: Ch. Links.

– (2010): „Pop-Islam revisited: Wohin entwickelt sich die transnationale Jugendbewegung der ‚neuen Prediger' in Europa und in der Arabischen Welt?" In: Hunner-Kreisel, Christine / Andresen, Sabine (Hg.): *Aufwachsen in muslimischen Lebenswelten. Aufwachsen und Bildung in deutscher und internationaler Perspektive.* Wiesbaden: VS-Verlag, S. 109–124.

Hafez, Farid (2018): „Zwischen Fundamentalismus und Emanzipation. Die Frage nach dem muslimischen Subjekt vor dem Hintergrund des antimuslimischen Rassismus/der Islamophobie." In: Hunner-Kreisel, Christine / Wetzel, Jana (Hg.): Rassismus und Rassismuskritik als Querschnittaufgabe in der Sozialen Arbeit. Perspektiven für Wissenschaft und Praxis. *Neue Praxis. Zeitschrift für Sozialarbeit, Sozialpädagogik und Sozialpolitik.* Sonderheft 15, S. 70–77.

Isik, Tuba (2015): „Dispositiv Muslim in Deutschland – ein nie endendes Unterfangen." In: Isik, Tuba / Schmitz, Sabine (Hg.) (2015): *Muslimische Identitäten in Europa. Dispositive im gesellschaftlichen Wandel.* Bielefeld: transcript, S. 43–64.

Linnemann, Tobias / Ronacher, Kim Annakathrin (2018): „Reflexion von Weißsein und Rassismus – produktive Verunsicherung und wichtige Ressource für die Soziale Arbeit." In: Hunner-Kreisel, Christine / Wetzel, Jana (Hg.): Rassismus und Rassismuskritik als Querschnittaufgabe in der Sozialen Arbeit. Perspektiven für Wissenschaft und Praxis. *Neue Praxis. Zeitschrift für Sozialarbeit, Sozialpädagogik und Sozialpolitik.* Sonderheft 15, S. 91–104.

Marmer, Elina (2018): „Kritisches Weißsein als Perspektivwechsel und Handlungsaufforderung." In: Blank, Beate / Gögercin, Süleyman / Sauer, Karin E. / Schramkowski,

Barbara (Hg.): *Soziale Arbeit in der Migrationsgesellschaft. Grundlagen-Konzepte-Handlungsfelder.* Wiesbaden: Springer VS, S. 291–302.

Mecheril, Paul / Melter, Claus (2010): Gewöhnliche Unterscheidungen. Wege aus dem Rassismus. In: Mecheril, Paul / Castro Varela, Maria do Mar / Dirim, Inci / Kalpake, Annita / Melter, Claus (Hg.): *Migrationspädagogik.* Weinheim, Basel: Beltz.

Mecheril, Paul / Thomas-Olalde, Oscar (2011): „Die Religion der Anderen. Anmerkungen zu Subjektivierungspraxen der Gegenwart." In: Allenbach, Birgit / Goel, Urmila / Hummrich, Merle / Weißköppel, Cordula (Hg.): *Jugend, Migration und Religion. Interdisziplinäre Perspektiven.* Baden-Baden: Nomos-Verlag, S. 35–66.

Nökel, Sigrid (2002): *Die Töchter der Gastarbeiter und der Islam. Zur Soziologie alltagsweltlicher Anerkennungspolitiken.* Bielefeld: transcript.

Okcu, Büşra (2018): „‚Es hat sehr viel mit Empathiegefühl zu tun …'. Zur Bedeutung von Religion für Sozialarbeiter*innen muslimischen Glaubens in Beratungsprozessen." In: Hunner-Kreisel, Christine / Wetzel, Jana (Hg.): Rassismus und Rassismuskritik als Querschnittaufgabe in der Sozialen Arbeit. Perspektiven für Wissenschaft und Praxis. *Neue Praxis. Zeitschrift für Sozialarbeit, Sozialpädagogik und Sozialpolitik.* Sonderheft 15, S. 124–136.

Ostermann, Änne (1996): *Zwischen Kopftuch und Minirock. Zum Problem der Toleranz.* HSFK-Standpunkte, Nr. 2/1996, Frankfurt/M.

Said, Edward (1981): *Orientalismus.* Frankfurt am Main: Fischer.

Sadjed, Ariane (2013): Fallstricke der Säkularisierung. In: *APuZ* 24/2013, S. 17–20.

Shooman, Yasemin (2012): „Das Zusammenspiel von Kultur, Religion, Ethnizität und Geschlecht im antimuslimischen Rassismus." In: *Aus Politik und Zeitgeschichte,* 32 (H. 16–17), S. 53–57.

Soliman, Asmaa (2018): „Gegenöffentlichkeiten. Kritische Stimmen zu anti-muslimischem Rassismus." In: Hunner-Kreisel, Christine / Wetzel, Jana (Hg.): Rassismus und Rassismuskritik als Querschnittaufgabe in der Sozialen Arbeit. Perspektiven für Wissenschaft und Praxis. *Neue Praxis. Zeitschrift für Sozialarbeit, Sozialpädagogik und Sozialpolitik.* Sonderheft 15, S. 137–145.

Tietze, Nikola (2001): *Islamische Identitäten. Formen muslimischer Religiosität junger Männer in Deutschland und Frankreich.* Hamburg: Hamburger Edition.

von Wensierski, Hans-Jürgen (2012): Das islamisch-selektive Bildungsmoratorium – Zur Struktur der Jugendphase junger Muslime in Deutschland. In: Ecarius, Jutta / Eulenbach, Marcel (Hg): *Jugend und Differenz.* Springer VS, Wiesbaden, S. 213–224.

von Wensierski, Hans-Jürgen / Lübcke, Claudia (2007): *„Als Moslem fühlt man sich hier auch zu Hause". Biographien und Alltagskulturen junger Muslime in Deutschland.* Opladen u. a.: Barbara Budrich Verlag.

Internetquellen

https://www.zhdk.ch/forschung/iae/glossar-972/post-koloniale-theorie-und-dekoloniale-perspektiven-3836 (Stand 17. 12. 2018).

https://www.welt.de/debatte/kommentare/article169627929/10-Thesen-fuer-ein-weltoffenes-Deutschland.html (Stand 17. 12. 2018).

Martina Loth / Dilek Aysel Tepeli

„Vater, woran glaubst du?" – „An Stock, Stein, Natur." Ein Beitrag über Identitätsfragen junger Alevitinnen und Aleviten

Abstract

„Father, What Do You Believe In?" – „In Stick, Stone, Nature." A Contribution on Identity Questions Among Young Alevis

This article examines the changes and challenges faced by young adults of Alevi origin in their everyday lives vis-à-vis Alevi identity issues. Over the course of its history, Alevis have been suppressed as a minority by the Sunni majority in Turkey, but the last five decades point to a sequential transformation process based on: secularism, culturalism and political recognition. From the 1980s onwards, a religious character has resurfaced once again, adding another layer to this complex redefinition of ‚who they are.' In contrast to former generations, the younger generation has been grown up after the abandonment of the collective dissimulation strategy (takiye) of their religion and the turning point to a public Alevi movement. However, the experiences of suppression and marginalization are still alive to many of them. The article shows how crucial this is by exploring intergenerational relationships as well as socializational conditions of the milieu of origin. We notice how fragile the adolescence phase is for the youths who seek to find out who they are and what it means to be an Alevi. Furthermore, we address the experiences of stigmatization by their Sunni fellow as well as intergenerational continuities and discontinuities within the experience of being an Alevi. In essence, the article zooms in at how young adults are dealing differently with the lack of transmission of Alevi (religious) values and general knowledge and how they find creative ways to build up their multiple identities. The youth organization of the Alevi community in Germany (Bund der Alevitischen Jugend Deutschland e.V., BDAJ) offers an orientation for many adults.

The illustrated difficulties of searching and finding Alevi religious identities help to question the idea of possible categories of being religious or being non-religious, especially in a postmodern society in which young adults are facing individualism and value-oriented identities.

Einleitung[1]

Aktuelle wissenschaftliche Debatten, wie auf dem Symposium der Akademie der Weltreligionen im Frühjahr 2017[2], veranschaulichen, dass im Alevitentum gegenwärtig ein radikaler „Wandlungs- und Neudefinierungsprozesses" stattfindet, der mit einer „Neuinterpretation kollektiver Geschichte und Neuverhandlungen geschichtlicher Erinnerungen" einhergeht (Baumann 1998, S. 288). Die alevitische Bewegung in Deutschland und in der Türkei seit Ende der 1980er (vgl. Kap. 2), hat „eine grundlegende Transformation des alevitischen Selbstverständnisses und der alevitischen Praxis hervorgerufen" (Sökefeld 2008a, S. 9), sodass wir es gegenwärtig „nicht nur mit einer Wiederbelebung, sondern sogar mit einer Rekonstruktion des alevitischen Glaubens zu tun" haben, die „zu einer Art neuer Religion mit alten Wurzeln" führen werde (Spuler-Stegemann 2003, o. S.).

Da der religiösen Redefinition eine politische, kulturelle und säkulare Phase vorausgingen (Dreßler 2002, S. 175), existiert heute ein Spektrum von Interpretationen wie religiös, mystisch, sozialistisch, kurdisch-national oder auch türkisch-national, philosophisch, säkular oder – wie später im Fall von Zeynep ausgeführt wird – vererbt und als negative Fremdzuschreibung wahrgenommen (vgl. Kap. 4). Hierbei ist das Verhältnis zum türkischen bzw. kurdischen Nationalverständnis ebenfalls vielschichtig. Zwar kam das Laizismus-Prinzip der Trennung von Religion und Staat der Minderheitensituation der Alevit*innen entgegen und in der bis heute anhaltenden Verehrung für Mustafa Kemal Atatürk wird er sogar von einigen als Heiliger angesehen. Doch kam es in der Zeit der Republik zu einer „Schaukelpolitik des türkischen Staates gegenüber den Aleviten zwischen Versuchen der Einbindung, ja auch des Bietens einer – wenn auch kurzzeitigen – Öffnung, und blutiger Abwehr" (Spuler-Stegemann 2003, o. S.). Diese Politik „hing mit der Einschätzung zusammen, insbesondere die kurdischen Aleviten zum einen dazu auszunutzen, um das Lager der Kurden zu spalten, zum anderen sie mit der gnadenlosen Bekämpfung der Kurden zusammen zu dezimieren" (ebd.).

Doch was macht eigentlich wen zu Alevit*innen und wie spiegelt sich die ungelöste Identitätsproblematik des Alevitentums in den subjektiven Selbst- und Weltdeutungen und Erfahrungen von jungen Erwachsenen der zweiten und

1 Dilek A. Tepeli und Martina Loth sind beide Hauptautorinnen und haben den Artikel zu gleichen Anteilen verfasst.

2 Das Symposium „Alevitentum im Gespräch mit Wissenschaft und Christentum" vom 08. 04. 2017 wurde veranstaltet von der Akademie der Weltreligionen – in Kooperation mit der Evangelischen Zentrale für Weltanschauungsfragen (EZW), der Christlich-Islamischen Begegnungs- und Dokumentationsstelle e.V. (CIBEDO) und der Alevitischen Gemeinde in Deutschland e.V. (AABF).

dritten Generation[3] in ihrem Alltag wider? Wie erleben sie die fehlende Institutionalisierung des Alevitentums in ihrer Identitätsausbildung?

Christel Gärtner stellt heraus, dass „religiöse Identität von Jugendlichen sich in Abhängigkeit von gesellschaftlich-historischen und sozialisatorischen Bedingungen konstituiert“ (Gärtner 2013, S. 212f.). Vor diesem Hintergrund ist die Phase der Adoleszenz für die Identitätsbildung besonders relevant, insbesondere bezogen auf Tradition und Innovation sowie auch Religiosität (ebd., S. 212). Daher werden wir im Folgenden eine kurze historisch-kulturelle Einordnung des Alevitentums in der Türkei und in der deutschen Diaspora nachzeichnen (vgl. Kap. 2) und im anschließenden zweiten Teil nach den Besonderheiten der Identitätsbildung in der Adoleszenz von jungen Erwachsenen mit familiärer Migrationsgeschichte fragen (vgl. Kap. 3). Im dritten Teil verdeutlichen wir anhand kontrastierender empirischer Fälle die Auseinandersetzung der jungen Erwachsenen mit ihrer alevitischen Identität – ihrem *Selbstverständnis*, ihrem *Religionsverständnis* sowie ihren *intergenerationalen Beziehungen* (vgl. Kap. 4). Abschließend diskutieren wir die Ergebnisse (vgl. Kap. 5).

Empirische Grundlage und Feldzugang

Das empirische Material stammt aus den Promotionsprojekten von Martina Loth und Dilek Tepeli und umfasst narrative Interviews und Gruppendiskussionen mit jungen Erwachsenen mit sunnitischem oder alevitischem Hintergrund.

Martina Loth führte im Zeitraum Oktober 2017 – Januar 2018 insgesamt acht Interviews mit Alevit*innen im Alter von 19–25 Jahren. Allesamt sind Mitglied einer Jugendgruppe des Bundes der alevitischen Jugend (BDAJ e.V.) in einer Großstadt im Ruhrgebiet.

Dilek Tepeli erhob zehn Gruppendiskussionen und fünf narrative Interviews mit Jugendlichen und jungen Erwachsenen zwischen 16–30 Jahren im Zeitraum

3 Wir verstehen Generation dabei nach Bohnsack in Anlehnung an Karl Mannheim als einen konjunktiven Erfahrungsraum und Generationenzusammenhang bzw. generationsspezifische Gemeinsamkeiten, die über milieuspezifische Differenzen hinweg gemeinsam geteilte kollektive Erfahrungen von Gleichaltrigengruppen (Peergroups) umfassen. Diese Gleichaltrigengruppen eröffnen gemeinsame Problemlagen kommunikativ, die von vielschichtigen Erfahrungsräumen, wie der Milieuspezifik, Geschlecht oder Generation überlagert sein können. Hieraus kann ein gemeinsam geteilter „existentieller Hintergrund“ abgeleitet werden (Bohnsack 1989, S. 11). Generation meint hier also eine zeitgeschichtliche Problematik, mit der die Zugehörigen einer Generation über subkulturelle Grenzen hinweg, konfrontiert sind. (Bohnsack 1989, S. 12). Was die Jugendphase demnach ausmacht ist, dass Adoleszente sich mit der älteren Generation auseinandersetzen müssen, ganz gleich welchen sozialen Milieus oder Subkulturen sie angehören (ebd., S. 11).

Mai 2017 – Mai 2018. Es handelt sich um gemischte und homogen zusammengesetzte Gruppen sunnitischer und alevitischer Zugehörigkeit sowie Einzelinterviews mit Sunniten*innen und Alevit*innen[4].

Unsere Datenerhebung erfolgte also in den Jahren 2017 und 2018, als die politischen Spannungen in der Türkei nach dem 2016 ausgerufenen Ausnahmezustand und das Verfassungsreferendum zur Etablierung des Präsidialsystems durch die islamisch-konservative *Adalet ve Kalkınma Partisi* (*Partei für Gerechtigkeit und Aufschwung*, kurz: AKP) ihren Höhepunkt fanden. Das Referendum spaltete auch die Türkeistämmigen in Deutschland in antagonistische Lager von Erdoğan-Befürwortern („Evet“[„Ja“]) und Erdoğan-Gegnern („Hayır“[„Nein“])[5]. Diese Spannungen im Herkunftsland Türkei wirkten sich deutlich auf die Erhebungssituation aus. Ein Vergleich der beiden Forscherinnen illustriert die Bedeutung dieser Spannungen: Martina Loth konnte als „autochthone“ Forscherin im Feld Vertrauen durch ihre Kenntnisse der türkischen Sprache, der alevitischen Kultur und bereits erfolgter Forschung zu Alevit*innen gewinnen. Dadurch, dass sie nicht selbst türkeistämmig ist, bestand auch keine Gefahr, dass sie einem „feindlichen“ Lager oder der sunnitischen Gruppe hätte angehören können. Dilek Tepeli dagegen wurde aufgrund ihrer türkeistämmigen Herkunft entweder mit Misstrauen oder Vertrauen begegnet. Dies rührte insbesondere daher, dass es nicht eindeutig war, welcher Religionsgemeinschaft oder politischen Richtung sie angehörte. Die fehlende Eindeutigkeit ihrer Zugehörigkeit zum Aleviten- oder Sunnitentum oder ihre Haltung zu Erdoğan konnte so – insbesondere in den Erzählungen über negative Erfahrungen mit der Referenzgruppe der Sunnit*innen oder der Ablehnung von Erdoğan – in einigen Gesprächen zu Unbehagen führen, wie nach manchen Gruppendiskussionen mitgeteilt wurde. So dokumentieren sich die religiösen und politischen Spannungen zwischen den Türkeistämmigen bereits im Feldzugang.

4 Die Interviewpartner*innen wurden durch sich selbst oder die Auswahl durch andere als junge Erwachsene oder Jugendliche eingestuft. Zum Adoleszenzbegriff und der Bedeutung von Altersstufen schreibt King: „Die Erscheinungsformen wie die Dauer, die biographische Bedeutung und die Altersgruppen haben sich gewandelt (…). Anfänge und Ende von Jugend haben sich weiter verschoben oder sind offener geworden. Klassische Endpunkte der Jugendphase – der Beginn einer Berufsbiographie oder eine Familiengründung – haben an normativer Verbindlichkeit verloren und variieren in ihren Bedeutungen im Lebensverlauf. Ehemals scheinbar festgefügte Differenzen zwischen Lebensphasen, insbesondere jene zwischen Jugendlichen und Erwachsenen haben sich verwischt und vielfach entgrenzt“ (King 2013, S. 12).

5 Die Türkeistämmigen in der Diaspora haben mit 46 % an der Wahl teilgenommen. Von diesen haben laut Spiegel Online 59,1 Prozent „Evet (ja)“ und 40,9 Prozent „Hayır (Nein)“ gestimmt. In Deutschland war die Zahl der Befürworter*innen mit 63 Prozent etwas höher als der Durchschnitt der Auslandswähler*innen (vgl. Spiegel Online 2017. Zu den in die Diaspora „importierten“ Konfliktlinien vgl. Uslucan, Hacı-Halil 2017).

Der Transformationsprozess des gegenwärtigen Alevitentums in der deutschen Diaspora und seine Ursprünge

Das heutige Alevitentum geht hervor aus dem Kızılbaş-Alevitentum, welches im späten 15. und im 16. Jahrhundert im Rahmen der Auseinandersetzungen zwischen dem Osmanischen Reich und den aufstrebenden Safawiden entstand (Gorzewski 2010, S. 27) und die Alevit*innen in entlegene Bergdörfer vertrieb (Spuler-Stegemann 2003, o. S.); sowie aus dem Bektaschiten-Orden, der sich auf Hacı Bektaş Veli (13.Jh.), den Gründer des anatolischen Alevitentums, zurückführt (Kaplan 2004, S. 127). Die Grundlage für das spätere Alevitentum bildeten allerdings Bewegungen, die bereits auf vorislamische Zeit zurückgehen (Gorzewski 2010, S. 26)[6].

Ein zentrales Element des Alevitentums ist neben der besonderen Verehrung Alis, des Schwiegersohns und Cousin des Propheten Mohammed, eine immanente Gottesvorstellung (Aksünger 2013, S. 19). Diese führt anders als bei der Sunna dazu, dass Alevit*innen mehr diesseitsbezogen denken und handeln würden (Kehl-Bodrogi 1988, S. 110). Da das Alevitentum kaum schriftlich festgelegte oder allgemeingültige Dogmen hat (Kehl-Bodrogi 1998, S. 122), beinhaltet es eine Offenheit für Veränderung. Die Religiosität sei zudem stärker auf den Alltag ausgerichtet, was Kehl-Bodrogi mit dem Leben als isolierte Gruppe erklärt (ebd., S. 121). Die Zugehörigkeit zum Islam wird insgesamt in Frage gestellt und ist umstritten. So werden Alevit*innen von der Orthodoxie nicht als Teil der Muslim*innen anerkannt (ebd., S. 120f.).

Das Alevitentum in der Türkei

Alevit*innen wurden primär in der spätosmanischen und frührepublikanischen Zeit als religiöse Minderheit Gegenstand von Unterdrückung und Vertreibung (Hendrich 2008, 42). Für die ursprünglich dörflich beheimateten Aleviten*innen führte die seit den 1960er Jahren zunehmende Landflucht in der Türkei zu enormen soziokulturellen Umwälzungen. Riten der Dorfstruktur konnten nicht mehr praktiziert werden und in der Stadt wurde das Umfeld als feindlich gesehen, da Vorurteile gegenüber Aleviten*innen Allgemeingut waren (Sökefeld 2008a, 14; Kehl-Bodrogi 1988, 230). Aus diesem Grund verheimlichten Alevit*innen auch in der Zeit der Republik ihre eigene Identität und praktizierten *Takiye*, obwohl die Verfolgung nicht mehr staatlich durchgeführt wurde (Tezcan 2016, 160). Sökefeld versteht unter *Takiye* „(…) eine defensive Strategie, die das

6 Diese Bewegungen wurden unter anderem durch Einflüsse des Manichäismus, Zoroastrismus, Mazdakismus sowie auch des Christentums und des Buddhismus geprägt (vgl. ebd.).

Ziel hat, nicht aufzufallen und die verwendet wird, um in einer ablehnenden und potentiell feindlichen Umwelt, die Verleumdungen für bare Münze nimmt, möglicher Verfolgung zu entgehen" (Sökefeld 2008a, 9). Die Kulturtechnik der *Takiye* ist aus der Angst vor Verfolgung entstanden und ein „Ergebnis der Jahrhunderte langen Erfahrung, im Osmanischen Reich als ‚Ungläubige' abgestempelt zu werden" (ebd.).

Alevit*innen sympathisierten zunehmend mit säkularer bis anti-religiöser, linksorientierter Politik (Gorzewski 2010, S. 11) und waren involviert in die sich Ende der 1970er Jahre zuspitzende Polarisation zwischen Linken und Ultranationalisten (Dreßler 2008, S. 285). Es kam zu Massakern in Maraş (auch Kahramanmaraş genannt, 1978) und in Çorum (1980) (Massicard 2013, S. 31).

Die Urbanisierung in der Türkei fiel zeitlich mit der Abwanderung vieler Türk*innen nach Westeuropa zusammen. Im Zuge des Anwerbeabkommens zwischen Deutschland und der Türkei kamen seit den 1960er Jahren auch sehr viele Alevit*innen in die Bundesrepublik (Sökefeld 2008b, S. 199)[7]. Über die Hälfte der rund eine Million Alevit*innen in Europa leben in Deutschland (Aksünger 2013, S. 19f.).

Von der *Takiye* zum *Coming-Out* in der Diaspora

Erst in der Diaspora haben Alevit*innen Anerkennung und Selbstbewusstsein erlangt (vgl. u.a. Aksünger 2013; Sökefeld 2008a). Unsere Interviewpartner*innen wurden alle *nach* dem Jahr 1988 geboren, welches den Wendepunkt alevitischer Identität und das *Coming out* der Alevit*innen in der deutschen Diaspora markiert. Grund für diese Wende war die weltweite Identitätswelle in den 1980er Jahren (Tezcan 2012, S. 84), die in den späten 1980ern zur „Renaissance der Aleviten" und parallel zu der wieder erstarkenden islamistischen Bewegung führte (Dreßler 2017, S. 28ff.). Nach dem Militärputsch 1980 lebte zudem die „Türkisch-Islamische Synthese"[8] auf, die anders als die westliche Orientierung des Kemalismus, eine Symbiose aus Türkisch- und Sunnitischsein darstellte (Dreßler 2017, S. 25), die auch in Deutschland unter vielen Alevit*innen zu einer Angst vor sunnitischer Assimilierung führte (Sökefeld 2004b,

7 Alevit*innen hatten eine höhere Bereitschaft abzuwandern als Sunnit*innen, „aufgrund ihrer schlechteren wirtschaftlichen Situation und geringeren gesellschaftlichen Integration" (Kehl-Bodrogi 2006, 7).

8 Dazu stellt Sökefeld Folgendes fest: „Die ideologische Basis des türkischen Nationalstaats ist die Vorstellung einer geeinten und homogenen Nation. Jeder Türke hat an erster Stelle teil an dieser Nation und leitet von ihr seine grundlegendste Identität und Zugehörigkeit ab. Er oder sie mag Kurdisch sprechen oder Alevit sein, aber das darf das prinzipielle Türkentum (türklük) nicht in Frage stellen" (Sökefeld 2004b, S. 172).

S. 53). Martin Sökefeld geht davon aus, dass in Folge dieser alevitischen Bewegung in Deutschland erstmals eine Generation junger Alevit*innen auftreten könne, für die es normal sei, sich als Alevit*in zu bekennen und die nie die Erfahrung von *Takiye* gemacht habe (Sökefeld 2008a, S. 9). Elise Massicard stellt zudem heraus, dass sich Alevit*innen im Kontext der politischen Freiheit in Deutschland in einer Weise mobilisieren konnten, die in der Türkei undenkbar gewesen wäre (Massicard 2013, S. 185).

Nur wenige Jahre nach dem *Coming-Out* erlebte die Gewalt und Unterdrückung gegenüber Alevit*innen in der Türkei 1993 aber einen erneuten Höhepunkt. In der zentralanatolischen Stadt Sivas wurde das Hotel Madımak, in dem eine alevitische Kulturveranstaltung stattfand, von einer zuvor in einer Moschee aufgehetzten fundamentalistischen Menschenmenge in Brand gesteckt. Dabei starben 37 Personen, darunter 33 Festivalteilnehmende (Massicard 2001, S. 156). Dieses Massaker führte zu einer Mobilisierung und Widerstandsbewegung in Westeuropa, wo im folgenden Jahr über 100 neue alevitische Vereine und auch der Vorläufer der heutigen alevitischen Gemeinde Deutschland (AABF) gegründet wurden (Gorzewski 2010, S. 81).

Alevitische Interpretationsvielfalt innerhalb der Diaspora

Hinsichtlich der nunmehr voranschreitenden Formierung des Alevitentums in Deutschland geht Andreas Gorzewski davon aus, dass sie mit einer Transformation überlieferter Traditionen und Rituale sowie deren Anpassung an einen deutschen Kontext einhergeht (Gorzewski 2010, 285). Handan Aksünger kommt bei der Untersuchung der Vereinsstruktur der alevitischen Gemeinden zum gleichen Schluss wie Martin Sökefeld (2008a) und Krisztina Kehl-Bodrogi (2006), nämlich, dass „die Aleviten eine strategische Integrationsorientierung verfolgen“ (Aksünger 2013, S. 229). Einen wichtigen Schritt stellt hierbei der Alevitische Religionsunterricht dar, der im Jahr 2002 erstmals in Berlin anerkannt wurde (Tezcan 2016, S. 161)[9] sowie die Anerkennung als „Religionsgemeinschaft im Sinne des Grundgesetzes“ (Kehl-Bodrogi 2006, S. 15). Kehl-Bodrogi weist aber darauf hin, dass die Interpretationsvielfalt, die viele „als ein wesentliches Kennzeichen des Alevitentums begreifen und nicht aufgeben

9 In der Türkei ist es nach wie vor nicht möglich alevitische Kinder in alevitischer Lehre zu unterrichten, stattdessen müssen sie am verpflichtenden sunnitischen Islamunterricht teilnehmen (Tezcan 2012, 83). In Deutschland ist die Erteilung von alevitischem Religionsunterricht mittlerweile in acht Bundesländern möglich und die in großer Zahl erforderlichen Lehrkräfte werden an zwei Standorten ausgebildet (s. Symposiumsbericht Kalbarczyk und Loth 2017, S. 90).

möchten“, im Rahmen der schulischen Wissensvermittlung nicht zu halten sein wird (ebd., S. 16).

Denn wie eingangs angesprochen lassen sich zahlreiche Interpretationen des Alevitentums antreffen. So lässt sich das Alevitentum als Teil der Zwölferschia verorten – eine Ansicht, die nur von wenigen Alevit*innen selbst geteilt wird. Einige betrachten das Alevitentum als eine mystische Organisationsform; und wieder andere sehen im Alevitentum den wahren Islam verkörpert oder auch den „türkischen Islam“ (Kalbarczyk / Loth 2017, S. 89). Das Gegenstück hierzu bildet der kurdisch-nationale Diskurs, „in dem das Alevitentum als ein kurdisches Phänomen betrachtet wird“ (Kehl-Bodrogi 2006, S. 6). Linke, atheistisch orientierte Alevit*innen, begriffen alevitische Symbole und Traditionen als sozialistisch und deuteten sie zu Symbolen des Klassenkampfs um (Dreßler 2002, S. 173). Für einige ist das Alevitentum also keine Religion, sondern eine Weltanschauung und Philosophie und viele finden sich unter dem Dach des „Yol“(dt.: Weg), der spirituellen Wegrichtung, wieder. Alle diese Spielarten sind auf die eine oder andere Weise auch in Deutschland vertreten, sowohl als Eigen- als auch als Fremdzuschreibungen (Kalbarczyk / Loth 2017, 89).

Festzuhalten bleibt, dass die verstärkt religiöse Deutung des Alevitentums „charakteristisch für die jüngere Neubestimmung alevitischer Identität“ ist (Dreßler 2002, S. 176) und synchron auch politische und kulturelle Deutungen weiter fortbestehen. Die Neubestimmung des Alevitentums als religiös ist einem historischen Prozess des „Identity Switching“ geschuldet, indem es „(…) in der Republikgeschichte nacheinander zunächst säkular, dann kulturell, in einer dritten Phase politisch und schließlich religiös (…)“ umdefiniert wurde. Diese Umdeutung unterlag der Einbettung alevitischer Identität in den Wandel religiös-politischer Diskurse innerhalb der Türkei (ebd., S. 175).

Selbstverständnis alevitischer Identität im Verhältnis zum sunnitischen Islam

Zu den umstrittensten Identitätsmerkmalen des Alevitentums gehört die Verbindung zum Islam. Die sunnitisch-türkische Religionsbehörde „Diyanet“ erkennt eine Eigenständigkeit der Alevit*innen in der Türkei nach wie vor nicht an und verortet sie im Sinne der Türkisch-Islamischen Synthese unter dem Dach des sunnitischen Islam (Kalbarczyk / Loth 2017, S. 89). Zu dem Verhältnis zwischen Alevit*innen und Sunnit*innen schreiben İsmail Engin und Erhard Franz, dass die gegenseitigen Charakterisierungen und Zuschreibungen sich im Laufe der Zeit in den kollektiven Gedächtnissen der Gemeinschaft festgeschrieben hätten und zu Traditionen geworden seien (Engin / Franz 2001, S. 275). Hülya Taşcı stellt bei den von ihr interviewten Alevit*innen in Bezug auf das Intergruppenverhältnis zu den Sunnit*innen fest, dass das Miteinander mit diesen eine *religiöse* Grenzziehung beinhaltet (Taşcı 2006, S. 381). Diese Grenzziehung zu den Sunnit*innen wird von vielen Autor*innen als ein wichtiger Bestandteil alevitischer Identität identifiziert und setzt sich demnach intergenerational und transnational auch in der Diaspora fort (vgl. Taşcı 2006, S. 381; Kaya 2009, S. 62; Loth 2014, S. 205f.).

Während sich in der Türkei ein Teil der Alevit*innen diese eigenständige Interpretation aus Furcht vor Gewaltakten nicht zu eigen machte (Kehl-Bodrogi 2006, S. 15), nutzt ein Teil der Alevit*innen in Deutschland diese Positionierung auch, um sich „bewusst vom Islam, den Muslimen und ihrem ‚negativen Image' in Deutschland abzugrenzen, und um von der Mehrheit der Deutschen Anerkennung zu erfahren" (Hendrich 2008, S. 46f.). Gleichzeitig gibt es Alevit*innen, die eine Chance darin sehen, genau diesem Image entgegenzuwirken, in dem das Alevitentum als liberale Strömung *innerhalb* des Islam gesehen wird[10].

Heuristischer Rahmen: Identität und Adoleszenz

Identitätsfragen sind in individualisierten, pluralisierten und enttraditionalisierten Gesellschaften immerzu auch mit Zweifeln und Unsicherheiten darüber verbunden, wer eine Person oder Gruppe ist oder sein möchte. Die Ungewissheit über die eigene Identität ist aufs Engste mit der Vervielfältigung an Handlungsoptionen und Lebensentwürfen in der Spätmoderne verflochten, denn „wer nach seiner Identität fragt, ist sich ihrer nicht (mehr) gewiss" (Straub 2000, S. 280). Auch der oben diskutierte, komplizierte und zum Teil in sich widersprüchliche Diskurs um die Bestimmung einer kollektiven alevitischen Identität, vollzieht sich also in einem Rahmen spätmoderner Gesellschaften, in dem solche Identitätsfragen zunehmend dringender geworden sind und an Bedeutung gewonnen haben (vgl. Straub 2000).

Der auf den Psychoanalytiker Erik H. Erikson zurückgehende, viel diskutierte Begriff der Identität bezieht sich auf die *Gleichheit einer Person*, die sich trotz psychosozialer Veränderungen im Laufe einer Biographie und trotz unterschiedlichen Handelns in verschiedenen Kontexten, sowie Rollen und Zugehörigkeiten, durch *Kontinuität* und *Kohärenz*[11] auszeichnet (vgl. Straub 1998; 2000). Nach Erikson besitzen Personen ein Gefühl dafür, eine persönliche Identität zu haben. Sie nehmen die „Selbstgleichheit" und Kontinuität ihrer

10 Diese Sichtweise begegnete uns in mehreren Gesprächen am Rande der eingangs erwähnten Konferenz „Alevitentum im Gespräch mit Wissenschaft und Christentum".

11 Vgl. ausführlich zu den zentralen strukturtheortischen Begriffen der Kontinuität und Kohärenz (Straub1998; 2000).

eigenen Existenz wahr, ebenso erkennen auch andere sie immer wieder als dieselben an (Erikson 2015 [1966], S. 47).

Von diesem *strukturtheoretischen Begriff personaler Identität* grenzt Jürgen Straub den Begriff der *qualitativen Identität* ab. Von *qualitativer Identität* wird dann gesprochen, wenn es um einzelne Prädikate, um inhaltliche Bestimmungen von Gruppen oder Personen geht und um das, was Menschen sich selbst oder anderen an spezifischen Eigenschaften und Orientierungen zuschreiben. Es geht also um „unmittelbare oder indirekte Selbstbeschreibungen" von Personen (Straub 2000, 280f.), um ihre *Grundüberzeugungen*, die sich auf die „Gesamtheit aller ‚inhaltlich' bestimmbaren Werte, Wissensbestände, Glaubenssätze, Meinungen, Einstellungen, Orientierungen, Interessen, Wünsche, Motive, Gefühle, individuellen Eigenarten und Eigenschaften, sozialen Rollen und Funktionen, die eine Person charakterisieren" beziehen, „sowie die mit all dem verwobene, in soziale Beziehungen, gesellschaftliche Institutionen sowie kulturelle Traditionen eingebettete Handlungs- und Lebenspraxis dieses Menschen, mithin sein praktisches Selbst- und Weltverhältnis sowie das bewusste Selbst- und Weltverständnis eben dieser Person" (Straub 1998, S. 91). Identität ist somit nicht losgelöst von anderen, sondern ein soziales und relationales Konstrukt (Straub 1998, S. 87; 2000, S. 280). Denn die personale Identität ist immerzu auch an identitätsrelevante Bezugskollektive und symbolische Ordnungen gebunden, die dem Subjekt bestimmte qualitative Identitätsprädikate auferlegen (Straub 2000, S. 282).

Die Vermittlung von diesen kollektiven Selbstbildern und Mythen (aber auch damit verbundene Chancen und Forderungen bestimmter Kollektive), geschieht innerhalb des Sozialisationsprozesses, indem Individuen ihre Identität ausbilden, die je nach sozialem Herkunftsmilieu variiert (Gärtner 2013, S. 213). Identität ist dementsprechend nichts, das man einfach hat, sondern sie muss ausgebildet werden: „Identität als spezifische Subjektivierungsform erwirbt man in Übergängen bzw. in psychischer Bearbeitung von Übergängen und Transformationen, nicht in starren gleichbleibenden Situationen" (Straub 1998, S. 92). Diese Übergänge hat Erikson in seinem acht-stufigen psychosozialen Modell der Identitätsausbildung eindrücklich dargelegt. In jeder Phase der Identitätsentwicklung müssen Individuen eine psychosoziale Krise[12] lösen (vgl. Erikson 2015 [1966]). Insbesondere in der Phase der Adoleszenz, welche als ein besonders herausragender Aspekt des Lebenszyklus gilt, geht es um die geistige Reifung, die es dem jungen Menschen ermöglicht soziale Verantwortung zu übernehmen (ebd., S. 91). Die Adoleszenz ist die abschließende Stufe der

12 Krise meint einen entwicklungsbezogenen „Wendepunkt, eine einschneidende Periode vermehrter Verletzlichkeit und eines erhöhten Potentials, und damit die ontogenetische Quelle für Stärke oder Fehlanpassung in der Generationenabfolge" (Erikson 2015 [1966], S. 96).

Kindheit und stellt nach Erikson eine „normative Krise“ dar, die als eine Phase von gesteigerten Konflikten, aber auch Wachstumspotentialen für den jungen Menschen zu verstehen ist (ebd., S. 144). So macht Erikson deutlich, dass man „diese Periode als ein *psychosoziales Moratorium* bezeichnen [kann], während dessen der Mensch durch freies Rollen-Experimentieren sich in irgendeinen der Sektoren der Gesellschaft seinen Platz sucht, eine Nische, die fest umrissen und doch wie einzig für ihn gemacht ist“ (ebd., S. 137f; Herv. durch die Autorinnen). Denn in der Adoleszenz müssen sich die jungen Erwachsenen auch mit essentiellen Identitätsfragen ihrer Herkunft und Zukunft auseinandersetzen (Gärtner 2013, S. 214). Christel Gärtner weist in diesem Zusammenhang nochmals auf die Relevanz der gestiegenen Handlungsoptionen in der Moderne und die gesteigerten Wahlmöglichkeiten der Jugend hin, die normativ mit der Forderung nach Individualität einhergehen und zu Überforderung im Sinne fehlender Orientierung führen können (ebd., S. 213). Da das Moratorium in intergenerationale Beziehungen eingebunden ist, entscheidet seine Qualität darüber, ob es den jungen Menschen gelingt Haltungen und Dispositionen wie Vertrauen oder Autonomie zu entwickeln, die es dem Adoleszenten ermöglichen Handlungsoptionen wahrzunehmen und Krisenbewältigung leisten zu können. Insbesondere, aber nicht ausschließlich, sind die Eltern-Kind-Beziehungen hierfür bedeutsam (ebd., S. 213f.), denn die „adoleszente Auseinandersetzung und Entwicklung vollzieht sich zwischen Familie, Gesellschaft und Peers“ (ebd., S. 213).

Für Adoleszente mit Migrationshintergrund kommt bei dieser dargestellten Auseinandersetzung und Entwicklung folgende Besonderheit hinzu: Sie müssen einen doppelten Transformationsprozess durchlaufen: den Übergang von der Kindheit zum Erwachsensein sowie die mit der Migration selbst verbundene Transformation. Dies gilt nicht nur für Heranwachsende, die selbst migrieren. Denn auch die Adoleszenz der Kinder der zweiten Generation ist von den Folgen der Migration für die Familie und die Art der Verarbeitung durch die Eltern geprägt (King / Koller 2006, S. 11).

Traumatische Erlebnisse der Elterngeneration können an die Kinder weitergegeben werden, die sich in der teils bewussten, teils unbewussten Weitergabe von historischen Verletzungsverhältnissen ausdrücken (vgl. Straub 2014) und aufgrund der geschilderten (Verletzungs-)Historie des Alevitentums eine wichtige Rolle für unsere Interviewpartner*innen spielen könnten.

(Be-)Deutungen alevitischer Identität

Im Folgenden wollen wir anhand kontrastierender Fälle einen Teil des Spektrums alevitischer Identität aufzeigen. Diese skizzenhafte Darstellung soll das *Selbstverständnis*, das damit verbundene *Religionsverständnis* sowie die *inter-*

generationalen Beziehungen und *Verhältnisse* aufspüren. Denn aus der Innenperspektive von Personen kann es bei der Bestimmung alevitischer Identität um „nahezu alles und jedes" gehen (Taşcı 2006, S. 377) und die Antwort auf die Frage „Wer bin ich?" bzw. nach der inhaltlich-qualitativen Identität stellt einen nie abgeschlossenen Akt dar (ebd., S. 378).

Im ersten Teil der Analyse sollen die vielfältigen Selbstverständnisse aus biographischen und in Gruppendiskussionen hervorgebrachten Erzählungen herausgearbeitet werden und aufzeigen, welche Erfahrungen die jungen Erwachsenen mit ihrer *Zugehörigkeit zum Alevitentum* machen, was sie mit ihrem Alevitischsein verbinden und inwiefern sie sich darauf beziehen. Im zweiten Teil soll an einem Fallbeispiel die Fremdwahrnehmung und geschilderte Zuschreibung von außen thematisiert werden[13].

Alevitischsein als politisches Engagement: „Man tut halt Vieles für seinen Glauben"

Im Selbstverständnis von Umut[14], der im „Bund der Alevitischen Jugendlichen in Deutschland e.V." (BDAJ) organsiert ist, lassen sich Aspekte eines transnationalen und intergenerationalen Verhältnisses zu seiner alevitischen Identität aufzeigen.

> (…) ich stehe auch öffentlich dazu, dass ich Alevite bin, zwar nicht in der Türkei da hab ich Angst, dazu steh' ich auch, aber in Deutschland gibt es ja Gott sei Dank die Meinungsfreiheit und die Religionsfreiheit und deswegen war ich auch auf ganz vielen Demonstrationen gegen Erdoğan oder mmh halt mmh ich war auf diversen Festivals Dersim-Festival und auch Dersim-Seminare und man kommt da viel rum man tut halt Vieles für seinen Glauben und ich bin halt stolz dass ich halt so viel- ich finde immer man kann, man kann viel dazu beitragen auch wenn's nur wenig is' zum Beispiel dieses auch Wahlen wenn man wählen geht dieses Evet-Hayır-Dings [Übersetzung und Anmerkung der Autorinnen: „Ja-Nein-Dings", Umut bezieht sich hier auf das Verfassungsreferendum vom 16. April 2017]ne' diese ganze Evet-Hayır-Sache au- auch mmh es ist zwar nur eine Stimme die ich habe aber die Stimme kann viel bewegen deshalb, muss man immer seine Chance nutzen, und das tu' ich auch denke ich. (Umut, 21 Jahre)

Zunächst führt er selbstbewusst an, zu seinem Alevitischsein im öffentlichen Raum zu stehen und es nicht zu verheimlichen, wie es in der Türkei üblicherweise von seiner Eltern- und Großelterngeneration gemacht worden war. So berichtet Umut im Interview davon, dass seine Eltern nicht nur in der Türkei,

13 Mit dieser Darstellung soll nicht in Abrede gestellt werden, dass junge Erwachsene vielfältigen Erfahrungsräumen angehören (vgl. Bohnsack 1989) und somit unterschiedliche Selbstverständnisse nebeneinanderstehen und sich überlagern können.

14 Alle Namen und personenbezogenen Daten sind zwecks Personenschutzes anonymisiert.

sondern auch in der Diaspora ihre religiöse Identität verheimlichten und demnach *Takiye* betrieben. Umut dagegen löst sich von dieser kollektiven Praxis seiner Familie und bricht mit ihr. Dies stellt einen Wandel im Umgang mit der Abweichung der alevitischen Identität von einer Generation zur anderen dar. In der Türkei allerdings wäre ein solcher Wandel für ihn nicht möglich gewesen, da er das Praktizieren von *Takiye* dort nicht aufgeben würde. Er relativiert demnach seine Aussage des selbstbewussten Inszenierens seiner alevitischen Identität nach außen und bezieht sich auf zwei entgegensetzte, antagonistische öffentliche Räume von Freiheit und Repression: Im Herkunftsland Türkei leitet ihn nicht Selbstbewusstsein, sondern – analog zur Elterngeneration – die Angst davor, seine alevitische Identität preiszugeben. Angst stellt eine Emotion dar, die vor einer bedrohlichen Situation warnt und schützen soll. Diese Angst lässt vermuten, dass sie familiär vermittelt und verinnerlicht wurde, auch wenn Umut selbst nicht in der Türkei aufwuchs, so wird die Verletzung der Eltern an ihn weitervererbt (vgl. Straub 2014, S. 77f.). Im familialen Erfahrungsraum hat er gelernt, dass Alevitischsein im öffentlichen Raum der Türkei ein Stigma darstellt und man seine tatsächliche soziale Identität zum eigenen Schutz nicht preisgeben sollte (vgl. Goffman 1975)[15].

Mit seinem „Alevitischsein" verbindet er relational zum nationalen Kontext Anerkennung aufgrund von Religions- und Meinungsfreiheit und Unfreiheit aufgrund der Repressionen im Herkunftsland der Eltern. Der Bezug auf Religionsfreiheit hebt Alevitischsein als Religion hervor, gleichzeitig nennt Umut aber keine religiösen Inhalte. Er selbst bezieht sich auf politische Aspekte, wie die Teilnahme an Demonstrationen gegen die repressive Politik gegenüber Alevit*innen in der Türkei. Er sieht es gar als seine Pflicht an, sich für das Alevitentum einzusetzen, und glaubt, dass man „seine Chance nutzen muss". Auch wenn Umut keine religiösen Bezüge herstellt, ist Alevitischsein für ihn etwas Religiöses: Sein politisches Engagement gilt seinem Glauben und steht in der Emanzipationsbestrebung des jungen Erwachsenen von intergenerational vererbten Unterdrückungserfahrungen. Dieses Engagement für den eigenen Glauben stellt eine implizite Loyalität zwischen den Generationen dar, die sich nicht

15 Die Strategie der *Takiye* als Verheimlichung und Anpassen an das Handeln und die Normen der feindlich gesinnten Gruppe (vgl. Kehl-Bodrogi 1988, S. 249), lässt sich mit Goffmans Stigmatheorie als eine Form des Stigmamanagements begreifen, die auf jedwede Art von Abweichung zur Sicherung der eigenen Identität angewandt werden kann. Insbesondere dann, wenn es sich um ein „diskreditierbares", der Umwelt unbekanntes Stigma handelt, können Individuen durch Täuschen und Verbergen eine Beschädigung ihrer Identität abwenden (vgl. Goffman 1975). Die einst übliche Barttracht, mit der Aleviten ihre Identität und Verschwiegenheit sowie Abgrenzung gegenüber Fremden stolz zur Schau stellten, wurde kaum mehr getragen als sie in Berührung mit einem von Sunnit*innen geprägten sozialen Umfeld gerieten (Kehl-Bodrogi 1988, S. 233).

im selben Maße dafür einsetzen konnten (vgl. auch Kaya 2011, S. 149) und erfüllt Umut mit Stolz.

Umuts politisches Engagement für das Alevitentum wird durch seine Bezugnahme auf die Stadt Dersim und die Dersim-Seminare und -Festivals sehr deutlich, denn das Massaker von Dersim steht für die repressive Politik und Brutalität des türkischen Staates gegenüber seinen ethnischen und religiösen Minderheiten (vgl. van Bruinessen 1988, S. 6). Die Nutzung des Begriffs „Dersim" stellt ebenso eine Verweigerungshaltung dar, denn die Stadt wurde von der türkischen Regierung offiziell in Tunceli (dt. eiserne Hand) umbenannt.

Für Umut stellt Alevitischsein im Herkunftsland der Eltern demnach ein Stigma dar, in dessen intergenerationalen Erbfolge er sich als Kind einer alevitischen Familie einreiht (vgl. Goffman 1975). Durch die Migration seiner Familie nach Deutschland haben sich für ihn aber neue Möglichkeitsräume ergeben, die die Elterngeneration nicht hatte: Er wächst in einem Raum der Religionsfreiheit auf. Diese Möglichkeiten gebraucht er, um Handlungsmacht zu entwickeln und sich durch sein politisches Engagement für die Anerkennung und Aufwertung seiner Gruppenidentität einzusetzen, was für ihn sogar eine Pflicht darstellt.

Alevitischsein als „Pseudoreligion": „Vater, woran glaubst du?"

Einen Kontrast zum ersten vorgestellten Fall, in dem Alevitischsein als politisches Engagement verstanden wird, stellt der in keiner Gemeinde angebundene Ali dar, der mit seiner sunnitischen Frau über die (Nicht-)Religion seiner Familie diskutiert. Anders als Umut engagiert sich Ali nicht für seine qua Geburt erworbene alevitische Zugehörigkeit. Er stellt sich zudem als jemand dar, der kaum über religiöses Wissen verfügt. Seine Familie grenzt er von religiösen Alevit*innen als „pseudo" Aleviten ab.

> Lale: (…) also von der religiösen Seite wissen die [Lales Eltern], dass die Eltern auch nicht so religiös sind, nichts mit Aleviten zu tun haben, sie sind zwar Aleviten aber
> Ali: Pseudo, pseudo
> Lale: die haben, also dein Vater is' ja, der glaubt glaub ich
> Ali: Weißt du, weißt du was das Beste war als wir den gefragt haben, meine Schwester hat den mal gefragt. Vater woran glaubst du? Da sagt der Stock, Stein, Natur
> Interviewerin: lacht.
> (Lale und Ali, 29 und 30 Jahre alt)

Das intergenerationale Verhältnis von Ali und seinem Vater zeichnet sich durch den fehlenden Transfer religiösen Wissens aus: In dieser Reinszenierung eines Gesprächs zwischen seinem Vater, ihm und seiner Schwester zeigt sich, dass die Generation der Kinder kein Wissen über die Religion vermittelt bekommen hat, das es ihr erlauben würde, die Antwort des Vaters auf die Frage nach dem Glauben angemessen einzuordnen. Die Zuschreibung durch seine Frau, dass seine Familie Alevit*innen seien, wird von Ali mit einer doppelten Wiederholung und Bekräftigung durch den Begriff *„Pseudo, Pseudo"* abgewehrt. Der Begriff „Pseudo" verweist auf einen Schein und wird in der Regel abwertend gebraucht. Sein Vater ist in der Darstellung von Ali somit nur dem Anschein nach ein Alevit und eigentlich kein „Echter". Das fehlende Wissen über die Religion des Vaters führt dazu, dass die herkunftsspezifische Religion des Alevitentums von der Kindergeneration als unauthentisch und areligiös wahrgenommen wird. Die nicht näher ausgeführte dreiteilige Formel „Stock, Stein, Natur" bleibt aus Sicht der beiden Geschwister, aber auch aus Sicht der lachenden Interviewerin, die das Verständnis der beiden teilt, leer und impliziert keinen religiösen Gehalt. In dieser kurzen, formelartigen Antwort des Vaters zeigt sich die fehlende Kommunikation zwischen Eltern- und Kindergeneration sowie die fehlende Explikation des Glaubens. Es findet also keine Tradierung religiösen Wissens von einer Generation an die nachfolgende statt, was zu Missverständnissen führt. Die alevitische Lehre hat in ihrem Kern nämlich einen besonderen animistischen Bezug zur nichtmenschlichen Natur, denn die Existenz Gottes sei in der Vorstellung alevitischen Glaubens in der Natur und im Menschen zugleich aufzufinden (Kaplan/Öztürk 2006, S. 19, 30). Das Missverständnis zwischen dem Vater und seinen Kindern rührt zudem daher, dass beide Generationen unterschiedliche implizite Wissensbestände davon verinnerlicht haben, was Religion und religiös sein eigentlich bedeutet. Hierbei ist der Glaube des Vaters an „Stock, Stein, Natur" der negative Gegenhorizont zu dem, was von den Kindern als Religion verstanden wird. Der implizite Maßstab, an dem Religiosität von den Kindern gemessen wird, ist ein Religionsverständnis, das sich durch klare Definitionen, Rituale, Traditionen, Institutionen, Inhalte und Regeln wie im sunnitischen Mehrheitsislam, Christen-, oder Judentum bestimmen lässt, denn erst über diesen Vergleichsmaßstab der sogenannten Weltreligionen erhält die alevitische Religion ihren areligiösen Charakter. In der Interaktion des Paars herrscht demnach Übereinstimmung darüber, dass die Herkunftsfamilie von Ali keine „richtigen" Alevit*innen sein können und zeigt, dass das Alevitentum aufgrund der fehlenden Wissensvermittlung für die Kindergeneration inhaltsleer bleibt. Dennoch gibt es die kollektiv geteilten Vorstellungen von Ali und seiner Frau davon, dass es religiöse Alevit*innen gibt. Die eigene Familie entspricht aber als negativer Gegenhorizont nicht religiösen Alevit*innen, sie hat sogar nichts „mit diesen zu tun". In Alis areligiösem Selbstverständnis alevitisch zu sein verdeutlicht sich die Unmöglichkeit mit dem Vater in einen Dialog über das Alevitentum treten zu können und weist auf die fehlende Vermittlung kollektiver Erinnerungen und kollektiven Wissens hin (vgl. auch Kaya 2011, S. 153).

Individuelle Deutungsmöglichkeiten: „dass man sich halt seine eigene Meinung dazu bilden kann“

Duygu ist in einer alevitischen Gemeinde eingebunden und hat sich dort das in der Familie nicht tradierte Wissen eigenständig im Raum der Glaubensgemeinschaft (im „*Cem Evi*“) und der Gleichaltrigengruppe des Jugendverbands aneignen können. Trotzdem ist sie mit dem Problem des fehlenden Wissenstransfers von einer Generation zur anderen innerhalb der Familie konfrontiert. Sie sucht kreative und individuierte Umgangsweisen für diese Problematik. Anders als Ali, dessen fehlendes Wissen über das Alevitentum zu keiner Auseinandersetzung mit dessen Inhalten führt, eignet sich Duygu das religiöse Wissen individuell in der Gemeinde an und deutet das Alevitentum für sich als eine undogmatische Religion. Ähnlich wie im Fall von Umut praktiziert auch die Elterngeneration von Duygu *Takiye* und sie erfährt erst mit einem gewissen Alter von ihrer Zugehörigkeit zum Alevitentum. Anders als die Eltern bricht sie aber damit. Dass Duygu keine Verheimlichung ihrer Identität betreibt, zeigt das Gespräch mit der autochthonen Interviewerin, mit der sie offen über die Entdeckung ihres Alevitischseins spricht:

> Mmh also das kam so also ich wusste bis zum gew- bis zu einem gewissen Alter nicht, dass ich Alevitin bin halt also meine Eltern haben mir das jetzt nicht gesagt so. weil ich glaub das lag halt daran weil in der Türkei halt mmh die Aleviten ja auch mmh gefoltert und mmh geschlagen wurden halt verbrannt wurden, gejagt wurden halt so ähnlich wie bei Juden und mmh die hatten halt Angst dass ich dass mir halt was passieren könnte dann hab ich das erstmal erfahren halt dass ich Alevitin bin ich kannte mich trotzdem noch nicht so gut darin aus dann nach de- nach einer Zeit hab ich halt angefangen in die Gemeinde zu kommen durch mmh einen Cousin halt weil er hat mich mal halt gerufen (.) und dadurch ist eigentlich mein Interesse so e- erweckt wurden. (Duygu, 24 Jahre alt)

Duygu erklärt hier vor dem Hintergrund ihrer eigenen Deutung, wie es dazu gekommen ist, dass ihre Eltern ihr das Alevitischsein verschwiegen haben – es gab also eine Zeit in ihrer Biographie, indem es keinen Dialog mit der Elterngeneration über die familiale alevitische Zugehörigkeit gab. Ihr Vergleich zur jüdischen Unterdrückungsgeschichte plausibilisiert das Verhalten der Eltern. Der Vergleich mit der jüdischen Leidensgeschichte setzt Aleviten- und Judentum relational miteinander in Beziehung und verbindet die beiden Gruppen in ihrer kollektiven Erfahrung, nicht anerkannt und verfolgt worden zu sein. Aufgrund der Verfolgungserfahrungen der Eltern und deren verinnerlichter Angst, ihre eigene Identität preiszugeben, wurde der eigenen Tochter das Wissen um die familiäre Zugehörigkeit vorenthalten: Die Tochter soll vor ähnlichen Verletzungen geschützt werden. Dieses Verhalten der Eltern, das als *Takiye* gedeutet werden kann, untersagt es religiöse Glaubensvorstellungen gegenüber Fremden preiszugeben, ragt aber auch in Duygus innerfamiliären Raum hinein und führt dazu, dass ein Geheimnis zwischen ihr und ihren Eltern steht. Ihr religiöses Selbstverständnis ist aus diesem Grund eng mit den Gewalt- und Leiderfahrungen der Elterngeneration verbunden. Die Nicht-Tradierung und das Verheimlichen durchdringen somit den Innenraum der Familie mit der Folge, dass Duygu selbstständig im Verbund der alevitischen Gemeinde den Prozess ihres „Alevitisch-Werdens“ und der damit zusammenhängenden Wissensaneignung in ihrem engeren Familienkreis in Gang setzt. Denn in ihrer Familie kann sie keine Orientierung bezogen auf die alevitische Identität finden. Die Erfahrung des Schweigens über die alevitische Zugehörigkeit setzt sich demnach bei den Diaspora-Alevit*innen als historische Kontinuität fort, wird aber von der Adoleszenten gebrochen, welche sich in der Gemeinde mit ihrer religiösen Identität auseinanderzusetzen beginnt. Ihr fehlendes Wissen deutet sie so um, es als Möglichkeit der Individuierung zu nutzen:

> und ich argumentiere immer damit dass mmh halt Jesus war ja Jude //mhm// und seine Anhänger sind ja Christen und dass es bei uns genauso sein könnte so warum nicht ne, man weiß es ja nicht; es ist ja nicht irgendwie auf Papier geschrieben oder sonstwas und (.) was aufgeschrieben ist ist ja auch nicht immer hundertprozent richtig so und deswegen also ich find' das gut in unserer Religion, dass man sich halt seine eigene Meeigene Me- eigene Meinung dazu bilden kann. (Duygu, 24 Jahre)

Duygu zieht einen erneuten Vergleich zur jüdisch-christlichen Tradition heran, um der Interviewerin gegenüber ihren Standpunkt zu plausibilisieren. Der Vergleich soll helfen die alevitische Religion zu verstehen und zu erklären, warum Alevit*innen nicht zwangsläufig Muslim*innen sein müssen. Der Vergleich dient aus Duygus Perspektive dazu, etwas Unverständliches und Uneindeutiges erklärbar zu machen, nämlich die von ihr geteilte Vorstellung, dass eine wesentliche Figur des Alevitentums – der von Alevit*innen verehrte Cousin des Propheten, Ali, – ein Anhänger des sunnitischen Islams gewesen sei. Der Vergleich zwischen Jesus als Juden und seinen Nachfolgern den Christen soll diese scheinbare Unvereinbarkeit nachvollziehbar machen und das Argument, sich als Alevitin außerhalb des Islams zu verorten, stützen, obwohl diese Erzählung nicht den historischen Tatbeständen entspricht. In diesem Selbstverständnis dokumentiert sich demnach eine implizite Abgrenzung zum sunnitischen Islam.

Eine Kritik an der (fehlenden) Schriftlichkeit und der vermeintlichen Authentizität des geschriebenen Wortes generell bestärkt ihre Position: Schriftlich fixierte Überlieferungen müssen nicht zwangsläufig wahr sein, aus diesem Grund ist es kein Nachteil, dass ein solch überlieferter kanonischer Textkorpus im Alevitentum fehlt. Die Interviewte bewertet ihre Religion positiv, indem sie einen Aspekt, der zunächst problematisch erscheint, in etwas Kreatives und Emanzipatorisches umdeutet: Die fehlende Dogmatik im Alevitentum erlaubt eine individuelle Interpretation dessen, was unter Alevitischsein verstanden werden kann. Diese Flexibilität wird in der Wahrnehmung von Duygu als Bereicherung geschildert, nicht als Nachteil. In ihrer Darstellung scheinen sich schier endlose, niemals ganz abgeschlossene Deutungsmöglichkeiten über das Alevitentum aufzutun. Dies ermöglicht ihr eine individuelle und auch eine möglicherweise wandelbare Deutung dessen, was sie unter „ihrer" Religion versteht. An der Art der Erzählung kann gleichzeitig aber auch herausgelesen werden, dass die Adoleszente die fehlende Dogmatik und Schriftlichkeit im Alevitentum zwar positiv für sich umdeutet und in ihren Individuierungsprozess einbinden kann. Allerdings zeigt die zögernd von ihr hervorgebrachte positive Bewertung des Alevitentums als eine Religion, die die eine „eigene Meinung" zulässt, auch auf eine in ihrer Erzählung zugrunde liegende Spannung: Der individuelle Zugriff auf eine kollektiv geteilte Weltanschauung beinhaltet zwar fehlende Muss-Normen, dennoch wird die Adoleszente mit einer schier unendlichen Deutungsmöglichkeit konfrontiert und muss selbstständig entscheiden, an welcher der vielen nebeneinanderstehenden konkurrierenden Interpretationen sie sich orientiert.

Fremdwahrnehmung und Zuschreibungen gegenüber Alevit*innen

Da Identität in wechselseitigen Zuschreibungen und Positionierungen interaktiv hergestellt wird (vgl. Goffman 1975), soll nun auch eine Erzählung analysiert werden, die Erfahrungen mit anderen und auch die empfundene und erlebte Wahrnehmung durch andere umfasst. Am Fallbeispiel Zeynep, die aus einer alevitisch-sunnitischen Familie stammt, sollen diese Erfahrungen mit anderen veranschaulicht werden. Sunnitisch-alevitische Ehen und deren Kinder erfahren von außen wie innen häufig Stigmatisierung, beispielsweise durch die Großeltern und andere Verwandte (vgl. Balkanlıoğlu 2012; vgl. Kaplan/Öztürk 2006). Eine solche Erfahrung thematisiert auch Zeynep. Für Zeynep ist ihr Alevitischsein bedeutsam, weil (signifikante) Andere[16] innerhalb ihrer Familie sie als Alevitin stigmatisierten, obwohl ihr Alevitischsein für sie selbst ein bloß von außen zugeschriebenes und durch Geburt erworbenes Merkmal darstellt. In diesem Ausschnitt berichtet sie von ihrer Erfahrung, als Alevitin negativ wahrgenommen und stigmatisiert worden zu sein:

16 In der Rollentheorie von George Herbert Mead übernehmen Kinder in der Sozialisation durch Rollenspiele und Rollenübernahme die Perspektive bezugsrelevanter Personen, der signifikanten Anderen, wie beispielsweise Eltern, Geschwister oder Lehrer (Jörissen 2010, S. 97f.).

> Zeynep: Und, aber ich hab' auch immer gemerkt dass ehm eh, bei der Familie meiner Stiefmutter oder Familie meiner Mutter dass die immer was gegen Aleviten hatten, das hab ich immer gespürt sooo, ich gehört' nicht ganz dazu und Aleviten sind Ungläubige und ich wurd' dann auch immer anders behandelt ne also auch meine Geschwister und hab dann immer schon gemerkt, man gehört irgendwie nicht dazu, da is, da is irgendwas dazwischen. aber ich wusste nicht was es ist
> I:Mmh
> Zeynep: und auch als Kind auch gerade so in der Schulzeit ehm dass sunnitische Kinder mich halt fertig gemacht haben, weil ich nicht gefastet hab ne so
> I:Mmh
> Zeynep: dass, natürlich das haben die von zuhause aus so mitgekriegt ne, man muss fasten und Aleviten sind sooo und als wir dann älter wurden haben die sich auch so bei mir entschuldigt und meinten, irgendwie haben wir das nur wiederholt, was unsere Eltern gesagt haben, aber das is' ja voll dumm was wir damals von uns gegeben haben, wir waren unwissend ne
> I:Mmh
> Zeynep: klar sind Aleviten nicht dreckig oder sind nicht keine Ahnung alle Frauen sind Schlampen oder was auch immer, aber als Kind hat mich das geprägt, sodass ich auch oft das verleugnet habe, wenn ich in einen neuen Kreis kam, hab ich das gar nicht erwähnt, hab so getan als würde ich auch fasten ne und mich so versteckt weil mir das zu unangenehm war, darüber zu diskutieren
> I:Mmh
> Zeynep: und als so zu tun als wär ich jemand anderes also jetzt heute hab ich Selbstbewusstsein (im Nachhinein) ich bin Atheist, ich bin homosexuell, is' mir scheiß egal was ihr denkt (lachend) (Zeynep, 30 Jahre alt)

Zeynep spricht hier über ihre sensible Phase von Kindheit und früher Adoleszenz und erzählt von ihren Gefühlen und Erfahrungen als Abweichende – einmal in der Innensphäre, einmal in der Außensphäre von Familie. In dieser Erfahrung dokumentiert sich ein negatives „Wir-Bild", das von außen zugeschrieben wird und ihre Identität verletzt (vgl. Goffman 1975, vgl. auch Elias / Scotson 1993). Diese Verletzung geht von der eigenen sunnitischen Familie und anderen Heranwachsenden aus, die Zeynep abwerten, weil sie zum einen nicht die gleichen religiösen Rituale des Fastens durchführt, wie die Mehrheit der Sunnit*innen, und zum anderen weil ihr Vater ein Alevit ist und damit als „ungläubig" stigmatisiert wird. Auch hier zeigt sich – diesmal aus der Außenperspektive – was unter Religion verstanden wird und was nicht: Der sunnitische Islam bildet den Maßstab der Bewertung von Alevit*innen als „Ungläubigen" und damit als areligiös, gleichzeitig auch als regellos, anomisch und unrein, wie die Zuschreibung „dreckig" oder „Schlampen" zu sein verdeutlicht (vgl. Elias / Scotson 1993). Aus sunnitischer Perspektive sind Alevit*innenen demnach nicht religiös und werden mit dem pejorativen Begriff „Ungläubige" etikettiert (vgl. auch Kaya 2009, S. 137f.). In der Erzählung zeigt sich auch ein Imperativ, der von den sunnitischen Mitschüler*innen ausgeht: „Sei wie wir, sonst gehörst du nicht dazu!". Differenz und Andersartigkeit werden folglich nicht geduldet sondern abgewertet. Die von außen zugeschriebene Identität als Außenseiterin bestimmt also die Identitätsfrage, wer Zeynep ist, signifikant mit (vgl. Goffman 1975). Hierbei spielt Emotionalität eine wichtige Rolle. Diese drückt sich beispielsweise darin aus, dass Zeynep „spürte", nicht ganz zu ihrer Familie dazuzugehören. Die Erzählende reflektiert dies selbst, denn die Erfahrung der Nicht-Zugehörigkeit in ihrer Kindheit und Jugend prägte ihr Selbst- und Weltverhältnis und verletzte ihre Identität in einer sensiblen Phase der psychosozialen Entwicklung. Alevitischsein wurde von Zeynep als Stigma erfahren, als etwas das negativ und gar als normenlos bewertet wird. Um die Beschädigung ihrer Identität abzuwenden, nutzt Zeynep als junge Erwachsene eine kollektive Form des „Stigmamanagements", die Bewältigung und Abwendung von Stigmatisieurng (vgl. Goffman 1975), die bereits Generationen zuvor anwandten: das Verheimlichen und sich Verstellen (*Takiye*). Anders als Umut, der diese Strategie nur in der Türkei anwendet, wendet sie diese Strategie in der Migrationssituation an. Demzufolge setzt sich das Stigma Alevitischsein und der Umgang damit auch in der Diaspora intergenerational fort. Zeyneps Selbstverständnis und Zugehörigkeit zum Alevitentum ist durch Verheimlichung und der Angst davor geprägt, von anderen Adoleszenten mit Herkunft aus der Türkei gemieden und abgewertet zu werden.

Es zeigt sich folglich eine historische Kontinuität mit der eigenen Abweichung umzugehen. Die Vorurteile, denen die Adoleszente begegnet, werden von ihr als intergenerational durch die Eltern der sunnitischen Kinder tradiert mitreflektiert. In einer besonders sensiblen Phase ihrer Biographie nimmt die Erfahrung eine Außenseiterin zu sein einen wichtigen Teil ihrer Identität ein. Die psychosozialen Folgen dieser Erfahrung als anders wahrgenommen zu werden sind Ausgrenzung, empfundener Anpassungszwang und Verinnerlichung eines zugeschriebenen negativen Wir-Bilds in die Identität (vgl. Elias / Scotson 1993). Innerhalb ihrer Identitätsentwicklung entwickelt Zeynep aber Autonomie und Widerstandskraft gegenüber Abwertungen von außen. Sie vergemeinschaftet sich mit anderen abweichenden Gruppen wie Homosexuellen und begreift sich selbst explizit (ähnlich wie ihr alevitischer Vater) als atheistisch. An diesem Fallbeispiel wird deutlich, dass es sich beim Alevitentum nur noch um ein Herkunftsmilieu handelt, religiöse Inhalte sind nicht bedeutungsvoll. Mit Alevit*innen „sympathisiert" Zeynep dennoch, wie sie in einem Gespräch nach der Gruppendiskussion auf Nachfrage mitteilt. Sie sieht das Alevitentum als eine „friedliche" und „angenehme" Religion an und gibt aus der aktuellen Perspektive auch gerne an alevitische Wurzeln zu haben[17]. In der sexuellen Orientierung

17 Dreßler weist, wie schon erwähnt darauf hin, dass es historische Umdeutungen der alevitischen Identität gegeben hat (Dreßler 2002, S. 175). Zeyneps areligiöse alevitische Identität kann sich in diese Typologie als kulturelles Erbe einreihen.

von Zeynep liegt eine weitere Abweichung in ihrer Identität vor, die sie jedoch im Zuge ihrer Identitätsentwicklung und Emanzipation von *Takiye* nach außen trägt und sich nicht mehr verstellt.

An diesem Fall konnte gezeigt werden, wie das Alevitentum von sunnitischer Seite wahrgenommen wird und welche problematischen Verletzungen negative Zuschreibungen von außen auf die Identitätsentwicklung von jungen Erwachsenen haben. In diesem Fall sogar innerhalb des familiären Erfahrungsraums, der doch eigentlich Schutz und Geborgenheit gewähren sollte.

Fazit und Ausblick

Wir haben gezeigt, dass die eingangs geschilderten soziokulturellen und historischen Entwicklungen im Herkunftsland der Alevit*innen als auch in der Diaspora sukzessive zu Veränderungen der alevitischen Identität geführt haben: Es hat einen Bruch mit der kollektiven Praxis der *Takiye* gegeben, der in der deutschen Diaspora seinen Höhepunkt in der Anerkennung als eigenständige Religionsgemeinschaft fand. Großeltern-, Eltern- und Kindergeneration erleben demnach ganz unterschiedliche Erfahrungszusammenhänge ihrer alevitischen Identität – dennoch ist und bleibt die Erfahrung von Marginalisierung und Unterdrückung der Eltern- und Großelterngeneration für die junge Generation entscheidend und prägend. Denn die intergenerationalen Beziehungen und sozialisatorischen Bedingungen des Herkunftsmilieus müssen von den jungen Erwachsenen verarbeitet werden und beeinflussen damit die Herausbildung ihrer religiösen und nicht-religiösen Identitätsentwürfe. Weiterhin machen auch die Adoleszenten, vor allem während ihrer Schulzeit, häufig ebenfalls Stigmatisierungserfahrungen (vgl. Loth 2014). Wie unsere Beispiele zeigen, umfasst die Umbruchphase der Adoleszenz sowohl intergenerationale Kontinuitäten als auch Diskontinuitäten in der Erfahrung, alevitisch zu sein. Der vollführte kollektive Bruch mit der *Takiye*-Praxis, das *Coming-Out* des Alevitentums, die geringe bis fehlende Vermittlung religiöser Wissensbestände, das Verheimlichen der eigenen religiösen Identität (*Takiye*) und das spezifische (Verletzungs-)Verhältnis zu(m) Sunniten(tum) sind entscheidende herkunftsspezifische Bedingungen in der Herausbildung einer eigenen alevitischen Identität. Allerdings haben die kontrastiven Beispiele auch gezeigt, dass das Wissen um und die Einordnung von diesen Prozessen individuell und familiär bedingt sehr unterschiedlich verlaufen kann. Trotz des alevitischen *Coming-Outs* sehen wir, dass auch bei den Jüngeren die Biographien von der Migrationsgeschichte der Unterdrückung und des Schweigens und Verheimlichens geprägt sind – wenngleich für diese jüngere Generation die Möglichkeit gegeben ist, *Takiye* abzulegen, wie Martin Sökefeld (2008, S. 9) schreibt. Unsere Empirie zeigt dagegen jedoch, dass zum Teil auch junge Alevit*innen in der sensiblen Phase der Adoleszenz in unterschiedlicher Ausprägung das Schweigen weiterhin praktizieren (müssen) oder in einem sozialisatorischen Milieu des Schweigens aufwachsen. Eine alevitische Identität auszubilden stellt unter diesen familialen Rahmenbedingungen insofern auch eine Schwierigkeit dar, als dass familiäre, religiöse Wissensbestände von der Elterngeneration an die Kindergeneration kaum tradiert werden und es den Adoleszenten so an Orientierung fehlt. Am ehesten wird der jüngeren Generation noch Wissen – sowohl implizit als auch explizit – darum vermittelt, dass Alevitischsein ein Stigma darstellt. Darin zeigt sich signifikant die Weitergabe eines verinnerlichten Verletzungsverhältnisses und Angst vor erneuter Verletzung, welche sich im Modus des Schweigens und in Spuren der Vergangenheit teils bewusst, teils unbewusst an die Folgegeneration tradiert (vgl. Straub 2014). Gerade die fehlende Tradierung von alevitischen (Glaubens-)Inhalten führt zu mangelnden sozialisatorischen Ausgangsvoraussetzungen im familialen Erfahrungsraum, auch für die Verarbeitung von kollektiven Verletzungsverhältnissen. Dennoch bricht die Jugend zum Teil auch mit der *Takiye*-Praxis ihrer Eltern- bzw. Großeltern, steht aber gleichzeitig in intergenerationaler Loyalität zu den Verfolgungs- und Unterdrückungserfahrungen dieser.

Unser Beitrag zeigt somit Kontinuität und Wandel der alevitischen Identität in der Diaspora: Auf der einen Seite besteht die Erfahrung, eine Minderheit zu sein, fort. Unsere Fälle zeigen, dass *Takiye* zutiefst verankert sowie ein wesentlicher Bestandteil der intergenerationalen Beziehungen ist und dass negative Erfahrungen mit sunnitischen Gleichaltrigen fortbestehen. Diese können bei den Adoleszenten zu negativen psychosozialen Folgen wie empfundenem Anpassungszwang an die Lebensweise der sunnitischen Mehrheit, Verheimlichung, Leugnen der eigenen Identität und das Gefühl anders und nicht in Ordnung zu sein, führen. Auf der anderen Seite verändert sich das Gefüge insofern, als dass Alevit*innen in Deutschland anerkannt sind und ihre alevitische Identität offen zeigen können. Eine Chance für die Jugend ist ebenfalls, sich aus der Diaspora heraus politisch gegen die Unterdrückung und für den Schutz ihrer Verwandten und anderer Alevit*innen in der Türkei einsetzen zu können.

Die jungen Erwachsenen finden im Jugendverband BDAJ ein Vehikel, um sich unter Gleichaltrigen über ihre schwierigen Sozialisationsbedingungen und ihre alevitische Identität auszutauschen: Hier können sie sich miteinander vergemeinschaften und politisch für das Alevitischsein engagieren. Im Kreis der Gleichaltrigen und Gleichgesinnten können sie zudem gemeinsam die fehlende Tradierung von Wissen im Elternhaus ausgleichen und sich dieses eigenständig aneignen. Dass diese fehlenden Wissensbestände trotz bestehender Unsicherheiten auch gewisse Freiheitsgrade erlauben, wurde deutlich, indem die Adoleszenten dies als Flexibilität für sich umzudeuten versuchen. Denn mit ihren individuellen Deutungen können adoleszente Alevit*innen sich durchaus einreihen in die Wert-Orientierungen junger Menschen in Deutschland, unter denen sich der individuierte Glaube „am Maßstab subjektiver Authentizität" orientiert (Gärtner 2013, S. 230).

Das von uns illustrierte Spektrum alevitischer Identität und Interpretationen charakterisiert sich in seiner Binnendifferenz als pluralistisch, insofern als dass religiöse wie nicht religiöse, politische, kulturelle und familiär vererbte Formen eines Selbstverständnisses alevitischer Identität synchron nebeneinander bestehen. Diese Pluralität alevitischer Selbstverständnisse stellt somit ein Spiegelbild der soziokulturellen und historischen Entwicklungsprozesse des Alevitentums dar. Bei all dieser Pluralität bleibt aber doch der soziale Tatbestand bestehen, dass sich die Adoleszenten in der Phase des Heranwachsens mit den Sozialisationsbedingungen des familiären Schweigens oder der fehlenden Weitergabe religiösen Wissens mehr oder weniger bewusst auseinandersetzen (müssen) und ihre alevitische Identität unter diesen schwierigen Voraussetzungen ausbilden müssen.

Literatur

Aksünger, Handan (2013): *Jenseits des Schweigegebots. Alevitische Migrantenselbstorganisationen und zivilgesellschaftliche Integration in Deutschland und den Niederlanden.* Münster: Waxmann.

Balkanlıoğlu, Mehmet Ali (2012): „Alevi-Sünni evliliklerinin aile ilişkileri ile cocuk yetistirme üzerine etkileri ve sosyal damgalama." *Türk Kültürü ve Haci Bektaş Veli araştirma dergisi,* (62), S. 163–182.

Baumann, Gerd (1998): „Ethnische Identität als duale diskursive Konstruktion. Dominante und demotische Identitätsdiskurse in einer multiethnischen Vorstadt von London." In: Assmann, Aleida / Friese Heidrun (Hg.): *Identitäten. Erinnerung, Geschichte, Identität 3.* Frankfurt am Main: Suhrkamp Taschenbuch Verlag, S. 288–313.

Bohnsack, Ralf (1989): *Generation, Milieu und Geschlecht.* Opladen: Leske+Budrich.

Bruinessen, Martin van (1988): „Genocide in Kurdistan? The suppression of the Dersim rebellion in Turkey (1937-38) and the chemical war against the Iraqi Kurds (1988)." *University of Pennsylvania Press,* S. 1–12. Verfügbar: https://www.academia.edu/2521265/Genocide_in_Kurdistan_The_Suppression_of_the_Dersim_Rebellion_in_Turkey_193738_and_the_Chemical_War_Against_the_Iraqi_Kurds_1988_ [30.03.2018].

Bund der Alevitischen Jugend in Deutschland e.V. (2018): Organisationswebseite. Verfügbar: „https://www.bdaj.de"; [01.07.2018].

Dreßler, Markus (2002): *Die alevitische Religion – Traditionslinien und Neubestimmungen.* (Abhandlungen zur Kunde des Morgenlandes LIII,4). Würzburg: Ergon.

Dreßler, Markus (2008): „Religio-Secular Metamorphoses: The Re-Making of Turkish Alevism." *Journal of the American Academy of Religion,* 76 (2), S. 280–311.

– (2017): „Erdoğan und die ‚Fromme Generation'. Religion und Politik in der Türkei." In: *Aus Politik und Zeitgeschichte* (APUZ 9–10/2017). Türkei, S. 23–29.

Engin, Ismail / Erhard Franz (2001): *Aleviler/Alewiten. 1.Bd. Kimlik ve Tarih/Identität und Geschichte.* Hamburg: Deutsches Orient-Institut.

Elias, Norbert / Scotson, John L. (1993) [1965]: *Etablierte und Außenseiter* (1. Auflage). Frankfurt am Main: Suhrkamp.

Erikson, Erik (2015) [1966]: *Identität und Lebenszyklus.* Frankfurt am Main: Suhrkamp Taschenbuch Verlag.

Gärtner, Christel (2013): „Religiöse Identität und Wertbindungen von Jugendlichen in Deutschland." *Kölner Zeitschrift für Soziologie und Sozialpsychologie*, 65 (1), S. 211–233.

Goffman, Erving (1975): *Stigma. Über Techniken der Bewältigung beschädigter Identität.* Frankfurt: Suhrkamp Taschenbuch Verlag.

Gorzewski, Andreas (2010): *Das Alevitentum in seinen divergierenden Verhältnisbestimmungen zum Islam*, Bonner Islamstudien, Bd. 17. Berlin: EB-Verlag Dr. Brandt.

Hendrich, Béatrice (2008): „Alevitische Geschichte erinnern – in Deutschland" In M. Sökefeld (Hg.): *Aleviten in Deutschland – Identitätsprozesse einer Religionsgemeinschaften der Diaspora.* Bielefeld: transcript, S. 37–64.

Jörissen, Benjamin (2010): „Geist, Identität und Gesellschaft aus der Perspektive des Sozialbehaviorismus." In: Jörissen, Benjamin/ Zirfas, Jörg (Hg.): *Schlüsselwerke der Identitätsforschung.* Wiesbaden: VS Verlag für Sozialwissenschaften, S. 87–109.

Kalbarczyk, Nora / Loth, Martina (2017): „Alevitentum im Gespräch mit Wissenschaft und Christentum – Symposium an der Akademie der Weltreligionen, 8. April 2017, Universität Hamburg", *CIBEDO-Beiträge* 2017 (2) (Zum Gespräch zwischen Christen und Muslimen). Münster: Aschendorff Verlag, S. 89–91.

Kaplan, Ismail (2004): *Das Alevitentum – Eine Glaubens- und Lebensgemeinschaft in Deutschland.* Köln: Alevitische Gemeinde Deutschland e.V.

Kaplan, Ismail / Öztürk, Mürvet (2006): *Glaubenselemente im alevitischen und sunnitischen Selbstverständnis. Eine Synopse.* Köln: Alevitische Gemeinde Deutschland e.V.

Kaya, Asiye (2009): *Mutter-Tochter-Beziehungen in der Migration. Biographische Erfahrungen im alevitischen und sunnitischen Kontext.* Wiesbaden: VS Verlag für Sozialwissenschaften.

– (2011): „Geschlecht und soziale Vererbung". In: Allenbach, Birgit et al. (Hrsg), *Jugend, Migration und Religion. Interdisziplinäre Perspektiven.* Zürich und Baden-Baden: Nomos und Pano Verlag, S. 137–158.

King, Vera / Koller, Hans-Christoph (Hrsg.) (2006): *Adoleszenz – Migration – Bildung.* Wiesbaden: VS Verlag für Sozialwissenschaften.

King, Vera (2013): *Die Entstehung des Neuen in der Adoleszenz. Individuation, Generativität und Geschlecht in modernisierten Gesellschaften* (2. Auflage). Wiesbaden: VS Springer.

Kehl-Bodrogi, Krisztina (1988): *Die Kızılbaş/Aleviten. Untersuchungen über eine esoterische Glaubensgemeinschaft in Anatolien.* Berlin: Schwarz.

– (2006): „Von der Kultur zur Religion – Alevitische Identitätspolitik in Deutschland." In: *Max Planck-Institute for Social Anthropology (Hg.): Working Paper* No. 84. Halle/ Saale.

Loth, Martina (2014): „Wird die alevitische Jugend das Alevitentum reformieren? – Eine Generation auf der Suche nach einer Neuformulierung". In: Kreiser, Klaus et al. (Hg.): *Junge Perspektiven der Türkeiforschung in Deutschland.* Wiesbaden: VS Verlag für Sozialwissenschaften, S. 227–245.

Massicard, Elise (2013): *The Alevis in Turkey and Europe. Identity and managing territorial diversity.* London/New York: Routledge.

Sökefeld, Martin (2004b): „Über die Schwierigkeit, dem türkischen Nationaldiskurs zu entkommen: Aleviten in Deutschland und Hürriyet". In: Ders. (Hg.): *Jenseits des Paradigmas kultureller Differenz: Neue Perspektiven auf Einwanderer aus der Türkei.* Bielefeld: transcript, S. 163–180.

– (Hg.) (2008a): „Einleitung". In: Ders. (Hrsg): *Aleviten in Deutschland. Identitätsprozesse einer Religionsgemeinschaft in der Diaspora.* Bielefeld: transcript, S. 7–36.

– (2008b): „Sind Aleviten Muslime? Die alevitische Debatte über das Verhältnis von Alevitentum und Islam in Deutschland." In: Ders. (Hg.): *Aleviten in Deutschland. Identitätsprozesse einer Religionsgemeinschaft in der Diaspora.* Bielefeld: transcript, S. 195–218.

Spiegel Online (2017): „Verfassungsreferendum. So stimmten die Türken im Ausland ab." In: *Spiegel Online*, 18.04.2017, verfügbar: http://www.spiegel.de/politik/ausland/tuerkei-referendum-so-stimmten-die-auslandstuerken-ab-a-1143662.html; [01.08.2018].

Spuler-Stegemann, Ursula (2003): „Ist die Alevitische Gemeinde Deutschland e.V. eine Religionsgemeinschaft? Religionswissenschaftliches Gutachten." *Erstattet dem Ministerium für Schule, Jugend und Kinder des Landes Nordrhein-Westfalen,* verfügbar: http://www.inforel.ch/fileadmin/user_upload/dateien/215.AlevSpuler.pdf; [10.09.2018].

Straub, Jürgen (1998): „Personale und kollektive Identität. Zur Analyse eines theoretischen Begriffs." In: Assmann, Aleida / Friese, Heidrun (Hg.): *Identitäten.* Frankfurt am Main: Suhrkamp Taschenbuch Verlag, S. 73–83.

– (2000): „Identität als psychologisches Deutungskonzept." In: Greve, Werner (Hg.): *Psychologie des Selbst.* Weinheim: Psychologie Verlags Union, S. 279–301.

– (2014): „Verletzungsverhältnisse, Erlebnisgründe, unbewusste Tradierungen und Gewalt in der sozialen Praxis." *Zeitschrift für Pädagogik*, (6), S. 74–95.

Taşcı, Hülya (2006): *Identität und Ethnizität in der Bundesrepublik Deutschland am Beispiel der zweiten Generation der Aleviten aus der Republik Türkei.* Berlin: LIT-Verlag.

Tezcan, Levent (2012): *Das muslimische Subjekt. Verfangen im Dialog der Deutschen Islam Konferenz.* Konstanz: Konstanz University Press.

– (2016): „Islam." In: Dinzelbacher, Peter / Krech, Volkard et al. (Hg.): *20. Jahrhundert – Religiöse Positionen und soziale Formationen.* Paderborn: Ferdinand Schöningh, S. 151–171.

Uslucan, Hacı-Halil (2017): „Türkeistämmige in Deutschland. Heimatlos oder überall zuhause?" *Bundeszentrale für politische Bildung,* 10. März 2017, verfügbar: http://www.bpb.de/apuz/243864/tuerkeistaemmige-in-deutschland-heimatlos-oder-ueberall-zuhause?p=all; [05.03.2017].

The Authors

Jürgen Endres is a postdoctoral researcher at the Center for Research on Religion at the University of Lucerne. He studied political sciences, law and Islamic studies at the universities of Freiburg (Germany) und Hamburg and holds a PhD in Islamic studies from the University of Leipzig. His current main research interests are Islam in Switzerland, Muslim youths in Europe, radicalisation and Islamic extremism, and conflicts in the Middle East.

Giulia Evolvi is a Research Associate in Religion and Media at the Center for Religious Studies (CERES) at Ruhr University Bochum, Germany, where she coordinates the focus group "Materiality" for the Käte Hamburger Kolleg project. She obtained her PhD in Media Studies from the University of Colorado Boulder, United States, where she was affiliated with the Center for Media, Religion and Culture, and also holds a Master's degree in Religious Studies from the University of Padua, Italy. Her research interests are religious change in Europe, secularization, digital media, Catholicism, Islam and Islamophobia. She has published various articles and chapters on these subjects in publications such as *Media History*, *Social Compass*, and *Information, Communication & Society*.

Farid Hafez is currently lecturer and researcher at the University of Salzburg, Department of Political Science and Sociology. He is also a senior research scholar at Georgetown University's The Bridge Initiative, where he researches and writes about Islamophobia. In 2017, he was Fulbright visiting professor at University of California, Berkeley and in 2014, he was visiting scholar at Columbia University, New York. Since 2010 he has been the editor of the Islamophobia Studies Yearbook, and since 2016 the co-editor of the European Islamophobia Report. Hafez has received the Bruno Kreisky Award for the political book of the year for his anthology *Islamophobie in Österreich* (Studienverlag, 2009) co-edited with John Bunzl. Currently, his research focuses on Muslim youth movements in Europe. He earned his Ph.D. in Political Science from the University of Vienna.

Linda Hyökki is a Senior Research Associate at the Center for Islam and Global Affairs, Istanbul Sabahattin Zaim University. She received her Master's in Translation, Linguistics and Cultural Studies from the Johannes Gutenberg University of Mainz in 2011. Currently, her work focuses on Islamophobia and Muslim minorities in European contexts and she is working on a Ph.D. thesis exploring Finnish Muslim converts' experiences on Islamophobia at the Ibn Haldun University. In addition to Islamophobia Studies and Qualitative Research Methods, she is interested in Futures and is a Fellow at the Center for Postnormal Policy and Futures Studies. Hyökki frequently writes Op-Eds and academic blogs about her research in English and Turkish and she authored the Finland-chapter of the European Islamophobia Report for the years 2015, 2016, and 2017. In her native country Finland, she is affiliated with NGOs contributing to the empowerment of Muslim youth.

Rebekka Christine Khaliefi is a PhD student at the Department of Religious Studies at the University of Lucerne. Previously she studied sociology and philosophy at the Eberhard Karls University Tübingen and at the Sorbonne (Paris IV) in Paris. She completed her studies with the Magistra Artium (M.A.). From April 2015 to March 2016, she received a scholarship from the Graduate School of Humanities and Social Sciences of the University of Lucerne. Since April 2016, she has been working as a research assistant in the SNSF project about young Buddhists with Vietnamese origin in Switzerland and in Germany. Her main areas of interest are qualitative research methods, "second generation" and religion.

Katharina Limacher is a postdoctoral researcher at the Research Centre "Religion and Transformation in Contemporary Society" of Vienna University. She earned her Masters in Sociology and Religious Studies and holds a PhD in Religious Studies from the University of Lucerne. She worked as research associate at the Universities of Berne, Lucerne and Vienna and was a fellow at the Istituto Svizzero di Roma in 2016. Her fields of research interest comprise Hinduism in Europe, Sociology of Religion, as well as research at the intersection of Religion and Politics.

Rüdiger Lohlker is professor of Islamic Studies at the Department of Oriental Studies at the University of Vienna. Here, he is also head of a Training Course for Imams. His research focuses on the history of Islamic Ideas, Islam and the Arab World Online, modern Islamic movements and Jihadism, especially online. Lohlker is co-editor of the journal *Wiener Zeitschrift für Kunde des Morgenlandes* and editor of *Cyberorient.* As an advisor of Austrian ministries and European committees he is actively involved in science-policy dialogue.

Martina Loth is a PhD-Candidate at the Graduate School "Regulating Religious Plurality in the Region" at the Ruhr-University Bochum. Before that she was assistant to the Managing Director, German-Turkish Youth Bridge in Düsseldorf. Her educational background is a joint German-Turkish Master's Program in Social Sciences (GeT MA) at Humboldt-Universität zu Berlin and the Middle East Technical University Ankara. For her Bachelor's degrees she studies Comparative Studies of Culture and Religion at the Philipps-Universität Marburg, where she also had the chance to go abroad to spend two terms as ERASMUS-student at Boğaziçi University Istanbul.

Astrid Mattes is a postdoctoral researcher at the Institute for Urban and Regional Research at the Austrian Academy of Sciences. She studied Political Science and Comparative Religious Studies at the Universities of Vienna and Limerick and holds a PhD in Political Science. Previously she held pre- and postdoctoral positions at the Department of Religious Studies, the Department of Political Science and the Research Platform "Religion and Transformation in Contemporary Society" (University of Vienna) where she collaborated on multiple research projects in the fields of religion, politics and migration. Her main research interests are governance of diversity in liberal democracies, immigrant integration politics, religion politics, religious pluralism and Islam in Europe.

Silvia Martens holds an MA in Religious Studies (University of Erfurt) and a doctoral degree in Islamic Studies (University of Berne). She wrote her dissertation on conceptions and practices of charity work and volunteering among Muslims in Switzerland. Working at the universities of Berne and Lucerne, her current research and teaching activities focus on religious practices of Muslims in Switzerland, specifically the Muslim youth in Switzerland, as well as Islamophobia and religiosity and prejudice.

Christoph Novak read Political Science at the universities of Frankfurt and Vienna and continued his studies with an MA in Culture, Diaspora, Ethnicity at Birkbeck, University of London. From 2014 to 2016 he worked for Swiss Paraplegic Research (Nottwil, Switzerland) in the fields of Health Sciences and Disability Studies. He started his doctoral research on the politics of belonging of young Muslims in Zurich and Vienna at the Department of Political Science (University of Vienna) and the Dèpartent de sciences politique et relations internationales (Universitè de Genève) in 2015. In 2016 he was awarded a DOC-Fellowship and in 2018 received the dissertation award for research on migration, both by the Austrian Academy of the Sciences.

Anastas Odermatt studied religious studies and environmental sciences, philosophy and ethics in Lucerne, Zurich and Vienna. After lectureships at high school level and a private-sector involvement in an environmental communications agency, he has completed his master's degree in 2014. He is Scientist in Religious Studies and Research Staff at the Center for Religion, Economy and Politics (ZRWP) at the University of Lucerne. His studies and research priorities are religiosity and integration especially by youth and young adults and statistics of religion (www.smre-data.ch).

Andreas Tunger-Zanetti studied Islamic studies, Oriental languages and History at the University of Berne, supplemented by study stays in Vienna and Tunis. His doctoral thesis, completed in 1994 in Freiburg (Germany) and published in 1996, is about relations between Tunis and Istanbul, 1860–1913. After working as a foreign news editor in a regional Swiss newspaper from 1999 to 2006 he returned to academia. Since 2007 he coordinates the Center for Research on Religion at the University of Lucerne. His major fields of research are Islam in Switzerland and in Western Europe, religions in a religiously plural context, religion and the public sphere, processes of recognition in society and law, interreligious and intercultural dialogue.

Aysel Tepeli is a PhD-Candidate at the Graduate School "Regulating Religious Plurality in the Region" of the Center for Religious Studies in Bochum. She holds a master's degree in social sciences from the Ruhr-University Bochum. Her research focus lies on social and cultural psychology and sociology. In her current research project, she focuses on the relations between Alevi and Sunni youths and the meaning of past and present injuries between both groups for their identities and group interactions.

Jana Wetzel is a research assistant at the university of Vechta, Germany at the department of social work, at the chair of "Transculturality and Gender". She studied pedagogy and education at the University of Bielefeld, Germany. Her main research interests are critical migration pedagogy as well as racism and social work.